# BENJAMIN GRAHAM
## *on* INVESTING

# BENJAMIN GRAHAM
# on INVESTING

EDITED BY

## RODNEY G. KLEIN

COMMENTARY BY

## DAVID M. DARST

New York   Chicago   San Francisco   Lisbon   London
Madrid   Mexico City   Milan   New Delhi   San Juan
Seoul   Singapore   Sydney   Toronto

1 2 3 4 5 6 7 8 9 0   FGR/FGR   0 1 0 9

ISBN    978-0-07-162142-7
MHID      0-07-162142-3

*Printed by Quebecor World.*

McGraw-Hill books are available at special quantity discounts to use as premiums and sales promotions, or for use in corporate training programs. To contact a representative, please visit the Contact Us pages at www.mhprofessional.com.

This publication is designed to provide accurate and authoritative information in regard to the subject matter covered. It is sold with the understanding that neither the author nor the publisher is engaged in rendering legal, accounting, or other professional service. If legal advice or other expert assistance is required, the services of a competent professional person should be sought.

*—From a Declaration of Principles jointly adopted by a Committee of the*
*American Bar Association and a Committee of Publishers.*

For Marie

My inspiration for 27 years.

RODNEY

# CONTENTS

Preface ■ BY RODNEY KLEIN                                             xiii

## Part I ■ SEPTEMBER 1917–SEPTEMBER 1918

Introduction ■ BY DAVID DARST                                            3

### 1 | CURIOSITIES OF THE BOND LIST
*Issues That Sell on Illogical Bases—Misconceptions of Investors—*
*Some Foreign Issue Anomalies*                                         13

### 2 | VALUATION OF GREAT NORTHERN OIL CERTIFICATES
*Based on 1914 and 1916 Operations—Life of Mines—Comparison with*
*Porphyries—An Opinion on Present Market Price*                        19

### 3 | INSPIRATION'S DIFFICULTIES AND ACHIEVEMENTS IN 1917
*Ore Valuation and War Taxes—Costs and Profits—Investment Value of Stock*   27

### 4 | NEVADA CONSOLIDATED—A MINING PHOENIX
*A "Dying Mine" That Refuses to Expire—Its Changing Balance Sheet—*
*Investment Worth of Nevada's Stock*                                   35

### 5 | SECRETS OF INVESTED CAPITAL
*Tangible Assets as Revealed by the War-Tax Reserve—Real Versus*
*Book Values*                                                          41

### 6 | THE GREAT STEEL TAX MYSTERY
*Various Phases of the U. S. Steel Tax Situation—Other Steel and*
*Equipment Stocks—Excessive and Insufficient Tax Reserves*            49

## Part II ▪ September 1918–January 1919

Introduction ▪ by David Darst                                    59

**7 | AMERICAN AGRICULTURE AND VIRGINIA-CAROLINA**
*Are They Selling Out of Line?—Causes of America's Preeminence—*
*Fertilizers as War and Peace Essentials*                       65

**8 | HIGH YIELD AND SAFE INVESTMENTS**
*Opportunities Created by Unfounded Prejudices—Instances of Six Per Cent,*
*Safety, and a Probable Ten Point Profit—List of Bonds, Preferred Stocks, and*
*Common Stocks*                                                 75

**9 | HIDDEN ASSETS OF CONSOLIDATED GAS**
*Will It Sell at 150 Again?—Definite Statement of the System's*
*Earnings and Asset Values—Analysis of Important Bonds*         83

**10 | BARGAIN HUNTING THROUGH THE BOND LIST**
*Gilt Edged Railroad Issues at Attractive Prices—Some Cheap*
*Industrial Bonds—Peerless 6s—The Investment Mystery*          93

## Part III ▪ April 1919–December 1924

Introduction ▪ by David Darst                                   103

**11 | ATTRACTIVE INDUSTRIAL PREFERRED STOCKS**
*Importance of Exemption from Normal Tax—Recent Improvement in*
*Investment Status—Various Elements in Judging Values—Attractive*
*Issues Recommended*                                           131

**12 | NORTHERN PACIFIC OUTSTRIPS GREAT NORTHERN**
*The See-Saw Race of the Grangers— Physical and Financial*
*Peculiarities Analyzed—Northern Pacific's Hidden Assets—*
*A Preferred in Name Only*                                     139

### 13 | A NEGLECTED CHAIN STORE ISSUE

*The Inconspicuous Merits of McCrory—Its Present Low Price Makes
It Attractive—Comparison with Its More Pretentious Rivals*                            147

### 14 | THE ART OF HEDGING

*Maximum Profits and Minimum Losses—Convertible Issues as a
Trading Medium—Safety First Operations in a Dangerous Market*                         155

### 15 | WHICH IS THE BEST SUGAR STOCK?

*Strong Market Position of the Commodity—Comparative Analysis of
Five Listed Issues—Importance of Capitalization Structure and
Operating Efficiency*                                                                 161

### 16 | THE "COLLAPSE" OF AMERICAN INTERNATIONAL

*Great Expectations Cruelly Disappointed—Is the Stock Cheap at 42?—
Facts and Figures about the Company and Its Subsidiaries*                             169

### 17 | THE GOODYEAR REORGANIZATION

*Unofficial Insolvency Caused by Ill-Timed Expansion—Sudden Disaster
Follows Wonderful Growth—Details of Proposed Reorganization and
Discussion of Company's Prospects*                                                    179

### 18 | IS UNITED DRUG CHEAP AT 53?

*Factors in the Collapse from 83*                                                     189

### 19 | SPECULATIVE OPPORTUNITIES IN RAILROAD STOCKS

*New Conditions Affecting Railroad Values—An Attempt to Estimate
Future Earning Power—Detailed Discussion of Six Issues*                              199

### 20 | ARITHMETIC AND STOCK VALUES

*Capitalization Structure as Affecting Earning Power—Magical Results
of a Little Slight-of-Hand—Owning a Corporation on Margin*                           207

### 21 | A TRUE TALK ON BOND YIELDS, OR

*What Every Small Investor Should Know. A Financial Playlet with a Meaning*           217

**22 | THE UNSCRAMBLING OF READING**
*A Problem for the Stockholders—Earning Power before and after*
*Segregation—Mysterious Aspects of the Coal Properties*                225

**23 | HOW TO APPLY THE SCIENTIFIC THEORY OF SWITCHING TO CONCRETE**
    **CASES IN THE PRESENT MARKET**
*A Practical-Minded Scrutiny of the Comparative Merits of Many*
*Securities Active in the Market Today*                                233

**24 | EIGHT STOCK BARGAINS OFF THE BEATEN TRACK**
*Stocks that Are Covered Chiefly by Cash or the Equivalent—No Bonds*
*or Preferred Stock Ahead of These Issues—An Unusually Interesting*
*Group of Securities*                                                  245

**25 | EIGHT LONG-RANGE OPPORTUNITIES IN LOW-PRICED ISSUES**
*Two Varieties of "Cheap Stocks"—Eight Interesting Issues Discussed—*
*Intelligent Speculation versus Wild Gambles*                          259

**26 | SIX BARGAINS IN LOW-PRICED DIVIDEND PAYING STOCKS**
*Profitable Purchases among Business Men's Investments*                271

**27 | READING—THE MARKET'S "SLEEPING BEAUTY"**
*Reading's Powerful Exhibit Obscured by Misleading Comparisons—*
*Investment Facts and Speculative Possibilities*                       279

**28 | SIMPLE TESTS FOR DETERMINING THE VALUE OF RAILROAD PREFERRED STOCKS**
*What Investors Should Know—Recommendations and Cautions*              285

## Part IV  ▪  JANUARY 1925–JANUARY 1927

Introduction ▪ BY DAVID DARST                                         297

**29 | A DIVERSIFIED LIST OF LOW-PRICED STOCKS**
*Seven Dividend Payers Selling Under $25 per Share Which Are*
*Attractive for Immediate Income and Long Pull Prospects*             313

30 | ARE C. & O. HOLDERS UNFAIRLY TREATED?

*Analysis of the Van Sweringen Merger—How the Earnings of the*
*Constituent Companies Compare with Their Purchase Price*                    321

31 | EFFECT OF RAIL CONSOLIDATIONS UPON SECURITY VALUES

*How Merger Problems Are Being Solved*                                       329

32 | BARGAIN-HUNTING NOT THRILLING BUT—IMMENSELY PROFITABLE

*Some Current Examples of Bargains*                                          339

33 | A VICTORY FOR THE SMALL STOCKHOLDER

*Vital Defects of the Van Sweringen Scheme—Effect on the Merger*
*Situation—Value of Ches. & Ohio, Erie and Pere Marquette*                   349

34 | THE RIDDLE OF U.S. STEEL'S BOOK VALUE

*Is the Common Stock Worth $280 Per Share?—Assets Contrasted with*
*Earnings—Essential Characteristics of the Steel Industry*                   359

35 | MR. SHAREHOLDER—DO YOU KNOW WHEN PERIODIC STOCK DIVIDENDS
       HELP AND WHEN THEY HURT YOU?                                          371

36 | THE NEW ERA OF DISCRIMINATION IN THE SELECTION OF SECURITIES

*Lessons of the 1926 Market That Should Prove Valuable in 1927*              381


INDEX                                                                        393

# PREFACE

The genesis for this book dates back to 1983, when I had recently developed an interest in collecting old books about the stock market to add to my historical knowledge of the markets and Wall Street. While I hadn't refined my degree of interest, it had reached the point where my travels around the country had to involve stops at likely sources of such books: bookstores, flea markets, collectible shows, and antique stores. While bookstores that sold used books could be a prime source, many of the outlets mentioned had generally low yields, particularly since some stores threw out old market books, considering them worthless. But one day in July of 1983, I stopped in an antique shop in Akron, Ohio, and, while they had a large number of old and uninteresting books, they also had a large stack of early issues of the *Magazine of Wall Street*. I knew that Richard D. Wyckoff was its editor and publisher in the early years, but when I started to browse through the issues, I was surprised to find the name Benjamin Graham listed as the author of many articles.

I had been a student of Graham's back in 1960 at UCLA, having missed him in 1959 when I received an MBA at Columbia and he had already moved to Los Angeles. While I had obviously read his investment books, I hadn't realized that he was also a prolific writer of financial articles earlier in his career. Thus began my effort to locate all of the *Magazine of Wall Street* issues that contain his articles. Eventually this search also led to my collecting all of the magazines published by Richard Wyckoff.

With a major in mathematics, Benjamin Graham graduated from Columbia University in June of 1914. While not particularly interested in the study of economics as an undergraduate, through a chance meeting with a member of a New York Stock Exchange firm, he accepted employment at Newburger, Henderson & Loeb. Graham started his Wall Street career with basic duties in order to learn the business from the bottom up and to work into the job of selling bonds. Bonds, after all, were considered worthy of investment, while stocks were considered to be strictly speculative. Not having a prior financial education, he studied texts on bond investment and reports on railroad securities. Though not a part of his duties, he wrote an analysis of a railroad that concluded that the firm was in poor financial condition and its bonds were not investment grade. His analysis impressed his employer, and, at his own request, he became the statistical department.

By 1916 he had been successful in several security operations, including his first arbitrage, but his first serious financial setback was coming up. Poor results in a stock market partnership he had formed resulted in margin calls that he couldn't meet due to funds being tied up in a phonograph shop co-owned with a brother. While the market partnership continued, he obligated himself to monthly payments to make up deficits in his capital account, though later the investments improved and stayed profitable.

Having previously supplemented his Wall Street income with night-school teaching and tutoring, he started writing occasional monthly articles for the editorial pages of *Vogue* magazine. This situation ended when the publication hired an editor who took over his duties. It was at this point that he wrote his first financial article for publication, "Curiosities of the Bond List." *The Magazine of Wall Street* accepted the article and published it in its September 1, 1917, issue, quickly followed by another article in the next issue. The publication was particularly pleased with his articles and from then on he became a regular contributor to the *Magazine*, which was the circulation leader among financial magazines. In fact, in the next year he was offered the chief editorship of the *Magazine* along with a substantial salary and a profit share. In his memoir, Graham wrote that "writing had been my early love, and this was an opportunity to combine literature with finance." While Graham was tempted by the idea, the Newburger brokerage firm he worked for made him a better offer, and in the January 1, 1920, issue of the *New York Times*, the firm advertised that Graham "had been admitted to an interest in our firm."

Three years later Graham left the firm to embark on his own investment business, the first of various enterprises he started during his Wall Street career.

Graham has written that he quite liked *Magazine of Wall Street* publisher Richard Wyckoff and his wife. In fact, Graham's brother Victor went to work for the *Magazine* in 1920, selling advertisements, and eventually became the vice president for advertising. While Wyckoff was a noted market technician and advocate of tape reading, Graham did not believe in these concepts and continued to develop his methods of security analysis.

His last *Magazine of Wall Street* article appeared in January 1927, perhaps because he was preparing to start his Security Analysis course at Columbia in the Fall of that year. It was in this course that he met the eventual co-author of *Security Analysis*, David Dodd.

Rodney Klein
Los Angeles

# BENJAMIN GRAHAM
## *on* INVESTING

# PART I

# SEPTEMBER 1917–SEPTEMBER 1918

# INRODUCTION

BY DAVID DARST

According to Warren Buffett, Benjamin Graham (1894–1976) said that he wished every day to do "something foolish, something creative, and something generous." And how these pages are devoid of the first, yet filled with the latter two qualities! Three years after graduating in 1914 at the age of 20 from Columbia College, while working for the New York Stock Exchange member firm of Newberger, Henderson & Loeb, Graham began contributing the articles you are about to read, to *The Magazine of Wall Street.*

The six articles in Part I span the time period from September 11, 1917 to September 28, 1918. Against a background of European hostilities (World War I, which due to the loss of 40 million combatants and civilians came to be known as "The Great War," had begun in August 1914), the U.S. liner *Housatonic* was sunk by a German submarine on February 3, 1917. Congress declared war in April, and in December, the U.S. government took over the country's railroads. Corporate profits were constrained by higher taxes, price controls, and raw materials shortages. As measured by the Dow Jones Industrial Average, on significantly reduced trading volume, stocks fell –21.7% in 1917, with many individual issues faring even more poorly, particularly among the railroad stocks.

In 1918, the ebb and flow of armed conflict were a key determinant of securities prices. AT&T's operations were taken over in July by the U.S. Post

Office (and were re-privatized in 1919). Representing for many their first foray into securities ownership, more than one-half of America's adult population subscribed to the fourth and final Liberty Loan Drive of late September. After the armistice was signed on November 11, several leading shares were sold off as overall business activity declined with the cancellation of wartime orders and the nation's entry into a recession which ended in early 1919. For 1918 as a whole, the Dow Industrials rose +10.5%, though off −8% from their October 18 highs.

So these six essays, which begin when Graham was all of 23 years old, were conceived and written during challenging economic, financial, and geopolitical conditions. Other than a relatively circumscribed number of mining, rail, utility, industrial (leather, cigar, and canning firms come to mind), retailing (five- and ten-cent stores and mail order houses), and traction (street railway) issues of common stock, preferred, and (usually) senior or junior bonds secured by mortgage liens, investors faced a limited choice of industries and instruments. Mutual funds, exchange-traded put and call contracts, and inflation-indexed securities had probably not yet been dreamt of. Technology and pharmaceutical shares were virtually absent from the scene, as were insurance, banking, and airline companies, much less broadcasting, advertising, real estate, home construction, cable television, and gambling issues.

Aside from some historical insights and reflections upon the author's writing style, why on earth should any but ultra-fanatic investment readers care today about the soon-to-be century-old incunabula of an investment neophyte?

First, in these paragraphs, charts, and tables, investors can readily identify the true origins of serious, thoughtful, thorough security analysis. Even in Graham's earliest articles, we encounter *an emphasis on a bottom-up, fact-based evaluation of each company, as to its fundamental merits as a business.* In what may be the third and fourth sentences he ever published, Graham sets forth the foundation principles from which all of his later work flows:

"One often thinks of prices as determining values, instead of vice-versa. But as accurate as markets are, they cannot claim infallibility."

With unflinching honesty and realism, Graham recognizes that price is distinct from value. Graham identifies *price* as determined by the vagaries, whims, exigencies, enthusiasms, and desperations of the marketplace, populated by human beings. By means of rigor, selectivity, and discipline, he strives repeatedly to delineate *value* as determined by cash generation ability and the timing, duration, magnitude, and reliability of cash flows. Even in these early writings, Graham grounds his analysis not in hope and anticipation, but in facts and realism.

At the beginning of the twentieth century, Graham, the security analyst, marshals three sets of factors that determine the essential merits of a company, features that have lasting merit and enduring application in the twenty-first century. *Income statement* factors, which affect a company's *going concern* value, include: sales growth; profitability; and cash flow. *Balance sheet* factors, which affect a company's *liquidation value*, include: inventories; receivables; fixed assets; depreciation; capital requirements; and debt structure. *Qualitative factors*, which affect a company's ability to survive and prosper, include: the understandability of the underlying business; barriers to entry; technological obsolescence; power relationships with customers and suppliers (including labor); and competition.

The second major reason that careful study of these essays yields insight and understanding is because of the bright light these articles shed on the evolution of Benjamin Graham's thought processes. Consistently in studying Graham's work, readers encounter open-mindedness, flexibility, and common sense. While maintaining a balanced viewpoint toward the worth of a specific issue or industry sector, Graham displays time and again a willingness to carefully come to his own conclusions and to consider investing in what others were prone to shun or ignore.

Yet Graham does not espouse contrarianism just to be different or stand apart from the crowd. Graham's approach everywhere blends (and constantly urges) selectivity, patience, and caution. His paragraphs are infused with admonitions, counterfactual arguments, and diplomatically delivered injunctions. What this produces is a pervasive emphasis on the downside risk of any investment operation and plenty of "what if we're wrong?" warnings (today, this would be known as "stress testing").

Because of his primary emphasis on loss avoidance, Graham values protection of principal and he seeks always to invest with a margin of safety. Perhaps echoing Virginia Woolf's priceless resolution that "What Einstein, Planck, and Bohr have done with quantum mechanics, I will do with the written word," Graham shows himself very much to be a coeval not only of Woolf and the new physicists, but also of Marie Curie, James Joyce, the Dadaists, the Cubists, and the Futurists, Debussy, Satie, and Ravel, and other pathbreaking pioneers of his time. In his at first inchoate, and then increasingly mature work, Graham asserts that there is no such thing as a definite, proper value for a given bond, preferred, or common stock. Equally so, no magic calculation formula exists that will infallibly produce a specific intrinsic value number with absolute accuracy.

Step by step, Graham shows readers how to think about and bracket, instead of attempting to define with precision, a security's intrinsic value. Based on earnings, cash flows, dividends, coupons, capitalization structure, and a realistic assessment of the future, Graham comes to the conclusion that it is best to work with *ranges* of intrinsic values.

In Graham's opinion, long-term investment success comes from identifying a purchase price for an asset sufficiently below its intrinsic value, so that in time the investor will be able to profit as market prices begin to reflect the security's intrinsic value. Or to put it another way, one or more catalysts may emerge that awakens investors to a $100 bill on sale for 50 dollars.

Spurred on by vast reserves of intellectual curiosity, coupled with a natural didact's delight in switching on the bulb of understanding in others, from the very beginning, Graham is always looking to discover, establish, and refine concepts, standards, paths of logical reasoning, and general principles for evaluating, rejecting, selecting, and disposing of securities positions. Like the first layer of granite blocks that forms the base of the pyramids, Graham's love of learning and teaching inform every phrase and example in his canon.

Which brings forth the third principal impetus to start with the first essay in Part I, composed in September 1917, and to read through to the final essay in Part IV, completed in January 1927, almost ten years after Graham first began to give concrete expression to his character, instincts, and investing passion. Although the examples cited and the securities identified as attractive or unattractive for purchase are many decades distant from the landscape of current readers, Graham's reflections, analytical tools, and investigative methods transcend time and investment fashion.

Investors of and in every age can learn from and practically apply Graham's ways of framing key questions, big and small, his emphasis on the potential for error and the need for internal cross-checking and consistency, and his steadfast awareness of the potential for the market's short-term verdict to stray from underlying reality.

Focusing on the durable lessons of Graham's essays can provide guidance and suggest means of tackling investment valuation across global boundaries, in a wide range of economic and financial circumstances, and along the full spectrum of asset classes, instruments, and manager styles.

■    ■    ■

What shines forth in Graham's inaugural essay, "Curiosities of the Bond List," is the pellucid clarity and elegance of his examples and his willingness to drill down into specific discrepancies and peculiarities to illustrate a point or straighten out misconceptions.

Even as he recognizes the importance of considering interest-on-interest in bond investing, Graham describes the innate tendency of investors to disregard the capital gains effects on bonds purchased at a discount from par, as well as their aversion to purchasing bonds at a premium to par:

> The investor apparently imagines that by paying $1,180 for a $1,000 bond, [s]he must eventually lose $180. The fallacy of this argument is well illustrated by this very example. For it would require only $59 a year to yield a straight 5 per cent on the $1,180 investment . . . But since the 7s pay $70 per bond, there is a surplus of $11 per year, which if simply accumulated *without interest* (Graham's emphasis) would, at the date of maturity, amount to about $300—fully $120 per bond more than the premium paid. If interest is compounded on these surpluses, the gain over the 5 per cent bond would be considerably more.

In the same essay, after evaluating the conversion features, yields, and maturities of five Chicago, Milwaukee and St. Paul Railroad bonds secured by the same property mortgage, he ranks them as to relative attractiveness. Combing through several sets of railroad debt obligations, Graham searches for "circumstances which explain, but do not justify" yield variances between essentially similar issues.

Wherever he can, Graham is quick to point out subtleties and nuances that affect investment value: "The American Telephone & Telegraph 4s of 1929 have the additional value of being legal for savings banks in some New England states." And always in a polite and dignified way, he displays a willingness to take a stance and issue a call to action:

> These are times of rapidly shifting values, and the security owner should be on the alert to acquaint [her]himself with new conditions affecting [her]his holdings, nor hesitate to modify them when favorable opportunities are presented.

■　　■　　■

In "Valuation of Great Northern Ore Certificates," Graham reveals a willingness to go beyond the superficial in search of deeper meaning. Puzzlingly so in view of the market prominence of the trust certificates, in Graham's opinion, "Great Northern Iron Ore Trust annual reports are full of data but bare of information." He thus moves to rectify the situation and, by "eliminating items not properly included in the income accountant and making numerous other adjustments," he restates the Trust's earnings to the proper accounting standards of the time.

Graham considers several factors responsible for Great Northern Ore's relatively poor price performance, ranging from the micro—the abrogation of the Great Western lease, to the macro—the "disastrous" shortage of shipping tonnage capacity on the Great Lakes. After finding out from an interview with one of the Trustees that future production trends are unlikely to match the output of three years before, Graham concludes that the earlier period's certificate price level probably "represents the maximum appraisal under current conditions."

After: (i) restating the earnings of Great Northern Ore; (ii) evaluating the micro and macro factors affecting the Trust; (iii) comparing current with past production output, Graham chooses not to ignore the explicit signals being given off by the market. In view of the "strong accumulation which has been going on for some time past," which to him indicates, "when buying of this kind develops something favorable occurs in the near future, concluding that "therefore, we are favorably inclined toward Great Northern Ore."

■        ■        ■

In "Inspiration's Difficulties and Achievements in 1917," Graham examines the discrepancies arising from the company's keeping two sets of books, noting that Inspiration Copper's charges for depletion appear only in its tax return, and not in its published income account. This one fact leads Graham

on a three-stop journey, in which he shows how to: (i) estimate the extent
and actuarial net present value of Inspiration's ore reserves; (ii) calculate
with reasonable accuracy the company's costs of production and its
operating efficiency; and (iii) construct a business model of Inspiration's
profitability at several different levels of output.

As the *plein-air* painters were wont to do in Barbizon, France, in the
1870s, Graham then steps back from the canvas in order to furnish greater
perspective. He notes the advantages of copper mining companies over
most manufacturing enterprises:

> They do not tie up much money in inventories; they sell on a cash
> basis—and, most important of all, their yearly additions to plant are
> usually small.

■   ■   ■

"Nevada Consolidated—a Mining Phoenix" shows Graham's willingness to
swim against the current of prevailing opinion, when, in wry and ironic
prose, he takes issue with the consensus view that the company's reserves
were nearing exhaustion and Nevada Consolidated would soon be extinct:
"for a liquidating proposition, Nevada seems to possess extraordinary
vitality." To prove his point, Graham takes the reader through a careful
analysis of Nevada's "charge for depreciation, ore extinguishment, and
amortization of stripping expense."

Even as he repeatedly takes care to underpromise and overdeliver
("like most predictions, this is at best approximate"), Graham keeps readers
constantly aware of cash generation ability, the time value of a stream of
payments, and the crucial importance of compounding in the accumulation
of investment capital. His conclusion is direct and to the point:

> Some day the public will realize that a low cost, brilliantly managed
> copper mine like Nevada—rich in cash and free from debt—is fully as

safe an investment as many a railroad or industrial bond, and a great deal more profitable.

For readers who think they here detect the words and rationality of Warren Buffett, it is worth remembering that these essays emanate from Buffett's teacher, mentor, and friend. As Holinshed's *Chronicles of England, Scotland, and Ireland* were to Shakespeare's history plays, so too, in some measure, do Graham's writings inspire and inform Buffett's peerless pearls of investment wisdom.

■   ■   ■

This initial six-article group of Graham's writings comes to a close with another set of paired essays, "Secrets of Invested Capital," and "The Great Steel Tax Mystery: Secrets of Invested Capital—Part 2." By means of an ingeniously derived formula, Graham is able to determine (with an acceptable degree of accuracy) the level of a company's tangible invested capital. In the accounting leeway that was permitted in the early decades of the twentieth century, not all companies chose to reveal their tangible assets (Goodrich did, U.S. Rubber elected not to). The method by which Graham manages to prise this information loose from a company's Net Earnings and from its Wartime Excess Profits Tax Revenue, he would call "working backwards." Many modern-day practitioners would recognize this as "reverse engineering."

Graham is not reticent about naming specific over-goodwilled companies that "have possessed exceptionally liberal views on capitalization." But when considered in the aggregate, what most impresses Graham about the uses to which profits earned during wartime were put, is:

Not so much the large quantities of good will (sic) concealed in the plant account, but the extent to which most companies have succeeded

in replacing this original water by real assets, and in creating a
foundation of solid value for their junior issues.

The second of the paired essays addresses what the implications would
be for the estimate of tangible capital invested if the Wartime Excess Profits
Tax Reserve had been overstated or understated. Graham applies this more
flexible methodology to the analysis of several steel companies, including
U.S. Steel, Republic Iron & Steel, Baldwin, Lackawanna, American Steel
Foundries, and others.

Hypothesizing after significant digging that some companies have
understated and other companies have overstated their tax requirements,
Graham observes with his inimitable brand of finesse:

> Our conclusions are advanced not as positive statements of fact, but as
> tentative estimates based on available data. We will indeed vouch for the
> sufficient accuracy of our results *provided* (Graham's emphasis) the
> companies' figures from which we started are themselves accurate.

Discreet and tactful to the very end.

# 1

# CURIOSITIES OF THE BOND LIST

*Issues That Sell on Illogical Bases—*
*Misconceptions of Investors—*
*Some Foreign Issue Anomalies*

The test of the market, like that of Barrie's policeman, is popularly supposed to be "infallible." Economists picture a thousand buyers and sellers congregating in the market place to match their keen wits and finally evolve the correct price for each commodity. In the securities market particularly, the word of the ticker is accepted as law, so that one often thinks of prices as determining values, instead of vice versa.

But accurate as markets generally are, they cannot claim infallibility. While vagaries are to be found in both the stock and bond lists, the latter offers the better field for study since direct comparisons are easier, especially where two issues of the same company are selling out of line. The recent universal readjustment of bond prices has produced more than the usual number of such discrepancies, so that there are many opportunities for investors to exchange their holdings for issues "just as good," and returning a higher yield. Several of these anomalies will be discussed in the following paragraphs.

Let us first consider the case of Lorillard 7s, due 1944, and 5s, due 1951. The 7s are senior to the 5s in their claim on the company's assets, yet they are offered at 118, to yield 5.62 per cent., while par is bid for the 5s—a 5 per cent. basis.

## AN INVESTMENT MISCONCEPTION

Here then is an issue yielding five-eighths per cent more than a directly junior security. Moreover the 7s are a smaller issue, of nearer maturity. Of course the explanation of this discrepancy lies in the general prejudice against bonds selling at a high premium. The investor apparently imagines that by paying $1,180 for a $1,000 bond, he must eventually lose $180. The fallacy of this argument is well illustrated by this very example. For it would require only $59 a year to yield a straight 5 per cent on the $1,180 investment—the rate of the junior issue. But since the 7s pay $70 per bond, there is a surplus of $11 per year, which if simply accumulated *without interest* would at the date of maturity amount to about $300—fully $120 per bond more than the premium paid. If interest is compounded on these surpluses, the gain over the 5 per cent bond would be considerably more.

## A REVERSED CASE

The reverse side of the prejudice against premium bonds is found in the instance of Baltimore & Ohio convertible $4^1/_2$s, due 1933, compared with the Refunding and General 5s of 1995. *Both issues are secured by the same mortgage,* but the $4^1/_2$s sell at $87^1/_2$, yielding 5.70 per cent, while at 963/4 the 5s return only 5.16 per cent. This is all the more peculiar because the $4^1/_2$s have a conversion privilege which may conceivably become valuable; their maturity is much nearer, making for greater stability in market price; and their amount is limited to the bonds now outstanding, while the Refunding 5s may be increased almost indefinitely—in fact, the $4^1/_2$s are to be retired by an issue of Refunding 5s.

The cause of this discrepancy is probably twofold. In the first place, investors seem to prefer a 5 per cent coupon to any other. This is absolutely illogical, since a 4 per cent coupon on a bond bought at 80 is certainly no less attractive than 5 per cent on an issue costing par. Secondly, the public is wont to disregard that portion of the yield represented by the redemption at par of a bond purchased at a discount. The usual argument is that they don't expect to hold the bond to maturity, and therefore cannot count on receiving par for it.

This reasoning is fallacious, because it is not necessary to hold an issue until the due date in order to recover at least part of the discount. Each year as the maturity approaches, the market value of the bond should grow closer to par—unless its yield is increased as the result of general or special conditions. In the case of long term bonds the annual advance is imperceptible, but in short or medium maturities it is very evident. So with these Baltimore & Ohio $4^1/_2$s, their appreciation of 12 points to par will be spread over the comparatively short space of 13 years, adding a substantial amount to their yield.

The peculiar aspect of this question is the fact that the same investor who completely ignores the additional yield contained in a discount price is extremely adverse to buying a bond quoted at a premium. He is obsessed by the idea that the $180 premium on Lorillard 7s will have disappeared by 1941, but he pays little attention to the fact that by 1933 he will recover the $120 discount on Baltimore & Ohio $4^1/_2$s.

As it happens the straight yield on this latter issue at $87^1/_2$, considered as a stock, is practically equal to that of the General 5s, so that their other advantages described above render them a far more desirable security, even eliminating the discount element.

The Baltimore and Ohio new two-year notes, secured by 120 per cent in these Refunding 5s and Reading stocks, yield 5.73 per cent, against 5.17 per cent for the longer maturity. Their security is at least as good as that of the 1995 issue, and in the present unsettled bond market they can be relied on to display greater price stability because of their early redemption at par.

## THE ST. PAUL ISSUES

Almost the identical situation as in the B. and O. issues is presented by Chicago, Milwaukee and St. Paul convertible $4^1/_2$s of 1932, and convertible 5s of 2014. The 1932 maturity sells at $88^1/_4$ to yield 5.65 per cent., as against $97^1/_4$ and 5.14 per cent, respectively, for the long term issue. Both maturities are secured by the same mortgage, and in this case they are both convertible into common stock at par. The 5s of 2014 have some advantage in that their conversion privilege extends to 1926, four years longer than that of the 1932 issue. This feature is probably neutralized by the nearer redemption and limited amount of the latter bonds, so that the additional yield of more than one-half per cent makes these much more attractive.

There are three other St. Paul issues secured by the same mortgage as the foregoing, but not convertible. The $4^1/_2$s of 2014 sell at $93^1/_2$ and yield 5.39 per cent; the 4s, due 1934, yield 5.45 per cent at their present price of 84, while at $89^1/_4$ the 4s of 1925 return fully 5.65 per cent.

## OTHER DISCREPANCIES

Similar discrepancies in bonds of the same mortgage are afforded by three newly reorganized roads—St. Louis and San Francisco, Pere Marquette and Missouri Pacific. In the case of the Frisco 4s and 5s of 1950, the 4s at 61 yield 7.05 per cent against only 6.48 per cent for the 5s at 80—a difference of .53 per cent. Even figuring the straight yields as stocks, the 4s return 6.57 per cent, the 5s only 6.25 per cent.

This difference is probably caused by the much larger amount of 4s outstanding—a circumstance which explains, but does not justify the variance. But there are fewer Pere Marquette 4s than 5s of 1956, yet the 4s at 71 yield 5.92 per cent, against 5.76 for the 5s at 88.

The Missouri Pacific consolidated 5s present an even more glaring discrepancy. This issue is divided into three series, due 1923, 1926 and 1965, respectively. One would naturally expect the nearer maturities to sell at a lower basis—as is usually the case; e. g. the B. and O. 5s of 1918 yield only 5.12 per cent against 5.73 per cent for the 1919 issue. But the Missouri Pacific 5s of 1923 return 6.15 per cent at $94^1/_4$, the 1926 series yields 6.22 per cent at $91^1/_2$; while the 1960 maturity, which is the largest of the three series, is 90 bid—no better than a 5.60 per cent basis.

A simple analysis will indicate the absurdity of this situation. In 1923 the shortest maturity must be redeemed at par, an appreciation of 6 points. If the 1965 series is still selling on a 5.60 per cent basis, it will have gained only one-half of a point in the six years. In order to equal the advance of the 1923 issue, it would have to be selling at 96, which would be only a 5.25 per cent basis.

Incidentally it may be mentioned that the Missouri Pacific third extended 4s of 1938—which are an underlying mortgage on the main line—are now offered at 80 to yield 5.62 per cent.

It is interesting to observe that the General Electric debenture 5s of 1952 are still selling at 103, yielding 4.82 per cent, in spite of the fact that the new 6 per cent note issue due 1920, ranking equally with them, returns fully 5.70 per cent on its present price of $100^3/_4$. In the public utility field, mention may be made of the 5.37 per cent return of American Telephone and Telegraph collateral 4s of 1929 at 88, compared with 5.12 per cent on the newer 5 per cent issue due 1946 at $98^1/_4$. The 4s have the additional advantage of being legal for savings banks in some New England States.

## N. Y. CENTRAL CON. 4'S

Another important railroad issue is the New York Central consolidation 4 per cent mortgage, due 1988. These bonds are virtually senior to the refunding $4^1/_2$s of 2013, by which they are to be refunded. They are additionally favored by their limited authorized amount, and they yield 5.24 per cent at 77, against 4.82 per cent for the $4^1/_2$s at $93^3/_4$.

In the same way Norfolk and Western General 6s of 1931, which underly the consolidated 4s of 1996 recently sold at $112^7/_8$, a 4.72 per cent basis, against a yield of 4.56 per cent for the junior issue at 88.

Finally we shall invade the foreign government field and consider the peculiar case of the Japanese $4^1/_2$ per cent issues of 1925. These are outstanding in two series, the "seconds" having a junior claim on the earnings of the government tobacco monopoly. Nevertheless, both series have been usually quoted at the same price, and on some occasions recently the second $4^1/_2$s actually were selling above the first series. This seems strange, considering that the Cuban 5s of 1914, which follow the 1904 issue in their lien on the customs revenues, are now quoted six points under the older issue.

## AN INTERESTING CASE

In some respects the most interesting discrepancy of all is to be found in the Japanese $4^1/_2$s "German stamped," which sell about seven points below the plain bonds. Although these bonds were once the property of German subjects, they are accorded exactly the same treatment as any other bonds of that issue as far as interest payments are concerned, although probably not included in the frequent purchases for the sinking fund. The punctual payment of both principal and interest is guaranteed on the face of the bond even to the citizens of hostile countries—which, as a matter of fact, does not apply in this case anyway, since the bonds are now the bona-fide property of American citizens.

A painstaking scrutiny of the bond list would probably disclose other discrepancies of the same nature as those discussed above. This article has limited itself to issues of general interest, and hopes to find some utility in suggesting to investors here and there the possibility of advantageous exchanges. These are times of rapidly shifting values, and the security owner should be on the alert to acquaint himself with new conditions affecting his holdings, nor hesitate to modify them when favorable opportunities are presented.

# 2

# VALUATION OF GREAT NORTHERN ORE CERTIFICATES

*Based on 1914 and 1916 Operations—*
*Life of Mines—Comparison with*
*Porphyries—An Opinion on*
*Present Market Price*

For the average investor the annual reports of the Great Northern Iron Ore properties have been full of data but very bare of information. Instead of the familiar statement of a corporation to its stockholders they represent the accounting of trustees to beneficiaries. Hence there is no question of profit and loss, but only of receipts and disbursements. All expenditures, for instance, are lumped together for current operation or temporary investment.

Moreover, the organization of the properties is highly complicated. The trustees act both as administrators of the trust and as agents for the proprietary companies; and the latter are at the same time lessees, lessors and (since 1914) operators. Consequently the public's knowledge of the actual operations and earnings of Great Northern Ore is remarkably limited, considering the market prominence of the shares. Some utility may attach therefore to the

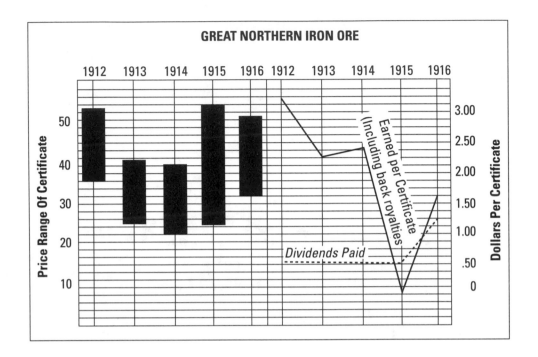

**GREAT NORTHERN IRON ORE**

following analysis of the trustees' reports. Its purpose is first to transform the financial statements into an intelligible income account and then to place a definite value upon the certificates on the basis both of their earning power and the expected life of the mines.

## TRUST FORMED IN 1907

As is well known the Great Northern Iron Ore Trust was formed in 1907 by the Great Northern Railway to administer the income from various iron mines controlled along its lines. The holder of each share of railway stock was given a share of interest in the Ore Properties, making a total of 1,500,000 shares outstanding, with no par value. Some of the mines had been owned outright by the railroad, and the remainder were held under lease or varying royalties and for various periods. But all these properties had in turn been leased or sub-leased to outside operators. In many cases the royalties received from the latter were no larger than those paid to the underlying owners, and these unprofitable "leases of the second class" were gradually disposed of by the trustees. Seven of the mines owned in fee had been leased for the life of the property at a sliding scale of royalty, which has averaged under 16¢ per ton. As will be seen, these "old leases" have supplied a large proportion of the output but only a small part of the total income.

All the remaining mines (some owned, others held under lease) had been leased to U. S. Steel Corporation, represented by the Great Western Mining Co. The contract provided for annually increasing production at an average royalty of $1.18 net per ton. In 1912 the output under this lease approximated 7,500,000 tons and the net royalties exceeded $9,000,000. At this time the Department of Justice, for some unaccountable reason, began to question the legality of the Great Western lease and its threat of prosecution under the Sherman Act compelled the Steel Corporation to exercise its option of cancelling the contract to take final effect at the end of 1914.

## STATE OF UNSETTLEMENT

The abrogation of this important agreement plunged the affairs of the properties in a state of great unsettlement, from which they have not yet completely recovered. Some of the mines relinquished by the Steel Corporation were leased to others, a number have been operated by the trustees, and the remainder were still idle at the close of the last fiscal year. Consequently the 1916 report is probably not as good an index of the properties' normal earning power as that of 1914, the last year of the Great Western lease. We intend accordingly to value the certificates on the basis both of 1914 and 1916 operations.

Taking the Trustees' report for 1914, but eliminating items not properly included in income account and making numerous other requisite adjustments, an earnings statement is evolved, as in Table I.

### TABLE I

GREAT NORTHERN ORE'S EARNINGS IN 1914

| | | | |
|---|---:|---:|---:|
| Receipts from "old leases" | | | $336,202 |
| Receipts from Gt. Western Lease | | $11,161,627 | |
|    Less freight | $3,440,398 | | |
|    Underlying royalties | 2,167,648 | | |
|    Proportion not accruing to ctfs | 1,736,260 | 7,344,306 | 3,817,323 |
| Miscellaneous receipts | | 207,496 | |
|    Less property account credits | | 49,466 | 158,030 |
| Trustees misc. income, less expenses | | | 47,126 |
|    Total income | | | $4,358,681 |
| Expenditures | $3,479,822 | | |
| Less chargeable to property account | 2,682,370 | | 797,452 |
|    Net income | | | $3,561,229 |
|    Per certificate | | | 2.37 |

It thus appears that the actual earnings in 1914 were $2.37 per certificate, against 53¢ net per certificate received by the Trustees in the form of distributions by the proprietary companies.

The next step in valuing the certificates is the determination of the life of the mines on the basis of present ore reserves and 1914 production.

## LIFE OF MINES

For greater accuracy we will consider the "old leases" and the Great Western lease separately. From estimates made by the Great Western Mining Company, it appears that on December 31 last, the lands formerly under lease to that company contained about 203,000,000 tons of ore. Production in 1916 aggregated 6,014,000 tons, so that if the 1914 rate of output were maintained in the future these mines would be exhausted in 34 years.

Earnings from these properties in 1914, including for convenience miscellaneous receipts less expenses, totalled $2.15 per share. By the so-called 7 per cent and 4 per cent standard of valuation, the interest of each certificate in these earnings would be worth $25.40. Briefly explained, the earnings of $2.15 would allow a 7 per cent return on the valuation of $25.40, and in addition yield an annual excess ($.372) which if compounded at 4 per cent will upon the exhaustion of the mine in 34 years amount to the full $25.40.

Ore remaining in the mines held under the "old leases" on December 31 last, according to estimates made by the Minnesota Tax Commission, equalled 89,350,000 tons. Since the 1914 output from this source was 1,825,579 tons, this rate of production would give the properties in question a life of 49 years. Earnings from the "old leases" amounted to only 22¢ per share. Applying the above method of valuation, the interest of each certificate in the old leases is shown to be worth only $2.86.

The total value of the earnings from all properties will thus equal $28.26 per share. On December 31 last net current assets were $5.40 per certificate. Adding these items we have a final present valuation of $33.66 for each certificate on the basis of 1914 operations.

Before commenting on this result let us apply the same process to the 1916 report. Here the earnings from the Great Western lease have disappeared and their place is taken by a number of new leases and by the Trustees' own operations. (Table II.)

Of course the relatively poor earnings in 1916 were due chiefly to the decline in production following the abrogation of the Great Western lease—but also largely to the disastrous shortage of tonnage space on the Great Lakes. Shipments from mines formerly operated for the Steel Corporation

**TABLE II**

GREAT NORTHERN ORE'S INCOME FOR 1916

| | | |
|---|---:|---:|
| Receipts from "old leases" | | $562,705 |
| Receipts from "new leases" | | 984,967 |
| Net proceeds of direct operations | | 544,994 |
| Miscellaneous receipts | $858,761 | |
|    Less prop. acct. credits. | 373,130 | 485,631 |
| Est. val. of 659,000 tons shipped from | | |
|    Hill & Walker mines, accruing to ctfs., but | | |
|       not included above | | 659,000 |
|    Total earnings | | $3,237,297 |
| Expenditures | $1,480,796 | |
| Less charg. to prop. acct. | 820,671 | 668,125 |
|    Net earnings | | $2,569,172 |
|    Per certificate | | $1.71 |

were only 3,902,000 tons, against 6,014,000 tons in 1914. The output of the "old leases" increased 1,382,000 tons, but owing to the low rate of royalty the advance in earnings from this source totalled only $226,000.

## AN ABNORMAL YEAR

Assuming provisionally that future operations will proceed only at the 1916 rate, the method of valuation employed above would yield the following results:

| | Life of Mines | Earned per ctf. 1916 | Value per ctf. |
|---|:---:|:---:|:---:|
| "Old leases" | 28 | $0.375 | $4.17 |
| Other mines and misc | 52 | 1.335 | 17.56 |
| Net current assets | | | 5.40 |
| Total | | $1.71 | $27.13 |

From the point of view of the Trustees, 1916 was a particularly abnormal year, inasmuch as they were required to assume the operating management of some of the mines—a development not contemplated at the time of forming the Trust. Accordingly they have made strenuous efforts to again place under lease the various properties relinquished by the Steel Corporation. I am informed that contracts have now been actually completed covering the last of these mines, so that beginning with next year all of the Great Northern Ore Properties will again be leased to outside interests.

For business reasons the terms of the most recent agreements cannot be published, but enough data is contained in the last annual report to indicate how earnings under the new regime will compare with those from the Great Western Lease. In 1914, a year of abnormally low iron ore prices, the net royalties paid by the Steel Corporation averaged $1.28 per ton. In 1916 with ore quotations nearly 50¢ above the preceding five year average, the properties directly operated showed profits of only $1.21 per ton. Even more significant is the fact that the average rate of royalty received from the new leases was only 81¢ per ton.

As for future production under the new management, I have been told by a Trustee that it will exceed substantially the 1916 figures (especially since the lessor companies control their own cargo space), but it will not equal the enormous output of 1914. In other words, it appears that neither the production nor the royalty rate can be counted on in the future to reach the figures reported under the Steel Corporation lease. Consequently the valuation of $33.66 per share on the basis of 1914 operations must be regarded as the maximum appraisal of the certificates under present conditions.

## MINES NOT INEXHAUSTIBLE

Although the Trustees use every opportunity to emphasize the fact that the Properties' ore reserves are being constantly depleted, a hazy notion seems prevalent that the mines are practically inexhaustible. It is true that in 1907 the Properties were estimated to contain 470,000,000 tons of ore, but nearly two-fifths of this total has since been disposed of, as indicated by the following summary:

| | | |
|---|---:|---|
| Original reserves | | 470,000,000 tons |
| Ore mined | 75,000,000 | |
| Leaseholds of the second class, relinquished | 104,000,000 | 179,000,000 tons |
| Ore remaining | | 292,000,000 tons |

It must further be remembered that a large proportion of the Properties are held under leases, expiring between 13 and 40 years. The two best producing mines, namely the Dean and Leonard, are held under leases expiring

**TABLE III**

COMPARISON WITH THE PORPHYRIES

|  | (Sep. 7) Present Price | Minimum Value | |
|---|---|---|---|
|  |  | Based on 1916 Operations | Based on Prospective Operations |
| Chino | 53 | $78 | 97 |
| Utah | 97 | 140 | 161 |
| Nevada | 22 | 31 | 33 |
| Ray | 26½ | 31 | 39 |

|  | | Maximum Value | |
|---|---|---|---|
|  |  | Based on 1916 Operations | Based on 1914 Operations |
| Great Northern Ore | 34 | 27 | 33½ |

in 15 and 13 years respectively. Of course, these leases may be renewed, but a higher underlying royalty may then be charged (as recently in the case of the Leonard mine), and in any case their approaching maturity will involve an uncertain factor.

Perhaps largely because of the general ignorance of the actual earning power of the certificates, Great Northern Iron Ore has always been a favorite medium of market manipulation. But despite the many bull campaigns of the last decade, the certificates have yet to pay an annual dividend larger than $1.25. Elsewhere in this article appears a graphic giving the range of prices, dividends, and actual earnings during the past five years. Whatever speculative fascination these Great Northern Iron Ore certificates may exert, the conclusion appears inevitable that at 34 they constitute a relatively unprofitable investment.

There is another side to this question however, and the answer to it cannot be deduced from the statistics. We refer to the strong accumulation of Great Northern Ore which has been going on for some time past. The evidence of this is found in the character of the fluctuations of the stock. What the basis for this accumulation is, we do not know, but past experience tells us that when buying of this kind occurs something favorable develops in the near future. Notwithstanding its low dividends and yield, therefore, we are favorably inclined toward Great Northern Ore.

# 3

# INSPIRATION'S DIFFICULTIES AND ACHIEVEMENTS IN 1917

*Ore Valuation and War Taxes—Costs and Profits—Investment Value of Stock*

The history of Inspiration has repeated itself, after an interval of exactly two years. On July 1, 1915, mining had not yet started; on July 1, 1917, operations had completely ceased. By April, 1916, the output had reached the calculated nominal rate of 10,000,000 lbs. per month. This month the company has announced that operations are again at normal. The demoralizing influence of the Arizona strike last summer can best be perceived by the fact that when operations recommenced it took almost as long to attain the standard production as when first the mine was opened. To pursue the parallel, it is strange that April, 1918, finds Inspiration at the same price level as two years before. The coincidence is so striking that a table of production and prices seems apposite. (See Table I.)

From November on, the price range in both periods has been very similar. The stockholder will devoutly pray that the analogy be continued through the rest of the year. He recalls that in August, 1916, the public suddenly realized that Inspiration had become a real mine, and the price shot up to 69 $^5/_9$ in the next month; outstripping Chino—its constant rival—by ten

## TABLE I

INSPIRATION COPPER—PRODUCTION AND PRICES

|  | Production | | Average Price | |
|---|---|---|---|---|
|  | 1915–16 lbs. | 1917–18 lbs. | 1915–16 | 1917–18 |
| July | 1,095,909 | Mine idle | $30^3/_4$ | $57^1/_2$ |
| August | 2,189,425 | Mine idle | $34^1/_2$ | $54^1/_4$ |
| Sept. | 2,746,066 | 2,250,000 | $38^3/_4$ | 51 |
| Oct. | 4,017,604 | 2,400,000 | $44^1/_2$ | $46^1/_4$ |
| Nov. | 4,855,526 | 2,250,000 | $44^1/_4$ | $41^1/_2$ |
| Dec. | 5,541,140 | 5,600,000 | 45 | $42^1/_2$ |
| Jan. | 5,354,815 | 5,000,000 | $45^1/_2$ | $45^1/_4$ |
| Feb. | 7,931,022 | 6,200,000 | $45^3/_4$ | $46^1/_2$ |
| March | 9,594,762 | 8,750,000 | $46^1/_2$ | 45 |
| April | 10,122,686 | *10,000,000 | $45^3/_4$ | 47 |

*Estimated.

points. In November the high record of $74^3/_4$ was made. A year later it was back to 38. Since then the mine and the stock have been recovering together—the former more rapidly.

On March 25, 1916—just eight months after mining began—an initial dividend of $1.25 was declared. The next quarter saw the rate raised to $2, at which it has since remained. There had been much fear of a reduction to $6 last month because of the strike, rising costs and heavy taxes, so that the maintenance of the regular dividend for the current quarter came rather as a pleasant surprise.

## FEATURES OF ANNUAL REPORT

The justification of the continued $2 payments is found in the annual report for 1917, recently made public. Despite the large decline in production—equalling one-third the 1916 output—the income account shows earnings after war taxes and depreciation of $9.37 per share. Although $8.25 per share had been disbursed in dividends, the net current assets had actually increased by $1,688,729 to $14,482,945—or $12.25 per share.

Certain features of the report are worthy of special comment. Inspiration is the first of the larger copper companies to publish the amount of Federal taxes levied against 1917 income. The figure is surprisingly low. Income and Excess Profits taxes together equalled but $1,185,249. If these taxes were computed upon the earnings as reported, a little algebra would show that the 6 per cent. Income Tax must represent more than half of this total, thus reducing the Excess Profits Tax to less than $500,000.

A paragraph in the report, however, contains an interesting sidelight on the method employed by the mining companies to deal with the difficult question of depletion in relation to war taxes. Inspiration has made a valuation of the developed ore as of March 31, 1913, and has then deducted from earnings for ore extinguishment an amount equal to the proportion of this value represented by the tonnage extracted during the year. This charge to earnings for depletion appears only in the company's tax return, and not in its published income account.

## ORE VALUATION AND WAR TAXES

I understand from an official of the company that the basis of valuing the ore reserves is substantially as follows: First, the copper content of all the ore is estimated, from which allowance is made for losses in tailings in order to obtain the amount of recoverable copper. The March, 1913, selling price, say, 15¢ is applied to this copper content to arrive at the gross value of the metal. From this sum is deducted first the estimated costs of production and then the entire value of the equipment. There is left the *net value* of the copper ore. But these proceeds are to be obtained over a series of years, and are therefore less valuable than a corresponding lump sum paid over on March 31, 1913. It was finally necessary, therefore, to compute the then present worth of each year's production according to approved actuarial methods, and the result was the valuation of the ore-bodies prescribed by the U. S. Treasury. The company is naturally averse to giving out figures on this delicate point, but the writer is convinced that the additional valuation referred to in the report must equal several times the fixed asset account in the balance sheet, and that therefore the depletion charged to earnings for taxation purposes no doubt will run into a few million dollars annually. This element is of great general importance in its bearing upon the war taxes of the coppers as a class. Apparently the burdens imposed by the War Revenue Act will not be nearly as heavy as their relatively small capitalization led investors to fear.

Another feature of interest in the report is the very moderate increase in the cost of production. Considering the sharp advances in wages and material prices, and especially the difficulties incident to the strike, one would have expected a disastrous jump in operating expenses. Under these conditions, holding down the costs to 10.44¢ per pound—an increase of but 1.77¢—must be regarded as quite an achievement. But these figures do not tell the whole story. The management purposely treated a lower grade of ore than the previous year, thus adding to the cost per pound. The operating cost per ton—the true measure of efficiency—increased only 6¢, from $1.95 to $2.01. In other words, the costs per unit increased by 3%—a really remarkable performance.

## PROBABLE COSTS AND PROFITS

The output of copper in the first six months exceeded the rate of 130,000,000 pounds per annum, but the shutdown in the summer reduced the year's total to 80,567,000 pounds. We are thus led to inquire what should be the company's earning power at present prices and costs, but with *normal* production. The latter figure let us set at 120,000,000 pounds. This was the 1916 output, and indications point to a similar production for the current period, which so far has closely paralleled the performance of two years ago. It represents only 80% of the plants' capacity and makes allowance therefore for a temporary curtailment of operations.

The 1917 costs (excluding Federal taxes and depreciation) averaged 10.47¢ per pound, permitting a net profit of say 13¢ on 23 1/2¢ copper. There is reason to believe that should expenses rise appreciably in 1918, they would bring a compensating increase in the selling price of the metal, since a number of high cost producers find it difficult to operate successfully on the present margin. Thirteen cents should therefore represent a reasonable profit for Inspiration under war conditions. On 120,000,000 pounds, the earnings would total $15,600,000. From this sum are to be deducted Federal Taxes which we estimate—very roughly, of course—at around $2,000,000. There remains $13,600,000, or $11.50 per share as the net profit applicable to dividends and depreciation. The depreciation charge in both 1916 and 1917 was fixed at $750,000, or about $.64 per share, but for reasons touched upon later this sum has not been deducted from the earnings applicable to dividends.

Profits of $11.50 per share for the stock under present conditions would justify the continuance of the $8 dividend rate, especially in view of the company's strong current asset position. The estimate of war taxes is of course predicated on the assumption that the reserve in the 1917 report has been correctly figured.

The copper companies in general have great advantages over most manufacturing enterprises. They do not tie up much money in inventories, they sell on a cash basis—and, most important of all, their yearly additions to plant are usually small.

Hence practically all the earnings are available for dividends. Inspiration is faced with an important piece of construction that some day must be undertaken, but it is unlikely to affect the dividend policy to any extent. I refer to the need of a leaching plant for handling the oxidized material which constitutes about 23 per cent. of the developed reserves. These important ore bodies cannot be treated by the concentrating methods used for the sulphide material, and will require a special reduction process. The company has experimented successfully on this class of ore, and refers to the favorable results of the large scale operations effected by New Cornelia. The latter mine recovered about 80 per cent. of the copper content. I believe that Anaconda announced an extraction of around 83 per cent. of its oxidized tailings. (Inspiration has been saving about 90 per cent. of its copper in sulphide form.)

There is no immediate need for the leaching plant and because of the prohibitive price of machinery the company has wisely postponed this addition until after the war. The cost will eventually be met out of earnings; but by that time the company will undoubtedly have accumulated a cash reserve for the purpose (if it has not already done so) so that this expenditure should not encroach on dividends.

## INVESTMENT VALUE OF STOCK

Is Inspiration cheap at the present price? The question can be answered mathematically by computing the minimum value of the stock both on $23^1/_2$¢ and $14^1/_2$¢ copper—the latter representing what many would call the lowest limit. But first the life of the mine must be estimated.

In the 1915 report Inspiration summarized its ore reserves as follows:

|  | Tons. | Per cent. Copper |
|---|---|---|
| Sulphide ore | 46,252,000 | 2.01 |
| Low sulphide ore | 28,698,000 | 1.26 |
| Oxidized ore | 17,460,000 | 1.31 |
| Mixed ore | 4,731,000 | 1.31 |
| Total | 97,141,000 | 1.63 |

No attempt has been made to develop additional ore since then, but mining operations have disposed of 9,268,000 tons of slightly less than average grade, leaving reserves of 87,874,000 tons at the beginning of 1918. Taking the 1916 production as an index—5,316,000 tons—the *minimum* life of the mine would be about 16 years.

**TABLE II**

<small>INSPIRATION IN WAR AND PEACE</small>

|  | "War Conditions" | "Peace Conditions" |
|---|---|---|
| Price of copper | 23$^1/_2$¢ per lb. | 14$^1/_2$¢ per lb. |
| Cost of copper | 10$^1/_2$¢ per lb. | est. 8¢ per lb. |
| (Excl. taxes and depreciation) |  |  |
| Net earnings | $13.20 per share | $6.60 per share |
| Federal taxes (estimated) | 1.70 per share | (1916) .34 per share |
| Balance for dividends | 11.50 per share | 6.26 per share |
| Minimum life of mine | 16 years | 16 years |
| Minimum Value of mining property | $91.42 per share | $49.77 per share |
| Net current assets 12/31/17 | 12.25 per share | 12.25 per share |
| Total minimum value | $103.67 per share | $62.02 per share |

Having determined the normal production and the minimum life, we can set down the mathematical valuation of Inspiration stock under both war and peace conditions as in Table II.

These appraisals are based upon the standard tables of Mr. H. C. Hoover, once a mining engineer, but now Food Administrator. The earnings will net 8 per cent. upon this valuation, and a sufficient annual surplus besides (if compounded at 4 per cent.) to replace the original investment at the end of 16 years.

The reason for not deducting depreciation in computing the per share earnings should now be evident. The equipment is expected to outlast the mine, and hence the investor is himself depreciating it when laying aside (theoretically) his sinking fund. Should the mine actually last fifty years, the equipment might have to be renewed, but then the whole basis of valuation would have to be radically revised upward.

This point draws attention to the fact that our valuations are based upon present ore reserves, which are practically certain to be increased later. Only a fraction of the mineral lands have been explored, and when development work is resumed there is no reason why Inspiration should not duplicate the recent success of the other large porphyries. It will be remembered that Nevada has increased its recoverable ore in three years from 39,000,000 to 68,000,000 tons.

If it is true, as many experts claim, that 14$^1/_2$¢ copper is a long way off our "peace valuation" of $62 would represent the height—or rather the depths—of conservatism. But earnings even on a $14^1/_2$¢ market would justify a $5 dividend rate—by no means a niggardly return on the present market price.

The porphyry coppers in general have not earned the dazzling percentage upon their market price shown by some of the steel issues. But they have no bonds or preferred stocks; all the property and earnings belong to the common stockholders, and no panic or depression can ever send them on the rocks. The investor in the coppers at these levels is sure to get his money back before the mine gives out—with an excellent return in the meantime—and each increase in metal prices, ore reserves, or productive capacity makes his holdings more valuable. One of the newest and best examples of this type of investment is Inspiration Copper, which in an industry long distinguished by able management, has established an enviable record for productive efficiency.

MARKET STATISTICS

|  |  |  | Dow Jones Avgs. | | 50 Stocks | | | Breadth |
|---|---|---|---|---|---|---|---|---|
|  |  | 40 Bonds | 20 Inds. | 20 Rails | High | Low | Total Sales | (No. issues) |
| Monday, | April  8... | 75.01 | 77.69 | 79.53 | 68.29 | 67.76 | 242,400 | 156 |
| Tuesday, | April  9... | 75.77 | 77.40 | 79.21 | 67.86 | 67.42 | 170,900 | 172 |
| Wednesday, | April 10... | 75.83 | 76.85 | 78.90 | 67.54 | 67.07 | 190,200 | 157 |
| Thursday, | April 11... | 75.85 | 75.58 | 78.00 | 67.04 | 66.22 | 343,500 | 195 |
| Friday, | April 12... | 75.91 | 76.25 | 78.45 | 66.84 | 66.23 | 211,400 | 153 |
| Saturday, | April 13... | 75.91 | 76.01 | 78.26 | 66.71 | 66.42 | 115,100 | 127 |
| Monday, | April 15... | 75.92 | 77.51 | 79.15 | 67.57 | 66.88 | 305,600 | 161 |
| Tuesday, | April 16... | 75.98 | 77.21 | 78.98 | 67.70 | 67.14 | 360,300 | 150 |
| Wednesday, | April 17... | 75.93 | 76.89 | 78.60 | 67.23 | 66.68 | 336,200 | 189 |
| Thursday, | April 18... | 75.91 | 78.11 | 79.28 | 68.07 | 67.29 | 523,200 | 173 |
| Friday, | April 19... | 76.05 | 78.60 | 79.38 | 68.70 | 68.07 | 521,200 | 187 |
| Saturday, | April 20... | 76.16 | 79.73 | 79.52 | 68.78 | 68.29 | 302,400 | 147 |

# 4

## NEVADA CONSOLIDATED— A MINING PHOENIX

*A "Dying Mine" That Refuses to Expire—Its Changing Balance Sheet— Investment Worth of Nevada's Stock*

In December, 1912, the Nevada directors declared an extra dividend of 50 cents per share, which they were careful to point out was not a payment from earnings but a return of capital made out of the reserve for ore extinguishment. It chanced that in the annual report published shortly afterwards the tonnage of recoverable ore showed a decrease for the first time since operations commenced. From these two events originated the famous theory of the exhaustion of Nevada, which completely dominated its market action for many years, and even now persists in the minds of many an investor.

The sad story of the gradual extinction of Nevada is shown in Table I.

After having mined nearly twice as much ore as it started with in 1907, Nevada still has left about *five times the original tonnage*. The map shows that large portions of the company's property are as yet unprospected, and the management is now very optimistic as to the possibilities of future additions to the ore reserves. On the basis of last year's record tonnage removed, the

## TABLE I

RECOVERABLE ORE

| | |
|---|---|
| Sept. 30, 1907 | 14,433,000 tons |
| 1908 | 20,000,000 tons |
| 1909 | 29,000,000 tons |
| Dec. 31, 1910 | 40,361,000 tons |
| 1911 | 40,853,000 tons |
| 1912 | 38,854,000 tons |
| 1913 | 39,108,000 tons |
| 1914 | 41,020,000 tons |
| 1915 | 50,525,000 tons |
| 1916 | 67,993,000 tons |
| 1917 | 70,025,000 tons |
| Total tonnage mined to date. | 25,841,000 tons |

minimum life of the mine is now $17^1/_2$ years against 15 years for Inspiration. For a liquidating proposition, Nevada seems to possess extraordinary vitality.

Although last year established a record for tonnage mined, the production of refined copper suffered a substantial decline from 90,735,000 lbs. to 82,040,000 lbs. This was due chiefly to a reduction in the grade of ore mined in the open pit from 1.53 per cent to 1.28 per cent. In addition the percentage of copper recovered showed a slight shrinkage, so that the extraction per ton fell from 24.12 lbs. to 21.81 lbs. per ton.

Judged from the assay of remaining ore reserves, the decline in the grade of ore mined should prove a temporary factor. The open pit ore averages 1.415 per cent copper and the richer material in the Ruth underground working brings the grade of the total up to 1.58 per cent. The falling off in recoveries is explained by the crowded conditions at the mill due to the treatment of foreign ore from Consolidated Coppermines. Steps have already been taken to meet this difficulty, with the result that the extraction in the fourth quarter reached 73.94 per cent, which is better than the average for 1916.

Table II gives the latest income account of the company. Of the net profit $8,297,946, or $4.15 per share, was paid in dividends and $528,706 was charged off for plant alterations, leaving a final addition to surplus of $661,082, or 33¢. per share. To this sum must be added an item of $108,434 representing the earnings of the subsidiary Nevada Northern RR., in excess of dividends paid to the parent company.

## TABLE II

INCOME ACCOUNT FOR 1917

|  |  |  | Per Pound |
|---|---|---|---|
| Sales of Copper |  | $19,484,271 | 23.75c |
| Operating Expenses (excluding taxes and depreciation) | $10,254,466 |  | 12.50c |
| Less other income | 2,088,702 |  | 2.54c |
| Net Operating cost | $8,165,764 |  | 9.96c |
| Taxes | 896,458 |  | 1.09c |
| Depreciation and Depletion | 934,517 |  | 1.14c |
| Total Cost |  | 9,996,739 | 12.19c |
| Net Profit |  | $9,488,532 | 11.56c |
| Profit Per Share, $4.75 |  |  |  |

In the statement, the company's figures have been corrected to include an additional $165,800 for taxes, to bring the allowance made during the year up to the final estimate. On the other hand the management explains that the price actually received for copper was over 2¢ more than the stated average of 23.75¢, because the unsold copper (in accordance with previous custom) has been inventoried at $13^1/_2$¢. The writer has calculated that there were 14,000,000 lbs. of finished copper at hand at the end of the year, which must already have been sold at $23^1/_2$¢—an advance of 10¢ over the carrying price.

On the basis of the selling value of the copper produced, the year's earnings were therefore about 70¢ per share more per share than reported—in all, about $5.50 per share.

It will be observed that the net operating costs before taxes and depreciation averaged 9.96¢ per pound against 7.62¢ the previous year—the difference of 2.34¢ representing the increase in mining expense due to war causes other than taxes. Taxes increased from .51¢ to 1.09¢ per pound, bringing the total advance in costs up to 3.43¢ per pound. In the operating expense of both years has been included a charge of 30¢ per ton of ore mined—about $1^1/_2$¢ per pound—for the amortization of prepaid development expense. The latter item represents chiefly the cost of removing the capping, or layer of waste material, which covers the commercial ore in the open pit. The expenditure for this purpose each year is carried to a deferred asset account, which at the same time is being extinguished by the 30¢ charge for each ton mined.

A careful analysis of the Nevada's charge for depreciation, ore extinguishment, and amortization of stripping expense brings out some very striking facts as to the ultimate financial condition of the company—and incidentally sheds much light upon the much discussed capital distributions referred to in the opening paragraph.

Let us assume for the sake of simplicity that no new ore is discovered, that last year's rate of production is maintained and that therefore the mine is exhausted in the middle of 1935. Also that the present charges for depreciation, etc., are continued without change. Following is a chronology of future events in the life of Nevada, *as they would appear on the books*.

1. By 1925 the mill and smelter will have disappeared from the balance sheet through depreciation charges which have already reduced their book value by 47 per cent. Needless to say these plants (which are well maintained) will be far from a heap of ruins in eight years, and although theoretically extinct, will probably be operating at full blast.

2. By 1927 the stripping of the present ore reserves in the open pit will be completed and the prepaid expense item in the balance sheet will begin to contract rapidly, through the 30¢ per ton operating charge.

   (It is impossible to make a similar forecast for the Ruth mine, but this is of minor importance.)

3. By 1928 the entire cost of the ore in the ground will have been extinguished and although the mine will then have remaining over twice as much ore as at first reported, this property will be given no value in the balance sheet.

4. By 1931 the cost of stripping the pit ore will have been completely amortized by operating charges. This means that in the last three years of production there will be no stripping expense to charge off,—an item which now represents $1^1/_2$¢ per pound of the cost of production.

But as these assets gradually fade from the balance sheet, what will take their place? The answer is *cash*,—unless (1) new properties are purchased, or (2) the surplus is reduced by dividends in *excess of profits*. If we suppose that neither course is followed, but that Nevada pays out all it earns from now on, keeping the surplus at the 1917 figure, Table III shows the present tendency of Nevada's balance sheet carried forward into the future. Like most predictions, this is at best approximate—especially in the treatment of the prepaid expense.

Table III demonstrates that the purchaser of Nevada at $20 per share need not worry particularly about the exhaustion of the mine in 1935.

**TABLE  III**

BOOK VALUE OF NEVADA'S ASSETS PER SHARE

|  | 1913 | 1917 | 1925 (est.) | 1928 (est.) | 1931 (est.) |
|---|---|---|---|---|---|
| Mine | $2.16 | $1.63 | $.43 |  |  |
| Mill and Smelter | 3.24 | 2.62 |  |  |  |
| Prepaid Expense | 1.64 | 2.72 | 2.72 | $2.12 |  |
| Net Current Assets (Includes Investments) | 3.02 | 8.16 | 11.98 | 13.01 | $15.13 |
| Total Book Value Per Share | $10.06 | $15.13 | $15.13 | $15.13 | $15.13 |

Three years before that time the company will have converted all its assets into liquid form, ready either for distribution or for the purchase of new properties.

Regarded from another standpoint, on $23^{1}/_{2}$¢ copper Nevada can maintain its former charges for depreciation, etc., pay dividends of $4.50 per share and still keep its $20,000,000 surplus intact. On $14^{1}/_{2}$¢ copper, assuming 1915 costs, it can earn $2.50 per share after all charges. The stockholder could therefore collect dividends of between $2.50 and $4.50 for thirteen years, and at the end of that period still have an equity in net current assets of $15 per share, together with three years more of production at the present rate,—but eliminating the stripping charge of $1^{1}/_{2}$¢ per pound from operating costs. If additional ore is developed, as the officials expect, the value of the stock will increase.

Nevada differs from the other porphyries in that its stockholders do not have to establish a sinking fund out of dividends for the return of their capital. The company is doing that for the investor—and at a more rapid rate than is necessary. In this connection, the meaning of the capital distributions should now be clearer. They do not represent the directors' belief that the exhaustion of the mine is imminent, but merely a division of part of the cash with which—through depreciation charges—the fixed assets have been gradually replaced in the balance sheet. Unless more of such distributions are made, Nevada will soon be converted from a mine into a bank.

Marketwise, Nevada has never been much in the limelight. In the past, when it wasn't condemned as a "liquidating proposition" it was disdained as a minority issue. Time brings its revenges. Utah Copper, which controls Nevada, is now in its turn controlled by Kennecott, and the Nevada stockholder has welcomed his patronizing big brother into the ranks of the minority.

Some day the public will realize that a low cost, brilliantly managed copper mine like Nevada,—rich in cash and free from debt—is fully as safe an investment as many a railroad or industrial bond, and a great deal more profitable.

# 5

# SECRETS OF INVESTED CAPITAL

*Tangible Assets as Revealed by the*
*War-Tax Reserve—Real Versus*
*Book Values*

The War Revenue Act of last October established certain relations between the Invested Capital, the Net Earnings and the Excess Profits Tax of a corporation, so that if any two of these elements are known the third can be deduced from them. Consequently in those cases where a company has accurately reported its earnings and tax reserve, a set of formulae can be employed to determine what figure it has used for its Invested Capital in making its tax return.

Needless to say, the Capital reported to the Treasury Department is often very different from that shown in the balance sheet. The published valuation of a company's plant account will rarely reflect its original cost, but includes usually unstated amounts of a commodity variously termed "good will," "intangible assets," or simply "water." But the Invested Capital figures we obtain from the War Tax Reserve are based upon the actual cash outlay and thus enable us to determine the tangible asset value of the preferred and common stock.

Before considering the individual issues it might be well to discuss the importance of the information we are seeking.

Only a few years ago the average industrial common stock was little more than a vehicle for speculation. Its market price was determined primarily by manipulation. The only factors of intrinsic worth that received any consideration were current earnings and future prospects. It was taken for granted that the issues had little or no tangible value; the exact amount of water in the capitalization was of small importance; and it made little difference whether the good will was plainly stated—e.g. as by Goodrich—or concealed in the plant account as in the case of U. S. Rubber.

## IMPORTANCE OF TANGIBLE VALUES

But the war has rapidly been transforming these out and out speculations into semi-investment and even pure investment issues. Hence the public is gradually coming to apply *investment* standards to determine their value, and the question of their tangible asset backing is finally assuming considerable importance. A dozen times a year we are regaled with analyses of U. S. Steel Common's tangible asset value, showing that all the pristine water has been carefully evaporated and replaced by "bricks and mortar." The Goodrich balance sheet is now eagerly scrutinized to find out what progress is being made towards substantiating the once completely ethereal common.

There are many circumstances to justify the newly awakened interest in tangible values. The most obvious of these is the tax law which differentiates sharply between real and imaginary assets, penalizing water heavily through higher levies. But this is only one aspect of the whole fabric of government control, which in fixing prices and compensation looks behind the balance sheet figures to the actual cash investment involved in each enterprise.

A perhaps more important element is also involved. With the largely increased capacity of our plants we may eventually enter a period of severe competition in which profits will be restricted to a reasonable return on the value of the producing assets.

For these reasons the question of real capital invested must be differently regarded than in 1912. It is no longer a matter of slight importance that Goodrich reveals and U. S. Rubber conceals the tangible value of its common stock. Whatever clues the 1917 Tax Reserve can afford us towards securing such information should therefore be entitled to due attention, even if in some cases they be incomplete or approximate. We propose, therefore, to work backwards from the Tax Reserves of leading industrials, to see what we can learn therefrom as to the tangible value of their common stocks.

Lack of space prevents a complete exposition of the mathematical process involved in determining the Invested Capital, so that only a few of the more important points can be touched on here. Since the typical Tax Reserve represents the sum of the Excess Profits and 6% Income Tax, it is first of all necessary to separate these two elements—as is done in the formulas herewith (the accuracy of which can easily be verified by practical tests.)

## FORMULA A

$$\text{Excess profits tax} = \frac{100 \times \text{total tax} - 6 \times \text{net income}}{94}$$

In formula A we have two known factors—the Net Income and the Excess Profits Tax—from which the unknown quantity (Invested Capital) remains to be determined. For this purpose a series of five formulas have been constructed, corresponding to the five "brackets" or rates of tax,—varying from 20% to 60%. In the case of General Electric for example, which reaches the 35% rate, formula B is employed:

## FORMULA B

$$\text{Invested capital} = \frac{3500 \times \text{net income} - 10,000 \times \text{excess profits tax}}{275 + 20 \times \text{exemption}}$$

In this instance, the exemption evidently stands at the maximum,—9%. Where the pre-war profits fall somewhere between 7% and 9% of the Capital, the exact rate of exemption must be determined by trial and error. Readers interested in checking over results can easily do so by applying the proper rates of tax to our figures for Invested Capital given herewith. The Excess Profits and Income Tax levies thus obtained will be found to correspond almost exactly with the company's stated Tax Reserve.

## METHOD EMPLOYED

With this article appears a table showing the invested capital of a number of important companies, the amount of good-will included in their assets, and finally the tangible value of the common stock as of December 31st last, compared with the present market price. The steel and equipment issues are omitted from this table since they are reserved for treatment in a subsequent issue. It must be remembered in connection with our results that their accuracy is directly dependent upon that of the Tax Reserve as published by the company considered. In cases where a larger reserve than necessary has been set aside—for conservative or other reasons—the invested capital will accordingly appear smaller than it really is. For this reason companies stating their tax reserves as an exact figure admit of more accurate treatment than those publishing a round or approximate amount.

In view of the references in the above paragraphs it is perhaps natural that we devote some space to the asset value of U. S. Rubber common. According to our computation the $130,000,000 plant account on December 31st, 1916, contained practically $70,000,000 of water—an amount equal not only to the entire common issue, but to half the preferred stock as well. The accumulated surplus, however, had created a dollar for dollar backing in tangible assets for the preferred and about $20 per share of real value for the common. The 1917 earnings have since raised this value to $30 per share.

These figures are startling and may well be challenged as inaccurate. It happens that they are substantiated by figures contained in the official circular describing the U. S. Rubber 5% bonds sold in 1917. The appraised value, as of October 31, 1916, of the tangible assets securing the $60,000,000 issue is here given as $124,000,000. In other words, the margin of tangible assets for the

APPROXIMATE TANGIBLE ASSET VALUES OF INDUSTRIAL COMMON STOCKS AS DETERMINED FROM THEIR WAR TAX RESERVES (FINAL 000 OMITTED IN TABULATION)

| Company | Earned 1917 Before Taxes | Tax Reserve | "Invested Capital" | Tangible Capital (Deducting Permitted Allowance for Good-Will) | Book Capital Dec. 31, 1916 | Good-Will Concealed in Property Account | Tangible Asset Value of Common Dec. 31, 1917 | Present Market Value of Common |
|---|---|---|---|---|---|---|---|---|
| American Can | $18,000 | $6,000 | $48,000 | $31,500 | $93,500 | $62,000 | $0 | $48 |
| Am. Smelt. & Ref. | 23,931 | 3,850 | 147,000 | 117,000 | adj.167,000 | 50,000 | 85 | 78 |
| Am. Woolen | 14,126 | 3,000 | 63,700 | 51,900 | 71,400 | 19,500 | 88 | 58 |
| Central Leather | 22,250 | 6,000 | 76,000 | 61,400 | 93,400 | 32,000 | 98 | 71 |
| Corn. Products Ref | 14,850 | 3,500 | 58,700 | 42,800 | 92,800 | 50,000 | 44 | 44 |
| General Chemical | 10,775 | 1,800 | 46,000 | 46,000 | 46,000 | | 200 | 185 |
| General Electric | 34,193 | 7,289 | 145,000 | 145,000 | 135,600 | | 160 | 147 |
| Goodrich | 12,794 | 2,250 | 65,300 | 47,900 | 49,300 | 1,400 | 45 | 45 |
| Nat'l Cloak & Suit | 2,570 | 524 | 11,200 | 7,900 | 8,000 | 100 | 37 | 70 |
| Nat'l Enameling | 5,345 | 1,100 | 25,100 | 20,280 | 29,985 | 9,705 | 100 | 53 |
| Sears, Roebuck | 19,002 | 3,977 | 80,200 | 66,600 | 60,000 | | 90 | 136 |
| Underwood Type | 3,027 | 500 | 12,600 | 10,100 | 10,100 | | 80 | 103 |
| U. S. Ind. Alcohol. | 12,350 | 5,240 | 22,430 | 18,500 | 30,500 | 12,000 | 120 | 128 |
| U. S. Rubber | 18,800 | 3,465 | 90,000 | 70,000 | 140,000 | 70,000 | 32 | 62 |
| Virginia Car. Chem. | 10,885 est. 2,500 | | 36,100 | 26,400 | 62,400 | 36,000 | 50 | 55 |

common and preferred stocks was only $64,000,000—leaving but $2,000,000 or $6 per share for the common. These figures are even less than our own—the difference being accounted for partly by our inclusion of the earnings from October 31, 1916, to the end of that year. With this adjustment made the two appraisals are close enough to indicate the substantial accuracy of our method.

It turns out finally that Goodrich—despite its $58,000,000 of acknowledged good-will—has a greater tangible asset backing per share than U. S. Rubber. In 1913 this value was practically nil. It has since grown to $45 per share and is now equal to the market price of the issue.

## THE CASE OF U. S. ALCOHOL

A very similar development is shown by U. S. Industrial Alcohol, which apparently has included in its property account good-will to the full amount of the $12,000,000 common stock. Consequently at the outbreak of the war the junior issue had a tangible asset value not exceeding $20 per share, which three years of prosperity has since increased to no less than $120. In this case, however, the market price has more than kept pace with the growth of tangible assets—an exception to the general rule, explained by the strong technical position of the issue.

National Enameling & Stamping affords another example of the influence of recent prosperity on tangible values. We find that about one-third of the plant account—i.e. $9,700,000—represents good-will, and that therefore the asset value of the common in 1914 was about $60 per share. Since then over $40 per share has been added to surplus and reserves, so that the common has today a dollar for dollar backing in tangible assets.

In a recent article on American Smelting & Refining in THE MAGAZINE OF WALL STREET, the original amount of water in its capitalization was referred to as an unknown quantity of large proportions. The War Tax Reserve enables us to determine an approximate valuation of these intangible assets, which according to over computation must have amounted to about $50,000,000, or the entire amount of the original common. Substantial profits have accumulated since those early days, however, and the writer would now set the real asset value of "Smelters" as nearly $85 per share—somewhat above its present market price.

## AMERICAN CAN

On the other hand, the Tax Reserve of American Can, if reliable, would place the company in a class with U. S. Rubber from the standpoint of fluid ingredients. Our formulae result in an Invested Capital of only $48,000,000, which would probably include a permitted good-will allowance of 20% of the stock issues or $16,500,000. This would leave but $31,500,000 of tangible capital, against a book capital and surplus of $93,500,000—a small discrepancy of $62,000,000. Such a mass of water, if actually present, would have acounted for not only the entire common stock, but half of the preferred issue as well. Against this handicap the accumulated surplus has been able to make little headway. The tangible value of the preferred is now about $90 per share and no solid value has yet been created for the common. Of course, this analysis would be too severe in proportion as the company has over-stated its tax reserve, which it presents as the round sum of $6,000,000. But admitting that our results are merely approximate, it is evident that the original promoters of "Can" possessed exceptionally liberal views on capitalization—a fact which undoubtedly has been one of the prime causes of the aversion shown by investors to the securities of this company, like those of U. S. Rubber, in the past. It remains to be seen whether the large earning power recently developed will succeed in overcoming what once was certainly a well-founded prejudice.

It will be noted from our table that American Woolen is credited (or debited) with a good-will item of $19,500,000—almost equal to the entire common issue. The same is true of Corn Products Refining, which the war has at last enabled to cope with its $50,000,000 burden of intangible values. Even Central Leather reveals about $32,000,000 of good-will—$80 per share of common—which large surplus earnings have since replaced by tangible assets.

Those companies which report the amount of their good-will in their balance sheets generally appear to have based their tax return on an Invested Capital corresponding very closely with their book capital. Examples are Sears Roebuck, which on December 31st last had a tangible asset value for the common of $90 per share—also National Cloak & Suit, Underwood Typewriter and Goodrich.

## GRADUAL ELIMINATION OF WATER

Two companies in the list have no good-will stated in their balance sheet and none concealed in their property account. As might be expected, these are General Electric and General Chemical,—the aristocrats of the industrial group, with an investment rating established long before the war. An interesting detail crops up in connection with General Electric. The company's book capital and surplus on December 31, 1916, was $135,000,000 but its tax reserve indicates an Invested Capital of about $145,000,000. Evidently the company had understated its assets in the balance sheet by about $10,000,000—a truly exceptional case. But in order to take full advantage of the Invested Capital provisions of the War Revenue Act, the company has found it desirable to bring these hidden assets to light, and for this purpose created the Special Reserve of $12,000,000, which has given rise to so much comment among the followers of the stock.

If these results are viewed as a whole, the striking fact is not so much the large quantities of good will concealed in the plant account, but the extent to which most companies have succeeded in replacing this original water by real assets, and in creating a foundation of solid value for their junior issues. The public has long had a general idea as to which companies were over-capitalized and which have been most successful in remedying this defect. But the question of tangible value has now assumed far greater significance than ever before because of the gradual progress of many of these issues into the investment class. The foregoing investigation—while to some extent approximate in its results—should provide a certain amount of definite information on this highly important question.

# 6

## THE GREAT STEEL TAX MYSTERY

*SECRETS OF INVESTED
CAPITAL—PART 2*

*Various Phases of the U. S. Steel Tax
Situation—Other Steel and Equipment
Stocks—Excessive and Insufficient
Tax Reserves*

In my previous article on this subject I pointed out that by deriving the Invested Capital on which a company's Tax Reserve has been based, we might reach one of two opposite conclusions. Assuming that the Tax Reserve is correct as reported, we can determine absolutely what is the tangible capital invested and therefore the asset value of the common stock. But on the other hand, it frequently happens that the capital indicated by the Tax Reserve is larger or smaller than the figure established by independent and authentic information. In such cases it is evident that the War Tax has been under or over-stated, and we are accordingly led to correct the company's Income Account, decreasing or increasing the percentage reported as earned upon the stock.

## U. S. STEEL CORPORATION

In a discussion of this kind the Steel Corporation must inevitably claim considerable attention. A scrupulous author hesitates to add to the already overflowing sea of literature on this single enterprise, but the importance of the subject and the novelty of some of the conclusions to be advanced must excuse us for recurring to this sadly threadbare theme.

The Steel War Tax has always been a mystery to those who understood its implications. That the figure was enormous was not surprising—the perplexity was caused by the extremely high *percentage* borne by the Tax Reserve to the Earnings. The Corporation reported net for preferred dividends of $224,000,000 after deducting $233,000,000 taxes. The latter apparently claimed *over* 50% of the net income—an unparalleled proportion, contrasting with 33% for Republic Iron and Steel and approached only by companies (e.g. Midvale) whose Invested Capital was reduced by the absence of preferred stocks.

Could Steel's actual capital be so small compared with its earnings, that it must turn over to the Government a much larger percentage of its profits than any similar company? Our computation showed that using the above figures for income and taxes, the capital indicated would be only $462,000,000 against a book figure of nearly $1,400,000,000. This discrepancy was so striking as to prove conclusively that either the tax has been greatly overstated or earnings understated—or both.

A new factor has been injected into the situation by the recent publication of Secretary McAdoo's testimony on August 14th last before the House Committee on Ways and Means. Here he analyzes a number of actual returns made to the Treasury Department by large Corporations, whose names are replaced by letters. For the first of these, Corporation A, he gives the following data:

| | |
|---|---|
| Invested Capital for 1917 | $1,427,233,403 |
| Invested Capital for Pre-War Period | 1,132,459,896 |
| Net Income, 1917 | 568,964,090 |
| Excess Profits Tax for 1917 | 173,504,430 |

There is only one enterprise in this country—or in the world—to which the above figures could apply. Since this is a real and not a fictitious example, it is undeniably a transcription of the tax return of the U. S. Steel Corporation.

We immediately remark that Steel paid a smaller war tax than it reserved. Adding in $23,728,000 for Income Tax, as easily determined, the total levy is "only" $197,230,000–$36,234,000, or $7 per share, less than the published figure.

There is nothing astonishing about this discovery since we have pointed out that the reserve set up in the report was inexplicably large. The really extraordinary aspect of Mr. McAdoo's testimony is found in the statement of Invested Capital and Net Earnings. The accepted figure of Steel's 1917 earnings was $457,684,000 subject to tax; but according to the Treasury Department taxable earnings were fully $111,000,000, or $22 per share, more. Again the Capital, Surplus and Reserves at the beginning of 1917, as shown in the balance sheet, totalled about $1,360,000,000, which was generally held to contain somewhere between $500,000,000 and $700,000,000 of good will (of which not more than $175,000,000 could be included in Invested Capital because of the 20% limitation). But Secretary McAdoo here places the Invested Capital at $1,427,000,000, actually a larger figure than that claimed by the balance sheet.

Here are two mysteries indeed, and important ones—because if we accept the apparent significance of the Treasury's data, we should have Steel earning $105 before taxes and *over* $68 *per share after taxes*—compared with the recognized figure of $39.15. Not only that, but we should have an asset value of $1,067,000,000 behind the common—*or more than* $200 *per share at the beginning of* 1917.

A careful study of all the ramifications of the War Revenue Act as applied to U. S. Steel results in the following possible explanation of the wide divergence between the figures given by the Treasury and by the annual report. The Steel Corporation is a holding company, its property being the securities of its subsidiaries, and its income the dividends and interest received from them. According to Article 78 of Regulation 71, construing the Excess Profits Tax, affiliated companies may, and sometimes must, make a joint return covering their combined capital and income. If this had been done by all Steel *subsidiaries* together—but excluding the Corporation itself as merely the holding company—the large net income reported to the Treasury would be explained as suggested in Table I.

The close correspondence of this total with the Treasury figures lends plausibility to our explanation. It is strange that the $75,000,000 deducted from earnings for reserves has escaped general attention. These allowances—equivalent to $15 per share—represent in principle an appropriation of *surplus* against possible eventualities, and as such are not recognized by the Treasury as charges against the year's operations—although they are thus treated by the Corporation.

There would seem to be a disadvantage in the subsidiaries' making the return instead of the Corporation itself as a unit, because by doing the former, the interest on the Steel Corporation's bonds cannot be deducted from earnings. But this is more than compensated for by the fact that the assets represented by these bonds can be included in Invested Capital, since the bonds are not the liability of the subsidiaries. This fact would account for the large Invested Capital revealed by the Treasury Department. In Table II we show how the latter figure might be reconciled with the Corporation's own statement, as modified by prevalent notions as to the original good-will included therein.

Of course, in this table the good-will has been arbitrarily valued so as to make the final figures correspond—but it is sufficiently close to generally accepted ideas (based on the investigation of the Commissioner of Corporations) to make the above analysis worth considering as a possible solution of the great Steel Tax Mystery. Incidentally we would point out that after subtracting the $150,000,000 good-will allowed, and the $260,000,000 *net* for U. S. Steel bonds proper, we have left a tangible Invested Capital of $1,017,000,000 as of December 31, 1916. This is equivalent to an asset value for Steel Common of about $140 per share at the beginning of this year (after restoring the $75,000,000 reserves written off earnings in 1917).

If we finally pass on to the other steel issues, we immediately strike another puzzle—the relation of Lackawanna's War Tax to Republic Iron and Steel. Note these figures.

|  | Lackawanna | Republic |
|---|---|---|
| Book Capital | $52,912,000 | $70,945,000 |
| Taxable Income | 26,147,000 | 24,454,000 |
| Tax Reserve | 10,040,000 | 8,597,000 |

Since Lackawanna's book capital is so much smaller—due to the absence of preferred stock—it would be thought to pay a very much larger percentage of its earnings in taxes than does Republic. On the basis of book capitals, therefore, we should expect either a smaller tax for Republic or a larger tax for Lackawanna. Here is an opportunity to bring our algebraic formulas into action. Sure enough, the Tax Reserves indicate an Invested Capital of $61,200,000 for Republic and $57,370,000 for Lackawanna—in one case *less*, in the other *more* than the balance sheet figures. It will suprise no one to learn that Republic's tangible investment is less than its annual report shows, but no one would have supposed (or will now believe) that Lackawanna's property account *understates* its real assets. We must look further into this question.

Our figure of $61,200,000 for Republic's Invested Capital would include a good-will allowance of about $10,400,000, bringing the tangible capital down to $50,800,000. This is by no means a bad showing, since it gives the

**TABLE  I**

DEVIATION OF THE TREASURY FIGURES FOR U.S. STEEL'S 1917 EARNINGS.

| | | |
|---|---:|---:|
| Net before Taxes, as stated in the report | | $457,700,000 |
| ADD: | | |
| Interest and premium on Corporation's bonds (not a charge against subsidiaries' earnings) | | 22,100,000 |
| Profits of subs. on sales to other subs. of material still held by latter—excluded from Corporation's Income Account | | 14,100,000 |
| Increase in Contingent and other Reserves | $19,300,000 | |
| Less charged to Surplus | 4,000,000 | |
| | | $15,300,000 |
| Reserve for excess of cost over pre-war value—    Inventories | | 29,800,000 |
| Plant | | 29,800,000 |
| (Note: Last three items have been charged to Income, but are not allowed as Deductions by Treasury Dept.) | | |
| Total Earnings as Reported to Treasury Dept. | | $568,800,000 |

common an asset value of $94 at the end of 1916, and fully $142 at the beginning of the current year.

At this point Mr. McAdoo's testimony again intervenes. In the list of twenty-two returns presented, (Company "C") has been quite generally identified with Republic Iron & Steel. Here are the figures:

C "Company"

| | |
|---|---:|
| Invested Capital | $70,827,000 |
| Taxable Income 1917 | 24,124,000 |
| Excess Profits Tax | 6,258,000 |

Republic

| | |
|---|---:|
| Invested Capital | $70,945,000 |
| | (Book Figures) |
| Taxable Income 1917 | 24,454,000 |
| Excess Profits Tax | 7,574,000 |
| | (Indicated by Reserve) |

If ("Company C") is really Republic Iron & Steel in disguise then in its report to the Collector it has evidently used its full book capital and surplus, without any deduction for intangible assets. This basis of calculation naturally results in a smaller tax ($1,316,000 less) than the reserve set up in the report, which has been shown to be computed on a capital of $61,200,000. Was Republic trying "to get away with something" in its statement to the Treasury? Dr. Adams, discussing these figures in general, makes several cryptic references to returns based on excessive capitalization. After weighing all the aspects of the case we are led to the peculiar—but not altogether impossible—hypothesis that Republic has tried to hold down its tax *return* by reporting as large a capital as possible; but in its statement to stockholders it has followed the conservative plan of *reserving* the maximum amount that might be required, if the Treasury rejected its book figures for Invested Capital.

So much for Republic. The Lackawanna case is not so complicated. It appears to furnish an obvious example of *understatement* of tax requirements. On the basis of the full book figure for Invested Capital, the resulting Income and Profits Taxes would be $10,540,000—or just $500,000 above the reported reserve. This difference would not have much importance, being a matter of only $1.45 per share. But if we were to assume the same amount of intangible assets as indicated by the Republic reserve—about $20,000,000—then after including $7,000,000 of this for permitted good-will, we should have an Invested Capital of but $40,000,000. On this basis the Profits Tax would amount to no less than $11,050,000, and the total tax to $11,950,000—reducing the reported 1917 earnings by $5.45 per share and bringing them down to $40.45, or $11.45 below Republic's record. We point out incidentally that the Invested Capital indicated by Lackawanna's Tax Reserve would give the stock a tangible value on January 1, 1918, of $195; the book value is $185; and the value, assuming $20,000,000 good-will, would be $126 per share.

Lackawanna is not the only company which has evidently understated its tax requirements. This distinction is shared by Baldwin—the smallness of whose tax reserve appears to have escaped general notice. Its estimate of a $1,750,000 tax on over $10,000,000 of earnings implies an Invested Capital of fully $60,000,000. But by writing off $15,800,000 for patents and good-will last year, Baldwin admitted that its tangible investment at the beginning of 1917 was no more than $33,000,000, and allowing $8,000,000 for permitted good-will its Invested Capital would have been only $41,000,000. To determine the proper figure for Baldwin's tax reserve it is advisable to consider the joint report of this company and its subsidiary, the Standard Steel Works. Our calculation shows a total tax requirement of $3,930,000, whereas the *reserves* of the two companies add up to only $2,517,000—a discrepancy of $1,413,000 or over $7 per share for the common. Counting in the assets of Standard Steel Works, Baldwin common has now a tangible value of about $123 per share.

**TABLE II**

DEVIATION OF THE TREASURY FIGURES FOR U. S. STEEL'S INVESTED CAPITAL, DEC. 31, 1916.

| | | |
|---|---:|---:|
| Total Assets shown in Balance Sheet | | $2,083,000,000 |
| LESS: | | |
| Current Liabilities | $ 92,900,000 | |
| Obligations of Subs. owned by Public | 174,000,000 | |
| Carnegie bonds owned by Corporation | 159,500,000 | 426,400,000 |
| Indicated Invested Capital of Subsidaries | | $1,656,600,000 |
| ADD: | | |
| Surplus of Subs. on sales to other Subs. not yet included in Corporation's Surplus | | 35,900,000 |
| Written off Property Account and charged to Surplus 1901-8 | | 163,700,000 |
| Written off Inventory and charged to Income 1916 | | 15,600,000 |
| | | $1,871,800,000 |
| Less: Original Good Will included in Assets        est. | | 594,100,000 |
| Tangible Invested Capital of Subsidaries | | 1,277,700,000 |
| Add: 20% of Stocks allowed for Good-Will        sur. | | 150,000,000 |
| Invested Capital—Treasury Department Figure | | $1,427,700,000 |

It is difficult to derive dependable information from the American Locomotive tax return,—first, because this article is written just as the annual report goes to press, so that we have available only the statement for the last half of 1917. Secondly, the tax reserve for this period includes an unstated amount for Canadian duties, which makes it impossible to separate the U. S. War tax. If we accept a published estimate that Canadian taxes accounted for about one-quarter of the total we should then derive an intangible asset item of about $25,000,000—the par amount of the common stock. Accumulated surplus would now give the common an asset value of around $87 per share.

American Steel Foundries is unique among the equipments in that its Tax Reserve indicates an Invested Capital almost identical with the balance sheet figures. The absence of good-will here might seem unlikely at first, but when it is recalled that the readjustment in 1908 reduced the capitalization by $15,000,000, the approximate correctness of our results is again substantiated by external facts. The tangible value of Steel Foundries on January 1st last appears to have been well over $170 per share.

Railway Steel Springs—which has recently shared with Steel Foundries in a belated recognition of intrinsic value—provides an interesting example of over-stated taxes. The reserve here is $3,500,000 against earnings of $8,808,000; which results in a capital of only $18,000,000, against a book figure of $34,000,000. Allowing for permitted good-will in the former amount, the intangible assets in Railway's balance sheet should then total $21,500,000—all the common and over half the preferred. When the writer called this fact to the attention of an official of the company, the latter admitted that the Tax Reserve was overstated—in order to be conservative, said he, and not to lead the stockholders to clamor for unduly large dividends. If for argument's sake, we place the actual good-will item at $13,500,000 (the amount of common), the tax would be reduced by $835,000 or over $6 per share.

In leaving this subject, we would point out that our conclusions are advanced not as positive statements of fact, but as tentative estimates based on available data. We will indeed vouch for the sufficient accuracy of our results *provided* the companies' figures from which we started are themselves accurate. What we have said in effect is that *if* X Corporation has really earned the income and paid the tax it has reported, then it must necessarily have used our specified figure for Invested Capital—and the present tangible value of its common stock must consequently be so much per share. Some of our figures, therefore, may have no value whatever, merely because the company in question has made inaccurate or misleading reports. But we do claim sufficient reliability for our results in general to prove that that market value of American industrials no longer exceeds their tangible assets; and that whatever burdens they may have to bear in the future, over capitalization will not be one of them.

# PART II

# SEPTEMBER 1918– JANUARY 1919

# INRODUCTION

BY   DAVID   DARST

By late 1918, the tragic, multiyear, multi-nation war in Europe was nearing an end. Calendar year 1919 would feature strikes by organized labor, higher consumer price inflation, rising interest rates, a bear market in rail stocks, and significant gains in oil shares. From its opening level of 82.60, the Dow Jones Industrial Average reached a yearly high of 119.62 on November 3 and closed at 107.23, up +30.5% for the year.

In these four investment essays published between September 1918 and mid-January 1919, our 24–25-year old Benjamin Graham begins to extend the range and depth of his analysis.

A recurrent theme in Graham's work is the determination of what factors are significant and relevant in determining intrinsic value—in bonds, in preferred stocks, and in common shares. Graham is quick to point out that such factors are not the same ones for all industries, and in some cases, the investor should be wary of being misled by a superabundance of superfluous and/or misleading figures. Constantly aware of the imprecision of investment analysis, Graham pushes the reader to assess whether a security's intrinsic value is roughly equal, appreciably higher, or appreciably lower than its market price.

Another subject that permeates these early essays—and Graham's entire canon—is the Janus-like message of yield. Graham is faithfully and eternally attentive to how yields can reflect the vagaries of the business cycle, shifts in a company's fortunes due to technological change, and managerial skill and character (or lack thereof). For Graham, a high yield can contain the semiotics of attractiveness, or equally, of danger. In his opinion, lofty yields in and of themselves are not worth sacrificing safety of principal.

In his focus on the entire capitalization of a company's balance sheet, Graham presages a post–2000 investment approach, that of capital structure analysis. Over and over, Graham reminds investors to consider who is in line before, and after, their own investment position in the balance sheet hierarchy. Does the common stock investor have a little or a lot of debt or preferred stock above his or her standing in the company's capitalization structure? Depending on the industry, the position of the company, and the economic outlook, Graham can argue in favor of, or against, "a lot of debt and preferred ahead of the common."

What can we possibly hope to gain from these early writings? After all, even though he was a quick study and mature beyond his years, at the same time, Graham was young, junior, and possibly even a little bit jejune when he wrote these essays. Social and economic conditions, financial market structures, patterns of investor behavior, and geopolitical realities were so different back then! How relevant and useful can these analyses be? Why should we care about par amounts that have long since ceased to be meaningful, industries that have long since declined, companies that have long since disappeared, and bonds that have long since matured?

In short, just as we need to read *The Bible,* Shakespeare, *The Koran,* the *I Ching, Beowulf, Don Quixote, The Decameron, The Song of Roland, The Canterbury Tales,* and other great works to gain an appreciation of human nature, of the mysteries of our shared existence, and of what truly changes through the ages and what doesn't, we need to read and understand first-hand the thinking, the principles, the motivations, and the consummate genius and mental breakthroughs in Graham's oeuvre.

In fact, the classic works cited above draw often extensively from even earlier works, including: *The Epic of Gilgamesh;* the *Upanishads* and the *Bhagavad Gita;* the *Iliad,* the *Odyssey,* and the *Aeneid;* and *The Tale of Genji;* among others. When we read Benjamin Graham's earliest works, we evoke our financial origins and we return, like anadromous salmon, to unchanging investment truths, to the language of value and its meaning, and to deep layers of our investment consciousness.

Ever since its composition around 2100 BCE, the 12-book *Epic of Gilgamesh* has shed light on the ultimate meaning of life and humans' quest for immortality. The mystical and intense philosophical nature of the more than 100 texts of the *Upanishads,* the earliest of which date from 1000 BCE, assert to readers a divine consciousness and an individual soul, at times even equating the two. Drawn in 350 BCE from the *Mahabharata,* the 18-chapter, 700-verse *Bhagavad Gita* is still considered a font of eternal wisdom capable of inspiring any man or woman to supreme accomplishment, emancipation, purification, and enlightenment.

Linked to the invention of the Greek alphabet, the 15,693-line, 24-book, *Iliad,* dating from 850 BCE, has continued through the centuries to shape notions of glory, respect, wrath, and honor. Presumably composed shortly thereafter, its 12,110-line, 24-book sequel the *Odyssey,* makes use of nonlinear narrative, flashbacks, and storytelling, to define loyalty, choice, cunning, intelligence, homecoming, and revenge.

In order to emphasize Roman moral values and legitimize the imperial lineage, Augustus Caesar commissioned Virgil to compose the 12,000-line, 12-book Latin epic the *Aeneid,* consulted through the ages for its earnest depiction of piety, reason, and filial and patriotic duty. Composed around the same time (400 BCE–200 AD) as the *Aeneid,* the 24,000-verse, 7-book *Ramayana* depicts the duties of relationships and the qualities of leadership, equanimity, and justice.

Sometimes (and erroneously) called the world's first novel, *The Tale of Genji* was written in the early 11th century AD by Lady Shikibu Murasaki and from that time onward has powerfully influenced writers of fiction through its naturalness, narrative unity, passion, subtlety, and detailed psychological insights.

■      ■      ■

In "American Agricultural and Virginia-Carolina," Graham examines the reasons for the market preference accorded to American Agriculture and then assesses whether and to what extent it is still justified by existing prices. Graham identifies as a key factor American Agricultural's steady and gradually increasing dividend rate compared to Virginia-Carolina's more erratic dividend payments, including suspension of its dividends entirely for three years. Always looking at firms' balance sheets as well as their income statements, Graham cites American Agricultural's consistently larger working capital and lower bank debt relative to Virginia-Carolina's.

Pointing out that the recent prosperity of both firms was tied more to increasing fertilizer usage than to wartime demand, Graham downplays the 1911–1915 period and focuses instead on each company's asset value and earning power. Given the more rapid rate of then recent profit growth for Virginia-Carolina and its improved working capital position, *at current price levels,* Graham concludes that Virginia-Carolina common and preferred shares "constitute decidedly the more attractive purchase."

■    ■    ■

"High Yield and Safe Investments" searches for exceptions to "that ancient and deep rooted misconception . . . that a high yield must necessarily signify greater risk than a low yield." Although Graham points out that one hundred bonds picked at random from the 4.5% yield level will likely produce a lower percentage of defaults than the same number of issues yielding 6%, he also feels that the careful investor may find high-yielding yet secure investments among: (i) securities that are "safe but unseasoned;" and/or (ii) securities "safe but affected by investors' prejudice, never or no longer justified."

Graham sees no lack of attractively yielding yet safe bond, preferred, and common stock issues for the discerning and disciplined investor willing to investigate the facts and details of specific issues "on a level-headed basis:"

> Contrary to general opinion, prices do not always anticipate changed conditions, nor even immediately reflect them. The Law of Inertia holds in finance as everywhere else, and broad intervals often elapse before investors accommodate their judgment to the new order of things.

Graham admonishes readers that "unless shrewd judgment is exercised, the gain in income return is likely to be offset by painful losses in principal. "Yet given the opportunity to investigate and select, yield and safety become perfectly feasible.

■   ■   ■

"Hidden Assets of Consolidated Gas" investigates whether the public utility stocks, and, in particular, the companies comprising the Consolidated Gas System, should have seen the worst with the cessation of wartime conditions and whether they could be expected to gradually regain their former prosperity.

Graham examines the elements adding to Consolidated Gas's earning power (such as undistributed profits of subsidiaries, excessive reserves charged to operations, and excessive taxes charged to operations) and the elements adding to asset value (such as the excess of its subsidiaries' equity market value over their balance sheet carrying values, and excessive contingency reserves carried as liabilities). After laboriously and meticulously assembling and analyzing the relevant data to arrive at "a basis for intelligent confidence in the intrinsic merits of this issue," Graham concludes that there is "real value behind this issue and with better times ahead, the investor at these levels should find the stock a very satisfactory purchase—although a little patience may be needed."

■   ■   ■

In "Bargain Hunting Through the Bond List," Graham conducts a detailed analysis of: Houston & Texas Central 5% First Mortgage bonds; East Tennessee, Virginia & Georgia 5% First Mortgage bonds; four Chesapeake & Ohio and four New York Central bonds; Granby Copper 6% First Mortgage bonds; Union Bag and Paper 5% First Mortgage bonds; Chile Copper 6% Convertible bonds; and Peerless Truck and Motor 6% First Mortgage bonds, to ascertain these bonds' degree of attractiveness according to the following criteria:

1. Small closed first mortgage on valuable property.
2. Net current assets exceed par value of the issue.
3. Minimum earnings greatly in excess of interest requirements.
4. Market price of stock many times the outstanding bonds.
5. Sinking fund will redeem entire issue before maturity.
6. Conversion privilege of potential value.

According to Graham, point four in the above listing ordinarily escapes the investor's attention, yet it is the "most significant index of the real security behind a bond issue." In his opinion, where the value of the stock greatly exceeds the funded debt, there is room for a severe shrinkage in the company's assets and earnings before the safety of the bonds is impaired.

# 7

# AMERICAN AGRICULTURAL AND VIRGINIA-CAROLINA

*Are They Selling Out of Line?—Causes
of America's Preeminence—Fertilizers
as War and Peace Essentials*

From the standpoint of investment rating American Agricultural Chemical maintains a marked superiority over Virginia-Carolina Chemical—a fact which is most clearly shown by our grouping of their respective securities (Table I).

Not only does "AGR" common sell at almost twice the price of "V C," but all its other issues are quoted on a lower income basis than the corresponding securities of its less favored rival. The price of the bonds is affected somewhat by their various conversion privileges, but the preferred stocks certainly reflect the public's estimate of the relative standing of the two concerns. We propose to examine the reasons for the preference accorded to American Agricultural, first determining to what conditions in the past it owes its origin, and then inquiring whether—and to what extent—it is still justified by the present situation.

## TABLE I

Amer. Agricultural vs. Virginia-Carolina

| | | Market Yields of Securities | | | |
|---|---|---|---|---|---|
| | | Due | Rate | Present Price | Yield |
| First Mortgage Bonds | AGR | (a) 1928 | 5% | $94^1/_2$ | 5.75% |
| | VC | 1923 | 5% | $93^1/_2$ | 6.50% |
| Debentures | AGR | (b) 1924 | 5% | $97^1/_2$ | 5.50% |
| | VC | (c) 1924 | 6% | $96^1/_2$ | 6.70% |
| Preferred Stock | AGR | | 6% | 92 | 6.52% |
| | VC | | 8% | 107 | 7.48% |
| Common Stock | AGR | | 8% | 100 | 8.00% |
| | VC | | 4% | 53 | 7.56% |

(a) Convertible into preferred stock at par.
(b) Convertible into common stock at par.
(c) Convertible into preferred stock at 110.

It may surprise some readers to learn that not only is Virginia-Carolina the older concern, but also that for many years it was far more highly regarded than American Agricultural. "V C" began operations in 1895, four years before "A G R" was organized under its present name. In 1902 Virginia common was regularly selling at twice the price of American—the highs for that year being $76^5/_8$ and $32^1/_4$ respectively. Virginia-Carolina maintained its lead well into 1912, but after that year American Agricultural forged ahead rapidly, as shown in our first graph. Observe how in eight years the relative position of the two companies had been almost exactly reversed.

| | VC | AGR |
|---|---|---|
| High, 1906 | 58 | $34^1/_8$ |
| High, 1914 | $34^7/_8$ | $59^1/_2$ |

The original cause for this market adjustment was a decline of about $2,000,000 in Virginia's net for the fiscal year ended May 31, 1911. Peculiarly enough, this reduction occurred in the face of a gain of nearly $6,000,000 in gross business. But for some reason, not fully explained, V C's margin of profit on sales contracted sharply in that year, and has since been maintained at a low level—so that while net available for interest charges was over 10% of gross in 1910, in 1911 it only slightly exceeded 6%; and the highest ratio since has been 8.5%, this last year. There is reason to believe that the decline in the percentage of net profits has been partly due at least to the adoption of more conservative accounting methods, and particularly to the establishment of adequate reserves for doubtful debts, etc.

## AGR TO THE FORE

Whatever was the cause thereof, in 1911 Virginia entered upon a four year period of very mediocre net profits, during which the highest amount earned on the common was $3.40 per share in 1914, and the lowest, 53¢ in 1913. In the meantime, however, the record of American Agricultural, while not exactly brilliant, had been far more substantial and encouraging. In 1910 both companies had earned $10.42 per share of common stock. During the next four years A G R's earnings did not fall below $5.23 per share and reached as high as $9.05—a very much better showing than that of Virginia-Carolina just mentioned.

But the chief cause of American Agricultural's market progress lay in its dividend policy. Although almost from the very first it had been earning a very substantial sum for its common, it was twelve years after organization before it began disbursements on the junior shares. But since the initial rate of 4% was established in 1912, it has never since been passed or reduced, and in the last two years it has been steadily advanced to the present figure of 8%. Virginia-Carolina's record has been much less regular, as is shown in full in Table II. It was particularly unfortunate for the Company that it advanced the rate to the highest figure of 5% in 1911, the very year that earnings suffered so pronounced a decline, so that profits were insufficient by $530,000 to meet dividends. Again

## TABLE II

DIVIDEND RECORDS OF COMMON STOCK

| Year | VC | AGR | Year | VC | AGR |
|------|------|------|------|------|------|
| 1896 | 1% | none | 1911 | 3% | none |
| 1897–1901 | 4% | none | 1912 | 3% | 4% |
| 1902 | 4³/₄% | none | 1913 | 1¹/₂% | 4% |
| 1903 | 2¹/₂% | none | 1914–15 | none | 4% |
| 1904–8 | none | none | 1916 | none | 4¹/₄% |
| 1909 | 3% | none | 1917 | 3% | 5¹/₄% |
| 1910 | 5% | none | 1918 Present rate | 4% | 8% |

in 1913 the 3% rate was maintained although earnings on the common had practically vanished, an even larger deficit then resulting—and it was found necessary to discontinue common dividends entirely for the next three years.

American Agricultural's record of earnings and dividends was thus sufficient to establish its investment superiority, but two other factors—of more or less importance—contributed to this result. Not only did Agricultural possess a consistently larger working capital than Virginia, but it was far more successful in restricting its bank loans. In 1913, when V C had notes payable of $9,900,000, A G R's debt to the banks was only $3,219,000.

## RECENT RECORD

Having thus analyzed the original causes of American Agricultural's ascendancy, we must now turn our attention to the effect of the war upon the two companies. Our second graph shows the development of earnings in the past four years. The first point we emphasize is that these fertilizer companies were immune from the general business prostration immediately following the outbreak of the conflict. The fiscal periods of V C and A G R end May 31 and June 30 respectively, so that their 1915 year coincides almost exactly with the first year of hostilities. Yet Virginia-Carolina (which alone reports its gross business) enjoyed a larger turn-over than in the previous year, and its earnings on the common were the best in its history, except for 1910. American Agricultural's showings were even better, and in the next four years the profits of both companies recorded steady increases culminating in the 1918 reports—which showed $35.00 earned on A G R common and $24.25 on V C common.

Since 1914 Agricultural has earned $86.50 for each share of common and has paid out $18.50 in dividends, leaving $68 added to surplus—about 70% of the present market price. In the same period V C earned $53.10 per share and disbursed $4.50, making $48.60 added to surplus—over 90% of the current price.

These are truly excellent earnings and prospects for the immediate future are said by both companies to be extremely favorable—the only drawback being the great scarcity of labor.

While the war continues, the fertilizer companies are certainly in a strong position. Their industry is recognized as most essential and farmers are being urged on every hand to increase their output through the use of soil enrichers. The demand for the food products made by the Southern Cotton Oil Company—Virginia-Carolina's large subsidiary—is certain to continue heavy.

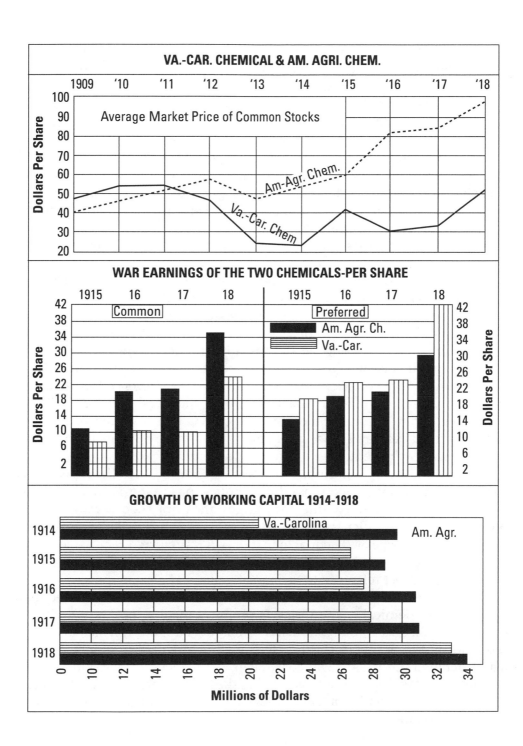

**VA.-CAR. CHEMICAL & AM. AGRI. CHEM.**

Average Market Price of Common Stocks

Am-Agr. Chem.

Va.-Car. Chem

**WAR EARNINGS OF THE TWO CHEMICALS-PER SHARE**

Common

Preferred

■ Am. Agr. Ch.

▤ Va.-Car.

**GROWTH OF WORKING CAPITAL 1914-1918**

Va.-Carolina

Am. Agr.

Millions of Dollars

On the other hand the particular strength of both companies lies in the benefits they will experience from the return of peace. They can look forward not only to regaining their fairly large export trade, which the war has almost completely suspended, but especially to a tremendous foreign demand for their phosphate rock, inspired by the long continued shortage of phosphoric acid. The recent prosperity of these two enterprises was not the result of orders for war munitions which will disappear with the advent of peace. Their product is intimately bound up with the food supply, and the period of intensive cultivation which is certainly ahead of us will mean an increased use of fertilizing material. We would point out here, as evidence of the stability of the business under all conditions, that as far back as our records go Virginia-Carolina's gross sales each year but one (1912) have exceeded the previous record.

From the comparative standpoint this survey of the recent record and future prospects of both companies leads us to an important conclusion. So great has been the transformation in their status since 1914 and so favorable is their outlook, that we assert that their showing in the 1911–1915 period has now no longer any bearing on their relative merits as they stand to-day. We mean that it is now no more logical to point to Agricultural's admittedly better record of five or six years ago as a cause of preference today, than it would be to use Virginia-Carolina's indisputable leadership prior to 1910 as an argument in its favor. In choosing between A G R and V C we must disregard the record before 1915 as ancient history, and base our conclusion solely on their recent achievements and present position.

The capitalization of both companies (shown in Table III) is so nearly identical that we are spared those difficult questions that arise in comparing two enterprises with very different charges ahead of their common stock. While V C has a smaller issue of preferred, its 8% rate makes its dividend requirement almost exactly equal to that of A G R preferred. The same can be said of the fixed interest charges. The two common stocks can, therefore, be compared by direct reference to their asset value and earning power.

It might be said in favor of V C that its business is better diversified than Agricultural Chemical's. The former's products include not only fertilizers and similar chemicals, but cotton seed oil, lard, soap, etc.—which are made and sold by the Southern Cotton Oil Company. In 1914, the only year for which detailed figures are available, the gross business of the Southern Cotton Oil subsidiary constituted over 60% of the total. In other words, the fertilizer department actually contributed less in the way of sales than did the food products and allied lines.

## TABLE  III

CAPITALIZATION OF THE TWO COMPANIES

|                       | Am. Agric. Chem. | Vir.-Car. Chem. |
|-----------------------|------------------|-----------------|
| Mortgage Bonds        | $8,252,000       | $12,300,000     |
| Debentures            | 9,100,000        | 4,609,385       |
| Total bonds           | $17,352,000      | $16,909,385     |
| Preferred Stock       | 27,648,200       | 20,012,255      |
| Common Stock          | 18,430,900       | 27,084,400      |
| Total capitalization  | $63,431,100      | $64,006,040     |

## HIGH ASSET VALUES

The asset value of A G R common is $189 per share and of V C common $165 per share—in one case nearly 200% and in the other 300% of the market price. Virginia's balance sheet, however, includes an unstated amount of good will in its property account, while American Agricultural ostentatiously carries this asset at $1.00. V C's good will certainly stands at a substantial figure. The plants of the Southern Cotton Oil Company were taken into the property account at $18,000,000, at the time of consolidation in 1907, although their book value was less than $10,000,000. On the other hand the absence of intangible assets in the case of A G R is due to a bookkeeping adjustment. Patents and good will were originally carried at over $16,500,000; but in 1912, $12,000,000 was transferred to the mining property account as a result of the re-valuation of the latter asset. The remaining $4,500,000 was charged off against surplus, chiefly in 1916.

The point is that Virginia-Carolina's phosphate lands have probably also greatly increased in value since their acquisition, so that if it followed the same procedure here as did the A G R, its good will account would also be greatly reduced. Of chief importance is the fact that the V C's property account—good will and all—stands at no higher a figure than A G R's; and with these assets it has been able to earn a larger net profit last year than did its rival. We would say, therefore, that V C common at 53 is backed proportionately by at least as large an asset value as is A G R. It has already been stated that in the past four years alone Virginia has increased the assets behind the common by 90% of its present market price, against 68% in the case of American Agricultural.

In the matter of working capital the advance of V C has been particularly noteworthy. Our third graph shows that A G R's 50% advantage in 1914 has now practically disappeared. Virginia's net current assets now cover all its bonds and preferred stock, except for $4,000,000; whereas in the case of Agricultural this difference is $11,000,000. While we have stated that in previous years A G R's bank borrowings were always much less than V C's, they are now $3,290,000 *greater*—$17,020,000 against $13,729,000. Finally, on May 31st last Virginia-Carolina had $6,776,000 cash on hand, against only $2,785,000 for A G R on June 30th. As regards current assets and liabilities the advantage appears now to have swung to Virginia-Carolina.

## LIBERAL EARNINGS

We come next to the all important consideration of earnings. Last year V C earned after taxes 45% of its market price against 35% for American Agricultural. The average for the past four years has been 25% and 23% respectively. Year by year Virginia's profits have been increasing at a more rapid rate.

The increase in the dividend rate on Agricultural common to 8% which has just been announced, has for the present raised the income return on this issue slightly above that of V C common. To our mind, however, the current dividend return is often an over-rated factor in determining values, particularly nowadays—and in these very instances—when disbursements are being changed almost from quarter to quarter.

Having examined the question from all angles, we reach the conclusion that V C common is a more attractive investment proposition at 53 (despite its slightly lower dividend returns) than is A G R at par. We think, in fact, that it ought to sell more nearly on the basis of its comparative earning power of last year—that is about two-thirds of the price of American Agricultural. Our view is, therefore, that V C is quoted possibly 12 points too low in relation to the present price of A G R.

## INVESTMENT VALUE

A similar verdict applies to the preferred stocks. V C preferred has a record of 8% paid continuously since 1895. In 1915, however, the first two quarterly installments were paid in scrip, redeemed the next year. This event seems to have hurt the investment rating of the issue considerably. The fact is that in the year the scrip dividends were paid, over 18% was earned on the preferred—a better showing than A G R's. The company had more than $4,000,000 cash on hand, its current asset position was quite comfortable, and the recourse to scrip appears merely as a measure of conversatism at the time when the early stages of war had made the outlook exceptionally uncertain. V C preferred is now as well protected by assets and earnings as A G R preferred; it is more nearly covered by working capital alone; and considering that it yields fully 1% in excess of the other issue, we believe it a more attractive investment.

No one can study the recent record of these two leading fertilizer companies without being impressed with their strong exhibit. They have more to hope and less to fear from the future than perhaps any other industry; and their issues rank high among the so-called "peace stocks." While both companies are, therefore, in an enviable position, our analysis would indicate that *at these levels* Virginia-Carolina Chemical common and preferred constitute decidedly the more attractive purchase.

# 8

---

# HIGH YIELD AND SAFE INVESTMENTS

*Opportunities Created by Unfounded
Prejudices—Instances of Six Per Cent,
Safety, and a Probable Ten Point Profit—
List of Bonds, Preferred Stocks,
and Common Stocks*

With the bond market moving too fast to be photographed—to say nothing of being analyzed—investment suggestions are out of date almost before the ink is dry. In the very course of writing this article, it has been necessary to change the viewpoint in order to conform to the rapid advance in bond quotations; and whereas a week or two ago the term "High Yield" would have denoted at least a $6^1/_2\%$ or 7% return, we must now regard anything above a 6% income basis as belonging to the high yield category.

This is an excellent opportunity to attack that ancient and deep rooted misconception—namely that a high yield must necessarily signify greater risk than a low yield. As applied to the general run of securities, this rule is obviously true enough—one hundred bonds picked at random from the $4^1/_2\%$ class will eventually be found to include a smaller percentage of defaults than the same number of 6% issues. But with individual securities the case may be very different; and there have been and still are innumerable examples of high yield obligations which are really better protected than many others selling on a lower basis. "Six Percent and Safety" is just as possible as 4% and safety—only it requires greater care and discrimination in selecting the investment.

The fact is that whereas ordinarily a high yield is due to uncertain security, in many particular instances the reason may have no connection with the intrinsic merits of the issue. It is here that the careful investor will find his opportunity and the signs whereby these bargains may be recognized are twofold:

A. Securities safe but unseasoned.
B. Securities safe but affected by investor's prejudice, never or no longer justified.

## SOME CHEAP 6% BONDS

An excellent example of a high grade bond selling on a high income basis because of lack of seasoning is found in the Wilson & Co. 1st 6s due 1941, which at this writing can be bought below par. The stable character of this company's business—meat packing—and its splendid earnings record in

### LIST I

ATTRACTIVE BONDS YIELDING 6% OR BETTER

|                                      | Due  | Price Nov. 12 | Yield  |
|--------------------------------------|------|---------------|--------|
| Armour Co. conv. 6s                  | 1924 | 99$^1/_2$     | 6.10%  |
| Bethlehem Steel Purchase Money 5s    | 1936 | 84            | 6.52%  |
| Braden Copper collat. 6s             | 1931 | 95            | 6.55%  |
| Chile Copper conv. 6s                | 1932 | 89            | 7.35%  |
| Granby Copper conv. 6s               | 1928 | 100           | 6.00%  |
| Missouri Pacific consol. 5s          | 1923 | 94            | 6.60%  |
| N. Y. Air Brake 1st 6s               | 1928 | 99            | 6.15%  |
| St. Louis, Iron Mt. & So. ref. 4s    | 1929 | 82            | 6.29%  |
| Texas Co. deb. 6s                    | 1931 | 100           | 6.00%  |
| Virginia-Carolina Chemical conv. 6s  | 1924 | 100           | 6.00%  |
| Wilson Co. 1st 6s                    | 1941 | 98            | 6.14%  |

recent years, should place its first mortgage bonds in the class of high grade investments.

In the same category may be placed Chile Copper convertible 6s due 1932, which having been brought out at the worst possible time speedily sustained a severe decline in market value, from which they have only recently been recovering. The present earnings of the mine cover interest charges with a wide margin to spare; and any possible reduction in the profit per pound during the next few years is certain to be more than compensated for by the increased output which peace will make possible. It is important to recognize that, first, Chile Copper is an enormous property with the strongest bankers and the best engineering talent behind it; second, there are 3,800,000 shares of stock with a market value of about $90,000,000 standing between these bonds and trouble. The history of mining shows that the convertible bonds of *good* copper companies have invariably been exchanged for stock—and there is little doubt but that the holders of Chile Copper 6s will some day find it to their advantage to exercise their conversion privilege.

The list of bonds which have been depressed marketwise by unjustified prejudice is a very long one. Contrary to general opinion, prices do not always anticipate changed conditions, nor even immediately reflect them. The Law of Inertia holds in finance as everywhere else, and broad intervals often elapse before investors accommodate their judgment to the new order of things. One or two examples from the past may win better attention for our comment on the present situation.

## LIST II

STANDARD INDUSTRIAL PREFERRED STOCKS

|  | Rate | Price Nov. 12 | Yield | Price to Yield 6% |
|---|---|---|---|---|
| Am. Agric. Chemical | 6% | 96$^1/_2$ | 6.09% | 100 |
| Am. Car & Foundry | 7% | 111 | 6.30% | 116$^3/_4$ |
| Am. Smelting & Refining | 7% | 110 | 6.36% | 116$^3/_4$ |
| Central Leather | 7% | 108 | 6.48% | 116$^3/_4$ |
| B. F. Goodrich | 7% | 104 | 6.73% | 116$^3/_4$ |
| International Harvester | 7% | 110 | 6.36% | 116$^3/_4$ |
| S. S. Kresge | 7% | 105 | 6.85% | 116$^3/_4$ |
| National Lead | 7% | 105 | 6.85% | 116$^3/_4$ |
| U. S. Steel | 7% | 112$^1/_2$ | 6.22% | 116$^3/_4$ |

## THE LESSON OF ALLIED BONDS

When the United States entered the war in April, 1917, two things must have been apparent to every thinking man. First the war was bound to be won in the end. Secondly, as long as the war continued the entire financial resources of the country would stand solidly behind the Allies. What else could these facts mean but that *every French and English loan* placed in this market was absolutely safe—because either the war would be over when they matured, in which case they would easily be taken care of; or else the United States itself would assume the burden, as part of its financial aid to the Allies. It might have been observed that our advances to France and England were running at the rate of six billions a year, while their net imports from this country were less than four billions. Evidently our loans to the Allies were covering not only their purchases in this market, but *their maturing obligations* as well.

In the long months when the United Kingdom $5^1/_2$s ranged below 90 and the French Municipals sold in the "early eighties," the writer presented these arguments to investors time and time again. Did they dispute his reasoning? No. But how many took advantage of this extraordinary opportunity? Very, very few. Most of them "did not like foreign bonds"—which meant that the handful of level headed investors who were superior to prejudice were enabled to make a veritable killing.

One other example, which has a bearing on the recommendations to be made. At the end of 1915, when railroad issues were quoted on a $4^1/_2$% basis, Railway Steel Springs, Inter-Ocean Plant, 5s could be bought at 92. The company was then in excellent financial condition; its earnings had reached record proportions; and there were two stock issues junior to the bonds to guarantee them against harm. But no bond house would have dared recommend them to an investor seeking conservative investments. The customer, finding this issue on the list, would have sniffed, "I ask them for high grade bonds and they try to palm off this low priced industrial. Fine people to trust my money to!" Whereupon he would have journeyed to another house and selected a list of railroad bonds beginning with Atchison general 4s at 94, and perhaps including some Saint Paul refunding 5s at 107 to bring up the yield.

The wisdom of this typical investor is shown by the sequel. In September last when railroad bond prices were at their lowest ebb, and the St. Paul 5s were selling at 77—a decline of nearly thirty points—the Railway Steel Springs Co. redeemed its remaining mortgage bonds at 105, thirteen points *above* the price at which they couldn't be sold because their yield was too high!

Perhaps this veracious tale may be found to have a valuable moral for present day conditions. Here are Texas Company debenture 6s selling at par and yielding a full point more than U. S. Steel sinking fund 5s. Mr. Average Investor remarks "I don't want an oil company bond," and picks out one of the old favorites (which sell five points too high just because they are old favorites). But the level headed buyer investigates the issue. He finds that these debentures are the company's only bond—a small issue with a large sinking fund just beginning to operate—that the company has poured tens of millions into its property out of its extraordinary earnings and continual stock issues, *without increasing its funded debt;* and that finally the equity of this issue measured by assets and earnings is so enormous that even a total collapse of the oil industry could scarcely destroy its value.

A very similar case is supplied by the New York Air Brake 6s also selling around par. The old-line investor thinks of the company as a mushroom war proposition, and views its bonds with cold suspicion. Yet this issue is so small Air Brake's net current assets are so large, and even its pre-war earnings so greatly in excess of interest requirements, that the safety of its first mortgage bonds is now independent of any fluctuation in the company's earning power.

## GRANBY 6s

Again there are the Granby Copper convertible 6s, also due in 1928, and selling around par. Many investors would not consider them because they don't like a mining company bond; others recall Granby's checkered career many years

### LIST III

SOUND INDUSTRIAL PREFERED STOCKS YIELDING 7% OR MORE

|  | Rate | Price Nov. 12 | Yield | Price to Yield 6% |
|---|---|---|---|---|
| Am. Locomotive | 7% | 100 | 7.00% | $116^3/_4$ |
| Bethlehem Steel | 8% | 104 | 7.69% | $133^1/_4$ |
| General Motors | 6% | $85^1/_2$ | 7.01% | 100 |
| Republic Iron & Steel | 7% | 100 | 7.00% | $116^3/_4$ |
| Pierce Arrow | 8% | 103 | 7.76% | $133^1/_4$ |
| Tobacco Products | 7% | 100 | 7.00% | $116^3/_4$ |
| Virginia-Carolina Chemical | 8% | 111 | 7.20% | $133^1/_4$ |
| Willys-Overland | 7% | 86 | 8.13% | $116^3/_4$ |

ago and raise their hands in protest at the suggestion. But there is an issue of only $2,500,000; which is being retired at the rate of over $500,000 per year, which comes ahead of $15,000,000 stock valued at over $12,000,000; and the interest on which should be earned *ten times* on $14^1/_2$ ¢ copper. Since the sinking fund must retire the entire issue before maturity, the owner is certain to get 110 for his bonds—the maximum price—if he holds on to them long enough. In other words, here is a combination of safety, six percent and ten points profit.

Very similar is the status of Armour and Co. 6% notes, due serially to 1924, and convertible at any time into 7% preferred stock at par. Some investors are frightened by the possibility of Government control of the packing industry. For the same reason it was so hard to dispose of the Am. Tel. & Tel. convertible 6s at 94 (now 104)—the most attractive offering of the year.

The public could not be made to see that in both cases *the disadvantage of Government control would fall entirely on the large stock issues, while the advantage of guaranteed earnings would directly benefit the bondholders.*

With practically a half billion of 8% stock in back of them, what had the A. T. & T. bondowners to fear for their interest? And with a hundred millions of Armour stock outstanding, the holders of the new notes have a comfortable buffer between them and confiscation. The new 7% preferred stock into which the Armour notes are convertible should eventually sell at 110; so that here is another instance of safety, six percent, and a probable ten point profit.

Virginia-Carolina Chemical 6% debentures due 1924, also sell at par. Four years of unprecedented prosperity has placed these bonds in the conservative investment class. The issue is small, the equity large, a sinking fund maintains the price, and a conversion privilege into 8% preferred stock at 110 (below the present price) carries prospects of a nice profit.

In the railroad group, there are not many issues yielding 6% which can stand the acid test of analysis. The Missouri Pacific reorganization has been so skilful and thorough, and the road's recent exhibit so encouraging, that the First and Refunding 5s due 1923 and the Iron Mountain division refunding 4s of 1929 can now be recommended without hesitancy.

## PREFERRED STOCKS

Industrial preferred stocks are more attractive now than at any time in their history. The status of most companies has improved so radically in recent years, that the dividends on their senior shares should henceforth be assured. Moreover, since the average yield of preferred stocks is still well above the prewar figure, the gradual return of interest rates to pre-war levels should effect a substantial advance in the price of these issues.

**L I S T   IV**

Common Stocks Which Are Conservative Investments

|  | Dividend Rate | Price Nov. 12 | Yield |
|---|---|---|---|
| Am. Telephone & Telegraph | 8% | 108 | 7.40% |
| Atchison, Topeka & Santa Fe | 6% | 96 | 6.25% |
| General Electric | 8% in cash | 156 | 9.12% |
|  | 4% in stock |  |  |
| Great Northern | 7% | 103$^{1}/_{2}$ | 6.76% |
| Union Pacific | 10% | 135 | 7.40% |
| Western Union Telegraph | 7% | 93 | 7.52% |
| Westinghouse Electric Manufacturing | $3.50 | 45 | 7.77% |

Our selection of preferred shares has been arranged in two groups. The first includes the standard seasoned issues, which in the old days were wont to sell around 6% basis, and which now yield between 6.30% and 6.75%. These are sound and desirable investments, which eventually should show a profit of from four to ten points.

Superficially regarded, the second list might present a rather nondescript appearance. All these issues yield over 7%, and some of them may shock the staid investor. But a careful analysis would demonstrate that every one of these high yielding preferred stocks is well protected by both asset value and earning power. The three motor issues have come through a trying period without hint of danger; their backing in fixed and current assets is relatively larger than many of the standard issues; and theirs is an industry which peace is expected to stimulate rather than contract.

In the same way, the tremendous equities accumulated for the benefit of such stocks as Republic Pfd., American Locomotive Pfd., and Bethlehem Steel 8% Pfd., in the past three years should carry them safely through a temporary period of depression—if that is in store—and should ultimately be reflected in a *permanently increased earning power* behind the senior shares.

## COMMON STOCKS

The best investment is a *good* common stock.

The stockholder, as a partner in a sound enterprise, may expect not only an attractive return on his capital, but an appreciation in value as the business expands and a surplus accumulates. Many an investor has remarked to the writer, "I never buy stocks. Let the other man speculate. All my money goes into bonds."

This is perhaps the best policy for those who are unable or unwilling to exercise care in the selection and periodic scrutiny of their investment. But numbers have found to their cost that the word "bond" contained no magic charm guaranteeing against loss—and others as they gained experience have learned conversely that "stocks" do not always signify speculation.

Conservative investments among common stocks may be divided into two classes. First, those that represent an unquestionably stable industry and possess a long established dividend record. Second, those whose prosperity is of more recent date, but which are placed on a solid basis through the (practical) absence of prior obligations.

Examples of the first type are Atchison among the rails, American Telephone & Telegraph among the utilities, and General Electric among the industrials. The holder of these stocks can view the past with satisfaction and the future with equanimity. The first two have come through the ordeal of Government Control unscathed—i. e. with dividends guaranteed. The third can look forward with especial confidence to coming industrial developments.

Westinghouse is in much the same position as General Electric, but belongs rather to the second group because its investment status is of more recent creation. A long article could be written about the transformation wrought in this company's affairs by the prosperity of the war period. With negligible funded debt and preferred stock, with current assets available to liquidate its note issue at maturity, Westinghouse comes into the reconstruction period with practically no charges ahead of its common stock. Its 7% disbursement has been earned with a greater margin than many bond interest requirements, and a plentiful surplus has been set aside to stabilize its dividend policy, should any lean years intervene. Westinghouse like General Electric possesses limitless possibilities, and the stockholder need never fear that the claims of prior issues may at any time endanger his interests.

There is a dangerous fascination about high yields which leads many experienced bankers to caution against them. It is perfectly true that unless shrewd judgment is exercised, the gain in income return is likely to be offset by painful losses in principal. Yet, given the opportunity to investigate and select, six per cent and safety becomes perfectly feasible—a fact which it has been the aim of this article to demonstrate.

# 9

## HIDDEN ASSETS OF CONSOLIDATED GAS

*Will It Sell at 150 Again?—Definite Statement of the System's Earnings and Asset Values—Analysis of Important Bonds*

That the public utilities have most to gain from the return of peace is obvious to all those who have watched the unequal combat between mounting operating expenses and stationary rates. Of course, the signing of the armistice cannot act immediately as the magic restorative of the pre-war margin of profit. The scaling down of material prices and wages may be a lengthy process, and many think that the levels of 1914 will never be seen again. Moreover, there is the likelihood of a contraction of industrial activity which, by reducing the utilities' gross earnings, would somewhat neutralize the benefits of lower costs.

Such considerations may restrain speculative enthusiasm in the public utility stocks, but they cannot overthrow the basic proposition that these companies have seen the worst and should gradually regain their former prosperity. What

## TABLE I

COMPANIES COMPRISING THE CONSOLIDATED GAS SYSTEM

A—Gas Companies
Consolidated Gas

| | | |
|---|---|---|
| Astoria Light, Heat & Power | | 100% |
| Central Union Gas | | 100% |
| New Amsterdam Gas | | 99.9% |
| New York & Queens Gas | | 100% |
| Northern Union Gas | | 100% |
| New York Mutual Gas | | 55.3% |
| Standard Gas Light | Pfd. | 95.4% |
| | Common | 96.8% |

B—Electric Companies

| | | |
|---|---|---|
| New York Edison | | 100% |
| New York & Queens Elec. | Pfd. | 65.6% |
| | Common | 83.5% |
| United Elec. Light & Power | | 99.9% |
| Yonkers Elec. Light & Power | | 100% |
| Brush Elec. Illuminating | | 100% |

C—Gas and Electric Companies

| | |
|---|---|
| Westchester Lighting | 100% |
| Northern Westchester Lighting | 100% |

D—Conduit Company

| | |
|---|---|
| Consolidated Tel. & Elec. Subway | 99.7% |

does this fact mean in the case of Consolidated Gas, which three years ago sold above 150, a few months ago around 83 and is currently quoted near par? If we were to assume that its former earning power will eventually be regained, then ought not its intrinsic value be fully as great as before—since the last two years, difficult as they were, could not have sapped its resources to any appreciable extent? If Consolidated Gas was actually worth 150 in 1916, then it should again be worth very nearly that figure in 1920.

At this point the reader interrupts sharply to inquire, "But was the price of 150 three years ago justified by the facts?" This is the crux of the matter. The investor is no longer willing to take values on faith. The old reliable stories of hidden assets, overstated earnings, etc., that did such staunch service in maintaining Con. Gas at a level certainly unjustified by its dividends, appear to have died out very suddenly when the stock broke under par. An attempt to revive them now will doubtless find a coldly sceptical audience, waiting "to be shown."

Now that the public is at last disposed to take a properly critical attitude toward this issue, the time would seem ripe for a real analysis of the Con. Gas situation. Instead of vaguely estimating the subsidiaries' earnings and assets, let us compile definite information on this subject, so that we can determine the value of Consolidated Gas stock in a logical manner—on the basis of a combined income account and balance sheet covering all the companies as one system.

## ANNUAL REPORT INADEQUATE

The source of our information will *not* be the ludicrously inadequate report that Con. Gas issues annually to its stockholders. Toward the Public Service Commission the company is far more confidential; in fact, it fairly deluges this august body with operating and financial statistics. In almost every case, data is available covering the 1917 year, but in a few unimportant instances we must utilize the 1916 figures. Our results are summarized in Tables I, II, III,—giving first, a list of the sixteen companies comprising the Consolidated Gas System; second, a comparative combined income account for 1916 and 1917; third, a consolidated balance-sheet as of December 31, 1917.

With these facts before us, we are in a position to test the numerous claims of "hidden values" that have been made for this issue in the past. These assertions may be summarized as follows:

I.  Elements Adding to Earning power.
    A.  Undistributed profits of subsidiaries.
    B.  Excessive reserves charged to operations.
    C.  Excessive taxes charged to operations.
II. Elements Adding to Asset Value.
    A.  Excess of par of subsidiaries' stocks over valuation in Consolidated Gas balance sheet.
    B.  Accumulated surplus of subsidiaries.
    C.  Excessive contingency reserves carried as a liability.

## TABLE II

CONSOLIDATED GAS CO. AND SUBSIDIARIES COMBINED INCOME ACCOUNT (EXCLUDING INTER-COMPANY ITEMS)

|  |  | 1917 | 1916 |
|---|---|---|---|
| Gross revenues | Electric | $34,153,000 | $32,094,000 |
|  | Gas | 29,164,000 | 27,632,000 |
| Total |  | $63,317,000 | $59,726,000 |
| Net after taxes (before deducting reserves) | Electric | $13,148,000 | $15,428,000 |
|  | Gas | 6,350,000 | 9,275,000 |
| Total |  | $19,498,000 | $24,703,000 |
| Other income |  | 1,220,000 | 1,176,000 |
| Total income |  | $20,718,000 | $25,879,000 |
| Deductions | Interest | 5,495,000 | 5,461,000 |
|  | Miscellaneous | 1,166,000 | 1,092,000 |
| Balance for dividends and reserves |  | 14,057,000 | 19,326,000 |
| Reserves |  | 7,176,000 | 6,618,000 |
| Dividends |  | 6,987,000 | 6,987,000 |
| Carried to surplus |  | 104,000 | 5,621,000 |
| Earned per share—before reserves |  | $14.08 | $19.36 |
| Earned per share—after reserves |  | 6.91 | 12.73 |

Let us take up these items one by one.

1-A. The report to the stockholders shows all the earnings of the Consolidated Gas Company proper and of the Astoria Light, Heat & Power Company, but only that part of the profits of the other subsidiaries which is paid out to the parent company as interest or dividends. In 1916, the undistributed profits of the subsidiaries figure out as $4.07 per share of Con. Gas stock, of which N. Y. Edison Company accounted for the equivalent of $3.60 per share. In 1917, however, the subsidiaries (other than Astoria) actually paid the holding company more than they earned; so that whereas the annual report shows earnings of $7.76 per share, on a combined basis, they total only $6.90.

1-B. The contingency and renewal reserves charged against earnings have often been characterized as excessive and as thereby bringing the apparent net profits below the actual figure. Following is the total provision made in 1916 and 1917 for repairs, renewals and contingencies:

|  | 1917 | 1916 |
|---|---|---|
| Expended for repairs. | $4,925,000 | $4,382,000 |
| Expended for renewals | 1,501,000 | 2,429,000 |
| Reserved for contingencies | 5,675,000 | 4,189,000 |
| Total | $12,101,000 | $11,000,000 |

These allowances total 19.1% of gross revenues in 1917 against 18.4% the previous year. Both Brooklyn Union Gas and Edison Electric Illuminating of Brooklyn charge about this percentage of gross for maintenance and depreciation, while Con. Gas and Electric of Baltimore has a somewhat lower ratio— about 17.50%. Considering that the Con. Gas Co. of N. Y. system has a net plant valuation of $323,000,000, an expenditure of $12,100,000 for repairs and depreciation—less than 4%—can hardly be regarded as excessive.

1-C. The assertion that Consolidated Gas has over-charged itself in the tax item is better founded, but the amount involved turns out to be rather small. The companies have regularly charged their earnings with the so-called Corporate Property Tax, which they have never had to pay—this item being included in another levy. In 1917, the taxes thus overstated aggregated $355,000, or about 35 cents per share, bringing the corrected net earnings up to $7.25 per share.

The influence of higher operating costs last year is clearly shown by the reduction of $5,205,000 in net compared with 1916, despite an expansion of $3,590,000 in gross. Of the decline in net earnings, about $1,600,000 was due to a cut in electric rates effective during the year. If in 1917, the system barely covered its dividend and reserve requirements, it is evident that the 1918 exhibit will be even poorer, since operating conditions have presented still greater difficulties in the current year; and for at least part of 1919 the stockholders must be prepared to see profits fall below the 7% dividend rate. Whether or not this prospect will affect the dividend policy must depend largely upon:

## II

### THE ASSET VALUE OF CONSOLIDATED GAS

From the combined General Balance Sheet, presented in Table III, the following book value of Consolidated Gas is deduced:

| | |
|---|---|
| 1. Par value of Con. Gas stock. | $ 99,816,000 |
| 2. Surplus—Con. Gas (proper) | 19,890,000 |
| 3. Premiums through sale of stock | 13,919,000 |
| 4. Surplus of subsidiaries | 47,954,000 |
| 5. Excess of par value of subsidiaries' stocks over price at which carried in Con. Gas balance sheet | 52,772,000 |
| | $234,351,000 |
| 6. Renewals and contingency reserve | $ 59,290,000 |
| | $293,641,000 |

Items 4 and 5, aggregating $100,000,000, are the real hidden assets, representing the excess of the book value of the subsidiaries' stocks as shown by their own balance sheets over the price at which they are carried in the Con. Gas investment account. N. Y. Edison stock, for example, with a par value of $66,000,000 and a surplus of $36,000,000, is valued on the holding company's books at only $39,000,000—an apparent understatement of no less than $63,000,000, or $63 per share of Con. Gas. These figures give Con. Gas stock a book valuation of fully $234 per share compared with only $113 in the company's balance sheet. To this large figure many claim that at least a part of the replacement and contingency reserve of $59,290,000 should be added—which would bring the actual value up to somewhere between $234 and $293 per share. These hidden equities in Con. Gas appear so large therefore, as to justify all the enthusiastic puffing of the stock in the past.

Nevertheless, it must be recognized that a good part of these enormous book values is indubitably the result of an inflated property account. Proof of this fact is provided by a comparison of the assessed value with the net balance sheet value of the system's real estate and plants. Considering all but the two Westchester companies, the balance sheet figures in 1914 exceeded the appraised value by no less than $121,000,000. In the past two years, however, the assessed values have been increased by fully $60,000,000, chiefly through the marking up of the "Special Franchise" account. The latter item takes into consideration the system's "incorporeal rights"—in other words, it includes an official valuation of the good-will.

The 1917 tax figures indicate an overvaluation of about $56,000,000 in plant and franchise account. To this sum ought to be added the $12,500,000 stock of the Westchester Lighting Company, which is carried by Con. Gas at a nominal figure and no doubt represents nothing but water, since the company is very heavily bonded. If the State Tax Commission's figures are assumed to represent the maximum value of the company's property—a pretty safe assumption, since they will certainly be used as a basis for rate decisions—then at least $68 per share must be deducted from the book value of the stock, bringing the corrected figure down to about $166 per share.

This then is a fairly accurate and official valuation of Con. Gas stock. Were the shares still selling between 140 and 150, one would hardly characterize this result as particularly bullish; but with the stock below par these figures have a different significance and should provide a basis for intelligent confidence in the intrinsic merits of this issue.

Another point of great importance is the continued strong liquid asset position of the system, which reports cash assets alone in excess of the total current liabilities. It is interesting also to observe that the bond interest of

**TABLE III**

CONSOLIDATED GAS CO. AND SUBSIDIARIES COMBINED BALANCE SHEET DEC. 31, 1917, EXCLUDING INTER-COMPANY ACCOUNTS

| Assets | | Liabilities | |
|---|---|---|---|
| Plant account | $382,341,000 | Capital stock—Consolidated | |
| Cash | 6,601,000 | Gas | $99,816,000 |
| Special deposits | 18,192,000 | Subsidiaries (outside interest) | 2,560,000 |
| Materials and supplies | 7,847,000 | | |
| Other current assets | 18,980,000 | Bonded debt | 114,584,000 |
| (Total current assets) | (51,620,000) | Current liabilities | 21,749,000 |
| Miscellaneous | 1,603,000 | Misc. reserves | 3,030,000 |
| | | Reserves for contingencies and renewals | 59,290,000 |
| | | Surplus—Consolidated Gas | 19,890,000 |
| | | Surplus—Subsidiaries | 47,954,000 |
| | | Surplus—Premiums on sale of stock | 13,919,000 |
| | | Excess of par value of Subs. securities over carrying price | 52,772,000 |
| Total | $435,564,000 | Total | $435,564,000 |

the companies as a whole has been covered with a good margin, even in this unfavorable year. In Table IV we list a few of the more important bond issues. The Convertible Debenture 6s, which can be exchanged for stock par for par, are not selling on a straight bond basis. But regarded as a one-year call on the shares, with the possible loss limited to four points, they are fairly attractive, although the writer prefers the American Telephone & Telegraph Convertible 6s. The mortgage security of the N. Y. & Westchester Lighting 4s is not especially strong, but the guarantee of Consolidated Gas should make them perfectly safe. After their recent twelve-point rise advance from 59, they are not quite as desirable as the N. Y. Gas & Electric 4s, due 1948 (a N. Y. Edison Company obligation, which is well protected directly by earnings). The New Amsterdam Gas 5s are not guaranteed and this particular company reports only a slight margin of earnings over fixed charges.

## TABLE IV

IMPORTANT BOND ISSUES OF THE CONSOLIDATED GAS SYSTEM

| Amount Outstanding | | Due | Price Nov. 25 | Yield |
|---|---|---|---|---|
| $24,874,000 | Consolidated Gas Convert. Deb. 6s | 1920 | 104$^1/_2$ | |
| 10,635,000 | New Amsterdam Gas Consol 5s. | 1948 | 85 | 6.10% |
| 15,000,000 | N. Y. Gas & Elec. Light, Heat & Power 1st 5s | 1948 | 96 | 5.27% |
| 20,930,000 | N. Y. Gas & Elec. Light H. & P. Pur. Money 4s | 1949 | 76$^1/_2$ | 5.62% |
| 8,488,000 | Westchester Lighting 1st 5s | 1950 | 92 | 5.55% |
| 10,000,000 | N. Y. & Westchester Ltg. Gen. Gtd. 4s | 2004 | 71 | 5.64% |

## CONCLUSION

Coming back to the stock, our analysis has disclosed both the favorable and unfavorable aspects of the situation. Current earnings are undoubtedly poor; but the company is in strong shape to meet this temporary setback. Unless the expected improvement in operation results fails utterly to materialize, there seems no reason to anticipate a cut in the dividend. If normal conditions return, the earnings should gradually approach the level of 1916—in which nearly $13 per share was earned on the stock.

Consolidated Gas has never been the gold mine that Wall Street liked to think it; but it is a financially sound, well managed utility, enjoying exceptional advantages through its unique location. There is a hundred dollars per share and more of real value behind this issue and with better times ahead, the investor at these levels should find the stock a very satisfactory purchase—although a little patience may be needed.

MARKET STATISTICS

| | 40 Bonds | Dow-Jones Avgs. | | 50 stocks | | Total | Breadth |
| | | 20 Inds. | 20 Rails | High | Low | Sales | (No. Issues) |
|---|---|---|---|---|---|---|---|
| Monday, Nov. 18 | 81.98 | 85.01 | 89.91 | 76.85 | 76.07 | 561,500 | 212 |
| Tuesday, Nov. 19 | 81.76 | 84.68 | 89.56 | 77.66 | 75.80 | 456,000 | 200 |
| Wednesday, Nov. 20 | 81.70 | 84.33 | 89.45 | 76.28 | 75.49 | 541,400 | 200 |
| Thursday, Nov. 21 | 81.68 | 83.84 | 89.28 | 76.54 | 75.53 | 564,800 | 210 |
| Friday, Nov. 22 | 81.42 | 82.60 | 88.45 | 76.13 | 74.76 | 673,600 | 238 |
| Saturday, Nov. 23 | 81.35 | 81.83 | 87.51 | 74.91 | 73.97 | 334,700 | 206 |
| Monday, Nov. 25 | 80.96 | 79.87 | 85.10 | 74.17 | 72.06 | 984,700 | 245 |
| Tuesday, Nov. 26 | 80.69 | 81.43 | 86.06 | 73.80 | 71.96 | 647,600 | 221 |
| Wednesday, Nov. 27 | 80.78 | 80.16 | 85.56 | 74.02 | 72.64 | 727,900 | 191 |
| Thursday, Nov. 28 | | | THANKSGIVING | | | | |
| Friday, Nov. 29 | 80.82 | 80.93 | 87.16 | 73.93 | 72.17 | 661,300 | 205 |
| Saturday, Nov. 30 | 80.91 | 81.13 | 87.03 | 74.05 | 73.48 | 277,500 | 175 |

# 10

# BARGAIN HUNTING THROUGH THE BOND LIST

*Gilt Edged Railroad Issues at Attractive Prices—Some Cheap Industrial Bonds— Peerless 6s—The Investment Mystery*

Nearly a thousand different bond issues are listed on the Daily Quotation Sheet of the New York Stock Exchange. If armed with a microscope and a set of Security Manuals, the statistician plows valiantly through this wilderness, he is certain to uncover a bargain or two in passing. A recent expedition of this nature has yielded the following results:

Among the score of bonds grouped under the heading of Southern Pacific, appears the following item; Houston & Texas Central 1st 5s, interest guaranteed, due 1937. Outstanding $1,389,000. Quite a few of these bonds have sold recently at 96; the last sale, however, was noted at 97, at which price the yield is 5.25%. Not such a wonderful return you say; but let us first see in what class the issue belongs.

According to the Railroad Manual, Houston & Texas Central 5s are a first lien on 453 miles of road, running into Houston. The bonded debt per mile figures out therefore at only $3,128. This is an extraordinarily low rate in any case, and especially so in view of the profitable character of the mortgaged line, as evidenced by the company's separate report.

The following comparison of these 5s with Atchison, Topeka & Santa Fe General 4s—typical of the highest grade railroad bonds—indicates the unique security enjoyed by the former issue:

|                                          | H. & T. C. 1st 5s | Atch. gen. 4s |
|------------------------------------------|-------------------|---------------|
| Yield                                    | 5.25%             | 4.70%         |
| Outstanding per mile                     | $3,128            | $17,600       |
| Interest charge per mile                 | 156               | 704           |
| Net Available for interest per mile, 1917 | 3,000            | 4,400         |
| Interest charges earned.                 | 19.2 times        | 6.3 times     |

The insignificant size of the Houston & Texas Central issue is explained by the fact that $6,711,000 of the bonds originally emitted have been retired at 110 by a sinking fund provided from the proceeds of land sales. Practically all the available land has now been disposed of. In the olden days, this fund was quite a nuisance to the bondholders, since otherwise the issue would have ranged well above the callable price. But the investor has a chance to purchase this gilt-edged issue thirteen points below its minimum price in the past.

To make assurance doubly sure, the H. & T. C. 1st 5s are additionally protected by the guarantee as to interest of the Southern Pacific Co.—which, while quite superfluous in this case, serves to intensify the attractive features of the issue. All told, this is about as safe an investment as can be found anywhere, and its yield is substantially higher than that of many other gilt-edged railroad bonds. Holders of the New Pennsylvania General 5s, Chicago & North Western General 5s or Wabash 1st 5s could very advantageously exchange into Houston & Texas Central 5s—provided bonds can still be obtained at or near the last sale price. This is the great difficulty in recommending bargains; they rarely remain on the counter long enough to be snapped up by the eager purchaser thereof.

## EAST TENNESSEE, VIRGINIA & GEORGIA 1ST 5s.

Another bond of much the same type as that just discussed is the East Tennessee, Virginia & Georgia 1st 5s due in 1930, which sold last at 95 to yield 5.60%. This is an underlying obligation of the Southern Railway and is secured by a first lien on the very important line running through Nashville and Chattanooga. The issue amounts to but $3,106,000, so that it is outstanding at the rate of but $5,650 per mile. For some peculiar reason these bonds are listed on the official Quotation Sheet as "divisional 5s" and on this account there seem to be a widespread notion that they are junior to another issue, called East Tennessee, Virginia & Georgia Consolidated 5s due 1956. Exactly the reverse is the case; in fact, the 5s of 1930 precede no less than four other mortages as follows:

| | |
|---|---|
| 1st Lien E. Tenn., Va. & Ga. 1st 5s | 1930 |
| 2d Lien E. Tenn., Va. & Ga. Con. 5s | 1956 |
| 3d Lien E. Tenn. Reorganization 5s | 1938 |
| 4th Lien Southern Ry. Con. 5s | 1994 |
| 5th Lien Southern Ry. Devel. 4s | 1956 |
|   Also | |
| 6th Lien Southern Railway Preferred Stock | |
| 7th Lien Southern Railway Common Stock | |

The holder of these bonds is not only "close to the rails" but is surrounded by layer upon layer of junior issue padding to absorb the stocks of a possible reorganization. It is particularly recommended that this obligation be purchased in place of Southern Railway consol. 5's, which sell at a higher price and yet are not as well secured as are the underlying E. T. Va. Ga. bonds.

## CHESAPEAKE AND OHIO ISSUES

The yield returned by the bonds of the Chesapeake and Ohio appears very attractive in view of the great progress made by the company in recent years. 'Tis true that the overlarge proportion of bonds to stock militates against the investment rating of its various issues. But this fault is even more pronounced in the financial structure of New York Central, the bonds of which sell relatively higher than do Chesapeake's. Table I gives a comparison of the leading issues of the two systems.

Solely from the investment standpoint, the most attractive of the Chesapeake issues is the convertible $4\frac{1}{2}$'s, which because of their near maturity in 1930 yield 7%. An investor who has purchased the New York Central ref. $4\frac{1}{2}$'s in the nineties should make up his loss much more easily by switching into the C. & O. convertible $4\frac{1}{2}$s. The latter bond constitutes an excellent business man's investment.

The higher yield of the N. Y. Central debenture 6's compared with the C. & O. convertible 5's is explained first by the fact that the former are a debenture, while the latter have a mortgage lien. Secondly, the Chesapeake 5's are now convertible into stock at 75 against 110 for the N. Y. Central 6's. This means that C. & O. shares need advance only eight points to show a profit to the purchaser of the 5's, whereas N. Y. Central must rise thirty-one points—a much less probable contingency.

## CHEAP INDUSTRIAL BONDS

The prosperity of the past few years has been reflected in the quotations for industrial bonds, which, in sharp contrast with railroad and utility obligations, have in many cases advanced above their pre-war level. Real bargains in the industrial list are therefore by no means easy to unearth; careful study—and above all an impartial mind—are required to dig them out.

The fact that Granby Copper 6's due 1928 have again sold under par calls attention to the excellent opportunity for conservative and profitable investment afforded by this issue. Granby 6's possess all the qualities of a desirable bond—as witness the following enumeration:

1. Small closed first mortgage on valuable property.
2. Net current assets exceed par value of the issue.
3. Minimum earnings greatly in excess of interest requirements.
4. Market price of stock many times the outstanding bonds.
5. Sinking fund will redeem entire issue before maturity.
6. Conversion privilege of potential value.

The fourth point ordinarily escapes the investor's attention, yet it is the most significant index of the real security behind a bond issue. Where the value of the stock greatly exceeds the funded debt, there is room for a severe shrinkage in the company's assets and earnings before the safety of the bonds is in any way impaired. In the case of Granby 6's there is $15,000,000 stock with a market value of $12,000,000, junior to but $2,500,000 of bonds. In other words, the mortgaged property is here pledged at only 18% of its current realizable value.

Perhaps the most interesting feature of this issue is the large sinking fund of 10% of net earnings plus the fixed sum of $40,000. This provision is

## TABLE I

COMPARISON OF N. Y. C. AND C. & B. BONDS

| | New York Central | | | | Ches. & Ohio | | |
|---|---|---|---|---|---|---|---|
| | Due | Price | Yield | | Due | Price | Yield |
| 1st Lien 1st 3$^1/_2$s | 1997 | 72 | 4.90% | 1st 5s | 1939 | 98$^1/_2$ | 5.11% |
| 2d Lien Con. 4s | 1988 | 77 | 5.25% | Gen. 4$^1/_2$s | 1992 | 82 | 5.50% |
| 3d Lien Ref. 4$^1/_2$s | 2014 | 83 | 5.42% | Conv. 4$^1/_2$s | 1930 | 81 | 7.00% |
| Convert. Conv. 6s | 1935 | 99$^1/_2$ | 6.05% | Conv. 5s | 1946 | 87$^1/_2$ | 5.90% |

almost certain to retire the entire issue before maturity, and since the trustee must pay 110 for the bonds, if not obtainable for less, the patient bondholder could successfully hold out for the top price—and again a ten point premium in addition to his excellent return.

## UNION BAG AND PAPER 1ST 5's

A few years of great prosperity can entirely transform the status of a company's bond issue. The Union Bag and Paper Company of the old days was an overcapitalized, more or less shaky enterprise—a speculative proposition pure and simple. But the reorganized Corporation has worked itself into excellent condition of late; and the first mortgage 5's due 1930 stand well up under critical analysis—although they are selling at 87 to yield 6.70%. First there are only $3,000,000 left of the original issue of $5,000,000, and the remainder are being retired at a steadily increasing rate—now about $170,000 per year. Secondly, they are fully covered by net current assets, which fact is one of the best possible assurances of ability to repay. Both in 1917 and 1918 interest charges were earned no less than ten times over. Moreover, the bonds are protected by $10,000,000 stock, selling at 75, paying $8 dividends, and earning $20 per share. Evidently the company could meet a year or two of depression without the slightest danger to the bonds? When Union Bag succeeds in living down its past reputation, these 1st mortgage 5s should easily sell ten points higher.

## CHILE COPPER 6's.

Chile Copper Convertible 6s, due 1932, have lost about half of their ten point gain following the declaration of the armistice, and are now selling at $84\frac{1}{2}$. This means a straight yield of over 7%, which the amortization of the large discount brings up to about 8%. So liberal a return for a bond issue would imply more or less serious doubts as to the safety of principal or interest, yet an analysis of this undertaking reveals elements of fundamental strength which should entitle the 6% bonds to a higher investment rating.

The cause of this exceptionally low price can be traced primarily to their ill-times offering at par in April 1917. The sudden collapse of the bond market at this juncture left most of the issue in the hands of the underwriters, and the process of investment absorption, or "digestion," has necessarily been slow. There is no doubt, also, that the foreign location of the property has been held against it by the conservative. There has been a deal of fine talk about the coming period of American investment in foreign fields: but is does appear as if we have a long educational process to undergo before Yankee dollars will respond readily to the call of Wladikawkas or Hu-Kuang. For here is Chile Copper—an enterprise originated, financed and managed by Americans—in a country certainly more amenable to our control than any European state—which can contend with only meagre success against the provincial spirit of American investors.

The bases of Chile Copper's strength are its huge ore reserves, its large productive capacity, and its ability to produce at relatively low cost. With four hundred million tons of developed ore, the exhaustion of the mine can be ignored as a factor. Current production is approximately 100,000,000 pounds per annum, the projected output is 300,000,000 lbs. Since the interest charges on the $35,000,000 6s and the $15,000,000 prior 7s aggregate $3,150,000, a profit of three cents per lb. on the present scale, or only one cent on the ultimate output, will serve the funded debt. In this connection it should be noted that only about 50% of the principal of the 6s has been paid in, so that present interest charges are about $1,000,000 less than the above calculation indicates.

The method of dealing in the part paid receipts is somewhat peculiar. If a bond is purchased at 84½, the transaction would be settled as follows:

| | |
|---|---|
| Price of $1,000 bond at 84½% | $845 |
| Less unpaid installment | 500 |
| Net Cost | $345 |

It should be pointed out that the part paid receipts are dealt in "flat," so that the accrued interest is not added to the purchase price. The company has the right to call the second installment on May 29.

## PEERLESS TRUCK AND MOTOR 6s.

Bonds have their mysteries no less than stocks. The prize puzzle of the bond field does not appear on the Stock Exchange Quotation Sheet, but is probably presented by the unlisted First Mortgage Notes of the Peerless Truck and Motor Corp., which are now selling at 87½ to yield about 8¼%.

These Notes were brought out in 1915 by a very reputable syndicate and made an excellent showing at the time. The three annual reports published since then have all been very favorable as far as the notes were concerned. The company's accounting methods seem to have been extremely conservative; nevertheless interest charges have been earned at least five times over during this period. Furthermore, the working capital position has been kept consistently strong, and on Dec. 31, 1917—the last report available—cash assets alone exceeded all current liabilities. Considering the fact that the bonds were covered one and one-half times over by net current assets— entirely outside of the Plant Account—it is difficult to imagine how they could ever get into trouble.

But most important of all is the fact that the company last year retired well over $1,750,000 of these bonds, leaving hardly more than $3,000,000 now outstanding. The funds were obtained by the sale to the Government of the unprofitable Long Island plant.

In view of the excellent showing that this security makes from every standpoint, it is difficult to understand the extraordinarily low price at which the notes have sold since shortly after their issue. For one thing it is known that the underwriting syndicate have never made an effort to maintain the quotation. Again certain losses sustained by a subsidiary on shell contracts appear to have frightened bondholders, but these were all charged off against the earnings of 1916.

The writer has investigated the affairs of the Company as thoroughly as available data will allow, and has been totally unable to discover an adequate reason for the large discount at which the notes are now selling. Either there is a particularly elusive snare here—or else the Peerless 6s are one of the greatest bargains to be found in the wide realm of corporation bonds.

# PART III

# APRIL 1919– DECEMBER 1924

# INRODUCTION

BY DAVID DARST

Beginning in March 1919 and continuing through December 1924, Benjamin Graham published more than 25 articles in *The Magazine of Wall Street.* In the last three quarters of 1919, seven articles appeared (Graham was 25 years old), followed by 4 articles in 1920, four articles in 1921, two articles in 1922, three articles in 1923, and eight articles in 1924 (when Graham reached his thirtieth birthday). These investment essays covered a wide range of topics and varied in length.

Following the postwar recovery of 1919, the five years from 1920 through 1924 featured the following: at the beginning of the period, significant inflation followed by meaningful deflation; restrictive (in 1920) and then expansionary (in April and September 1921) monetary policy by the still-new Federal Reserve board; a horrific bomb blast that killed 30 people on September 16, 1920 outside of J.P. Morgan & Co's headquarters at 23 Wall Street; the death in office (on August 2, 1923) of U.S. President Warren Gamaliel Harding; and unmistakable signs of growing American economic might, significant oil discoveries within the continental United States, and the emergence and expansion of the automobile, aviation, and radio industries.

After reaching a January 3 high of 109.88, and from the year's opening level of 108.76, the Dow Jones Industrial Average closed the year 1920 at 71.95, down −32.9%. Calendar years 1921 and 1922 witnessed improving business, consumer, and investor confidence, reflected in gains for the Dow Jones Industrials of +12.7% and +21.7%, respectively. Viewed in hindsight,

1923's decline of –3.3% for the Dow Industrials, to a closing level of 95.52, represented but a brief corrective phase in what would turn out to be an epic bull market run for equities.

Reflecting significant growth in the utility and construction sectors, 1924 saw General Electric rise from $194 to $322 per share and the Dow Industrials rise +26.2%, closing on December 31 at its high for the year: 120.51. Tellingly, November 1924's New York Stock Exchange trading volume of 42.8 million shares eclipsed the previous all-time record monthly volume peak (reached in April 1901), and the Dow Industrials surpassed the record high that had been established in 1919.

Some of Graham's most fundamental investment thoughts, so eloquently and indelibly elucidated in his classic bestsellers *Security Analysis* and *The Intelligent Investor,* first began to be reified in many of the deeply penetrating and analytical essays that he composed over the ten-year period from 1917 to 1927 for *The Magazine of Wall Street.* Among the successful practitioners of Benjamin Graham's ideas are Warren Buffett, Charlie Munger, William Ruane, Jonathan Goldfarb, Irving Kahn, Seth Klarman, Scott Black, Walter Schloss, Jean-Marie Eveillard, Tom Knapp, Ed Anderson, Mario Gabelli, Warren Parkkonen, Stan Perlmeter, Rick Guerin, and Jeremy Grantham. Some of Graham's principles that appeared in his two masterworks include:

1. **Viewpoint and Approach:** Equity investors should proceed as if they are considering purchasing part ownership of a business. As a result, short-term price fluctuations should be of less concern than the basic soundness, defensibility, and durability of a company's business model. "In the short-term, the stock market behaves like a *voting machine* (subject to fads and fashions), but in the long-term, the stock market behaves like a *weighing machine* (reflecting the true worth of a business)."

2. **Investment versus Speculation:** "An investment operation is one which, upon thorough analysis, promises safety of principal and a satisfactory return." Operations not meeting these requirements are speculative.

An *investment operation* is one that can be justified on both qualitative and quantitative grounds. Investment is grounded in the past, whereas speculation looks primarily to the future. A cynic's definition of an investment is: "an investment is a successful speculation and a speculation is an unsuccessful investment." [In Warren Buffett's words: "A great investment opportunity occurs when a marvelous business encounters a one-time huge, but solvable, problem."]

3.  **Intrinisic Value vs. Book Value**: *Intrinsic value* represents what an investor can *get out* of a company, and *book value* represents what has been *put into* the company. *Intrinsic value* is "that value which is justifiable by the facts, e.g., the assets, earnings, dividends, and definite prospects, as distinct, let us say, from market quotations established by market manipulation as distorted by psychological excess." *Book value* shows: (i) how much capital is invested in the business; (ii) the ease or stringency of the company's financial condition (i.e., the working-capital position); (iii) details of the capitalization structure; (iv) an important check on the validity of the reported earnings; and (v) the basis for analyzing the sources of income.

4.  **The Role of Market Prices**: "In common stock investing, the danger of paying the wrong price is almost as great as that of buying the wrong issue." To regard investment quality as something independent of price is a fundamental and dangerous error. Nearly every issue might conceivably be cheap in one price range and dear in another.

5.  **Margin of Safety**: When a common stock is available on the market at a price which is at a discount to its intrinsic value, a *margin of safety* exists which increases its suitability as an investment.

6.  **Security Analysis**: The value of analysis diminishes as the element of chance increases. Security analysis can be any or all of the following: descriptive; selective; or critical. The major obstacles to successful security analysis include: (i) incorrect data; (ii) the uncertainties of the future; and (iii) the irrational behavior of the market. Abnormally good

or abnormally bad conditions do not last forever. "The common stock investor is neither right nor wrong because others agreed or disagreed with him/her; he/she is right because his/her facts and analysis are right."

■    ■    ■

"Attractive Industrial Preferred Stocks" points out the advantage of preferred stock dividends, which are exempt from the U.S. government's so-called Normal Tax, over ordinary bond interest payments, which are generally subject thereto. While the true worth of any asset depends primarily upon its asset value and its earning power, and because the merit of a preferred stock stems principally from the sufficiency of the issuer's earnings to meet dividend requirements, "it is especially important that these charges be covered with a fair margin in poor years."

According to Graham, another very useful standard of assessing the value of a preferred stock issue is the relation of the equity capitalization (the total market value) of the common stock to the total par value of the preferred stock. Assuming that a company's stock price reflects to some degree the intrinsic worth of its common shares, then the total common equity capitalization-to-total par value of the preferred stock ratio provides a reasonable measure of the level of equity protecting the preferred stock, its senior sibling on the balance sheet.

A third measure used to appraise preferred stocks is the amount of net current assets (after deducting all prior liabilities, including bonds and notes) available to cover the total amount of the preferred issue outstanding. Graham then proceeds to evaluate 41 preferred stocks, selecting eight issues based on their yield and the criteria described above. In characteristic Graham fashion, he discusses the disadvantages of non-cumulative preferred stocks ("the dividends suspended in bad years can never be recovered, no matter what prosperity follows . . . Why take even an infinitesimal chance?"). Graham then displays his straightforward willingness to express his opinions: "on this account we would select American Linseed Preferred as a stunning example of an issue not to buy."

■   ■   ■

Graham continues the side-by-side physical, operational, and financial analysis of railroad magnate James J. Hill's two sibling issues in "Northern Pacific Outstrips Great Northern." After losing and then regaining its leadership over Great Northern in traffic and earning power, Northern Pacific, the latter road, is affirmatively judged to be a better investment purchase based on:

1. Record prior to government control,
2. Results under federal operation,
3. Relative growth of fixed charges, and
4. Northern Pacific's valuable land grant.

It is a source of great puzzlement for Graham how, with 20% less freight capacity and 10% less locomotive power, Northern Pacific is able to handle as much traffic as Great Northern. After careful research, he is able to conclude that "with a 40% larger haul for its traffic, Northern Pacific must evidently be able to keep its equipment in use a larger proportion of the time, and thus get along with a smaller quantity of freight cars." Northern Pacific is also able to translate its higher traffic density into lower transportation costs, the chief source of Northern Pacific's advantage. Delving into each road's fixed interest requirements, Graham finds that an apparent sizeable advantage of Great Northern virtually disappears when both lines are evaluated on an apples-to-apples basis. Given the financial and operating superiority of Northern Pacific over Great Northern, the extreme disparity in the two lines' land holdings— 4.8 million acres for Northern Pacific, compared to 101,543 acres for Great

Northern—makes it seem to Graham that it is "only a question of time when Northern Pacific, for ten years the 'underdog,' shall once more claim the ascendancy."

■    ■    ■

"A Neglected Chain Store Issue" conducts a comparative analysis of the common shares of four publicly traded five-and-ten-cent chain store companies: Woolworth, S.S. Kresge, S.H. Kress, and McCrory. In his examination of these issues, Graham goes beyond such obvious metrics as revenues and net earnings, observing that a company's superiority in sales may be offset by proportionately higher levels of debt on its balance sheet or an overly elevated valuation. Graham points out that "while Woolworth may be earning *seventeen* times as much as McCrory, its market valuation is *fifty* times as great" (Graham's emphasis).

In passing, Graham notes the better protection afforded by Kresge preferred shares relative to the preferred shares of Kress:

> It is nothing short of ludicrous that Kress preferred should be quoted above Kresge preferred, as the former has not a single point in its favor. Not only is Kresge in a much stronger position with respect to both assets and earning power, but its past record shows a healthier and more rapid growth.

Returning to McCrory, Graham expresses astonishment that: (i) its tangible assets per share ratio equals that of Woolworth, which sells five times as high as McCrory; and (ii) it is the only one of the four five-and-ten-cent chain store common stocks selling for less than the real assets behind it. Seeking an explanation for McCrory's anomalous pricing, Graham suggests the absence of dividend payments and the low growth rate in its working capital (in the prior two years, sales have doubled while net current assets have increased by only 23%). In Graham's opinion, the latter factor represents a serious objection to an unreservedly favorable assessment of McCrory's common stock.

Although tempted by the example of Kresge's financials having been in a position similar to McCrory's two years earlier and Kresge's having since experienced a doubling in its stock price, Graham notes that margin pressures have prevented McCrory from achieving Kresge's steady increase from year to year in the net earnings for the common stock. In the final analysis, "there are possibilities of a sharp expansion in net profits, dependent upon the capabilities of its management." Graham concludes that "it is a good stock for the patient investor, the kind that usually makes the largest profits and incidentally isn't worried by day to day fluctuations."

■    ■    ■

In "The Art of Hedging," Graham uses the examples of Southern Pacific convertible bonds and Gilliland Oil convertible preferred shares to demonstrate the favorable risk-reward characteristics of convertible hedging. In such an operation, the investor purchases the convertible security and sells short the equivalent amount of the underlying common stock. Should the stock price rise, the investor can exchange the convertible for the common stock in order to cover and close out the short position at a minimal loss. On the other hand, a decline in the common stock price tends to not be matched by a similar percentage selloff in the convertible bond or convertible preferred stock, due to the preferential position of such instruments in a company's capital structure.

Graham reveals similar hedging principles in the case of buying common stock subscription rights at a small fixed cost and selling short an equivalent amount of shares. In addition to common-stock hedging involving convertible securities or subscription rights (both of which involve being able to obtain at a fixed price the common stock that has been sold), hedging can also sometimes be carried out by selling securities against one another, with no other safeguard than the definite knowledge that the two prices are out of line. Such methods are demonstrated, involving: (i) Brooklyn Rapid Transit certificates of deposit versus BRT free stock; (ii) Interborough-Metropolitan $4\frac{1}{2}\%$ bonds versus I-M preferred stock; or (iii) the 4% Missouri, Kansas, & Texas bonds versus the 4% M.K.T. non-cumulative preferred stock.

■   ■   ■

"Which Is the Best Sugar Stock?" features a comparative analysis of the 1918–9 financial results of five listed sugar-producing issues—Cuba Cane; Cuban-American; Punta Alegre; Manati; and South Porto Rico. After noting the relatively arbitrary nature (and thus the capricious effect on earnings) of these companies' depreciation expenses, Graham identifies Cuban Cane as having generated, both before and after depreciation expenses, the largest 1919 earnings per dollar of market price of its common stock. Upon examining the capitalization structure of the five companies, Graham finds that Cuba Cane Sugar's significant amounts of bonds and preferred stock on its balance sheet mean that its profits are distributed over a relatively smaller common stock base than the other companies. The disadvantage of such a financial structure is the fact that under severe economic conditions, "the margin for the common shares quickly melts away, and before long even the payments on the senior issues are impaired."

This line of analysis leads Graham to the important concept, related to late 20th century notions of earnings-to-enterprise value metrics, of comparing the earnings of the five companies *to their total capitalization* instead of merely on their common stock. On this basis, in which all of the companies are put on the same level of capitalization, Cuba Cane drops from the top to the bottom of the five sugar firms, and Punta Alegre (followed closely by Cuban-American) jumps to first place. Additional insights are furnished by comparative operating data such as transportation costs, raw sugar yields, percentage of output refined in-house, and profits per pound.

In spite of its large production volume, Cuba Cane's high operating costs and its debt- and preferred-heavy capitalization structure render it susceptible and highly leveraged to sugar pricing:

> This is a combination which makes excellent earnings on the common during high sugar prices, but a very rapid shrinkage of profits when the price of the commodity declines. In a word, Cuba Cane common is essentially a speculative issue, carrying possibilities both of sharp advances and sharp declines.

Graham sums up by placing Cuban American, South Porto Rico, and Punta Alegre "rather closely together in the class of conservative common stocks. Manati is too high, and Cuba Cane must be regarded as essentially speculative."

■    ■    ■

In "The 'Collapse' of American International," Graham looks for the causes of the dividend omission and the 94-point price decline (from 132 to 38) in the shares of the supposedly sound American International, an enterprise launched under excellent auspices, devoted to foreign trade and investment, and guided by an illustrious 24-person Board of Directors drawn from the leaders of American banking and business.

Graham observes that "for months there had been persistent and mysterious selling of the stock which carried it steadily to lower levels," generating a suspicion of sales by insiders who must have known that the dividend would be passed. Placing aside moral concerns for the moment, Graham inquires, "what the public would chiefly like to know is whether the stock is still dear at 42."

In addition to conducting some operations in its own name, American International has acquired securities in no less than 24 companies:

- Group A: Eleven proprietary companies whose operations are included in American International's 1919 Report (these span the gamut of machinery, steel, shipbuilding, import-export, naval goods, and the importing and sale of tea)—in Graham's opinion, "the peculiar point about all of these is that none of them appears to have been a really big proposition."

- Group B: Three proprietary companies whose operations are not included in the American International's 1919 report (they are respectively involved in the manufacture of life-saving equipment, "the obtaining of concessions in China," and construction work in China)—Graham opines that, "none of the three companies appears very important."

- Group C: Ten outside investments (including participation interests in Pacific Mail Steamship Company, International Mercantile Marine, United Fruit, New York Shipbuilding, U.S. Rubber, International Products, Simms Petroleum, U.S. Industrial Alcohol, Symington Forge Company, and American International Terminals Company)—Graham notes that "the question of Outside Investments is of the utmost importance, not only because they represent $60 per share in book value of American International stock, but chiefly because, in 1919, they contributed over 88% of the total income available for American International Stock."

After making allowance for the fact that the market value of the ten outside investments has shrunk considerably, Graham believes it is reasonable to suppose that these participations are worth at least $40 per share. If so, such a valuation would approximately equal the recent stock price and still leave the assets invested in the 14 proprietary companies of Group A and Group B amounting to roughly *an additional* $54 per share.

Graham wraps up his analysis by concluding that: (i) "the company's foreign business has apparently been of insufficient size to swallow up the larger portion of its capital, even at worst;" and (ii) "the domestic investments should assure a minimum asset value and minimum income large enough to justify the purchase of the stock at or below present levels."

■    ■    ■

"The Goodyear Reorganization" seeks the origin of the fall of Goodyear Tire and Rubber "from the height of prosperity to the depth of insolvency in a bewilderingly short space of time." In 12 years, the company had increased its annual sales from $2 million to $200 million, while also expanding its assets and capitalization a hundredfold. Graham inquires whether it was purely an accident that one of the strongest and soundest enterprises in the country—with the highest reputation in the commercial and financial field—succumbed to a business depression which its rivals were able to withstand. The company's common and preferred stock prices declined more than 80% over the last three quarters of 1920.

One of the weakest points in Goodyear's strategy was management's decision to invest enormous sums in fixed assets just as the industrial boom was reaching its climax: in the fiscal year ending October 30, 1920, the company increased its fixed assets by 130%, and in the previous five years, by 750%. The lavishness and variety of the new fixed assets included: a plant in Ohio for the manufacture of commercial dirigibles; a plant purchased from Ford Motor Company in Long Island City, New York; coal properties in Ohio; cotton ranches in Arizona and California; facilities in Brazil; and rubber plantations in Indonesia. While a good part of these heavy outlays was financed through the sale of new common and preferred stock, a large portion of the remainder was paid for by substantially drawing down Goodyear's cash position.

Graham carefully and ingeniously pieces together a pro forma balance sheet reflecting Goodyear's Readjustment Plan for its prepackaged reorganization. On the assumption that the company is able to obtain the consent of the 25% of the creditors who had not yet voted in favor of the plan, Graham lays out Goodyear's likely capital structure (consisting of First Mortgage Bonds, Debentures, Prior Preference Stock, Preferred Stock, and Common Stock), working capital position, fixed charges, and earnings. At then current prices, and in view of the substantial prior claims on earnings of bond interest and Prior Preference dividend charges, Graham rates the heavily diluted common stock as an essentially speculative issue, "which will fluctuate widely with each relatively small change in the company's earnings." He sees the preferred stock as "also mainly speculative, since dividend resumption is not yet in sight."

■    ■    ■

In "Is United Drug Cheap at 53?" Graham wonders whether a 30-point, two-day decline in the common stock price (from $83 to $53) has made the company an attractive candidate for purchase. In conducting his analysis, Graham notes many companies' delays in releasing timely financial information, and in boldface type he calls on the New York Stock Exchange (the Securities and Exchange Commission did not yet exist) to do more to force firms to publish their results as promised:

> The organization of the New York Stock Exchange has apparently not yet reached the point where it can independently make sure that all the agreements contained in the listing applications are regularly observed. But when its attention is called to any default in this respect, it quickly and energetically brings pressure to bear to have the conditions remedied. Hence, if wide-awake stockholders will insist upon obtaining the reports at the periods agreed upon, they can get what they want.

Graham expresses dismay that if United Drug's stockholders had been appropriately informed of the company's sales, profits, and financial position, "some of the more alert and intelligent among them might have sensed danger ahead and acted accordingly." Since the end of 1919, the company's position was weakened by a number of unfavorable circumstances.

First, United Drug's plant and inventories expanded tremendously at the peak of cost inflation, threatening severe losses when they were marked down to a deflated valuation. Second, the company incurred heavy bond interest and sinking fixed requirements and minimum working capital levels that put its common stock dividend in jeopardy. Third, in connection with the 1920 acquisition of Boot's Pure Drug Company of England, United Drug indefinitely guaranteed 8% dividends on a large amount of Liggett International preferred stock. Fourth, the first half of 1921 witnessed significant contractions in revenues and profits versus the previous year.

Given these negatives, Graham concludes that further inventory writedowns are likely and the company's current common stock dividend is questionable. With the market also dubious about the business acumen and financial condition of United Drug's President Louis K. Liggett, "the stock holds forth very few attractions even at its present low price of 53."

■   ■   ■

"Speculative Opportunities in Railroad Stocks" sets out to discover: (i) the factors that will contribute most directly to an increase in a specific railroad's stock prices; and (ii) the prospects of such factors being realized in the near future. In order to intelligently do so, Graham points out that it is important to realize that in the past several years, the primary determinants of the prosperity of any one railroad have been transferred from its capitalization (a *fixed* element) to its operating costs (a *variable* element).

In Graham's opinion, the future earning power of a railroad is dependent on its gross revenues (determined by volume and freight rates) and its operating costs (determined by wages and material prices). He then calculates the theoretical future earning power of six low-priced railroad issues, which, Graham hastens to point out, appear to offer speculative possibilities. Graham selects as his favorite the St. Louis Southwestern Railway due to its extraordinary revenue growth. Even with a further shrinkage in traffic, the road is estimated to possess sufficient earning power to justify higher than current market prices.

His second favorite is Missouri, Kansas & Texas 7% preferred stock, due to its generous dividend, the fact that this preferred will soon be cumulative, and the small size of the preferred issue relative to the amount of common stock outstanding. Next in line are: Toledo, St. Louis & Western Railway common stock (due to its increased earning power); Pere Marquette Railway common stock (due to above-average earnings and a greatly reduced debt burden after its reorganization); Rock Island Railway (due to its position in a rapidly growing part of the U.S.); and Chicago & Eastern Illinois (based on Graham's expectations of lower operating costs in the future).

■   ■   ■

In "Arithmetic and Stock Values," Graham emphatically points out that "in the last analysis, earning power must always be the chief criterion of stock values—exceeding in importance asset backing, financial condition, and even dividend return." To Graham's way of thinking, earnings determine the real worth of physical assets, the degree to which a company's cash position is augmented or vitiated, and its dividend policy.

At the same time, it is important to consider not merely profits relative to a company's common stock, but *earnings relative to its total capitalization:* "the smaller the ratio of common stock to total capital, the less dependable are profits per share as an index of the company's real earning power." Through side-by-side depiction of: (i) Mack Truck and White Motor; (ii)

American Ice and All America Cables; and (iii) Associated Dry Goods and
May Department Stores, Graham shows that if White Motor, All American
Cables, and May Department Stores had been capitalized with more
preferred stock in place of common, on the same percentage basis as its
comparable company, each of these enterprises would have earned more,
not less, on its common stock than its evaluated neighbor.

Actual transformations of the capital structure produced similar results
for North America Company and for Julius Kayser (a glove manufacturing
concern), American Zinc, Virginia Iron Coal and Coke, and American Steel
Foundries. Graham takes pains to point out that in *prosperous years* (Graham's
emphasis), "the smaller the portion of common stock to total capital, the
larger the earnings per share," but when periods of economic difficulty cause
a significant profits decline, "then the situation is reversed." In such cases, it
turns out that the large earnings on common stock shrink rapidly, and
frequently the preferred dividends and even the bonds' scheduled interest
payments may be endangered. As a consequence, "a simple readjustment of
capitalization is found to produce dazzling effects on the earnings exhibit, but
analysis shows this stimulus to be entirely artificial."

Graham concludes that a company's optimal capitalization structure
may be importantly influenced by the characteristics of the sector in which it
operates, with steadier, more predictable-earnings industries justifying a
higher proportion of senior securities such as preferred stock.

■    ■    ■

In "What Every Small Investor Should Know," Graham entertainingly sets
forth, in the form of "a financial playlet with meaning," several key
principles of bond investing. First, when swapping from a higher-coupon
bond (such as a 5% issue maturing in 72 years and yielding 6.05%), into a
lower-coupon bond at a higher yield (such as a 4.5% issue maturing in
10 years, and yielding 7.30%), it is important to consider: (i) the *price* of the

two securities (and thus the cash received or given up in the swap) relative to (ii) the differential in cash income thrown off each year by the bonds' coupons.

Second, an investor does not have to hold a bond bought at a discount until maturity in order to realize some part of its annual advance in principal value (known in modern times as "accretion"), and the amount of the annual accretion is larger for bonds that have a shorter time period remaining to final maturity. Third, numerous accidents and anomalies appear from time to time in the bond market, and investors can take advantage of them by being attentive, flexible, and opportunistic.

■      ■      ■

"The Unscrambling of Reading" describes the government-mandated split-up of the so-called Reading Combination: (i) to separate the Central Railroad of New Jersey from the Philadelphia & Reading Railway; and (ii) to terminate the control exercised by these carriers over their iron and anthracite coal subsidiaries. Being prohibited from retaining an interest simultaneously in the coal and the railroad properties, Reading Common stock holders have to choose between one enterprise or the other. At the same time, the bonds and preferred stock issues of "Railway" and "Coal" need to be evaluated.

Graham notes "without prejudice and without responsibility" that while the Reading Coal shares are deemed to possess "remarkable possibilities," sworn affidavits presented to the U.S. Court in January 1923 assert that the Railroad *properties* are worth about twice as much as those of the Coal Company. As is his wont, Graham remarks that a comparison of the *earning power* of the two companies can shed light on the relative attractiveness of each. As a result of separating out the Coal and Iron companies' earnings from those of the Railroad, Graham finds that the Reading Railroad Company proper, owing to its unusually strong and conservative capitalization structure, would have shown a larger dividend balance *minus* the coal and iron properties than on the old basis, with the income of the coal and iron companies included.

Graham remains puzzled, and more than a little skeptical, that Reading Coal's earnings have supposedly been understated in the past, especially since "mining in the Schuylkill field, where Reading Coal has its properties . . . is much more expensive than in the Lehigh and Wyoming fields." He concludes that Reading (Railway) Common is unusually attractive at then current levels and has much more proven investment merit than the Coal shares, particularly in light of its large and current earning power and its exceptionally low fixed changes.

■   ■   ■

In "How to Apply the Scientific Theory of Switching to Concrete Cases in the Present Market," Graham reviews four of the primary advantages of switching (swapping) between one security and another: (i) increased safety; (ii) higher yield; (iii) greater opportunity for capital gains; and (iv) improved liquidity/marketability. Although an ideal swap may "secure the advantage desired without any offsetting loss," in reality investors may have to accept a sacrifice in one objective in order to capture a significant gain in another. For example, Graham feels it is generally a good idea to forego a little bit of yield in order to capture greatly enhanced safety.

Some of the swaps that had turned out well in the previous few years included: switching, in 1921, from two-year U.S. Treasury bonds into 17-year Treasuries, which increased current income and produced significant capital gains when yields subsequently declined; and swapping, in 1914, from railroad stocks into industrials, with a switch back into the rails on favorable terms in 1923. Graham points out that the attractiveness of a given swap may vary according to the investor's personal circumstances, tax status, and risk tolerance.

Particularly compelling, yet frequently overlooked, swap opportunities are often available in switches out of common stock into convertible bonds or convertible preferred shares of the same issuer, at a considerable pickup in income safety and downside protection (should the common stock price decline), with only a small sacrifice in current yield. Graham works through the details of common-to-convertible switches in Consolidated Textile, Illinois Central, California Petroleum, and the Foundation Company, among others. Similarly motivated swaps may also be beneficial between ordinary preferreds and guaranteed preferreds of the same issuer.

Desirable switches frequently present themselves between stocks or straight bonds of different companies. Examples include income-driven switches from Atchison 4% bonds into St. Louis Southwestern 4.5% bonds, from St. Paul 4% bonds into St. Louis 5% bonds, and from Rock Island 4% bonds into Toledo, St. Louis & Western 4% bonds.

Stressing that bondholders need to pay more attention to unfavorable factors than to favorable factors, Graham issues a reminder that one prime requisite of safety for bonds is "a large aggregate of junior securities to absorb fluctuations in earning power." For this reason and because of its scant coverage of fixed charges, a representative swap is recommended from Interboro Rapid Transit 5% bonds into either the Brooklyn-Manhattan Transit 6% or the Third Avenue 4% bonds.

Graham concludes with a brief survey of typical motivations for common stock swaps between different companies, including: from New Haven Railroad into Kansas City Southern, due to financial concerns about the former but not about the latter; from Ontario & Western Railroad into Wabash, due to the overly large amount of shares outstanding of the former relative to the latter; from the Delaware, Lackawanna & Western Railroad into Reading, due to the significantly larger revenues, net earnings, and dividend coverage of the latter; from Pittsburgh & West Virginia into Pere Marquette, due to its relative earnings and dividend superiority; from Anaconda to Kennecott Copper based on the latter's ability to earn and pay a $3.00 dividend to stockholders while Anaconda had to suspend its dividend; from Ray Copper to Wright Aero, for the same reason; and from American Agriculture Chemical to Atlas Tack because of the heavy burden of the former's unpaid cumulative dividends.

■   ■   ■

"Eight Stock Bargains Off the Beaten Track" describes a group of unusually interesting common stocks that Graham is considered to have pioneered the study of: stocks that are characterized by two general features: (i) they do not have bonds or preferred stock ahead of them; and (ii) they have cash assets exceeding all or a great part of their market prices. According to Graham, such stocks tend to be neglected, not generally known among the investing public, and their trading volumes tend to be thin. As a result, these issues, also known as "Cash Asset Stocks," should be purchased "at a price and not 'at the market.'"

Graham's first example is Tonopah Mining, which, owing to depressed silver prices and investor despair over the company's efforts to develop new properties, is priced at $1.38 per share, even though the company has $4.31 per share in liquid assets. NYSE-listed Transue & Williams Steel Forgings Corporation is trading at $28.00 per share, paying a $3.00 dividend and has a solid book value of $37.21 per share, of which $18.56 per share is in cash. Another inconspicuous issue is Crex Carpet, a manufacturer of well-known floor coverings. In spite of its irregular earnings and dividend record, Crex Carpet's market price of $29.00 per share has a wealth of assets behind it: $16.97 per share in cash, an additional $22.93 per share in other current assets, and $73.77 in fixed and other assets. Observing that "certain needed changes to management have apparently been initiated," Graham doubts that the assets of Crex Carpet will remain priced in the market so far below their liquidation value.

Two pipeline companies make Graham's Cash Asset Stock list, each carrying an exceptional cash position, possessing strategically-positioned fixed assets and providing a generous dividend return. Driven down by investors' fears over competing modes of transportation and/or competing pipelines, their stock prices are trading below book value as follows:

| Company | Stock Price Per Share | Cash per Share | Fixed and Other Assets Per Share | Total Book Value Per Share |
|---|---|---|---|---|
| Cumberland Pipe Line | $128.00 | $83.90 | $86.86 | $170.76 |
| Southern Pipe Line | $95.00 | $78.73 | $38.44 | $117.17 |

Despite having net cash assets of $15.85 per share versus current sales per share of $13.00 (known as a "100% plus Cash Assets Stock"), Crescent Pipe Line is a pipeline company that does not pass muster with Graham. Crescent is a small connecting line which appears to be in danger of losing its business entirely due to changing conditions. The prior year's earnings were only $0.73 per share and the company passed its dividend. Graham articulates an extremely important lesson from the Crescent situation:

> It is a very fine thing to be able to buy a certificate representing $1.00 cash in the bank for 90 cents—but your profit on the deal is strictly limited to 10 cents. And if a long interval must elapse before the $1.00 is paid over, you may find your profit a very small one, considering the time involved.

Graham reminds investors that "cash assets are a great source of strength, but a moderate source of profits." They will appeal strongly to the investor, but their speculative possibilities are limited. He then directs his focus to Pennok Oil, selling at $15.50 per share due to investors' fear of overproduction, oil price weakness, and depletion of a deep sand well. Pennok's cash assets are $8.08 per share, and its fixed and other assets amount to $7.63 per share.

Due to uncertainties about the life of its copper ore reserves, Shattuck-Arizona Copper changes hands at $10.50 per share, with $2.88 per share in cash, $1.65 per share in other current assets, and $17.02 per share after substantial deductions for depletion and depreciation. In effect, the market is valuing Shattuck-Arizona's mines and equipment at zero in spite of its copper earnings, its low operating costs, and its large reserves of lead ore.

A threatened lawsuit by the U.S. government alleging a multi-million dollar overpayment has caused investors to sell the stock of Wright Aeronautical down to $10.50 per share, even though the company has cash on the balance sheet amounting to $16.25 per share. Fixed and other assets on the balance sheet total another $10.97 per share. Graham's considered view is that the stock is trading virtually at rock-bottom prices, and if the government's litigation proves unsuccessful, "Wright Aero will be worth at least $30.00 per share."

■   ■   ■

In "Eight Long-Range Opportunities in Low-Priced Issues," Graham distinguishes between two types of low-priced stocks, the "artificial" type (because perhaps too great a number of shares are outstanding) and the "genuine" type, which is produced by a small valuation in relation to a company's total revenues and assets. The latter condition tends to be caused by poor earnings and narrow profit margins, heavy debt obligations, or both. Graham also feels that genuinely low-priced issues tend "to yield a most pronounced response to favorable developments," such as improving sales or expanding profit margins. Even though the opportunities for large profit are offset by correspondingly magnified risks, "it may be good business to risk (where such risk can be afforded) a few dollars now and then if there is a fair chance of a profit of several hundred percent." In other words, a highly favorable risk-reward ratio.

Graham presents the first of the eight low-priced issues, International Agricultural priced at $5.00 per share. The company emerged from a 1923 recapitalization with its bank loans (a fixed and overdue obligation) transformed into a new 7% cumulative preferred stock (the dividend payments on which are discretionary). Graham's favorable view of the stock derives from its greater financial flexibility and its exposure to a potential agricultural revival after a protracted depression. Somewhat similar considerations provoke a positive stance toward Wabash Railroad at $16.00 a share, with limited fixed charges, adequate working capital, improving earnings, and its reorganization behind it rather than in front of it. Graham also notes another point in the stock's favor: Wabash's "withholding of dividends from the non-cumulative preferred has been storing up equity and treasury strength for the benefit of the common."

Graham observes a stock market behavioral tendency in the early 1920s that has held true in the decades since:

> . . . a peculiar weakness of the stock market—its proclivity for paying attention to only a single factor governing an issue, and losing sight of other frequently more important elements.

Simms Petroleum represents a different type of low-priced issue, at $14.00 per share, displaying the credentials of an earnings- and balance sheet-driven attraction. With new management and its oil production having expanded from 1 million barrels in 1921 to nearly 4 million in 1923, Simms common stock sells for 2.8 times earnings and has virtually no fixed obligations ahead of it. In light of its excellent earnings and strong working capital position ($6.00 per share in net current assets), Graham feels it is likely that Simms will declare a dividend in the current year and rates that the stock "rather unusually cheap for long-pull speculation."

Selling at 6 times earnings (a 16% earnings yield) and yielding 8%, Waldorf System common stock at $15.00 per share offers exposure to a prosperous and growing chain-restaurant system doing business at 115 locations, primarily in New England. Graham's prediction that the stock can sell at $22.00 or higher is based on the fact that "the peculiar strength of these merchandising companies is their ability to increase sales and maintain profit margins in good times and bad."

Salt Creek Producers and Mountain Producers originally constituted a single enterprise in the Salt Creek oil field in Wyoming and are still closely related from an operating, capitalization, and earnings standpoint. Their appeal stems from: (i) substantial earnings and a remarkably strong cash position despite a low oil price; (ii) steadily increasing oil production with their long-life properties only 20% developed; (iii) an unusually favorable operating contract with the Standard Oil interests; and (iv) dividend yields exceeding 8.5%. Graham likes both companies and prefers Salt Creek Producers due to its stronger cash position.

A very different security in a very different industry is represented by Metro-Goldwyn 7% preferred stock selling at $15.00 per share. Graham considers the issue "undoubtly an attractive speculation" because of its strong asset backing and the company's earnings covering the preferred dividend requirements 4.5 times.

Graham considers Landover Holding Corporation, the last of the eight low-priced issues treated here, perhaps the most unique security of the group. As an outgrowth of the liquidation of the automobile maker Willys Overland common stock is selling at $8.50 per share, as are shares of Landover Holding Corporation. The Willys Overland shares are distributable to Landover stockholders after July 1928 and they are heir to approximately $12 per share in cash, subject to the settlement of a federal lawsuit alleging the government's overpayment during wartime to Duesenberg Motors, a former subsidiary of Willys Corporation. Upon weighting the merits (or the lack thereof) of the government's case, Graham points out that "so far these war-contract suits have proved generally unsuccessful." In any event, the purchaser of Landover common stock has a good chance to receive a cash dividend of up to $12.00 per share in perhaps a year or so.

In his inimitably reserved style, Graham notes: "It looks as if a handsome reward may be reaped for a little patience."

■    ■    ■

In "Six Bargains in Low-Priced Dividend Paying Stocks," Graham points out that "wisely chosen, strongly entrenched dividend-paying common stocks prove on the whole the most profitable purchases, considering both income and principal value. It is highly instructive to observe how Graham's security selection criteria are applied across several different industry sectors. Within the steel industry, Graham's choice falls on American Steel Foundaries, the leader in railroad steel casings and car wheels, the latter offering "stable replacement demand with no debt outstanding and a preferred issue equal to one-third the size of the common." The company's stock represents 75% of its total capitalization. Net current assets account for 60% of the total capitalization, and with dividends paid continuously since 1920, a dividend payout ratio of only 33% of earnings, and a dividend yield of 8%, Graham rates American Steel Foundaries "a decidedly attractive common stock."

Graham is similarly attracted to Cuban American Sugar, owing to its size, financial stability, low production costs, and its 9.4% dividend yield. Another issue favored by Graham is White Eagle Oil, due to its continuous $2.00 annual dividend payments (producing a yield of 8.3%) and the fact that its current assets amount to over seven times its current liabilities.

In a natural transition from oil to motors, Paige-Detroit Motor (yielding 8.3%) is Graham's selection in the sector, based on its remarkable sales and profits growth, its large earnings above cash dividends, and the fact that the company's working capital exceeds the total of its bonds and preferred stocks outstanding.

Because of its excellent track record, an expansive acquisition, and the possibility of a dividend increase, Graham also likes Weber & Heilbroner, a retailer of furnishings and men's clothing. At $16 a shares, the stock yields 6.2%.

Graham's final dividend pick is Columbian Carbon, whose chief product is carbon black, derived from natural gas and used as a major constituent in printers' ink and in the manufacture of tires. The reasoning behind Graham's favorable view of the stock include: a simple capital structure (with no debt or preferred stock), an excellent cash and working capital position, earnings 50% above the current dividend rate, and a yield of 9.8%.

■   ■   ■

In "Reading—The Market's 'Sleeping Beauty,'" Graham examines the reasons why, in spite of the company's record and financial position (ranking it as one of the strongest railroads in the country), Reading Company's common stock sells at such a lower multiple of earnings and such a higher dividend yield than many of its railroad peers, including Delaware, Lackawanna & Western, Norfolk & Western, Southern Pacific, Lehigh Valley, and Chicago & Northwestern.

Probing deeply, Graham traces the causes of Reading's relative undervaluation to: (i) litigation and uncertainty over the company's segregation and spinoff of its valuable coal properties; and (ii) the phenomenally high earnings generated by Reading in the first eight months of 1923. Graham counsels that "when [railroad] earnings are suspiciously high or low, look at the maintenance account." On this measure, he finds that Reading has *not* spent low sums on maintenance to augment its earnings; on the contrary, it spent an abnormally high 36.4% of its gross revenues on maintenance expenses. By shedding light "on the vexing question of how the mind of the market works," Graham comes to the conclusion that two additional reasons for the relative undervaluation of Reading common stock are: (i) investors' expectations that the company's dividend is unlikely to be increased in the near future; and (ii) the fact that "the twin angels of Wall Street—Merger and Distribution" [Spinoff]—are hovering over other railroad shares, particularly Lehigh Valley, and Delaware, Lackawanna & Western. In Graham's sagacious words, "in a speculative market, what counts is imagination and not analysis," and "in the stock market, facts are important, but emphasis is all important."

As a consequence, Reading Company remains a "Sleeping Beauty awaiting its Prince Charming (in the prosaic form of a bull pool) to stir it into life and reveal its charm to an appreciative public."

■    ■    ■

"Simple Test for Determining the Value of Railroad Preferred Stocks" points out one of the most common pitfalls of preferred stock investing. Such erroneous thinking occurs when an investor considers an issue's dividend secure due to the fact that it is covered several times by the company's earnings, even through a more senior security (with prior claim on those earnings) may just barely cover its fixed changes. Graham asserts a fundamental principle of investing in preferred stock issues:

> Evidently there is only one scientific way to measure the margin of safety behind a preferred dividend—and that is to figure the number of times that earnings will cover the bonds' fixed charges and the preferreds' dividends combined.

Graham also points out that bond interest is not always an accurate indication of a company's true fixed charges. For example, Rental Expense may be *added to,* and Fixed Income Receivable may be *subtracted from,* such fixed charges. As a better measure of fixed charges, Graham favors taking the difference between a company's Net Income After Taxes and its Surplus Available for Dividends. In general, preferred stocks' yield differentials relative to each other tend to be significantly explained by their respective margins of safety above *fixed changes and preferred dividends combined.*

Besides the safety of a preferred stock's dividend, other important selection criteria include: (i) whether the dividend is cumulative; (ii) if cumulative, how much back dividends have accumulated; (ii) whether the issue is a participating preferred; (iv) whether the preferred stock is convertible; and (v) if participating and/or convertible, the position and prospects of the underlying common stock. Graham also points out that a preferred stock cannot be worth more than a common stock *in the same position:*

> If a common stock has just as large earnings applicable to it and no greater deductions ahead of it, it must be more valuable than a similarly situated preferred—because the "common stock" is entitled to *all* [Graham's emphasis] future earnings and the preferred only to a restricted portion thereof.

Graham provides an important reminder of the limitations of fundamental research: "investment analysis is of little value when applied to the more speculative issues." If the investor feels that the railroad sector's inherent difficulties will persist, "then most of the preferred issues of the weaker roads would seem too risky to be bargains at these levels." On the other hand, if the investor expects a new era of prosperity for all the railroads, "then well-selected common [stock] issues would seem to offer better opportunities for realizing on his [or her] convictions."

# 11

# ATTRACTIVE INDUSTRIAL PREFERRED STOCKS

*Importance of Exemption from
Normal Tax—Recent Improvement in
Investment Status—Various Elements
in Judging Values—Attractive
Issues Recommended*

After a rueful quarter of an hour with their income tax, many investors have recently been imbued with a more wholesome respect for the merits of preferred stocks. For, in the case of the moderately well-to-do, the normal tax of 6% and 12% has made up by far the greater part of the total payment. Hence the advantage of dividends, *which are exempt from normal tax*, over ordinary bond interest, which is subject thereto, has been brought home in very concrete fashion while making out the tax return. An income of $1,000 from dividends was found to be equivalent to over $1,130 in corporation bond interest.

## GREAT IMPROVEMENT IN POSITION

In this connection it should be pointed out that the investment quality of industrial preferred stocks has improved immeasurably during the past four years. The vast accumulation of undistributed profits has been building up increasingly large equities behind the senior shares, and has thus established them on a permanently higher plane of security.

It is particularly impressive to note exactly how much in dollars per share has been placed behind these issues since 1914. The figures are accordingly given for a large number of companies in Table 1.

Just as in the case of the common shares, the great improvement in the standing of preferred issues has not escaped market recognition. Despite the higher interest rates now prevailing—which would ordinarily make for lower *prices* of fixed income bearing securities—industrial preferred stocks now sell on a substantially higher level than before the war. The comparative figures given in columns one and three of the table show that in some instances (notably Corn Products and American Linseed) the advances rival those of the common shares. The declines seem to be restricted to three of the "Tobacco Trust" issues.

## THE REAL BASIS OF VALUE

The value of any investment depends primarily upon its assets value and earning power. The former is relatively less important in the case of preferred stocks than in that of bonds. For if *interest* is once defaulted then (theoretically at least) the principal becomes immediately due, and the investor has recourse to all the assets to make good the par amount of his holdings. Thus in the event of default on bond interest evidently the value of the assets behind the issue assumes chief significance. With preferred stocks, however, there is no such thing as default, and the stockholder has direct recourse to the assets only in the rare cases of voluntary liquidation. The leading consideration must, therefore, be the sufficiency of earnings to meet dividend requirements. Since continuity of payments is extremely desirable, it is especially important that these charges be covered with a fair margin in poor years.

Accordingly, there has been compiled and set forth in Table 1 the average annual earnings on the various issues for the four years before the war and the four years during the war; that is, 1911–1914 and 1915–1918. All the companies considered make excellent exhibits for the latter period—whereat no one will be greatly surprised. But there is a significant divergence between the pre-war records of the various industrials; some having earned preferred dividends with a consistently large margin, and others either scantily covering or else failing to meet this requirement. While it is not to be claimed that

## TABLE I

ATTRACTIVE PREFERRED STOCKS

| Preferred stock of | Rate | Price (Apr. 1) | Yield | Priced Jan. 1, 1914 | Surplus & Reserve Inc'd per Share | Earned Per Share 1911–1914 | Earned Per Share 1915–1918 | Net Current Assets Per Share | Equity Measured by Value of Common |
|---|---|---|---|---|---|---|---|---|---|
| [1]Westinghouse Elec. | 7% | 63 | 5.56% | 58 | 1915–1918 | 92.5% | 282.0% | $490 | 1625% |
| General Chemical | 6 | 103 | 5.82 | 108 | 119 | 22.8 | *57.2 | 74 | 185 |
| Sears Roebuck | 7 | 120 | 5.83 | 121 | — | 103.0 | 176.0 | 312 | 1312 |
| American Tobacco | 6 | 101$\frac{1}{2}$ | 5.96 | 102$\frac{1}{2}$ | 17 | 29.3 | 25.1 | 100 | 156 |
| Am. Agric. Chem. | 6 | 100 | 6.00 | 91 | 29 | 11.1 | 20.6 | 37 | 111 |
| Woolworth | 7 | 116$\frac{1}{2}$ | 6.00 | 112$\frac{1}{2}$ | 107 | 41.3 | 63.3 | 135 | 496 |
| Am. Sugar Ref. | 7 | 116$\frac{1}{2}$ | 6.00 | 114 | 21 | 12.7 | 21.8 | 81 | 117 |
| U. S. Steel | 7 | 114$\frac{3}{4}$ | 6.07 | 106$\frac{1}{4}$ | 121 | 14.8 | 49.2 | — | 138 |
| Am. Car & Foundry | *7 | 115 | 6.09 | 114 | 45 | 11.8 | 22.3 | 109 | 91 |
| Barrett Mfg. | 7 | 115 | 6.09 | 102 | 95 | 19.7 | 44.8 | 141 | 253 |
| Liggett & Meyers | 7 | 111$\frac{1}{2}$ | 6.28 | 11$\frac{1}{2}$ | 41 | 41.3 | 41.6 | 58 | 195 |
| United Cigar Stores | 7 | 111 | 6.31 | 111 | 95 | 46.3 | 67.7 | 198 | 265 |
| Lorillard | 7 | 109 | 6.42 | 110$\frac{1}{4}$ | 76 | 33.2 | 43.4 | 130 | 318 |
| Central Leather | 7 | 108 | 6.48 | 95 | 80 | 11.4 | 32.2 | 136 | 95 |
| May Dept. Stores | 7 | 108 | 6.48 | 100 | 99 | 26.1 | 37.0 | 142 | 166 |
| Cluett-Peabody | 7 | 108 | 6.48 | 96 | 48 | [2]21.5 | 32.5 | 117 | 162 |
| Railway Steel Spgs | 7 | 108 | 6.48 | 97 | 60 | 7.7 | 25.4 | 37 | 78 |
| Goodrich | 7 | 108 | 6.48 | 80 | 135 | 13.0 | 46.5 | 170 | 158 |
| Am. Cotton Oil | *6 | 91 | 6.59 | 93 | 33 | 11.2 | 17.7 | 49 | 98 |
| General Motors | 6 | 90$\frac{1}{2}$ | 6.63 | — | — | [3]43.0 | 100.0 | [4]310 | 500 |
| Amer. Locomotive | 7 | 105 | 6.67 | 97 | 39 | 7.0 | 22.4 | 97 | 67 |
| Corn Products | 7 | 105$\frac{1}{2}$ | 6.63 | 65 | 58 | 6.9 | 24.5 | 50 | 100 |
| General Cigar | 7 | 105 | 6.67 | 100 | 30 | 28.3 | 28.8 | 140 | 198 |
| Am. Beet Sugar | 6 | 90 | 6.67 | 72 | 90 | 18.4 | 53.2 | 145 | 228 |
| Am. Smelt. & Ref | 7 | 104 | 6.73 | 98$\frac{3}{4}$ | 29 | 21.0 | 30.0 | 46 | 85 |
| Baldwin Loco. | 7 | 104 | 6.73 | 102 | 136 | 12.1 | 37.5 | 64 | 88 |
| Nat. Cloak & Suit | 7 | 104 | 6.73 | — | 89 | 20.1 | 33.1 | 114 | 200 |
| Standard Millings | 6 | 89 | 6.74 | 63 | 108 | 11.3 | 24.5 | 74 | 121 |
| Republic Iron & St'l. | 7 | 103 | 6.79 | 80$\frac{1}{2}$ | 156 | 7.8 | 42.0 | 58 | 90 |
| Pressed Steel Car | *7 | 102 | 6.86 | 96 | 34 | 9.8 | 20.2 | 42 | 70 |
| Tobacco Products | 7 | 101 | 6.93 | 83 | 38 | 9.2 | 25.0 | 83 | 210 |
| Loose Wiles | 7 | 100 | 7.00 | 102 | 65 | [5]10.7 | 18.3 | 106 | 105 |
| Vir.-Car. Chem | 8 | 113$\frac{1}{4}$ | 7.06 | 98$\frac{3}{4}$ | 62 | 11.4 | 26.5 | 81 | 80 |
| National Enameling | 7 | 99 | 7.07 | 75 | 93 | 8.0 | 30.4 | 67 | 95 |
| U. S. Rubber | *8 | 111$\frac{1}{8}$ | 7.20 | 101$\frac{1}{4}$ | 52 | 13.2 | 22.8 | 57 | 48 |
| Am. Sumatra Tob. | 7 | 95 | 7.36 | — | 130 | 13.6 | 51.0 | 188 | 446 |
| Worthington Pump | 7 | 94 | 7.46 | — | *127 | — | 56.2 | 329 | 280 |
| Willys-Overland | 7 | 93$\frac{1}{4}$ | 7.50 | 78 | 79 | — | 32.7 | 53 | 200 |
| Allis-Chalmers | 7 | 92 | 7.61 | 44 | 51 | 2.3 | 19.9 | 100 | 52 |
| Bethlehem Steel | 8 | 105 | 7.62 | — | 140 | — | 87.0 | — | 136 |
| Am. Linseed | *7 | 90 | 7.78 | 29 | 30 | 1.2 | 10.1 | 52 | 49 |

[1] Par, $50. [2]1912–14. [3]Adjusted. [4]Dec. 31. 1917. [5]1916–1918. *Non-cumulative.

post-war conditions are going to be identical with pre-war conditions, yet the investor will in general feel safer with those issues which have *always* given a good account of themselves in the past.

In cases where the earnings record for a number of years is either unavailable, or irrelevant because of radical changes in the company's position, another very useful standard of value may be employed. This is the relation of the *market value* of the junior issue to the par amount of the preferred stock. For if it is assumed that the market price reflects fairly closely the intrinsic worth of the common shares, then we have here an accurate measure of the equity protecting the senior issue. This appraisal is not based merely on the book value of the assets, nor upon the previous earning power; but takes into account also the company's future prospects, the management, and every other factor that might remotely affect the value. Bear in mind that it is not only the *price per share* of common that counts in this analysis; equally important is the relative size of the two issues. The equity behind Westinghouse Pfd., represented by the common selling at 46, is much larger than that behind Cities Service Preferred, though the common is quoted at 350. For in the first case there are fourteen times as many common as preferred shares; in the latter there are nearly twice as many preferred as common. This standard of value is applied in column 6, in which the market value of the entire common issue is divided by the number of preferred shares, to show the additional equity behind the latter.

Another element usually referred to in appraising preferred stocks is the amount of net current assets applicable to the senior issue. This factor is of chief significance as indicating the company's general financial condition. But in the case of preferred shares selling at a considerable discount this element often assumes direct importance, as establishing a minimum liquidating value. The arguments in favor of American Hide & Leather Preferred, for example, formerly centered on the fact that the working capital, exclusive of plant, greatly exceeded that issue's market price. A separate column in Table 1 has been devoted to a statement of the dollars per share of preferred, represented by net current assets—after deducting all prior liabilities, including bonds and notes.

## THE MOST ATTRACTIVE ISSUE

Having established these criteria of preferred stock values, we next proceed to select those issues which meet the requirements most satisfactorily *in proportion to their dividend yields*. The results of a careful investigation are embodied in Table II, which sets forth a list of eight of the most attractive preferred

## TABLE II

SELECTED LIST OF ATTRACTIVE PREFERRED STOCKS BASED ON TABLE I

|                                    | Rate Cum. | Price      | Yield  |
|------------------------------------|-----------|------------|--------|
| Westinghouse Electric (Par $50)    | 7%        | 63         | 5.55%  |
| Woolworth                          | 7         | 116$\frac{1}{2}$ | 6.00   |
| United Cigar Stores                | 7         | 111        | 6.28   |
| General Motors                     | 6         | 90$\frac{1}{2}$ | 6.63   |
| Am. Beet Sugar                     | 6         | 90         | 6.67   |
| Republic Iron & Steel              | 7         | 103        | 6.79   |
| Am. Sumatra Tobacco                | 7         | 95         | 7.36   |
| Willys-Overland                    | 7         | 93$\frac{1}{4}$ | 7.50   |

issues, arranged in order of dividend return. Needless to say, the presence of Willys-Overland Pfd. and the absence of General Chemical Pfd., for example, do not imply that the former is regarded as a safer investment. General Chemical Pfd. is omitted because there are more attractive issues of *the 6% class;* Willys-Overland is recommended because, as compared with its 7.50% return, its exhibit is remarkably good.

Although Westinghouse preferred yields only 5.55%, it is nevertheless included because of two factors—its giltedged security and its participating privilege. The small size of the issue, relative to the common, makes its protection by assets and earnings easily the strongest on the entire list. Failure to pay the meagre $280,000 dividend requirement is almost inconceivable. Consequently the security can well be compared with that of many medium grade bonds yielding no more. For if the investor pays an 8% normal income tax next year, the 5.55% return on Westinghouse Pfd. is equivalent to over 6% on a non-tax-free bond.

Furthermore, the present yield of this issue does not exhaust its possibilities. Westinghouse Pfd. participates equally with the common in any disbursement above 7% ($3.50). Since the latter rate is now paid on both classes, any increase in the common dividend would mean an equal gain for the senior issue. Considering that earnings have averaged 18% to 20% on the common, with every indication of continued prosperity, an 8% rate—or even higher—on Westinghouse Pfd. is far from impossible.

While the next two issues are both giltedged, the somewhat higher yield of United Cigar Stores, Pfd. should make it more desirable than Woolworth, Pfd.

For the analysis in Table 1 shows that in all factors bearing on value—earning power before and during the war, current asset value, and common stock protection—the Whelan issue makes an even better exhibit than Woolworth Pfd., excellent as is the latter. The key to the strength of Cigar Stores Pfd. is the small size of the issue, only $4,527,000, compared with $27,000,000 common, selling above 130. If the common stock earnings dropped from $13 to only $2 per share, preferred dividends would still be covered $2\frac{1}{2}$ times.

Dissimilar as they at first appear, Am. Beet Sugar Pfd. and General Motors Pfd. have several other points in common besides their price and yield. Both are characterized by absence of funded debt, a strong working capital position, and a really excellent earnings record. Because of recent fundamental changes in the company's organization, it is difficult to find an accurate basis on which to value the present General Motors Pfd. (or debenture stock, which is essentially the same). The approximate figures given in the table indicate a technically stronger position than that of American Beet Sugar Pfd. If either of the two is compared with so highly regarded an investment as American Agricultural Chemical Pfd., it must be admitted that the latter makes a less brilliant showing—despite its ten point higher price. Moreover, if the pre-war record of Corn Products Pfd., or the non-cumulative feature of American Cotton Oil Pfd. is considered, it becomes evident that either General Motors or Beet Sugar Pfd. affords greater security, without sacrifice of yield.

## CUMULATIVE VS. NON-CUMULATIVE

The disadvantage of *non*-cumulative preferred stocks must be obvious to any one who realizes that the dividends suspended in bad years can never be recovered, no matter what prosperity follows. On this account we would select American Linseed Pfd. as a shining example of an issue *not* to buy. The records show that it has paid no dividend at all in sixteen out of the last twenty years, the total payments averaging about 1% per annum. At the beginning of 1914 this stock sold at 29, so that the table shows that it has appreciated twice as much in market price as in asset value. Willys-Overland Pfd. yielding 1/4% less, is by all odds the better investment. Pre-war figures are not strictly comparable for Willys-Overland, because of the changes in capitalization. But during the past four years—not altogether clear sailing for the automobile companies—preferred dividends were earned $4\frac{1}{2}$ times. There is also a very substantial equity represented by $41,000,000 common stock selling at 116% of par ($25).

Since one can never be certain of the future, it is idle to ignore the noncumulative feature merely because the company has always paid dividends in the past. This was the attitude of those who paid fancy prices for St. Paul Pfd. a few years ago, and have now seen a year's payment withheld—never to be recovered. On this account we prefer American Beet Sugar Pfd. to American Cotton Oil Pfd., and we would rather own Virginia Carolina Chemical Pfd. than U. S. Rubber Pfd. (The latter's excellent earnings record is offset by its top-heavy capitalization and some what unsavory market reputation.) American Car & Foundry Pfd. is so strongly entrenched that here the non-cumulative provision would appear entirely insignificant. Still, why take even an infinitesimal chance, when there is Barrett Pfd. or United Cigar Stores Pfd. to buy instead?

Returning to our selected list, the next issue is Republic Iron & Steel Pfd., which requires little comment in view of the discussion in the March 29 article. American Sumatra Pfd., like Willys-Overland Pfd. (already discussed above), must be judged in connection with its high yield. By all our various standards, American Sumatra Pfd. shows up more favorably than Tobacco Products Pfd., which sells six points higher. If it is objected that Am. Sumatra's prosperity is all war-won, the reply is that even in the 1912–4 period preferred dividends were earned about twice over—a 45% better exhibit than that of Tobacco Products, and fully as good as that of the average industrial.

If space permitted it could be shown that Lorillard Pfd. is cheaper than Liggett & Myers Pfd., or Goodrich Pfd. than Central Leather Pfd., or National Cloak & Suit Pfd. than Cluett-Peabody Pfd. The holder of any preferred issue should be able to derive a fair idea of the relative desirability of his security by carefully examining the figures given in Table 1.

# 12

# NORTHERN PACIFIC OUTSTRIPS GREAT NORTHERN

*The See-Saw Race of the Grangers—*
*Physical and Financial Peculiarities*
*Analyzed—Northern Pacific's Hidden*
*Assets—A Preferred in Name Only*

On April 4, 1919, Northern Pacific sold higher than Great Northern—for the first time probably in ten years. Back of this incident lies an interesting tale of railroad development, centering about the great personality of James J. Hill. Great Northern has often been referred to as "Hill's favorite," and to his genius was largely due its erstwhile ascendancy over its sister road.

The varying careers of the two systems are pictured in striking fashion in the appended graphs, which show how Northern Pacific has first lost and recently regained its leadership in traffic and earning power. These graphs are constructed in a rather novel fashion. For instead of using two lines—one for each company—the *difference* between their respective figures is shown by a single curve. All of the elements considered—Gross Revenue, Net after Taxes, Earnings on Stock, and Average Quotations—follow the same course.

Practical interest will center chiefly about the relative movement of stock earnings and stock prices. Here the graph shows plainly that the market has lagged somewhat in reflecting Northern Pacific's recent substantial gains. In 1909 N. P. earned 1.62% more than Great Northern, and sold at practically the same level; in 1917 it earned 2.66% more and its price averaged about 6 points lower.

The question is thus raised whether Northern Pacific is not now a better investment purchase than Great Northern. After careful investigation, the writer concludes decidedly in the affirmative. His judgment is based upon the following considerations:

1.   Record prior to Government control.
2.   Results under federal operation.
3.   Relative growth of fixed charges.
4.   Northern Pacific's valuable land grant.

## RECORD PRIOR TO GOVERNMENT CONTROL

In 1917, the last year of private operation, the two Hill roads reported practically the same gross revenues, although three years before Great Northern's traffic was $6,500,000 larger. Northern Pacific's gain in net earnings is even more pronounced—this item being $4,990,000 larger in 1917, whereas in 1915 it was fully $4,117,000 smaller than Great Northern's, a difference equivalent to $3.65 per share. It is evident that N. P. must have been operated much more economically than the other road in 1917; but in seeking to analyze this advantage we run into all kinds of difficulties.

First, consider the question of maintenance. For years it has been apparent that Northern Pacific has been spending much less on the upkeep of its equipment than either Great Northern or the jointly owned C. B. & Q. In 1918, for example, with the same traffic on both roads, Great Northern expended $745,000 (or nearly 7%) more for this purpose than did N. P. In 1916 the difference was $1,704,000—in other words, 12.41% of gross for Great Northern, against 10.47% for N. P. From this incriminating evidence at hand, one would straightway conclude that N.P.'s operating expenses have been held down by neglecting its cars and locomotives. Yet on further investigation it transpires that Northern Pacific's unkeep costs per unit of equipment are actually higher than Great Northern's; and that the lower expenditure in the aggregate is

## TABLE I

EARNINGS UNDER FEDERAL CONTROL

|  | No. Pacific | Gt. Northern |
|---|---|---|
| Gross | $102,908,000 | $100,661,000 |
| Net after Taxes | 24,887,000 | 10,639,000 |
| Net after rents–actual | 28,209,000 | 11,979,000 |
| Net after rents–Gov. guar. | 30,090,000 | 28,754,000 |
| *Fixed charges (net) | 7,213,000 est | 7,815,000 |
| Bal for Divs.—guar. | 22,877,000 | 20,939,000 |
| Earned on stocks—guar. | 9.24% | 8.39% |
| Earned on stocks—actual | 8.48% | 1.67% |

* Includes war taxes and corporate expenses but excludes items prior to 1918 and depreciation of equipment.

due to its owning a much smaller number of engines and freight cars. But how—one asks—can Northern Pacific handle as much traffic as the parallel line, when it has 20% less freight capacity and 10% less locomotive power? Surely it must hire more equipment from other roads, or lend less to them. Wrong again! In 1917, Northern Pacific's *net income* from hire of equipment was $1,237,000—against only $511,000 for Great Northern.

Here is a company with the same traffic and much less equipment, yet it can spare more cars and engines to other lines. What is the reason? Does it get more freight in a car, or more cars to a train? Not at all: its trainload has regularly been less than "GNR's," although in 1917 the difference was only 9 tons. After careful search, the answer finally appears. In 1917 the average haul per ton was 385 miles, or 111 miles more than for Great Northern. This is in itself a peculiar circumstance, since the latter operated 8,232 miles of main track against only 6,522 for the other line—a difference of over 26%. With a 40% larger haul for its traffic, Northern Pacific must evidently be able to keep its equipment in use a larger proportion of the time, and thus get along with a smaller quantity of freight cars.

## GREATER TRANSPORTATION EFFICIENCY

Northern Pacific's heavier traffic density ($13,526 per mile against $10,504 for Great Northern in 1917) also stands it in good stead when it comes to transportation costs. This is the chief source of N. P.'s advantage, since Great Northern's

**TABLE II**

NORTHERN PACIFIC'S LAND SALES

| Year | Acres sold | Proceeds | Price per Acre |
|------|-----------|----------|----------------|
| 1912–13 | 526,374 | $3,040,126 | $5.75 |
| 1913–14 | 588,734 | 3,458,379 | 5.88 |
| 1914–15 | 1,004,018 | 4,124,580 | 4.11 |
| 1915–16 | 1,283,069 | 6,432,518 | 5.01 |
| 1916 (6 mos) | 741,863 | 3,789,570 | 5.11 |
| 1917 | 994,635 | 7,775,603 | 7.82 |
| 1918 | 162,315 | 1,989,261 | 12.25 |
| Total 1912–8 | 5,301,008 | $30,610,007 | $5.77 |

expenses are here $4,550,000 larger. Just how Northern Pacific does the trick cannot be fully explained, particularly since the other road does not publish detailed figures of its operating expenses. In looking through some State Commission reports, the writer came across the significant fact that during 1916 Great Northern's fuel bill for train locomotives was $1,000,000, or 20%, larger than Northern Pacific's figure, although its gross business was but $1\frac{1}{2}$% greater. This is a big item, and there are doubtless similar reasons to account for the remaining difference.

## UNDER FEDERAL CONTROL

The word has gone forth that the railways are to be returned to their owners—willing or unwilling—at the end of 1919. Wall Street thus appears in the unprecedented position of putting its trust in Congress to stand between the stockholders and the alarming deficits now being rolled up by their properties. It is devoutly to be wished that such childlike confidence will not be misplaced. And yet—January 1 is but six months away, Congress has much to do, and a definite plan of relief is still far from passage. This is not an especially pleasing position for the security owner who sees the 1918 earnings of his railroad about 50% of the 1917 figures. The writer has always claimed that there is much mental satisfaction—if not eventual financial advantage—in holding stock of a carrier which has prospered under Government control, rather than one of the numerous "lame ducks."

Now, while it cannot be said the Northern Pacific has made a brilliant showing under Messrs. McAdoo and Hines, its setback has indeed been relatively slight—for the net earnings after rents, as shown in Table I, were only $1,921,000 less than the guaranteed compensation. Great Northern, on the other hand, has been a very poor proposition for Uncle Sam, returning a deficit of no less than $15,775,000, after charging the rental paid to the stockholders.

The extraordinarily poor showing of "G. N. R." is due chiefly to its very heavy maintenance expenses, which were more than $7,000,000 in excess of Northern Pacific's outlay for this purpose. But even in transportation costs, N. P. has continued its progress, and reports a relative saving here of over $6,500,000. It is difficult to determine the exact significance of Great Northern's far heavier upkeep expenditures in 1918. But the advantage in transportation economy is certainly of prime importance—and promises to show up strongly after the roads are returned.

## FIXED CHARGES

So far, we have been considering only the question of gross and net revenues. An equal influence on the dividend balance is exerted by the fixed charges, which must next claim our attention. Even experienced investors are quite generally under the impression that Great Northern's interest requirements are much lower than Northern Pacific's. But an examination of the past, the present, and the future status of the roads in this respect, reveals the inaccuracy of the popular ideas on the subject.

The 1917 report of the two systems showed interest charges of $12,244,000 for Northern Pacific, compared with $6,773,000 for Great Northern. But much of the significance of this contrast disappears when it is remembered that Great Northern *excludes* from its income account the interest paid on its share of the C., B. & Q. collateral 4s, due 1921, offsetting it against the dividends received on the Burlington stock. Northern Pacific more properly includes both items in its statement, thus making an apparent but not a real difference of $4,254,000. The actual excess of Great Northern's interest charges in 1917 was only $1,217,000.

But even this difference has practically disappeared because of the sale by Great Northern in Sept., 1917, of $20,000,000 5% notes. On this account, the 1918 report will show an additional charge of $667,000, while Northern Pacific's interest payments decreased $100,000.

As for the future course of interest charges, attention must here be directed to the large land holdings of Northern Pacific, through the sale of which an annual reduction is made in the amount of prior lien bonds outstanding. Because of its importance, this land grant will be given further consideration below. We would merely remark that indications point to a speedy disappearance of Great Northern's present slight advantage in the matter of interest charges. In fact, in a few years "the shoe should be on the other foot."

## MISCELLANEOUS CHARGES AND INCOME

But the question of fixed charges does not depend solely upon the companies' bonded debt. There are several other items—often of great significance—which serve either to increase or reduce the burden of interest payments. Take the question of rentals; both of leased lines and of equipment. Where these rentals are *paid*, they are practically equivalent to interest on the money which would have been necessarily borrowed if the properties had been built instead of leased. Similarly, where a road derives income through renting its property to others, this is properly an offset against the interest it pays on the investment involved.

The writer has always believed, therefore, that in order properly to study the element of fixed charges, the difference between "other income" and "other deductions" should be added to or substracted from the interest payments. When this practice is applied to the two roads under discussion, Northern Pacific is found to enjoy a great advantage. For in 1917 its other income (excluding C., B. & Q. dividends) was $1,350,000 *more*, and its rentals and other deductions $209,000 *less* than in the case of Great Northern. The final result was that a margin of $4,996,000 in net after taxes was increased to an advantage of $6,463,000 in surplus available for dividend—equivalent to $2.66 per share.

## THE LAND GRANT

Northern Pacific's land holdings have been briefly referred to above, in connection with the future course of its interest charges. This is an element of such importance, however, that it is remarkable that it is hardly ever referred to—if at all in analyses of the company's status. Table II shows that Northern Pacific has been enjoying a steady income of large proportions through the sale of its farm lands, which are located principally in Montana and Washington. On Dec. 31 last there remained 4,800,000 acres available for sale. Assuming these holdings have an average value of $6 per acre—in 1918 the land brought $12.25—there is here a "hidden asset" worth $30,000,000, which is steadily being converted into cash. The funds so realized are applied to the retirement of the prior lien bonds and so increase the net income available for dividends. Great Northern's land holdings, however, are entirely negligible, now aggregating only 101,543 acres.

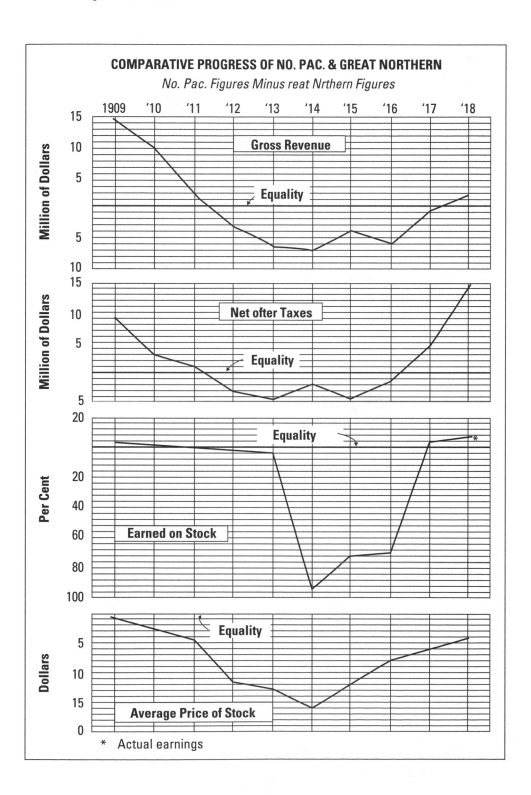

## CONCLUSION

Every Wall Street man is aware that Great Northern "preferred" is not a preferred stock at all. When the old common was retired in 1901, the present issue was left as the only class of stock, and thus became common in everything but name. The retention of the old title is generally regarded as illogical, but harmless. Yet the writer has seen not only experienced investors, but even Wall Street brokers themselves, list Great Northern among their preferred stocks. When the common stock of National Sugar Refining was retired in 1913, the old preferred was exchanged for new common stock. The same should have been done long ago in the case of Great Northern preferred.

The above is not entirely a digression, because the writer feels that Great Northern may be favored by some readers over Northern Pacific on account of the "preferred" in its title. With this error corrected the superior merit of Northern Pacific should now be entirely clear.

For on the basis of its operating and financial results we have shown that Northern Pacific is entitled to sell on at least as high a level as Great Northern—in fact should command a better price. If to these considerations is added the value of its land holdings—amounting to certainly more than $10 per share—it should then seem only a question of time when Northern Pacific, for ten years the "under dog," shall once more claim the ascendancy.

# 13

# A NEGLECTED CHAIN STORE ISSUE

*The Inconspicuous Merits of McCrory—
Its Present Low Price Makes It
Attractive—Comparison with Its More
Pretentious Rivals*

The recent death of F. W. Woolworth has attracted general attention to the five and ten cent store industry, of which he was the founder. While the organization that bears his name is at once the oldest and largest of its kind, there are several other systems of importance, the common stocks of which are publicly held.

In order of gross sales, these are S. S. Kresge, S. H. Kress and McCrory. Kresge and Kress (strange similarity of names) enjoy with Woolworth the advantage of listing on the New York Stock Exchange, but McCrory is an inactive issue, dealt in "over the counter" only. For this reason investors generally are but little acquainted with the latter company, their knowledge being restricted to the vague impression that this is a small and none too prosperous enterprise. Let us see to what extent this opinion is justified by the facts.

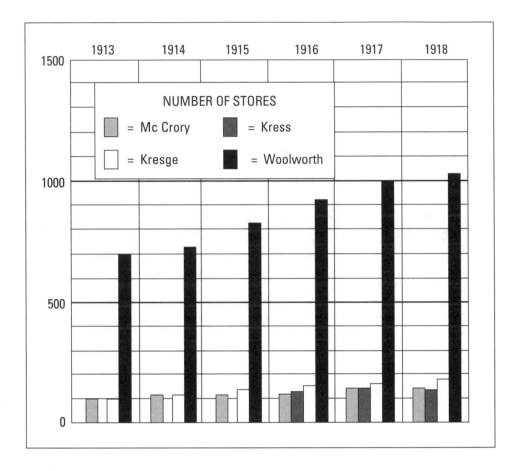

Since all five and ten cent systems operate under substantially similar conditions, they are especially well adapted to comparative treatment and a study of the bare figures should yield more than ordinarily illuminating results. But while the chain stores have of late supplied a favorite subject for investment house circulars, these have confined themselves simply to the presentation of a mass of statistics, without any serious attempt to draw helpful conclusions therefrom.

The investor is chiefly interested in knowing which of the four common stocks is intrinsically the cheapest at present market prices. Now if we merely compare the gross or net earnings of the various enterprises we will not get far in our investigation, because a company's leadership in gross business may be more than offset by heavier capitalization, or over-discount by its higher market price. We note for example that in 1918 Woolworth's sales were eleven

**TABLE I**

PERCENTAGE OF 1918 EARNINGS TO MARKET PRICE OF COMMON.

|           | Gross | Net After Taxes | Balance After Pfd. Divs. |
|-----------|-------|-----------------|--------------------------|
| Woolworth | 171%  | 9.4%            | 7.84%                    |
| Kresge    | 227   | 10.6            | 9.76                     |
| Kress     | 209   | 11.4            | 8.81                     |
| McCrory   | 768   | 27.8            | 20.96                    |

times, and its net profits seventeen times, greater than those of McCrory. For many readers this would seem conclusive evidence that Woolworth is a much more desirable investment. Yet it is of equal significance that the smaller company has only one-tenth as many shares, and that each share is selling at only one-fifth the price of Woolworth common.

In other words, while Woolworth may be earning *seventeen* times as much as McCrory, its market valuation is *fifty* times as great. Consequently McCrory earned last year 21 per cent on its market price, against only 7.48 per cent in the case of Woolworth. Despite the latter company's enormously greater business, from the standpoint of earning power, McCrory would appear more than twice as attractive at 25 as Woolworth is at 125.

## COMPARATIVE EARNING POWER

This primary test of value is applied to all common stocks in Table I, which shows the gross and net earnings (after taxes) *per dollar of market price*. Since Woolworth has not yet received its 1918 taxes, these are arbitrarily assumed at the 1917 figure. The table shows clearly that on the basis of last year's income account, McCrory common is selling far out of line with the other three issues—and in fact makes more than twice as good a showing on its present market price as does its nearest competitor, Kresge.

These results should be interesting enough to tempt us further into an examination of the tangible asset position of McCrory as compared with its more pretentious rivals. These figures, given in Table II, contain not a few surprises. In the first place it is rather startling to note that McCrory preferred, which goes begging around 92, has actually more tangible assets behind it per share than Woolworth preferred, one of the highest priced and best regarded issues of this type of investment. In this connection attention should be

drawn to the excellent showing made by Kresge preferred, which—because
of the small size of this issue compared with the common—is far better protected than many better known preferred stocks selling ten points higher. It is
nothing short of ludicrous that Kress preferred should be quoted above
Kresge preferred, as the former has not a single point in its favor. Not only is
Kresge in a much stronger position with respect to both assets and earning
power, but its past record also shows a healthier and more rapid growth. This
is true whether we consider the increase in number of stores or in gross sales
per store or in net profits per dollar of sales—all of which can be traced for the
form system in the accompanying graphs.

   But to return to McCrory it is indeed astonishing to discover that the tangible asset value per share of this humble common stock is fully as large as
that of Woolworth, which sells five times as high. Moreover, if allowance is
made for 1918 taxes (which are not provided for in the Woolworth balance
sheet), McCrory would actually be found to have *more* dollars of real assets
behind each share of common.

   If the very low market price of McCrory is taken into account, its tangible asset position—like its earning power—places it distinctly at the head of
the four companies. It is the only one of all the common stocks which is selling for less than the real assets behind it. These represent 160 per cent. of its
market price, against only 33 per cent. for Woolworth and Kress and 86 per
cent. for Kresge.

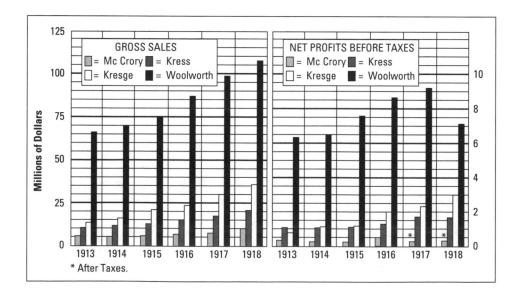

## REASONS FOR McCRORY'S BACKWARDNESS

McCrory is selling so much lower than its statistical position would justify (as compared with the other companies) that we are impelled to seek the reasons underlying its apparent bargain-counter (or five and ten cent counter) price. The first explanation that presents itself is the absence of a common dividend. This is an important drawback, it is true, yet not a fatal defect. The value of an industrial common stock is rarely definitely determined by its dividend rate at any particular time. Speculative issues have sold at fabulous figures while returning nothing whatever to their owners. But a more cogent argument is round right among the other chain store issues. The price of 160 for Kresge is certainly not governed by its $5 dividend, which gives it a yield of only 3.10 per cent. Even Kress, which pays $4, returns only 4.70 per cent. at its present price—less than a Victory bond. Woolworth has the greatest dividend yield of all despite its position as dean of the chain store issues. This could indicate the realization by investors that, in the last analysis, the current dividend rate is of less importance than the possibilities of future dividends, as measured by earning power and asset value.

In the case of McCrory, the withholding of dividends has enabled it to build up the uncommonly strong tangible asset position which we have already discovered behind its common stock. At the time of recapitalization in 1915, the company started off with $20 per share of real value for its junior issue. In three years and a half it has just doubled this figure, although the market price of the common has stood practically still. Incidentally this indicates that the *average* earnings since reincorporation have been about $5.60 per share, or 22 per cent. of its market price. Hence the investor need not fear that the 1918 exhibit may have been an isolated and misleading one.

## TABLE II

TANGIBLE ASSET VALUES DEC. 31, 1918.

|  | Per Share of Pfd. | Per Share of Common | % of Mkt. Price of Common |
|---|---|---|---|
| Woolworth | $265 | $41 | 33% |
| Kresge | 490 | 138 | 86 |
| Kress | 190 | 28 | 33 |
| McCrory | 272 | 41 | 160 |

## TABLE III

CAPITALIZATION AND DIVIDENDS.

| | Outstanding | Preferred Price | Rate |
|---|---|---|---|
| Woolworth | $12,500,000 | 116 | 7% |
| Kresge | 2,000,000 | 108 | 7 |
| Kress | 3,740,000 | 110 | 7 |
| McCrory | 1,179,000 | 92 | 7 |

| Yield | Outstanding | Common Price | Rate | Yield |
|---|---|---|---|---|
| 6.03% | $50,000,000 | 125 | 8% | 6.40% |
| 6.48 | 10,000,000 | 160 | 5 | 3.12 |
| 6.36 | 12,000,000 | 84½ | 4 | 4.70 |
| 7.61 | 5,000,000 | 25 | — | — |

## WORKING CAPITAL

A more valid objection to McCrory than the absence of dividends is based upon its current asset position. The trouble here is not that working capital is insufficient—this could have been more logically argued against Kresge—but rather that it has shown so few signs of growth in the past. Since December, 1917, net current assets have increased only $236,000, or about 23 per cent., while gross sales have practically doubled. The surplus earnings have gone chiefly into fitting up additional stores, and into advances to the subsidiary which acquires real estate for the new locations. With sales increasing so much faster than working capital, the company would doubtless find it hard to spare the cash for common dividends.

Now since the writer's purpose is not to sell McCrory stocks but only to analyze them impartially, he has no intention of belittling this really serious objection. No doubt this is the "true inwardness" of McCrory's extraordinarily low market price, which otherwise would have provided too good an opportunity to be neglected by the few who are really familiar with the company's affairs. One is moved to point out, however, that a very similar situation obtained with regard to S. S. Kresge, less than two years ago. This company's stock was then selling at 80, at which price it appeared a remarkable bargain in view of its exceptionally high earning power and asset backing. But its working capital had failed to keep pace with the rapid expansion of its business and was lower in proportion to sales than that of any of the other chain store systems, McCrory included. Hence the directors were, and still are, compelled to

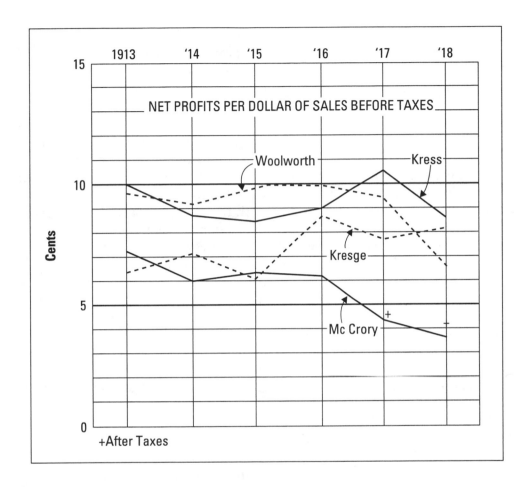

pursue a very conservative dividend policy. It is likely that even the insiders hesitated to buy into this extremely prosperous enterprise, because they feared it would be a long time before it could spare the cash for liberal dividends— unless new capital was raised, which seemed improbable. Nevertheless, value—like murder—"will out," and although Kresge has added only $1 to its dividend rate, its market price has doubled, as investors have at last realized its strong position and brilliant possibilities.

## WILL McCRORY FOLLOW KRESGE?

Encouraged by this example, the writer is tempted to utter a prediction that McCrory, marketwise, will prove a second Kresge, despite its handicap of insufficient operating funds and consequent deferment of dividends. But a fundamental element in Kresge's success is lacking in the case of McCrory—namely, the steady *increase* from year to year in the net earnings available for the common stock. The graphs reveal that practically all the advantage gained through the continuous expansion of McCrory's business has been lost through the equally persistent shrinkage in the net profit per dollar of sales. In 1913 the net earnings amounted to 7.24 per cent. of gross, whereas last year the ratio had fallen to 3.72 per cent. While some indeterminate portion of the poor showing of 1918 and 1917 is due to war taxes (not stated separately by McCrory) comparison with the other companies shows that this factor cannot account for all of the trouble. No doubt the great increase in the cost of goods purchased, coupled with the necessity of retaining a fixed selling price, had a good deal to do with this unsatisfactory showing.

It would be easier to grow enthusiastic over McCrory's future if, like Kresge, it had doubled its net profits in six years, instead of maintaining them practically unchanged. But what McCrory lacks in progressiveness it makes up in stability, since in no year in the past seven has less than $4 been earned per share of common stock. It ought to be asked further whether there is any good reason why McCrory should not be able to establish a ratio of net profits to gross sales, somewhat approximating that of the other three systems. With a $10,000,000 business this year, it should not be greatly handicapped in its purchases, and by skilful management it should be able to achieve considerable improvement in this respect.

## THE CRUX OF THE PROBLEM

Here we have the fundamental elements in the McCrory situation. The stock is undeniably selling at much less than is warranted by its present asset value and earnings. This would indicate the belief by investors that the company may be going backward—or at least is stagnating—a belief strongly supported by McCrory's inability to increase its net earnings during the last seven years. But in the vitally important respects, the company has not stagnated. Since 1916 its gross business has increased faster than that of Kress or Woolworth, and nearly as fast as that of Kresge; and it leads all the rest in the relative growth of the number of stores. McCrory is therefore in a fundamentally sound position, and there are possibilities of a sharp expansion in net profits, dependent upon the capabilities of its management.

All things considered, it is difficult to imagine McCrory's being worth less than 25 under any circumstances, while there are good reasons to look forward to seeing its price much higher one of these days. It is a good stock for the patient investor, the kind that usually makes the largest profits and incidentally isn't worried by day to day fluctuations.

# 14

## THE ART OF HEDGING

*Maximum Profits and Minimum Losses—Convertible Issues as a Trading Medium—Safety First Operations in a Dangerous Market*

Webster defines "to hedge" as "to protect oneself from loss by betting on both sides." Hedging as a commercial operation is practiced quite generally among flour millers and cotton spinners. While the details thereof might appear rather complicated, in essence it consists of selling "futures" short at the time the staple is purchased, so as to guard against fluctuations in price during the period of manufacture.

In the securities market a form of hedging very common on foreign Stock Exchanges is the use of puts or calls against long or short stock respectively. If a man purchases one hundred shares of U. S. Steel at 106, for instance, he might limit his possible loss by buying also a put good for thirty days at 102. This means that however low the stock may break, he has the right to sell it at any time within the next month at 102, so that his maximum loss under the worst possible conditions would be $400 plus the cost of the put (and commissions). This arrangement is often preferable to a stop loss order, because it guards against loss through a temporary fluctuation. Should Steel drop to $101\frac{1}{2}$ and then rally to 115 during the month, the man with a stop loss order at 102 would have been forced out at his limit, while a put would have carried him safely through to a large ultimate profit.

The purpose of this article is not, however, to discuss either hedging in commodities or the use of privileges in trading, although both might well deserve extended treatment. We intend to discuss a similar class of market operations, which is little understood or appreciated even by professionals, and which nevertheless affords the opportunity of excellent profits with very moderate risk.

## HEDGING BETWEEN BONDS AND STOCKS

What we have in mind is the simultaneous purchase of one security and sale of another, because the first is relatively cheaper than the second. Where the security bought sells lower than the one sold, there must be good reason for believing that the price of the two will come closer together,—and conversely for the opposite circumstance.

Without further tarrying on the general theory involved, let us hasten to a concrete example. On November 2, last, let us say, we purchase $10,000 of Lackawanna Steel convertible 5 per cent bonds, due 1950, and at the same time sell short 100 shares of Lackawanna Steel stock at 100. Should Lackawanna continue its head-long advance, we might be forced to convert our bonds into stock, in order to make delivery of the shares we sold. In this case our operation would have proved unsuccessful—we should have lost $25 and commissions. But if the stock declines it is evident that the bonds will not suffer as severely, because their investment rating alone assures them of a certain minimum value. In actual fact, at this writing the stock is down to 83, while the bonds hold firm around 94. We could therefore undo our little operation by selling the bonds for $9,400 and buying back our stock for $8,300. This would show a net credit of $1,100, from which expenses and the original difference of $25 are to be deducted, still leaving a net profit of over $1,000.

Here then was a venture which under the most unfavorable conditions could have shown a maximum loss of only $56.50, but contained by no means remote possibilities of a thousand dollar profit. Not a bad chance, was it? Add further that it required little capital (as the money really tied up was negligible), and that the carrying charge was insignificant since the bond interest almost offset the dividends on the stock. How much safer this is than the ordinary market commitment is apparent when we consider that the man who bought the 100 Lackawanna at par is out $1,700, if he still holds it; while on the other hand if Republic had been sold short when *it* reached par, the speculator would soon afterwards have faced a forty point loss.

This is a good opportunity to point out the technical difference between hedging, as described above, and arbitraging. An arbitrage is supposed to assure a definite profit within a fairly definite time. If, for instance, it had been possible (as no doubt it was for the bond specialist) to buy Lack. Steel convert. 5s at par, and simultaneously sell the stock at $100\frac{1}{4}$, such an operation would have constituted a real arbitrage. For the bonds could have immediately been converted and the new stock delivered, with a $25 profit.

The arbitrageur always expects to exchange the security he buys for the one he sells; the hedger will only do so if he must, and usually suffers a small loss thereby. His profit is found in selling out what he buys and buying in what he sells at a more favorable difference, or "spread," than at the beginning of the operation. The arbitrageur may of course delay converting in the hope of undoing his operation to better advantage in the market. He then becomes a hedger, but with an assured minimum profit instead of merely a minimum loss.

The relation of these two operations is very prettily shown by the Southern Pacific situation last October. At that time any one could have sold a large quantity of stock and replaced it by the convertible 5 per cent bonds at apparently $\frac{1}{4}$ point cheaper. In reality, however, the adjustment of accrued dividend and interest on conversion would have made the bonds about $\frac{1}{4}$ point higher than the stock. The supply of bonds was forthcoming from specialists who had been able to sell stock on rallies, above the corresponding price of the five per cent bonds, and who were about to present the bonds for conversion. They of course were glad enough to obtain an extra $\frac{1}{4}$ point profit by buying the stock and selling the bonds instead of converting. As it turned out the trader who took over the bonds on this basis would have fared better than the original owner, because on the subsequent break he could have bought back the stock and sold his bonds at a five points difference. This would have meant about $4\frac{1}{2}$ points "easy money" for a shrewd hedger.

Even experienced "hedge artists" often forego the chance of excellent profits because they wait in vain for the possibility of loss to be reduced to too small a figure. For example, in the ill-fated boom of Allied Packers stock last October, it sold at 66, while the convertible 6 per cent bonds were quoted at 91. Each $1,000 bond was convertible at any time for thirteen shares of stock, so if bought at 91 they constituted a call on the stock at $70 per share. The purchase of eight bonds at that time, together with the sale of 100 shares of stock at 66, would have subsequently shown no less than $3,200 profit, for the stock sold down to 26 with the bonds at 82. On the other hand, no matter how much higher the stock might have gone, the loss on this deal was absolutely limited to $400—the difference between 66 and 70. In this case, however, the temptation was to buy the bonds, and to wait for the stock to go a little higher before selling. Alas! the wait would have been in vain.

## PREFERRED STOCKS

Convertible preferred stocks present the same opportunities for hedging operations as do the bonds. A current example is Gilliland Oil preferred, which is exchangeable at any time for twice as many shares of common. On January 15, the preferred could have been bought at 100 and the common sold at 49. The maximum loss, in case of a great advance of the common, would have been two points per share of preferred, which in fact would have been made up by the $2 dividend coming off the latter on February 2. As it happened, two days later the common was down to 43, while the preferred was actually higher at 101. Thus on a hundred shares of preferred and two hundred common, there was a chance for $1,300 gross profit in two days, with negligible risk.

If someone with a little nerve had sold Pierce Arrow at 99 against a purchase of the preferred at 110, his courage would have been well rewarded. Yet his very greatest loss could not have exceeded eleven points, since the preferred is exchangeable for common, share for share—and in addition had the advantage of an 8 per cent dividend against nothing on the common. There is today a difference of about thirty-five points between the two issues, so that this not especially risky operation would now show a profit of well over twenty points.

Rights to subscribe to new stock can sometimes be made the basis of profitable hedging operations, especially when the stock is selling close to the subscription price. In such cases the rights can be bought and the stock sold against them, with the idea that should the shares fall below the subscription figure the rights can then be discarded and the stock bought in at a profit. Unfortunately for such schemes, inside manipulation usually keep up the price of the issue until the rights expire, in order to stimulate subscriptions. The severe declines, as in the case of Sinclair Oil and Pan American Petroleum, usually come a little after the expiration of the rights,—that is, too late for value to the hedger. Studebaker and Saxon Motors are recent instances of the stock falling below the offering price of the new stock before the last day for subscribing.

## THE "STRADDLE"

Perhaps the best way to operate with rights is to straddle,—that is to play the market for both an advance and a break. This can be done by selling only half the stock corresponding to the rights purchased. It is very important here that the price of the rights be very low, and they still have a substantial period to run. A good current example is that of Simms Petroleum. On January 15, when the news of salt water in the Homer Field was published, this stock declined to 47, and the rights to 1. The latter entitled the holder to obtain one new share of Simms for each two rights, on payment of $47.50, the privilege expiring February 2. Since the oil stocks were then in a highly speculative position, Simms Petroleum held possibilities, of either a big further slump or a radical recovery within the next two weeks. It appeared a good idea, therefore, to purchase say 400 Simms rights at 1, and sell only 100 shares of the stock against them at 47. The trader would then have been in a position to make profit from a wide move in either direction. Had the stock fallen to 40, for example, he could have covered his 100 shares with a gain of $650, and throw away his rights, which cost him $400 leaving him still over $200 to the good. On a recovery to 55, however (which subsequently happened) he would have used 200 of his rights to replace his short stock, and disposed of the other 200 rights at a nice profit. The reader can easily calculate that in this case he would have made $300, less commissions.

Operations of this kind, involving rights, are very similar to the use of puts and calls for hedging purposes alluded to at the beginning of this article. Rights to subscribe are neither more nor less than calls issued by the company. But practically speaking, these rights usually carry a more attractive option, in proportion to their cost, than does the ordinary 30-day privilege.

In the types of hedging heretofore considered the trader is always in a position to obtain the security he has sold, at a fixed price—either through conversion or by subscription. Yet one is often justified in selling one security against purchase of another, with no other safeguard than the definite knowledge that the two prices are far out of line.

On December 29 last, B. R. T. certificates of deposit sold at 5, while the undeposited stock was quoted above 10. It was true that the deposit agreement made withdrawal unusually difficult, but this was an entirely inadequate reason for the free stock selling at twice the price of the certificates. The two represented exactly the same property rights, and further there was enough stock in the control of the committee to enable it most probably to force the undeposited shares to accept their reorganization plan, when finally adopted. Hence the investor was running very little risk in buying

200 B. R. T. certificates at 5 and selling 100 shares of free stock against them at $10^{1}/_{4}$. Temporarily the spread might have widened perhaps, but ultimately the two prices were bound to approach each other. The latter happened very quickly in effect, as a few days later the certificates had advanced to 7 while the stock remained at $10^{1}/_{4}$. Today the trader could sell his certificates at 10 with a gain of $1,000, and cover his stock at $13^{1}/_{4}$—a loss of only $300— showing an excellent net profit on a very modest commitment.

A very similar opportunity was presented last November, when Interborough-Metropolitian $4^{1}/_{2}$s broke to $13^{3}/_{4}$, while the preferred stock was selling at $12^{1}/_{2}$. Considering the priority of lien "enjoyed" by the bonds, a spread of only $1^{1}/_{4}$ points between the two issues was ridiculously small. This has now widened to six points (which is still insufficient), but which nevertheless would allow a handsome profit to the man who bought the bonds and sold the stock at $13^{3}/_{4}$ and $12^{1}/_{2}$ respectively. At the present time one or two of the Missouri, Kansas & Texas bond issues—the St. Louis Division 4s, for example,—can be bought only a few points above the 4 per cent non-cumulative referred stock; while in view of the large accruals of interest and their prior lien, they should of right be selling at a much wider spread.

## DISCREPANCIES ARE COMMON

Discrepancies of this kind occur in almost endless variety and most of them can be availed of to advantage. But in many cases the outside trader cannot conveniently go short of the overvalued security, because of the difficulty of borrowing for an indefinite period and the interest problem. Nevertheless those who are holding the issue which is selling too high have every reason in the world for switching into the cheaper security. In the very first article of the present writer to appear in THE MAGAZINE OF WALL STREET (in September, 1917), he pointed out that there was no adequate reason for the ten point spread then existing between Japanese $4^{1}/_{2}$s, "plain" and "German Stamped." The man who exchanged from the former into the latter would now be ahead exactly ten points, since the Stock Exchange has abolished the stamp discrimination entirely as to these bonds, so that they all have exactly the same value.

The latter point is made in order to indicate that the three operations of switching, arbitraging and hedging all have very much in common, and that we may easily pass from one to another. They are all based upon exact information and analysis, and their success is usually entirely independent of market movements. At the present time, when the outlook is so clouded with uncertainty, the trader might well turn his attention for a while to the unspectacular, but safely profitable, business of hedging.

# 15

# WHICH IS THE BEST SUGAR STOCK?

*Strong Market Position of the
Commodity—Comparative Analysis
of Five Listed Issues—Importance
of Capitalization Structure and
Operating Efficiency*

The sugar issues as a class enjoyed considerably more than the average advance in the bull movement of 1919, and in the February decline they suffered less than most other industrials. This favorable showing has been due primarily to the continued advance in the price of the commodity. During the war the price of sugar was fixed by the International Sugar Committee and the Sugar Equalization Board, which in the crop years 1917–8 and 1918–9 purchased the entire Cuban output at 4.60c. and 5.50c. respectively. For the current year the regulatory policy has been abandoned, and the price of the staple has advanced sharply in response to purely natural conditions. The scarcity of sugar—with which most of our readers are ruefully familiar—has been due, first, to the sharp falling off in European beet sugar production, secondly, to the shortage of tonnage for the transportation of the Javan crop, and thirdly, to a recent substantial increase in the per capita consumption of this country.

Cuba—far from the firing line—has been able to take advantage of this situation by raising record crops and selling them at record prices. Producers in Porto Rico and other islands have enjoyed similar prosperity. The sugar industry in the United States, which relies chiefly on beets, was severely handicapped during the last crop year by adverse weather.

The securities of eight companies engaged in the production of sugar are now listed on the New York Stock Exchange. Of these, five operate under substantially similar conditions and are therefore susceptible of fairly accurate comparison.

These five concerns are Cuba Cane, Cuban-American, Punta Alegre and Manati, located in Cuba; and South Porto Rico, operating in that island and in San Domingo.

Of the other three companies the most important is probably American Sugar Refining, which is primarily a refining enterprise, and is interested in raw sugar production only indirectly, through its stock holdings in six western companies. United Fruit Co. is the fourth largest factor in the Cuban sugar output, but its other interests are so numerous—comprising shipping, fruit growing, livestock, etc.—that it cannot well be compared with sugar producers, pure and simple. Finally there is the Am. Beet Sugar Co., the only direct representative of this industry on the New York Stock Exchange. Since beet sugar leaves the factory in the refined state, neither the selling price nor the operating costs of this enterprise is comparable with those of the cane sugar companies. Moreover the weather conditions affecting the size of the crop may be entirely different for the two industries—as indeed they were last year.

For the reason stated above, therefore, it seems advisable to confine this article to an intensive comparison of the five cane sugar producers, leaving the remaining companies—important as they are—out of the picture.

## THE 1919 REPORTS

In the last analysis that stock is cheapest which will ultimately yield the largest return on its purchase price. With this criterion in mind, we begin by examining the last annual reports of the five companies—all covering the crop year 1918–9—to determine therefrom the amounts earned on the respective common shares.

These preliminary results are given in Table I. Since what we are seeking is not merely the amount earned per share, but chiefly the relation of the earnings to the *price*, the figures are stated both in dollars per share and in percentage market value (market price as of March 23, 1920, being used). These profits are stated, moreover, both before and after deduction of depreciation and taxes. The amount charged to expense for depreciation is more or less arbitrary with each company, so that the net income can be made unduly large or small by curtailing or inflating this item. While these nothing voluntary about taxes, the possibility of modification of at least the excess profits levy gives a comparison of profits before the tax deduction considerable potential value.

The table would indicate that, both before and after these two deductions, Cuba Cane Sugar earned last year the largest percentage of its present market value. On the second basis its figure of 16.2% earned on the price of its common compares with 16.1% for South Porto Rico Sugar, 1.5% for Cuban-American, 14.5% for Punta Alegre and 8.6% for Manati.

Cuba Cane leads therefore from the standpoint of 1919 earnings per dollar of market price of the common stock. Does this fact make Cuba Cane intrinsically the most attractive of the five issues? This question suggests a new consideration—one much too little regarded in view of its vital importance—namely the capitalization structure of the various companies. Cuba Cane Sugar's good showing is due in great measure to the very large proportion of its total securities represented by bonds and preferred stock, bearing a fixed charge of 7 per cent. Hence the surplus profits are distributed over a relatively small common stock issue, making the earnings per share in prosperous years unduly high as compared with other companies having a larger proportion of common stock to total securities. In times of depression, however, the margin for the common shares quickly melts away, and before long even the payments on the senior issues are impaired. This danger is clearly reflected in the lower

## TABLE I

EARNED ON COMMON SHARES—1918–19.

|  | Before Depreciation and Taxes | | After Depreciation and Taxes | |
|---|---|---|---|---|
|  | Per Share | % of Mkt. Price | Per Share | % of Mkt. Price |
| Cuba Cane | $13.11 | 27.3% | $7.76 | 16.2% |
| Cuban-Amer. | 117.66 | 25.9 | 67.67 | 15.0 |
| So. Porto Rico | 49.10 | 21.7 | 36.78 | 16.1 |
| Punta Alegre | 17.21 | 20.5 | 12.21 | 14.5 |
| Manati | 20.60 | 17.8 | 10.00 | 8.6 |

## TABLE II

RELATION OF CAPITAL STRUCTURE TO EARNINGS.

| | | Present Capitalization. | | | Common Stock | | |
|---|---|---|---|---|---|---|---|
| | Bonds | % of Total | Pfd. Stk. | % of Total | No. of Shrs | Mkt. Value | % of Total |
| Cuba Cane | $25,000,000 | 25.3% | $50,000,000 | 50.5% | 500,000 | $24,000,000 | 24.2% |
| Cuban-Amer | 2,000,000 | 3.7 | 7,893,000 | 14.4 | *100,000 | 45,000,000 | 81.9 |
| So. Porto Rico | | | 5,000,000 | 28.4 | 56,028 | 12,880,000 | 71.6 |
| Punta Alegre | | | | | 228,600 | 18,782,000 | 100.0 |
| Manati | | | 3,500,000 | 23.2 | 100,000 | 11,600,000 | 76.8 |

### Per Cent. Earned on Total Capitalization—1918–'19.

| | Before Depreciation and Taxes | After Depreciation and Taxes |
|---|---|---|
| Cuba Cane | 10.7% | 8.0% |
| Cuban-Amer. | 24.9 | 14.0 |
| So. Porto Rico | 17.2 | 13.4 |
| Punta Alogre | 19.9 | 14.5 |
| Manati | 13.1 | 8.2 |

* To be exchanged for 100,000 shares par $10.

price of Cuba Cane preferred compared with the others.

## THE CAPITALIZATION STRUCTURE

The significance of this point becomes immediately apparent when we compare the earnings of the various companies on their *total capitalization* instead of merely on their common stock. This capitalization is computed by valuing the bonds and preferred stock at par, and the common shares at market value. The 1919 results on this basis are given in Table II, and indicate that both before and after deductions for taxes and depreciation Cuba Cane now makes the *poorest* showing of all, instead of the best. In fact, before these deductions, Cuban-American actually reveals an earning power about two and one-half times as great as does the larger company.

To demonstrate the practical bearing of this matter, let us suppose that Cuban-American reorganized its securities so as to conform to the capitalization structure of Cuba Cane. This it could easily do by offering to issue 7 per cent bonds or preferred stock at par in exchange for three-quarters of the new common (par $10), valued at 45. If that were done, Cuban-American's capitalization would then consist of about $43,000,000 in bonds and pr ferred, and 250,000 shares of common. This would make it almost the exact replica of Cuba Cane, but on just half as large a scale. With such an arrangement, however, Cuban-American would have earned last year $37.30 per new share (par $10), before deduction of depreciation and taxes, against $13.11 for Cuba Cane. And yet the latter is now selling at a higher price!

A little "juggling of figures" can thus transform the apparent advantage of Cuba Cane in earning power into a woeful inferiority. It will doubtless be argued that all this is purely academic, since there is no possibility of any such readjustment in Cuban-American's securities as that imagined above. Admitted that the direct offer of exchange for senior issues is most unlikely, there is still the possibility that Cuban-American might seek to increase the earning power of the present common by the issuance of new bonds or preferred for the acquisition of new properties. Precisely this course was followed by American Steel Foundry. For when its directors realized that it could earn more on its common if part of its capitalization were in preferred stock they created a preferred issue and acquired the Griffin Wheel Co. With the proceeds.

A thorough discussion of the relation of capitalization structure to common stock values would require a separate article—and a long one at that. We cannot leave it however without drawing attention to the important influence of this element upon the exhibit of Punta Alegre Sugar. The securities of this company are all of one class—since the equivalent in common stock must be substituted for the convertible bonds. For this reason it ranks fourth in Table I, from the stand-point of actual earnings in 1919 on the present market value of the common stock. But when all the companies are reduced to the same level of capitalization—as is done in Table II—Punta Alegre Sugar jumps to the very first place. Cuban-American follows a fairly close second, with South Porto Rican Sugar a good third. Cuba Cane and Manati are far out of the running.

## OPERATING DATA

So far we have been dealing with the final results—which after all are the only things which really count. But in order to obtain some idea of how these results are likely to run in the future, it is necessary to pay some attention to the operating details reported by the various companies. The salient features are given in Table III, and exhibit a great diversity in costs and profits. The

## TABLE III

OPERATING DATA—1918–'19.

| | Production (350-lb. bags) | Gross Receipts (Per lb.) | Net Profit per lb. (Before Deprec. Tax) | Depreciation Charged | |
|---|---|---|---|---|---|
| | | | | Per lb. | % of Prop. Acot. |
| Cuba Cane | 4,319,189 | 5.90c. | .60c. | .12c. | 2.3% |
| Cuban Amer | 1,965,641 | 7.84 | 1.96 | .16 | 3.2 |
| So. Porto Rico | 618,400 | 6.28 | 1.58 | .35 | 5.6 |
| Punta Alegre | 605,150 | 5.90* | 1.31 | .27 | 5.7 |
| Manati | 507,366 | 5.90 | 1.56 | .31 | 3.7 |

* Estimated.

## TABLE IV.

PRICES AND DIVIDENDS.

| | Preferred | | | Common | | |
|---|---|---|---|---|---|---|
| | Price | Rate | Yield | Price | Rate | Yield |
| Cuba Cane | 82 | 7% | 8.55% | 47 | | |
| Cuban-Amer | 106 | 7 | 6.60 | 450 | $10 | 2.2% |
| So. Porto Rico | 110 | 8 | 7.27 | 230 | 20 | 8.7 |
| Punta Alegre | | | | 84 | 5 | 6.0 |
| Manati | 100 | 7 | 7.00 | 116 | 10 | 8.6 |

advantage enjoyed by Cuban-American in the matter of receipts per pound is clearly due to the fact that, alone of all five companies, it refines a portion of its output (about 30%) for which of course it obtains a higher price. To this cause is also due in part its leadership in net earnings per pound produced.

The outstanding feature of Table III is the very poor showing in profits per pound made by Cuba Cane. This figure is less than 40% of that reported by Manati, which is also under Rionda management. It must seem strange that the estates selected as the pick of all Cuba, entrusted to the foremost sugar men and supplied with the best scientific talent, should make such a miserable operating exhibit compared with any of the other companies. No doubt this disappointing element was chiefly instrumental in causing the Goethals investigation.

Opportunities for detailed comparison are lacking; for while Cuba Cane is most liberal with its information, this is rendered useless through the reticence of its competitors. One or two facts are perhaps worth stating. The cost of marine freight last year was about 10% higher for Cuba Cane than for Manati, although the latter's plantations are no nearer the Atlantic seaboard. The yield of raw sugar for Cuba Cane was 11.15% of the total cane ground, against 11.45% for Cuban-American, showing greater manufacturing efficiency for the latter, since the gross content of the cane was no larger. Cuba Cane, however, is making gradual progress towards obtaining a larger percentage of extraction.

## CONCLUSIONS

Coming now to a final valuation of the five issues, we must at the outset distinguish Cuba Cane from all the other companies. That enterprise is characterized by large production, high operating costs and heavy interest and preferred dividend charges. This is a combination which makes for excellent earnings on the common during periods of high sugar prices, but a very rapid shrinkage in profits when the price of the commodity declines. In a word, Cuba Cane common is essentially a speculative issue, carrying possibilities both of sharp advances and sharp recession.

The new 7% convertible debentures, however, having a first claim on the earnings and assets of the company, appear to be very well secured, and their conversion privilege into the common stock at 60 might some day acquire substantial value.

South Porto Rico Sugar yields the highest dividend return (see Table IV). As compared with the Cuban producers it enjoys the advantage of exemption from the one cent import duty levied on the latter. We would point out further that the depreciation charges of South Porto Sugar on paper bag basis were unusually large last year (Table III), a fact which made the final profits appear somewhat lower than was really the case. The company is planning to increase the output of its San Domingo central, and is said to have sold a good portion of this year's crop at excellent prices.

Between South Porto Rico Sugar and Cuban-American there is little to choose. The latter's stock should enjoy a much better market, now that the par is to be reduced from $100 to $10, and the dividend rate will no doubt be increased. And besides its reputation as the oldest and most successful Cuban producer should not be ignored in any comparison.

Punta Alegre made intrinsically the best showing of all the companies in 1919, but that was on the basis of its capitalization before the recent expansion. Since then it has increased its stock issue by 56% for the purpose of adding about 40% to its mill capacity. This disproportion would tend to diminish the attractiveness of the issue somewhat, especially as the new unit will be operating only partially during the current year of high prices. A good deal will depend on the success of this new venture, the prospects of which at this writing are said to be very favorable.

Manati Sugar, while a successful company, certainly seems to be selling too high compared with the other issues.

To sum up, we would group Cuban-American, South Porto Rico and Punta Alegre rather closely together in the class of conservative common stocks. Manati is too high, and Cuba Cane must be regarded as essentially speculative. If the writer must select one issue as "the best," he would name Cuban-American Sugar—but by a slender margin.—*Cuba Cane, Vol. 25, p. 750; Cuba Amer. Vol. 25, p. 338; Punta Alegre, Vol. 25, p. 676.*

# 16

# THE "COLLAPSE" OF AMERICAN INTERNATIONAL

*Great Expectations Cruelly Disappointed—Is the Stock Cheap at 42?—Facts and Figures about the Company and Its Subsidiaries*

Few corporate events in recent years have made as deep and painful an impression upon the financial world as the spectacular decline of American International from its high price of 132¼ in 1919, culminating in the passing of the dividend and the resultant break to a low of 38¼. Not, indeed, that the 94 point slump or the omission of the dividend were in themselves such striking occurrences. The Street unfortunately is fairly well inured to the bursting of bubbles. But American International from the very first was regarded as an entirely different and sounder proposition than the ordinary common stock. To begin with, it was supposed to have the finest Board of Directors in the country, comprising twenty-four of the leaders of American

**TABLE I**

COMPARATIVE INCOME ACCOUNT 1916–1919

| (In Thousands). | 1916 | 1917 | 1918 | 1919 |
|---|---|---|---|---|
| Interest and | $502 | $3,026 | $2,458 | $4,175 |
| Dividends | 3,338 | 3,804 | 5,388 | 8,158 |
| Operations | $3,840 | $6,830 | $7,846 | $12,328 |
| Taxes and Expenses | 1,356 | 3,084 | 4,130 | 7,606 |
| Net Income | $2,484 | $3,746 | $3,716 | $4,719 |
| Dividends | 375 | 1,574 | 1,817 | 2,398 |
| Adjustments | 165 | 588 | 336 | 495 |
| Surplus for Year | 1,944 | 1,584 | 2,235 | 1,826 |
| Earned on Average Capital | 15.68% | 14.81% | 12.40% | 12.43% |

banking and business. Secondly, every dollar of its $50,000,000 capitalization was issued for cash at par. And, thirdly, its field of activities—foreign trade and foreign investment—was considered to hold forth unusual opportunities for profitable growth.

Small wonder that an enterprise launched under these excellent auspices should have immediately taken rank as an investment favorite. It was well nigh universally regarded as an issue to be bought and "put away," with the confident hope that in a few years its value would have increased manifold. It is the sharp contrast between this great expectation and the disastrous event that makes the market collapse of American International an episode of such disturbing significance.

## ACCUSATION AND DEFENSE

The aim of this article is to reach as impartial a judgment as possible upon what has transpired. Many bitter things are being said on the subject; and while the criticisms may be wholly unfounded they are certainly not without provocation. For when the public is not told the "inside truth," it must necessarily decide by the outside appearances.

Now, the whole matter might be dismissed with the easy observation that where there are large possibilities of profit there must also be great risks of loss. Had things gone well the stockholders might have doubled or tripled their stake. Instead, ill fortune was encountered, and so half the investment was wiped out—unpleasant, but inevitable.

On the other hand the directors may say that the corporation is not responsible for the market action of its stock. The mere fact that dividends are suspended does not cut the intrinsic value in two. This action was taken in the interest of conservatism, and because adverse conditions involved a heavy strain (no doubt temporary) upon the cash resources. The company's assets are intact and its position fundamentally sound. So runs the official statement.

But by neither of these arguments can the management entirely escape blame for what has happened. If the decline in the market price really reflects an equal in intrinsic value, the disaster cannot be ascribed solely to bad luck. Exchange, it is true, has suffered extreme weakness this year, notably in the South American centers, where the corporation's subsidiaries do a large business. But in its most recent report, the president stated that these enterprises avoided at all times the accumulation of uncovered balances, and so eliminated direct risks from exchange fluctuations so far as possible. Nor should the decline in commodity prices have ordinarily involved an enormous loss to the company, for the total inventories carried at the end of last year amounted to only $15,000,000, or $30 per share. If, therefore, the actual worth of the enterprise has really shrunk 65% or $35,000,000 since last January, some suspicion of inexperience, or poor judgment, or mismanagement, might well arise.

However, if we accept the more optimistic view and consider that the break in the market price was greatly overdone—the intrinsic value having suffered to no such degree—even the responsibility for this collapse cannot be entirely avoided by the management. For months there had been persistent and mysterious selling of the stock which carried it steadily to lower levels. All this time the corporation gave no intimation that anything was wrong and countless investors bought the issue on the basis of the latest reports available, believing the stock to be a great bargain. In the light of what subsequently happened, Wall Street is now asking, "Who did all the selling before the dividend was passed?" Certainly not the general public, who were rather buying it, with misplaced confidence. Hence the men in the brokerage offices are saying that the selling must have been done by insiders, who knew the dividend was to be passed and who took advantage of the public's ignorance to sell out their holdings well in advance.

**TABLE II**

COMPARATIVE BALANCE SHEET 1916–1919

|  | (In Thousands). | | | |
| --- | --- | --- | --- | --- |
| Assets: | 1916 | 1917 | 1918 | 1919 |
| Investments | $23,227 | $27,314 | $27,847 | $30,816 |
| Cash and Call Loans | 2,954 | 2,375 | 1,638 | 7,768 |
| Other Current | 4,181 | 5,213 | 10,779 | 40,627 |
| Fixed | — | 1,732 | 2,040 | 2,433 |
| Miscellaneous | 43 | 472 | 1,557 | 1,943 |
| Total | $30,405 | $37,106 | $43,861 | $83,587 |
| Liabilities: | | | | |
| Capital | $25,000 | $29,970 | $29,970 | $50,000 |
| Surplus | 1,923 | 3,508 | 5,743 | 7,569 |
| Current and Reserves | 3,482 | 3,628 | 8,148 | 26,018 |
| Total | $30,405 | $37,106 | $43,861 | $83,587 |

In view of the high character of the men identified with American International these charges no doubt are entirely unfounded, but is it not their own fault that their secretive policy has permitted such rumors to gain credence? From this point of view there was much warrant for the phrase used recently by a prominent factor in Stock Exchange circles, who referred to "that disgraceful American International incident."

So much for the moral aspects of the case. After all what the public would chiefly like to know is whether the stock is still dear at 42, or whether its tremendous decline has not placed it on the bargain counter. The difficulty of answering these questions with any degree of accuracy must be obvious. Not only is it impossible even to surmise what has happened to the corporation in the past year; but even in the years for which reports are available the lack of definite figures as to investment holdings and gross earnings makes a valuation well nigh impossible. Nevertheless, we shall marshal what facts we have, with a view to giving some picture of what American International owns and does and possibly of reaching some fairly plausible conclusion as to the dearness or cheapness of the issue today.

## THE CORPORATION'S HOLDINGS

American International, in addition to conducting some operations in its own name, has acquired securities in no less than 24 companies. These are divided into appropriate groups, and briefly commented upon as follows:

### GROUP A.   PROPRIETARY COMPANIES—OPERATIONS INCLUDED IN 1919 REPORT

1.  Allied Machinery of America. Incorporated 1911. Capital $1,500,000, all owned by American International. Does a large export business in machinery and tools. Income account 1912–1916 is available, viz.:

| Year | Gross Profit | Net Income |
|------|-------------|------------|
| 1916 | $1,863,000 | $834,000 |
| 1915 | 662,000 | 467,000 |
| 1914 | 350,000 | Def.  22,000 |
| 1913 | 19,000 | Def.  29,000 |
| 1912 | 2,000 | Def.  41,000 |

2.  Allied Machinery Co. of France, Inc., 1916. Capital, fcs. 250,000—all owned by Allied Mach. Co. of America—French agency for machines, etc.
3.  Allied Machinery Co. of Italy. Incorporated 1918. Capital, lire 1,000,000, all owned by Allied Mach. Co. of America—Italian agency for machines, etc.
4.  Allied Construction Machinery Corp. Incorporated 1917. Capital $250,000. 84% owned by Allied Machinery Co. of America. In 1918 earned $275,000 gross and $50,000 net. Deals in construction machinery for export.
5.  Allied Sugar Machinery Corp. Incorporated 1916. Capital $200,000, 85% owned by Allied Machinery Co. of America. In 1918 earned $350,000 gross, but showed net loss of $82,000, after expenses.
6.  Horne Co. Ltd. Incorporated 1918. Capital, yen 600,000, all owned by Allied Machinery Co. of America. Controls Yamato Iron Works of Japan, and does an export business with the Orient.
7.  American International Steel Corp. Incorporated 1917. Paid in capital $100,000, all owned by American International. Does a general export business in steel, with numerous foreign connections.

8. American International Steel Corp., Ltd. Incorporated 1917. Paid in capital £3, of which £1 owned by American International. Is English agency of American International Steel Corp.

9. American International Ship Building Corp. Incorporated 1917. Capital $2,000, all owned by American International. Constructed and operated by Hog Island shipyard which built 122 ships for the Government. Corporation is no longer interested in this yard.

10. G. Amsinck Co. Incorporated 1916. Capital $6,000,000, all owned by American International. The corporation's recent troubles seem to have centered in this subsidiary, which does a large export and import business, chiefly with South America. In 1918 it reported gross income of $1,363,000, but a net loss—after expenses—of $2,123. In 1917 the net profits had been $470,000. Considering the size of American International, this does not appear to have been a subsidiary of exceptional importance—at least prior to 1919. On Dec. 31, 1918, it had total current assets of $11,383,000, of which $471,000 was in cash and $3,165,000 in inventory. Current liabilities were $8,526,000 of which $2,906,000 was in notes payable. Presumably at the present time its business and obligations are both on a much larger scale. It is stated that 40% of its requirements are financed by the banks and the balance by the parent company.

10. Carter, Macy & Co. Incorporated 1916. Capital $2,000,000, all owned by American International. Imports tea and sells same here and abroad. In the last 8 months of 1916 its gross profits were $423,000 and net $216,000.

11. Rosin and Turpentine Export Co. Incorporated 1916. Capital $800,000, all owned by American International. Deals in naval stores.

The peculiar point about all these subsidiaries is that none of them appears to have been a really big proposition, as far as can be judged by the meagre data at hand. It follows, therefore, that either some of these concerns have since done a far larger business than the reports of earlier years indicate, or else the major part of American International's operating profits came from its own business. These operating profits are stated separately in the income account for 1916–1919, in Table I. The only proposition which the statements mention as having been handled by American International direct was a sewerage construction job for Uruguay, the gross amount of which was $4,000,000, payable in bonds. One might suspect that part of the reported earnings were profits on the sale of securities, but the company insists that it does not speculate in stocks. This point is somewhat mysterious.

## B.  PROPRIETARY COMPANIES—OPERATIONS NOT INCLUDED IN 1919 REPORT

12.   American Balsa Co. Incorporated 1918. Capital $1,000,000, of which $693,600 owned by American International. Manufactures life-saving apparatus. In the last 4 months of 1918 its gross was $372,000 and net $225,000.

13.   China Co. Incorporated 1916. Capital $1,000,000, of which American International owns $500,000. Presumably intends to obtain concessions in China. Of the $1,000,000 capital, $950,000 represented "contracts and concessions." In 1918 its operations were only nominal.

14.   Siems-Carey Ry. and Canal Co. Incorporated 1916. Capital $500,000, of which American International owns $212,500. Its object is construction work in China. In 1918 operations were nominal, and showed a loss of $40,000.

None of the above three companies appears very important.

## C.  OUTSIDE INVESTMENTS

15.   Pacific Mail S.S. Co. Incorporated 1916, American International, together with W. R. Grace Co., acquired joint control of this enterprise.

16.   International Mercantile Marine. This interest was acquired in 1916, but the amount has not been published. In June, 1919, International corporation was unofficially reported to hold 82,745 shares of I. M. M. preferred, and the average cost is said to be about $75 per share.

17.   United Fruit. Interest acquired 1916. No further data available.

18.   N. Y. Shipbuilding. In 1916, corporation, together with W. R. Grace Co., Pacific Mail and International Mercantile Marine, acquired the entire property. Subsequently some stock was sold to the public.

19.   U. S. Rubber. Interest acquired 1917, but amount unknown.

20.   International Products. American International apparently owns some bonds of this South American packing concern. Amount unknown.

21.   Simms Petroleum. Corporation is said to have acquired 75,000 shares at 47. If this is true, the present price of 7 would mean a loss of $3,000,000 on this investment.

22.   U. S. Industrial Alcohol. An unstated interest in this company was acquired in 1917 and apparently disposed of in 1919.

In addition, the corporation was at one time interested in two other companies, probably of small importance, viz:

23.  Symington Forge Co., organized to carry out a munition contract. Stock since sold.

24.  American International Terminals Co. Now dissolved.


## THE OUTSIDE INVESTMENTS

Particular attention is directed to the item of investments in the comparative balance-sheet for 1916–1919, given in Table II. The changes in this account from year to year were chiefly due to the purchase of stock interests in outside companies (called participations), but they have also been affected by the transfer of the holdings in various subsidiaries from the investment account to the other assets. Furthermore temporary investments in bonds and notes amounting to $9,122,000 were made the first year. A large part of these were sold in 1917, while others may have been added subsequently. The following table summarizes the progress of the investment account, as far as can be gleaned from the reports and listing applications:

| Year | Securities | Book Cost, about |
|---|---|---|
| 1916—Pacific Mail, Int. Merc. Marine, United Fruit, N. Y. Shipbuilding | | $13,000,000 |
| 1917—U. S. Rubber, Int. Products, U. S. Industrial Alcohol (sold later) | | 2,500,000 |
| 1918—Unspecified | | 5,000,000 |
| 1919—Unspecified | | 8,000,000 |
| | | $28,500,000 |
| Proprietary Cos. and Misc | | 2,316,000 |
| Total Dec. 31, 1919 | | $30,816,000 |

The reports for 1918 and 1919 state that no important changes were made in the "participations group" of investments. This makes the disposition of the $13,000,000 spent in these years somewhat mysterious. About $3,500,000, apparently, went into Simms Petroleum, but the balance may be in the form of temporary holdings of bonds or notes.

This question of outside investments is of the utmost importance, not only because their book value represented $60 per share of Am. International stock, but chiefly because in 1919 they contributed $4,174,000, or $8.34 per share in interest and dividends. This was over 88% of the total income available for Am. International stock.

It is true that the market value of all these holdings has shrunk considerably of late, but their cost to American International was understood to have been far below the high levels of the past two years. It seems reasonable to suppose that these investments are now worth at least $20,000,000, or $40 per share. This would about equal the present price of the issue, and would still leave the assets invested in the proprietary companies, amounting last year to $27,000,000. That these should have been entirely destroyed is incredible, especially in view of the direct denial entered by President Stone, who declared that "statements that American International had made large losses in South America or anywhere else are untrue."

## CONCLUSION

After making allowances for the most unfavorable possibilities, it is hard to believe that American International is not worth more than 42. The chief result of this inquiry has been to indicate that the corporation's foreign business has been apparently of insufficient size to swallow up the larger portion of its capital, even at worst. If this is true, then the domestic investments should assure a minimum asset value and minimum income large enough to justify the purchase of the stock at or below present levels.

# 17

# THE GOODYEAR REORGANIZATION

*Unofficial Insolvency Caused by Ill-Timed Expansion—Sudden Disaster Follows Wonderful Growth—Details of Proposed Reorganization and Discussion of Company's Prospects*

In the midst of general commercial gloom, optimists have found much encouragement in the relatively few important failures recorded. To a great extent, however, this condition reflects not so much underlying financial strength, as a new technique in handling business troubles. For when difficulties occur, instead of appointing a receiver, the creditors now usually establish a committee to whom the affairs of the company are turned over unreservedly. Many concerns have thus been passing through the throes of insolvency, reorganization, or liquidation, without Dun's or Bradstreet's officially being any the wiser.

A striking example of these new financial methods is furnished by Goodyear Tire and Rubber, the affairs of which are now undergoing "readjustment." Had the present situation arisen a few years ago, a receivership

## TABLE I

GROWTH OF GOODYEAR'S BALANCE SHEET

### Oct. 31, 1915–1920 (,000 omitted)

Assets—

| | 1915 | 1916 | 1917 | 1918 | 1919 | 1920 |
|---|---|---|---|---|---|---|
| Fixed | 11,442 | 17,908 | 30,704 | 39,155 | 43,464 | *98,041 |
| Current | 14,838 | 81,309 | 51,858 | 54,464 | 76,813 | 55,036 |
| Liabilities— | | | | | | |
| Stock | 15,028 | 35,000 | 44,672 | 59,250 | 57,429 | 126,028 |
| Surplus and Reserves | 9,307 | 5,050 | 16,764 | 26,053 | 40,831 | −13,931 |
| Current | 1,945 | 9,167 | 21,126 | 8,314 | 22,017 | 40,980 |
| Total | 26,280 | 49,217 | 82,562 | 93,619 | 120,277 | 153,077 |

* Includes $3,568,445 due from Pres. Seiberling, later settled by transfer of fixed assets.

would have been inevitable, and the mortality records would have been swollen by a $66,000,000 failure—a figure that would put the famous Rumely insolvency quite in the shade.

## REMARKABLE INCIDENT

The downfall of Goodyear is a remarkable incident even in the present plenitude of business disasters. For the victims of deflation, though many, have for the most part, represented the weaker type of enterprise—either engaged in especially speculative undertakings, or equipped with insufficient capital, or in general established on an insecure, inflated basis. Goodyear, however, suffered from none of these weaknesses. But a short time ago it was considered one of the strongest and soundest enterprises in the country—the leader among tire producers, with the hightest reputation in both the commercial and financial field. And yet this company fell from the height of prosperity to the depth of insolvency in a bewilderingly short space of time.

A few figures paint the suddenness of the débâcle. In March, 1920, Goodyear common sold at 415. In the following July a stock dividend of 150% was paid, and the new shares sold at 136. At the same time the company offered for sale at par $30,000,000 of additional preferred and common. Less than three months later, its balance sheet dated Oct. 31, 1920, shows a profit and loss deficit of $15,670,000, with $19,000,000 in further losses expected on

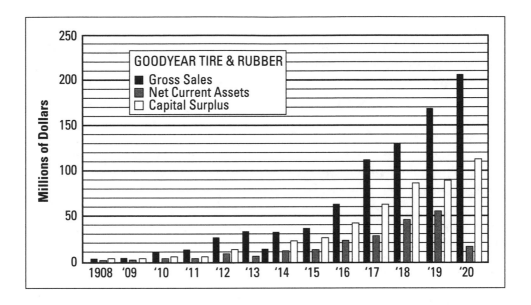

purchase contracts. In another three months (Dec. 31, 1920) the deficit had increased to $24,400,000, and the estimated loss on materials contracted for was placed at $18,247,000. In a year and a quarter the current liabilities rose from 22 millions to 66 millions, and the merchandise commitments to another 55 millions.

As this state of affairs became known to the public, the stock quotations fell precipitately. At the recent low prices of 11 and 25 for the common and preferred, the units of two shares of preferred and one of common, which had been offered last summer for $300, were worth only $61—about one-fifth of cost.

## GENERAL SIGNIFICANCE OF THE CATASTROPHE

In considering the Goodyear affair, three questions arise:

1. Just what is the present situation?
2. How was it brought about?
3. What are the prospects under the proposed readjustment?

It may be objected that it is idle to inquire into the cause of Goodyear's trouble. The stockholders can do nothing to retrieve the past; their hopes and fears are with the future. Yet for every investor, Goodyear stockholder or not, the sudden collapse of this enterprise raised a disquieting question. If Goodyear's reverses were the result entirely of ill-luck, and the most efficient management had been powerless to prevent them, then this incident would throw a very disturbing sidelight on the hidden risks underlying even the safest appearing industrial investment. It is important to ask, therefore, whether it was purely an accident that this company succumbed to a business depression which its rivals were able to withstand.

If we study the summary of Goodyear's financial history, given in Table I we quickly perceive the weak point in the company's armor. Two figures alone practically tell the story.

| | |
|---|---|
| Fixed assets Oct. 31, 1920 | $98,041,000 |
| Fixed assets Oct. 31, 1919 | 43,464,000 |
| Increase | $54,577,000 |

Just as the industrial boom was reaching its climax, Goodyear invested $54,000,000 in new plant facilities and subsidiary enterprises. In one year it increased its fixed assets by 130%; in five years by 750%. That the investment of these enormous sums in permanent assets at such a time constituted a grave error of judgment can hardly be denied. Huge inventory losses may be excused, perhaps, on the ground that the business stagnation came so swiftly and suddenly that escape was impossible—the only possible preparation being the voluntary curtailment of operations while the demand was at its height. But in its headlong expansion policy Goodyear went to the opposite extreme, and built new plants as if it thought the feverish activity of 1919 was merely the prelude to a new and unparalleled era of industrial prosperity.

Some idea of the lavishness and variety of these capital expenditures can be gleaned from the following partial chronology:

Feb., 1920. $2,000,000 guaranteed preferred stock of Goodyear Textile Mills of Cal. offered to public.

March, 1920. Naval Air Station at Akron, Ohio, purchased for manufacture of commercial dirigibles.

March, 1920. Reported that company intends establishing a plant in Brazil.

March, 1920. Company leases 5,200 acres of coal lands in Ohio.

April, 1920. Subsidiary buys Ford plant in Long Island City for $2,000,000.

May, 1920. Company buys a cotton ranch in Cal. for $1,000,000.

June, 1920. 7,800 acres in Arizona bought for raising cotton.

In the previous year the company had acquired 20,000 acres of rubber lands in Sumatra and had organized the Goodyear Tire and Rubber Co. of

Cal. with a capital of $20,000,000. No doubt much money was spent on these two ventures in 1920.

While a good part of these heavy outlays were financed through the sale of about $30,000,000 of new preferred and $8,000,000 of common, a large balance still remained to be paid for out of current assets. It was this drain on the cash resources at a critical time which brought disaster. For had the difficulty been confined to the shrinkage of inventory values, Goodyear no doubt could have pulled through, as did Central Leather, despite its colossal losses.

## DETAILS OF THE COMPANY'S PRESENT POSITION

The recently published Readjustment Plan contains a statement of the various obligations as of Dec. 31 last, and an outline of the proposed method of financing same through the issuance of new securities. No complete picture of the company's finances either before or after reorganization is given, however. This can be constructed only by a careful piecing together of the available material.

In Table II we give an approximate balance sheet as of Dec. 31, 1920, prior to the creation of the new securities. The deficit has increased to $24,400,000, and we assume, therefore, that the working capital has been correspondingly reduced since Oct. 31 by $7,880,000, and thus stands at only $5,200,000. Since current liabilities are stated at $66,000,000 we put the current assets therefore at $71,200,000.

### TABLE II

APPROXIMATE BALANCE SHEET
DEC. 31, 1920.

| | |
|---|---:|
| Assets— | |
| Fixed | $98,041,000 |
| Current | 71,267,000 |
| | |
| Liabilities— | |
| Stock | 126,028,000 |
| Deficit | 24,400,000 |
| Current | 65,964,000 |
| Reserves | 1,716,000 |
| Total | $169,808,000 |

## TABLE III

APPROXIMATE BALANCE SHEET AFTER REORGANIZATION (ALLOWING FOR $18,247,000 LOSS ON MERCHANDISE COMMITMENTS)

| Assets— | | Liabilities— | |
|---|---|---|---|
| Fixed | $98,041,000 | 1st Mtge Bonds | $25,000,000 |
| Net Current | 65,056,000 | Debentures | 25,000,000 |
| | | Prior Preference | 35,000,000 |
| | | Preferred | 65,000,000 |
| | | Reserves | 1,716,000 |
| | | Book value of 900,000 | |
| | | Shares Common | 11,381,000 |
| Total | $163,097,000 | Total | $163,097,000 |

This balance sheet, however, reflects in no way the commitments of $55,000,000 for future deliveries of merchandise, upon which an estimated loss of $18,287,000 will be sustained. If this loss were charged off, there would result an excess of about $13,000,000 of current liabilities over quick assets.

Table III summarizes the company's position after consummation of the readjustment, which will involve the issuance of the following securities:

A. $35,000,000 Twenty-Year First Mortgage 8% Bonds, presumably to be sold the general public.

B. $25,000,000 Ten-year 8% Debentures, to be used together with 250,000 shares of new common to pay off a similar amount of bank debt. These debentures are to be offered to present stockholders at par with a bonus of ten shares of common with each $1,000 bond.

C. $35,000,000 8% Prior Preference Stock. To be used to pay merchandise and contingent creditors and to fund one-quarter of the merchandise commitments. For this purpose the Prior Preference stock will be valued at 80, and evidently will be offered to stockholders at that price.

D. $65,000,000 7% Preferred Stock, to be exchanged share for share for present preferred.

E. 900,000 shares of common of no par value, to be exchanged share for share for present common (610,000 shares); to be given as a bonus with the debentures (250,000 shares); and for "other purposes" (40,000 shares).

Furthermore, there may be created an unstated amount of management stock to be entitled to aggregate dividends of not more than $30,000 per annum, in priority to the preferred and common; also to exclusive voting power for the election of majority of directors. This means that control of the company will be vested in the Creditors' Committee as long as any bonds or debentures are outstanding—quite probably for twenty years.

## WORKING CAPITAL AND FIXED CHARGES AFTER REORGANIZATION

The total par value of new securities to replace existing debt is thus $85,000,000. But since the Prior Preference stock is to be issued at 80, the actual amount realized will be $78,000,000. If from this figure the previous working capital deficit of $13,000,000 is deducted (which includes the future losses on merchandise contracts) the reconstructed company will start off with net current assets of about $65,000,000. This will cover the two bond issues fully and leave about $43 per share, for the Prior Preference stock. Valuing the fixed assets at their book figure of $98,000,000, the total assets behind the preferred works out at $117 per share; but for the new common, at only $12$^1/_2$ per share—or just about its present price.

Interest and dividends on the two bond issues and prior preference stock will aggregate $4,800,000. But to this must be added a sinking fund of $1,250,000 on the First Mortgage bonds, and another for the debentures, the amount of which is not stated but may be estimated at $500,000. These two items would make a total of $8,550,000 of charges ahead of the 7% preferred. Hence total annual payments of $13,100,000 would have to be met, before anything is available for the common. Nor will the sinking fund operations reduce these charges gradually, since whatever amount is thus saved in interest must go to redeem the Prior Preference stock.

## WHAT IS THE OUTLOOK?

The great obstacle to determining what are the reorganized company's prospects lies in the impossibility of selecting an average or normal year's operations on which to base an estimate of earning power. As the graph shows, in twelve years the company's sales grew from $2,000,000 to $200,000,000, and the assets and capitalization were similarly expanding a hundredfold. Hence the company's exhibit five or even two years ago may afford very little indication of future results.

One thing of course is clear—that for the time being sales cannot be expected to approach last year's record figure of $206,000,000. It is reported that the company will double its operations shortly, to a basis of 60,000 tires per week; but this schedule probably means gross business of less than $60,000,000 per annum. If we estimate the turnover under rather quiet (but not stagnant) conditions at, say, $130,000,000, and the ratio of profit after taxes at, say, 10% this would give net earnings of $13,000,000—or not quite enough to cover the preferred dividend. The bond interest should then be well secured, and the Prior Preference dividend covered with a fair margin, and doubtless paid. The situation of the preferred stock, however, would be dubious, with the likelihood against any disbursements for some time.

Another angle on the problem can be obtained by a comparison with Goodrich, the company's ancient rival. Since Goodyear preferred is quoted at only 30, it can be set off against Goodrich common, which sells about six points higher. In 1919 Goodyear's sales exceeded those of Goodrich by about 20%. We may assume that if Goodyear's gross is reduced to $130,000,000, the other company's might drop to $105,000,000. On a 10% profit basis, Goodrich's earnings could then be $10,500,000. Deducting note interest of $2,100,000 and preferred dividend of $2,660,000, the balance left for the 600,000 shares of common is $5,740,000 or $9.50 per share. From this point of view Goodrich common appears more attractive than Goodyear preferred. It has the further advantage of paying a $6 dividend—for the time being, at least—and not being in financial difficulties.

The 1920 Goodrich report is not yet available. Hence we do not know how its working capital has fared in the price readjustment. Last June it stood at $70,000,000—a comfortable figure—but if it has since shrunk considerably this factor may offset the apparent superiority over Goodyear.

## THE COMMON FUNDAMENTALLY SPECULATIVE

Our estimate of $13,000,000 net for Goodyear leaves nothing for the common. Its dilution through the issuance of the bonus stock makes the establishment of any large earning power in the near future rather improbable. At the present moment the salient point about the common is that the total market value of the new issue is only $11,000,000, as against a par value of $150,000,000 of prior securities.

This relationship is the earmark of an essentially speculative issue—the value of which will fluctuate widely with each relatively small change in the company's earnings. Goodyear common must, therefore, be regarded as a typical speculation; its market price will rise and fall with the general outlook of the tire industry.

The preferred stock is also mainly speculative, since dividend resumption is not yet in sight. It seems reasonable to assume that the re-establishment of normal conditions in the motor industry should enable the company to pay something on this issue. Hence at 30 the preferred stock appears a fairly attractive long-pull speculation. In this connection it must be remembered that Goodyear's troubles are mainly financial. Its products have not lost their prestige, and the valuable goodwill built up by years of national advertising and honest merchandise should be preserved unimpaired.

In valuing the Goodyear issues we have assumed that the reorganization plan is successfully completed. As this is written the company announces that while over 75% of the creditors have consented to the proposal, the co-operation of the remainder must be obtained. If the plan fails of adoption, a receivership will then appear inevitable, with more drastic treatment ultimately accorded the stockholders. This possibility has served to depress the current market price to a lower level than is warranted by the long-range prospects of the issues, especially of the preferred stock.

# 18

# IS UNITED DRUG CHEAP AT 53?

## *Factors in the Collapse from 83*

United drug common, which on July 25 sold at $83\frac{1}{2}$, on July 27 touched 54, a decline of $29\frac{1}{2}$ points or 35% in two days. Wall Street inured long since to such pyrotechnics, at first viewed the collapse with dull indifference. But finally the ticker flashed the news that Louis K. Liggett, president of the company, had placed his affairs in the hands of trustees. Here was the personal element, and immediately United Drug became interesting. The next day the affair progressed into the picturesque stage upon publication of an intimate letter from Mr. Liggett to his stockholders. This was headed, rather pathetically, "Dear Partner," contained a rather vague and emotional account of the president's difficulties, and insisted that the United Drug Company as such was in no way involved in his embarrassment, but on the contrary "is as sound as a nut."

The letter is extremely optimistic about the condition and prospects of the company. Mr. Liggett calls United Drug a "sounder industrial than any I know," and says it has no basic right "to be selling at its present price," because "the business has been in no way affected."

## PARADOXICAL

Yet, if these things are so, it is not entirely clear why Mr. Liggett should have come to grief. He insists he has not lost heavily in outside operations, nor gambled in stocks. It seems his financial troubles arise entirely from the decline in United Drug, and the decline in the United Drug is due entirely to his personal difficulties. This sounds paradoxical, to say the least.

At the outset we must express a doubt as to whether either statement is entirely accurate. The indications are first—which is of lesser importance— that Mr. Liggett's losses are not confined exclusively to United Drug; and second—of more significance—that the break in the stock has more behind it than the president's insolvency. There are grounds for both conclusions in the famous letter itself. For Mr. Liggett declares he holds 39,000 shares of United Drug and Liggett's International common, and that his assets have shrunk $5,000,000 in eight months. The range of prices during this period would point to a maximum loss of $2,500,000 from United Drug stock, leaving the balance of the same amount to come from other sources. As for the company itself, the letter also acknowledges that "these are tough times," that inventory losses in sugar, rubber, etc., have been taken, and that business for the first six months of 1921 fell 12% below 1920.

Highly distasteful as it is to discuss the financial reverses of an individual, any study of the United Drug situation must necessarily turn about Mr. Liggett's personal statement. For despite the shrinkage of 50% in the market value of the common stock since Jan. 1, this document contains the only information published regarding the company's operations so far this year. It is significant that the prospectus of the new 8% bonds, dated May 31 last, contained no figures more recent than Dec. 21, 1920. The writer is at present advised that a report will be published in "a week or ten days." But in the meantime seven full months have passed without the publication of a single figure. The bewildered and apprehensive stockholder is thus reduced to a critical and even skeptical examination of Mr. Liggett's manifesto for some clue as to the real status of his investments.

At this point a brief digression regarding earning statements may not be entirely inappropriate. When United Drug listed its stock in New York in October, 1916, its application contained an agreement "to publish quarterly an income account and a balance sheet." In common with a great many other corporations, this agreement has been quietly ignored from the very first, and for a full year at a time the stockholders have remained ignorant of their company's condition.

In the halcyon days of prosperity, the investor is satisfied with increased dividends and a rising market, and cares very little about dry statistics. But in these difficult times the security owner would dearly like to know as frequently as possible just how his enterprise is weathering the storm, and he is entitled to this knowledge. The organization of the New York Stock Exchange has apparently not yet reached the point where it can independently make sure that all the agreements contained in the listing applications are regularly observed. But when its attention is called to any default in this respect, it quickly and energetically brings pressure to bear to have the conditions remedied. Hence, if wide-awake stockholders will insist upon obtaining the reports at the periods agreed upon, they can get what they want.

A good many reasons are advanced by companies for their failures to publish statements as frequently as promised. Some are merely frivolous, such as the difficulty of computing income taxes—when the earnings can readily be stated before tax allowance. Others, with more logic, stress the difficulty of frequent physical inventories in their line of business. But the cold facts are that there are very few large corporations now whose offices are not supplied with a fairly accurate income account and balance sheet at least every quarter. United Drug Company itself is a perfect case in point. The last listing application was dated May 15, 1920, and contained an earnings statement and balance sheet for the quarter ended March 31, only 45 days before. It is now twelve weeks since May 15, but the earnings for the first quarter of 1921 are still to be made public.

It is at least possible that if last May the stockholders had been advised of the company's sales, profits, and financial position, some of the more alert and intelligent among them might have sensed danger ahead and acted accordingly.

## BRIEF HISTORY OF THE ENTERPRISE

Leaving the field of conjecture, it is time to consult the company's financial records for a more solid basis on which to rest our analysis of its present position. Handicapped as we are in that they reach no farther than Dec. 21, 1920, they may yet be found to shed some light upon subsequent developments.

The business was originated in 1902 by forty retail druggists, headed by Louis K. Liggett, as a co-operative proposition for manufacturing and dealing in various products usually sold in drug stores. From the first, therefore, the stockholders have been chiefly druggists owning so-called "Rexall" stores, who handled the company's merchandise. At the present time there are 8,000 such stockholder agents, while the total number of stockholders was last December unofficially placed at 16,600. In addition to manufacturing and distributing goods to retailers, the company also operates retail stores of its own, known as Liggett Drug Stores. In 1916, United Drug merged with the

Riker-Hegeman-Jaynes interests, increasing the number of its retail stores to 145. At the end of 1920, 226 stores were in operation.

Our graphs present a picture of the growth of the number of stores, total sales, net profits (before and after taxes) for the six years 1915–1920 inclusive. We also separate the sales of the retail and wholesale departments. It should be pointed out here that the annual reports all state earnings *before* allowance for taxes, which are deducted from surplus in the next year's statement. The result has been undoubtedly to give many people an impression of larger net profits than were actually realized. We have revised the income accounts to allow for war taxes, and have estimated the deduction for 1920.

In order further to picture the progress of normal earnings, apart from accidental charges or credits to income, we have eliminated from the statement for 1919 the profit of about $1,000,000 realized on the sale of Vivaudou, the perfume subsidiary, and also from the report of 1920 the loss of $687,000 written off for depreciation of inventories.

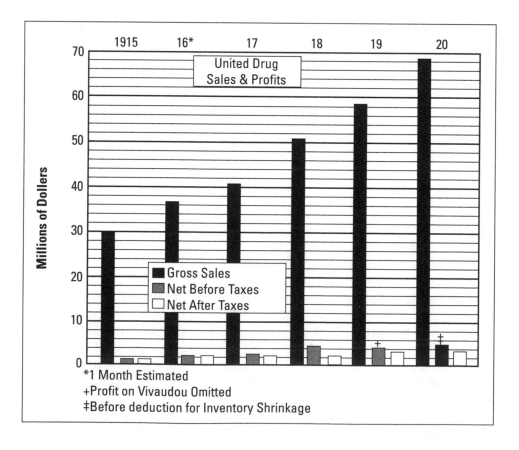

To reduce the profits to a proper per share basis, we have treated all the second preferred as the equivalent of common stock from the very beginning, as in fact it has practically all been converted into common. When the figures are thus recast so as to give an insight into the real performance of the company, we are struck by the exceedingly moderate earnings shown by the common stock. The 1920 profits, before inventory shrinkage, were the largest on record, and yet were only slightly above the 8% dividend rate established early in the year. The earnings for 1920 are referred to by Mr. Liggett as about $14.28 per share, but in reality were only $9 per share, after allowing for taxes and excluding the Vivaudou profit—properly a credit direct to surplus.

Taken in conjunction with the fact that the tangible asset value of the stock was but $40 per share, it is clear that the profits of $9 were far from justifying the high price of $175 touched by the issue in 1919.

## BALANCE SHEET ITEMS

Table I traces the development of the chief balance sheet accounts from 1916 through 1920. In the first three years we note that fixed assets were increased but moderately, financed through a corresponding small expansion in capitalization. Inventories, however, grew from $8,000,000 to $14,000,000 or 75% against a 40% increase in sales. Practically all this $6,000,000 addition to inventory was financed by the expansion of current liabilities. In 1919, the company sold $7,500,000 of preferred stock, increased its surplus by $1,600,000, and realized $700,000 on the sale of the intangible assets of Vivaudou. It also reduced its inventories slightly, despite a 14% addition to sales. These operations gave it a cash fund of $10,000,000 of which $3,000,000 was expended on new plants, and the balance of current assets—excluding inventory position. It ended 1919, therefore, in excellent financial condition.

In 1920, however, we witness a complete reversal of the tendency toward liquid strength exhibited the previous year. During the next twelve months fixed assets were expanded over $11,000,000 and inventories more than $9,000,000. Permanent capital raised, however, totalled only $2,400,000. The result was inevitably a tremendous increase in floating indebtedness, and the balance sheet shows notes payable of $20,790,000, against none in the previous report. Stated differently, whereas in 1919 the company had a balance of current assets—excluding inventories—over current liabilities of $3,100,000, in 1920 this figure was transformed into a deficit of $14,700,000.

The wisdom of separating inventories from the current assets in analyzing a company's position has been taught the investor by many hard experiences in recent months. In fact the basic difficulty with industrials as a whole may be summed up in the statement that *their inventories had ceased to be current assets.*

The financial condition revealed in the 1920 balance sheet called imperatively for new capital, and hence in June of this year, United Drug sold $15,000,000 of twenty year convertible 8% debentures. The cash thus received has undoubtedly placed the company in a much sounder liquid asset position.

## LIGGETT'S INTERNATIONAL

An event of first importance during 1920, was the acquisition of Boot's Pure Drug Co. stock of England and the merger of this enterprise with the British and Canadian subsidiaries of United Drug. The new combination started with annual gross sales of $37,000,000 of which $32,000,000 was contributed by the Boot's stores.

By thus adding over 50% to the business under its control, United Drug expects to and undoubtedly will effect important savings in overhead and operations. This was indeed a striking achievement of Mr. Liggett's, but we must not forget that corporations, like individuals, rarely acquire something for nothing. The price paid for the Boot's enterprise was apparently $22,000,000 of which $12,750,000 is in preferred stock (apparently 6%) of the English company. The capitalization of the new enterprise is certainly topheavy, since the preferred stock aggregates $20,500,000, against only $7,000,000 of common stock. Of the latter, $2,000,000 is called class B, has sole voting power, and is all owned by United Drug. The $5,000,000 of class A non-voting stock was offered to the public.

The net earnings, after preferred dividends but *before* British income tax, were estimated at $1,000,000, of which $290,000 would accrue to United Drug. But to obtain this moderate income, United Drug guaranteed the 8% dividend on $7,500,000 of Liggett's International preferred—thus assuming a contingent liability of $600,000 per annum. Even more, in order to persuade United Drug preferred stockholders to invest in the new International issue, those who subscribed were offered the right to exchange their present holdings, par for par, for additional guaranteed 8% stock. Hence, if all the preferred stock had been so exchanged, United Drug would now have substituted a yearly fixed charge of $1,200,000 for an optional preferred dividend payment of $1,050,000.

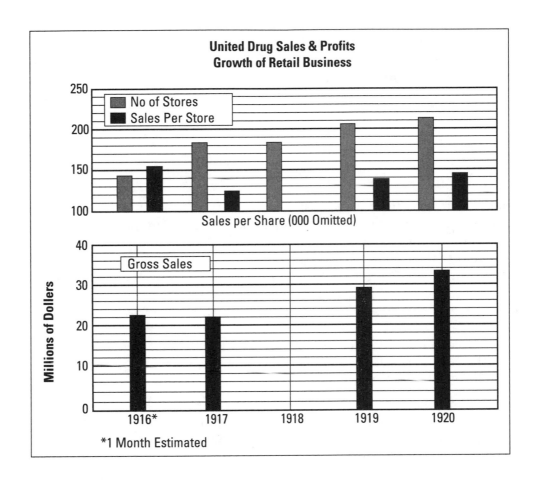

No figures have been published as to the amount of United Drug first preferred exchanged for the International preferred, so we do not know what is the company's liability on account of the guaranteed dividends. It is clear that the control of the Boot's Company must have been of great value in order to justify the assumption of a possible annual obligation of $1,800,000 to acquire it. This deal was effected on the eve of world-wide deflation, and whether all its results will be satisfactory is very much of a moot question.

The $15,000,000 bond issue referred to above has greatly added to the fixed obligations of the company. In addition to interest of $1,200,000 the first year, the company must pay $750,000 annually as a sinking fund. Furthermore it must maintain its current assets at 125% of current liabilities, including the bonds, failing which common dividends must be suspended until the required ratio is restored. On Dec. 31 last, current assets were $34,200,000 or only 135% of the current liabilities, which amounted to $25,370,000. If, therefore, the value of the inventories is reduced by only $2,500,000 (about 11%) the working capital would fall below the required percentage and common dividends would have to be deferred.

## CONCLUSION

United Drug has been a successful enterprise, conducted on sound principles, and enjoying very able leadership. But it started with practically no tangible assets behind the common stock; and while the earnings have been satisfactory, they have at no time compared with the war record of many other industrials. Yet, though denied the extreme benefits of inflation, United Drug has not escaped its ill effects. Since the end of 1919, its position has been greatly weakened by a number of unfavorable circumstances:

1.  Its plant account and inventory have both expanded tremendously at the peak of costs, threatening severe losses in marking them down to a deflated valuation.
2.  In floating its new bond issue the company has saddled itself with heavy interest and sinking fund requirements, and a working capital agreement which may seriously jeopardize the common dividend.
3.  It has rendered its future still more difficult by indefinitely guaranteed 8% dividends on a large amount of Liggett International preferred.
4.  Its business during the first half of 1921 was smaller in volume and no doubt much poorer in profits than in the previous year.

With the most recent figures more than seven months old, it seems rash to hazard an opinion on prospects and stock values. Yet, the writer believes that the facts set forth above make the maintenance of common dividends very questionable. Further than that, with the uncertain, but potentially heavy losses facing the company in inventory shrinkage, and with a dubious factor marketwise in President Liggett's trusteeship, the stock holds forth very few attractions even at its present low price of 53.

## UNITED DRUG CO. COMPARISONS

### (000 OMITTED)

### TABLE I

EARNINGS, DIVIDENDS AND PRICE RANGE, 1915–20.

| Year | Net after taxes | Preferred dividends | Balance for common | ¶Earned or common per share | Dividend paid on common | Price Range High | Low |
|---|---|---|---|---|---|---|---|
| 1915 | 1,606,000 | 525,000 | 1,081,000 | $8.71 | | | |
| *1916 | 2,198,000 | 525,000 | 1,473,000 | 5.05 | | 90 | 72 |
| 1917 | 2,817,000 | 525,000 | 2,292,000 | 7.86 | $3.75 | 80 | 64 |
| 1918 | 2,507,000 | 525,000 | 1,982,000 | 6.79 | 6.00 | $90^7/_8$ | 69 |
| *1919 | 3,896,000 | 700,000 | 2,696,000 | 9.00 | 7.50 | $175^1/_8$ | $90^1/_2$ |
| *1920 | 3,981,000 | 1,100,000 | 2,876,000 | 9.51 | 7.75 | 148 | 91 |
| 1921 (to date) | | | | | †8.00 | 106 | $52^3/_4$ |

\* Profit on Vivaudou omitted.
¶ See text.
† Annual rate.

### TABLE II

DEVELOPMENT OF BALANCE SHEET ITEMS, 1915–1920.

| Year | Inventory | % Sales | *Other current assets net | Fixed assets less reserves | Capitalization | *Surplus |
|---|---|---|---|---|---|---|
| 1915 | 5,509 | 18.3% | 229 | | | |
| 1916 | 8,074 | 22.2 | 1,226 | 6,079 | 37,464 | 1,410 |
| 1917 | 10,593 | 26.2 | Def.   887 | 7,332 | 38,149 | 2,385 |
| 1918 | 14,119 | 27.7 | Def.  3,927 | 7,257 | 38,184 | 2,762 |
| 1919 | 13,978 | 23.9 | 3,097 | 10,392 | 45,878 | 4,381 |
| 1920 | 23,116 | 33.8 | Def. 14,776 | 21,410 | 48,297 | 4,245 |

\* Adjusted for tax reserve.

# 19

# SPECULATIVE OPPORTUNITIES IN RAILROAD STOCKS

*New Conditions Affecting Railroad Values—An Attempt to Estimate Future Earning Power—Detailed Discussion of Six Issues*

The purpose of this article is to discuss a number of railroad issues which have good speculative possibilities, i.e., which under favorable conditions may increase substantially in market price. Our attention must therefore be confined to the low-priced issues, because—as is well known—they are subject to much wider fluctuations proportionately than the standard shares. To use a ready example, it would be by no means impossible for M. K. & T. new common to advance from 8 to 16 in a good rail market; but a corresponding doubling in the price of Union Pacific (from 120 to 240) is practically out of the question. In connection with the issues treated, we must inquire, first, "What are the factors which will contribute most directly to an increase in value?," and second, "What are the prospects of these factors being realized in the near future?"

But in order to judge intelligently of the position of the individual companies, it is essential that the reader have some idea of the very extraordinary present status of the railroads as a whole. The developments of the past few years have injected into the country's transportation system a new speculative feature of the greatest importance. For, in determining the prosperity of any one road the emphasis has been transferred from capitalization (a *fixed* element) to operating costs (a distinctly *variable* element). The test of strength has come to lie in a highly uncertain factor, and hence the status of the carriers as a class has grown essentially speculative.

Theoretical as all this may sound, it has so vital a bearing upon the future of the low-priced rails that some elaboration of the idea is necessary. Some two years ago, John E. Oldham once vice-president of the Investment Banker's Association, published a treatise entitled "A Comprehensive Plan for Railroad Consolidations," which included a study of the position of railway credit before Federal control. It was here pointed out that the distinction between the strong and the weak systems lay chiefly in their relative interest charges. In character of traffic, rates, and operating costs the two groups of carriers showed very similar results. By taking the so-called Test Period as a basis (July 1, 1914, to June 30, 1917), it appeared that while in the case of the strong roads only 11.5% of gross receipts were required for interest and other charges, the corresponding figure for the weak roads was almost double, or 22.2%. This latter amount represented nearly four-fifths of the net earnings of these systems, so that the small margin remaining was not sufficient to permit dividends on the stocks, or even to assure the safety of the bonds.

Hence the poor credit of second-grade roads was found to arise primarily from over-capitalization, in particular, from too large a proportion of bonded debt to gross revenues. But the enormous expansion of both receipts and expenses in recent years has greatly reduced the relative importance of the fixed charges. For, in 1920 interest requirements consumed only 7.7% of revenues, as against 11.7% four years previously. Given a normal operating ratio, any road would now have no difficulty in meeting its interest charges, and almost all would be earning substantial amounts on their stocks.

## OPERATING COSTS NOW THE RULING FACTOR

*The primary requisite of a prosperous railroad is therefore no longer conservative capitalization, but rather operating economy.* The extraordinary variations in the operating ratio since 1917 stand out most prominently when contrasted with its stability in previous years. (By operating ratio is meant the percentage of gross revenues consumed by all working expenses other than taxes.) From

1908 to 1917 this ratio was never more than 73% or less than $65\frac{1}{2}\%$; in five years the figure stood between 70% and 71%. But in 1918 it jumped to 81.4%, in 1919 to 85.1%, and in 1920 it reached the incredible figure of 94.5%. In that year, after making further deductions for taxes and equipment rentals, only 1% of the total receipts remained for interest and other charge—to say nothing of dividends. In 1921, however, another wide swing was registered in the opposite direction, the operating ratio having been reduced probably to about 84%.

The effect of such fluctuations upon the exhibit of any individual road is nothing short of magical. Take Rock Island as an example. A reduction of 10% in its operating ratio would mean an annual saving of about $14,000,000 (based on 1920 gross), equivalent to over $18 per share of common stock. Hence with revenues on their present scale, even a moderate change in the rate of expenses will profoundly affect the position of railroad stocks.

Given this kaleidoscopic background of the railroad situation, how shall we go about judging the position of the various low-priced shares? The difficulty lies evidently in finding some definite basis for an estimate of future earning power. The results of the pre-control days are certainly too

## TABLE I

SIX SELECTED LOW-PRICED RAILROAD ISSUES
ESTIMATED FUTURE EARNING POWER

| Road | Estimated Gross Revenues | Balance After Taxes (20% of Gross) | Equipment Rentals, etc. (Net) (Est.) | Interest and Other Deduction (Net) (1920 figures) | Preferred Dividends | Balance for Common | Per Share | Present Prices | % Earned on Present Prices |
|---|---|---|---|---|---|---|---|---|---|
| St. Louis Southwestern | $24,800,000 | $4,960,000 | | $2,140,000 | $1,000,000 | $1,820,000 | $11.08 | 21 | 52.4% |
| Pere Marquette | 32,300,000 | 6,460,000 | $1,500,000 | 2,097,000 | 1,072,000 | 1,791,000 | 3.98 | 20 | 19.4% |
| Rock Island | 113,000,000 | 22,600,000 | 3,500,000 | 10,502,000 | 3,640,000 | 4,948,000 | 6.65 | 31 | 21.4% |
| Chic. & East. III | 24,720,000 | 4,944,000 | 6,300,000 | 2,327,000 | 1,323,000 | 1,594,000 | 6.60 | $14\frac{1}{2}$ | 45.5% |
| | | | | | Balance for Preferred | | | | |
| M. K. & T | 58,400,000 | 11,680,000 | 1,400,000 | 7,793,000 | $2,493,000 | | *10.17 | *$25\frac{1}{2}$ Pfd. 24 | *40.0% †24.2% |
| Toledo, St. Louis & West'n | 9,400,000 | 1,880,000 | 500,000 | 463,000 | 917,000 | | †9.17 | Com. 14 | |

* Per share of Preferred.  † Per unit of one share Preferred and one share Common.

remote to be of much help under the present greatly changed conditions. On the other hand, the exhibit of the last four years have been so dominated by the distorting effects of Government operation as to make it a very questionable guide to future performance. The 1921 figures, of course, deserve careful attention; but in the present state of flux they can hardly be accepted as conclusive.

The facts at hand being thus insufficient for our needs, we are driven to supplement them with an admixture of theory. The future earning power of the carriers must be estimated—"guessed at" is probably the more accurate term—in accordance with some arbitrary principles. The two uncertain elements involved are the gross receipts and the operating costs—the former depending on both volume and rates the latter on wages and material prices.

In preparing the appended tabulation of expected normal earning power, the total revenues have been taken at 80% of the 1920 figures, while the net earnings, after taxes, are assumed to equal 20% of the gross. Neither of these percentages can be justified on mathematical grounds, but they represent the writer's best judgment on a very uncertain subject. The estimate of revenues is equivalent to a decline of about 12% from the 1921 totals, and at the same time operating costs are expected to be reduced far more radically.

After a careful study of the entire low-priced railroad lists, six issues have been selected as appearing to have the best speculative possibilities. The position of these companies is analyzed in Table I on the basis of theoretical future earning power, and in Table II on the basis of the actual operating results of the year ended November 30, 1921. In both cases the net fixed charges are taken from the 1920 reports, and hence are likely to be somewhat understated. The six issues chosen will now be discussed in the order of preference.

1. ST. LOUIS SOUTHWESTERN.—This common stock makes by far the best statistical exhibit in the entire railroad list. Its actual earnings for the past year were no less than $9.50 per share, or about 45% of the present price. The estimated future earnings are even larger, and, if realized, would exceed 50% of the current quotation of 21.

   This road also made an excellent showing in 1920, having earned $8.75 per share without reference to the Federal Guaranty. The latter result is the more noteworthy when it is considered that the company had expended over 40% of its revenues for maintenance. In the first ten months of 1921 this percentage was reduced to 35%, the saving in upkeep going to offset a loss of 20% in gross receipts. While the current maintenance figures are therefore a little low, it can hardly be asserted that the property is being skimped.

Those who remember the "Cotton Belt" as a struggling little system, its general reputation perhaps not of the best, may wonder at the reason for its sudden rise to prosperity. The primary factor has been an extraordinary growth in revenue, which expanded from $10,627,000 in 1915 to $31,020,000 in 1920—practically threefold. (In the same period the receipts of all the lines were a little more than doubled.) By far the greater part of this increase is due to heavier traffic, the higher rates having played a minor role.

The chief question in regard to St. Louis Southwestern is therefore whether it can retain the greater part of its increased business. Added point is given to this query by the fact that the decline in its gross last year has already been more substantial than the average. Yet, even allowing for a greater shrinkage in future traffic than is provided for in our tabular estimate, the Cotton Belt should still possess sufficient earning power to justify a higher price than 21 for its common stock.

2. MISSOURI, KANSAS & TEXAS NEW PREFERRED.—The prospects of the reorganized Katy were discussed in detail by the writer in a recent issue of The Magazine of Wall Street. While its very low price makes the new common decidedly attractive as a pure speculation, the 7% preferred has, of course, far more intrinsic merit. Its theoretical earning power is given in Table I as $10 per share, while the actual earnings last year were equivalent to about $7.90 per share. The recent exhibit would

## TABLE II

EARNINGS FOR THE YEAR ENDED NOV. 30, 1921†

| Road | Gross Revenues | Net after Rents | Maintenance Ratio | Balance for Common Stock | Per Share | % of Market Price |
|---|---|---|---|---|---|---|
| St. Louis Southwestern | $25,604,000 | $4,660,000 | 35.0% | $1,520,000 | $9.50 | 45.2% |
| Pere Marquette | 38,619,000 | 5,225,000 | 33.2% | 2,056,000 | 4.56 | 22.8% |
| Rock Island | 141,048,000 | 15,810,000 | 35.5% | 1,668,000 | 2.25 | 7.2% |
| Chic. & East Ill. | 28,171,000 | 2,447,000 | 42.8% | Deficit | | |
| M. K. T. | 65,035,000 | 9,629,000 | 37.0% | *1,936,000 | *7.90 | *31.0% |
| Toledo, S. L. & Western | 9,729,000 | 1,558,000 | 36.7% | *1,095,000 | ‡10.95 | ‡28.8% |

† See Text for Source of Figures.
* Preferred Stocks.
‡ Per Unit of one share Preferred and one share Common.

have been still better, were it not for the abnormal maintenance expenditures that always accompany a receivership.

Under ordinary circumstances a railroad common stock selling at 8 would seem to have better speculative possibilities than a preferred issue at $25^1/_5$. But M. K. & T. new preferred has three special points in its favor. The first is its 7% rate—as against 4% to 6% for most other railroad preferred stocks. This no doubt gives the preferred shares a claim on all the earnings that will be distributable for many years. Secondly, this issue will ultimately be cumulative, a feature which will greatly strengthen its position. And finally, there will be only one-third as many preferred as common shares, so that the entire senior issue is now selling in the market for no more than the entire junior issue. Because of these considerations, the writer believes that Katy preferred, in addition to representing a more conservative commitment, is likely to double in price almost as soon as the common.

3. TOLEDO, ST. LOUIS & WESTERN (CLOVER LEAF).—As this article is written, the final details are being wound up of a protracted litigation, which has kept the property under the cloud of receivership for many years. The matter under dispute was the validity of $11,527,000 collateral trust 4% bonds, issued to acquire Chicago & Alton stock. Under the settlement recently arranged, all of these bonds are to be cancelled, in return for a cash payment of $1,130,000 and various amounts of Alton and Clover Leaf stocks. To provide these securities the stockholders of the Toledo, St. Louis & Western will be required to contribute 10% of their holdings, against which they will receive scrip.

The elimination of these collateral trust bonds will cut the Clover Leaf's interest charges almost in two. Taken in conjunction with the recent excellent showing of the road, this development will result in a very substantial earning power for the stock. At present prices both the preferred and common issues offer separate advantages, and in buying into this situation it would probably be wise to acquire equal amounts of the two classes. A combination of one share each of common and preferred (4% non-cumulative) will cost only $38, and will give the investor a fixed interest in future earnings estimated at over $9, regardless of how they are ultimately divided between the two issues. The actual earnings the first year appear to have been nearly $11 on such a combination.

Special allowance must be made for the 10% reduction in holdings provided by the pending settlement, and also for a probable slight increase in fixed charges because of the cash payment to be made by the road. Nevertheless, the exhibit—both actual and potential—is extremely favorable, and would seem to justify substantially higher prices for both issues after the receivership is finally lifted.

4. PERE MARQUETTE.—This road was reorganized in 1917 with a greatly reduced bonded debt, and its record of earnings since then has been much better than the average. In 1919 it actually returned more than $9 per share on the common. It will be seen that the income available for dividends last year (Table II) was somewhat larger than our estimate of future earnings (Table I). The strong current exhibit is in some measure due to a reduction of maintenance charges to but 33.2% of gross—a figure which looks insufficient. The small sums expended on upkeep in 1921 may be explained as a reaction from the overliberal policy of the year before.

   There are two classes of 5% cumulative preferred stock ahead of the common. On the prior issue dividends have been paid regularly from the start. A dividend of 10% has just been paid on the second preferred, leaving 5% additional still accumulated up to January 1, 1922. If the road is able to continue its present showing, it should have no difficulty bringing its preferred payments up to date in a short time, after which the common may be in line for a small disbursement.

5. ROCK ISLAND.—The chairman of the Board recently announced that Rock Island closed 1921 with about $3 per share earned on the common. The figures for the twelve months ended November 30 show only $2.25 earned on the junior shares. These are based on the I. C. C. reports for gross and net, using the 1920 items of interest and other charges and credits. It should be pointed out in connection with all these figures that the totals of the monthly statements are often subject to rather substantial adjustments in the complete annual reports.

   While Table II shows only 7% actually earned on the present market price. Chairman Hayden's estimate is equivalent to nearly 10%. Furthermore, our estimate of future earnings is over $6.50 per share. Rock Island serves a rapidly growing territory, as is shown by the fact that its gross receipts were maintained in 1921 at very close to the 1920 record figure. The preferred dividends have been paid regularly from the outset, but the company suffers from the lack of an adequate medium for future financing. If this obstacle is removed, Rock Island common should eventually grow much more valuable.

6. CHICAGO & EASTERN ILLINOIS.—This is the youngest full-fledged member of the Reorganization Lodge, its final degree having just been awarded. The engineers who examined the property for the bankers

estimated the normal future balance available for interest charges at $5,300,000. This corresponds closely with the figure arrived at in Table I. On this basis the road should earn $6.60 per share of common stock, or 45% of its current price. The actual results in 1921, however, were very disappointing, as only a nominal balance was shown over interest charges. This unexpectedly poor exhibit was caused in good measure by the abnormally heavy maintenance outlay, which consumed no less than $45^1/_2$% of gross. There was also a peculiar shrinkage in the credit for equipment and joint facilities rentals. In 1920 the company had realized about $1,667,000 net from these sources, but last year this extra income well nigh disappeared.

Considering the low price of C. & E. I. common, the speculator may well afford to ignore the mediocre performance of last year, and place his reliance on lower operating costs in the future.

## APOLOGIA

Because of the wide range of the subject under discussion, it has been necessary to omit many details considered in arriving at the conclusions stated. Despite the great amount of time and care expended in this study, the recommendations made can be set forth only in tentative and undogmatic fashion. For the reader no doubt realizes to what extent more or less arbitrary estimates have unavoidably entered into these calculations. But, after all, judgment and not mathematical precision is the basis of all speculation, and it must not be forgotten that the opportunities herein described are primarily for the speculator.

# 20

# ARITHMETIC AND STOCK VALUES

*Capitalization Structure as Affecting
Earning Power—Magical Results of
a Little Slight-of-Hand—Owning
a Corporation on Margin*

*NOTE.—The influence of capitalization structure upon the earning power of common stocks is extremely important, but little understood. This article shows through actual examples how changes in the proportion of common stock to preferred will vitally affect the earnings per share. The application of this principle to certain issues has had a striking effect upon their market price.*

In a recent issue of THE MAGAZINE OF WALL STREET, one of the leading articles was devoted to a comparison of a number of listed common stocks from the standpoint of the percentage of current earnings upon their market price. It was pointed out very properly that in the last analysis earning power must always be the chief criterion of stock values—exceeding in importance asset backing, financial condition, and even dividend return. For it is the average rate of earnings which determines the real value of the physical assets, which weakens or strengthens the cash position, and which finally must control the dividend policy.

The study of corporation earnings as related to security values involves certain elements which usually receive slight consideration, yet which are not only interesting in theory, but often of great practical importance. Unless properly interpreted, a comparative table of earnings per share of common stock may result at times in quite misleading conclusions. For some of the companies showing the largest profits on their common may at the same time be earning a relatively small percentage of their total capitalization.

## WHAT IS CONSERVATIVE CAPITALIZATION?

In this article, capitalization is always measured by market value. (Par values are just as irrelevant here as the Prohibition Amendment. In fact, the removal of the par value is growing as customary among stocks as that of the appendix

JULIUS KAYSER & CO.

| | Old Capitalization | | | New Capitalization | | |
|---|---|---|---|---|---|---|
| | No. Shares | *Price | Total Value | No. Shares | *Price | Total Value |
| Preferred | 16,400 | 120 | $2,000,000 | 66,100 | 95 | $6,300,000 |
| Common | 60,100 | 100 | 6,600,000 | 115,000 | 20 | 2,300,000 |
| Total | | | $8,600,000 | | | $8,600,000 |
| Net Earnings (Average) | | | $1,500,000 | $1,500,000 | | |
| Per Cent of Total Capital | | | 17.4% | | | 17.4% |
| Balance for Common | | | $1,370,000 | | | $971,000 |
| Per Cent of Market Price | | | 20.8% | | | 42.2% |

* Price at Date of Recapitalization.

NORTH AMERICAN CO.

| | Old Capitalization | | | New Capitalization | | |
|---|---|---|---|---|---|---|
| | No. Shares | *Price | Total Value | No. Shares | *Price | Total Value |
| Preferred | | | | 300,000 | 32$\frac{1}{2}$ | $9,750,000 |
| Common | 300,000 | 65 | $19,500,000 | 300,000 | 32$\frac{1}{2}$ | 9,750,000 |
| Total | | | $19,500,000 | | | $19,500,000 |
| Net Earnings After Depreciation (Year Ended July 31, 1921) | | | $3,000,000 | | | $3,000,000 |
| Per Cent of Total Capital | | | 15.2% | | | 15.2% |
| Balance for Common | | | $3,000,000 | | | $2,100,000 |
| Per Cent of Market Price | | | 15.2% | | | 21.5% |

* Price at Date of Recapitalization.

among humans—and for the same reason, namely that it is of no earthly use and often causes grave annoyance.) For reasons that may soon appear clearer, the term "conservative" is usually applied to a capitalization structure wherein the amount of common stock represents a large percentage of the total. Conversely, it will be convenient to say that the smaller the ratio of common to preferred stock and bonds, the more "speculatively" is the company capitalized.

We are now ready for concrete examples. White Motor and Mack Truck naturally invite comparison, since both are leaders in the motor-truck industry and are fairly similar in size and market quotation. Taking the most recent estimates of 1922 profits, the two common stocks would size up as follows:

|  | Current Price Per Share | Current Earnings Per Share | Ratio of Earnings to Market Price |
|---|---|---|---|
| Mack Truck | 58 | $9 | $15\frac{1}{2}\%$ |
| White Motor | 50 | 7 | 14% |

On this basis, Mack would appear to be selling about 10% too low as compared with White, and therefore to have greater intrinsic merit at present prices. But let us consider these companies from another and more fundamental standpoint. How do their earnings compare with their total capital? Here is a different set of figures:

|  | Total Capitalization (M'ket Value) | Net Profits 1922 (est.) | Current Earnings on Total Capital |
|---|---|---|---|
| Mack Truck | $31,500,000 | $3,700,000 | 11.70% |
| White Motor | 25,000,000 | 3,500,000 | 14.00% |

The result of the second comparison directly contradicts that of the first. The company with the larger earning power on its common stock has a decidedly smaller earning power on its total capital. If on the first basis, Mack Truck appears to be selling 10% too low, on the second it would seem with greater reason to be selling 20% too high.

This paradox has a simple explanation. White Motors has only one kind of stock, but Mack Truck's capital is divided about evenly between 7% preferred (First and Second) and common. The effect of this arrangement is worked out in detail in the table. Since half of Mack's capital is restricted to a 7% dividend, the earnings above the dividend go to swell the percentage available for the common. White Motor, however, must evidently earn the same proportion on its common stock as it does on its total capital, because the two are identical. If White were to split up its capitalization on the same basis as Mack, then—as our table shows—instead of earning 14% on its common, this figure would be automatically raised to 20%.

## THE CASE OF AMERICAN ICE

The smaller the ratio of common stock to total capital, the less dependable are the profits per share as an index of the company's real earning power. To illustrate this point by an important example, in the table we analyze the 1921 results of the American Ice Co. A striking contrast is afforded by the inclusion of the corresponding figures of All America Cables, which sells at about the same price. (This is a listed issue of great merit, entirely neglected.) The cable company is readily seen to have a smaller capitalization and much larger earnings. Nevertheless American Ice common earned 18% on its present price, while All America shows but 12$^1$/$_2$%. The excellent exhibit of American Ice common is found, upon analysis, to be due not so much to extraordinary prosperity as to the fact that the common stock represents only 30% of the total capital. This means that whatever surplus is available above bond interest and preferred dividends is divided among a relatively small number of junior shares. Hence a very moderate increase in the percentage earned on the total capital results in a very substantial rise in the profits per share of common.

If All America Cables were anxious to mark up the earnings on its common stock, it would need only to exchange two-thirds of its present shares for new 7% preferred. In this way, as indicated in Table 2, it would achieve a capitalization structure similar to that of American Ice. Then, with the same earnings and the same total capital as before, it would be able to report earnings of 25% on its common stock, instead of 12$^1$/$_2$%.

A third example of our thesis is provided by a comparison of May Department Stores and Associated Dry Goods, as given in the table. Here again the company, which earns considerably more on its capitalization, shows a decidedly smaller percentage earned on its common stock. If May Department Stores had been capitalized on the same basis as Associated Dry Goods, it would have earned last year 21.9% on its common stock, against 16.6% for the other concern. Once more we observe that a simple transformation of common into preferred stock will suddenly double the apparent earning power of the junior issue.

At this point the reader well might ask: "If a little juggling of capitalization can work such wonders, why hasn't it been done?" The answer is that this very thing has been and is being done—both directly and indirectly.

The best example of a direct exchange of common for preferred stock, without trimmings and with the avowed purpose of marking up the earnings per share, is found in the case of North American Co. The directors here decided that the capitalization structure was too conservative, i.e. that too large a percentage of the total was in common stock, thus making too slow the annual increase in earnings per share. So in August, 1921, the company

---

## COMPARISON OF CAPITAL STRUCTURE

| | Mack Truck | | | White Motor Present Capitalization | | | White Motor Recapitalized on Basis of Mack Tk. | | |
|---|---|---|---|---|---|---|---|---|---|
| Capitalization: | No. Shares | Price | Total Value | No. Shares | Price | Total Value | No. Shares | Price | Total Value |
| First Preferred | 109,219 | 94 | $10,300,000 | | | | 250,000 | 50 | $12,500,000 |
| Second Preferred | 53,317 | 88 | 4,700,000 | | | | | | |
| Common | 283,109 | 58 | 16,500,000 | 500,000 | 50 | $25,000,000 | 250,000 | 50 | 12,500,000 |
| Total | | | $31,500,000 | | | $25,000,000 | | | $25,000,000 |
| Net Earnings, 1922 (Estimated) | | | $3,700,000 | | | $3,500,000 | | | $3,500,000 |
| Per Cent of Total Capital | | | 11.7% | | | 14.0% | | | 14.0% |
| Balance for Common | | | $2,562,000 | | | $3,500,000 | | | $2,500,000 |
| Per Cent on Market Price | | | 15.5% | | | 14.0% | | | 20.0% |

| | Ameican Ice | | | All Ameica Cables Present Capitalization | | | All America Cables Recapitalized on Basis of Amer. Ice | | |
|---|---|---|---|---|---|---|---|---|---|
| Capitalization: | No. Shares | Price | Total Value | No. Shares | Price | Total Value | No. Shares | Price | Total Value |
| Bonds | | | $5,569,000 | | | | | | |
| Preferred | 147,590 | 90 | 13,280,000 | | | | 180,000 | 100 | $18,000,000 |
| Common | 71,070 | 113 | 8,031,000 | 221,300 | $117\frac{1}{2}$ | $26,000,000 | 68,000 | $117\frac{1}{2}$ | 8,000,000 |
| Total | | | $26,900,000 | | | $26,000,000 | | | $26,000,000 |
| Net Earnings, 1921 | | | $2,769,000 | | | $3,256,000 | | | $3,256,000 |
| Per Cent on Total Capital | | | 10.3% | | | 12.5% | | | 12.5% |
| Balance for Common | | | $1,453,000 | | | $3,256,000 | | | $2,000,000 |
| Per Cent on Market Price | | | 18.1% | | | 12.5% | | | 25% |

| | Associated Dry Goods | | | May Department Stores Present Capitalization | | | May Department Stores Recapitalized on Basis of Assoc. Dry Goods | | |
|---|---|---|---|---|---|---|---|---|---|
| Capitalization: | No. Shares | Price | Total Value | No. Shares | Price | Total Value | No. Shares | Price | Total Value |
| First Preferred | 138,187 | 87 | $12,022,000 | 55,690 | 115 | $6,400,000 | 225,000 | 100 | $22,500,000 |
| Second Preferred | 67,250 | 90 | 6,053,000 | | | | | | |
| Common | 149,850 | 62 | 9,290,000 | 200,000 | 137 | 27,400,000 | 82,500 | 137 | 11,300,000 |
| Total | | | $27,365,000 | | | $33,800,000 | | | $33,800,000 |
| Net Earnings, 1921 | | | $2,836,000 | | | $4,053,000 | | | $4,053,000 |
| Per Cent on Total Capital | | | 10.4% | | | 12% | | | 12% |
| Balance for Common | | | $1,538,000 | | | $3,663,000 | | | $2,478,000 |
| Per Cent on Market Price | | | 16.6% | | | 13.4% | | | 21.9% |

issued one share of new 6% preferred stock and one share of new common, both par $50, in exchange for each share of old common, par $100.

This simple operation effected an immediate transformation in the exhibit of the company. The details are given in the table. Whereas the profits after depreciation for the year ended July, 1921, had been equivalent to 15.2% on the market price of the old common, the same earnings amounted to 21.5% on the corresponding price of the new common. More important still, the monthly increases in earnings were now made applicable to only 10 millions in market value of common, instead of 20 millions, as before; and so amounted to just twice as much per share. The result was a speedy and continuous advance in the price of the new stock. The preferred is now at 46 and the common at 100. Hence one share of each is together worth 146, against 65 for the old common at the time when the exchange was operative. And we have not considered the large additional value of subscription rights accorded in the interim.

A transaction similar in purpose and result, but more complicated in detail, was the recapitalization of Julius Kayser, the glove enterprise. The effect of this operation upon the position of the common is shown in the table. In this case the relative proportions of preferred and common were directly reversed. Whereas the company previously had about 2 millions preferred and 6.6 millions common, the new arrangement raised the preferred to 6.3 millions and reduced the common to 2.3 millions (initial market value).

This was undoubtedly a bold departure from accepted standards of conservative financing. On paper, however, it made the new common at 20 look far more attractive than the old at 100. For the same figure of average profits which gave an earning power of 20% to the old stock, worked out as 42% upon the market value of the new common. Without much trouble, therefore, the new shares have doubled in price; and at 46 they are still being recommended as among the most desirable of industrial common issues.

## INDIRECT METHODS

Where companies feel handicapped through having only one class of stock, they sometimes revise their capitalization through the payment of a large extra dividend in new preferred shares. Special distributions of this kind, amounting to 50%, have been made by American Zinc and by Virginia Iron Coal and Coke. Unfavorable market conditions directly following these operations make it difficult to judge to what extent the stockholders have benefited thereby.

A very interesting case of indirect capitalization is presented by American Steel Foundries. For many years this was the only one of the equipment companies without preferred stock. On this account, its large earnings during the war period did not show up as spectacularly as those of Baldwin or American Locomotive, and its stock ranged considerably lower. The situation was changed in 1919 through the acquisition of another large enterprise—Griffin Wheel Co.—by issuance of about 9 millions of new preferred stock. Since Griffin Wheel normally earned substantially more than the 7% dividend required by this preferred, its surplus profits now go to increase the earning power of American Steel Foundries common. The success of this transaction from a market standpoint is now becoming evident. Steel Foundries is keeping pace with the advance of the other equipment companies, whereas in the previous boom period it had lagged behind.

These concrete examples have been made so numerous in order to dispel a natural impression—namely that capitalization structure is primarily a theoretical conception, with remote practical significance. It must not be imagined, however, that the expedients described above can be applied indiscriminately to all companies, with unvarying success and without compensating disadvantages.

*In prosperous years* it is undeniably true that the smaller the proportion of common stock to total capital, the larger the earnings per share. The company with the most speculative capitalization makes the best showing. But when periods of depression bring a sharp shrinkage in profits, then the situation is reversed. Not only do the large earnings on such common stocks decline with alarming rapidity, but frequently the preferred dividend and even the bond interest is not covered, resulting in serious embarrassment. But the conservatively capitalized company has no problem of heavy fixed charges, and comes through hard times with far less difficulty.

The situation here has its direct counterpart in the stock market itself—among those who own their securities outright and those who carry them on margin. A rise in prices evidently brings a larger profit on the capital of the marginal trader than on that of the outright purchaser. But when prices break, the former's capital fades away just so much faster—and he has a debt to his broker to take care of, while the other man can sit tight and wait for the storm to blow over. In very analogous fashion, the common stock of a speculatively capitalized company represents *marginal* ownership of the enterprise. It will be found that in the major swings of the market, such issues usually fluctuate over a relatively wider range. They advance furthest in boom times, but suffer the greatest declines when prices break.

## AN IMPORTANT DISTINCTION

To what conclusions does this investigation lead? They might well appear contradictory and inconclusive. A simple readjustment of capitalization is found to produce dazzling effects upon the earnings exhibit, but analysis shows this stimulus to be entirely artificial. Yet if admittedly artificial is it necessarily meaningless, or even harmful? Like most general questions, this one must be answered by a distinction. There is such a thing as *over*-conservatism in capitalization, as well as *under*-conservatism. Concerns in a stable field of industry, normally exempt from wide fluctuation in earnings, are justified in having a reasonable part of their capital in the form of securities with fixed dividends or interest, so that the common stock may have the benefit of the profits which this capital regularly produces in excess of its annual cost. It has been considered quite proper, for example, that public utility enterprises should have by far the greater portion of their capitalization in senior securities—a financial policy which has often been carried to disastrous extremes. In the case of North American Co., however, the old common stock undoubtedly represented a much larger percentage of the total capital of the system than was usual, or probably necessary. Hence the recent readjustment may be characterized as a stroke of sound judgment; for while it substantially increased the earnings of the common shares, it did not expand the prior charges to an uncomfortable total. Similarly, American Steel Foundries was no doubt well justified in rearranging its capitalization to a basis comparable with that of the other equipment companies.

On the other hand, if the directors of White Motor were asked why they did not follow suit and recapitalize on the basis, say, of Mack Truck, they might plausibly point out that the absence of preferred dividend requirements stood the company in good stead during the trying times of 1920–1921. Hence White was able to continue its 8% ($4) common dividend, while Mack has yet to make its first cash payment on its junior shares.

Obviously there is more to this subject than can be presented in an article of this size. Scientific inquiry might determine what basis of capitalization is best adapted to various types of enterprises, so that the over-conservative might be readjusted with profit, and those too speculatively constituted might be avoided. In passing, the writer might express his opinion that the Five-and-Ten-Cent-Store companies, as a class, have not a sufficient percentage of preferred stock. Their remarkably stable record of earnings justifies a higher proportion of senior securities—which would mean of course correspondingly larger profits per share of common. From this point of view, the retirement of Woolworth preferred, just announced, while following conventionally accepted financial practice, might not prove truly beneficial to the common stockholders. One would imagine that the cash might more successfully be employed in the further expansion of that remarkable business. Undoubtedly Woolworth, Kresge, and similar issues, would have much better prospects of renewed substantial advances from their present high levels, if a good part of their common capitalization were transformed into preferred shares.

The analysis of security values is not an abstruse science. While in essence mathematical, it does not soar into the realms of calculus—in fact, it rarely gets as far as algebra. But, as the above discussion may illustrate, it does require a fair acquaintance with arithmetic.

# 21

# A TRUE TALK ON BOND YIELDS, OR

*What Every Small Investor
Should Know*

*A Financial Playlet
with a Meaning*

A Dialogue on Discounts between Mr. George Brokaw, Investment Dealer, and His Client, Mr. Henry Byer.

*Byer: Good morning, Mr. Brokaw. May I have a few minutes of your valuable time? I wonder if you've looked over that little list of mine and have any suggestions to make.*

Brokaw: Why yes. You know those Baltimore & Ohio 5s you're carrying—

*Byer: Well, aren't they perfectly good? I thought B. & O. is doing fine.*

Brokaw: Oh, they are a very fair bond; but I have a switch in mind for them by which you can increase your yield more than 1%, with exactly the same security.

*Byer: That sounds too good to be true. What's the secret?*

Brokaw: Simple enough. Just change your B. & O. 5s into the B. & O 4$\frac{1}{2}$s, secured by the same mortgage.

*Byer: That's strange; I didn't notice the $4\frac{1}{2}$s were selling so far below the 5s.*

*Brokaw:* They're not. They sell at 81. while the 5s sell at 83. But the $4\frac{1}{2}$s are due in 1933—less than 10 years—so their amortized yield works out at 7.30%, against only 6.05% for the 5s, which don't mature until 1995.

*Byer: So that's your brilliant idea! Well it's no good for me at all. It may be alright for the big institutions that buy bonds on your amortized yield basis. But I'm only a small investor and I've got to look at the coupon return. This discount business is largely bank. A fine game it would be for me to take $\frac{1}{2}$% less a year in the hope of getting a profit in 1933. In all probability I won't be holding the bonds by then. And anyway the 5s are just as likely as not to be selling at par or better in a few years. Some bond experts say long-term bonds are due for a big advance. With all due respect, Mr. Brokaw, that idea strikes me as the quintessence of tommyrot.*

*Brokaw:* Thanks for the compliment. But I'm not surprised to hear you talk like that. Ninety-nine per cent of the investors reason as you do, but they're all dead wrong. Are you willing to spend a few minutes to go into the matter in a logical way?

*Byer: I'm sure you could talk all day without selling me any such outlandish suggestion. Still your time is worth more than mine, and if you can afford to waste it, so can I. Proceed.*

*Brokaw:* You made an emphatic little speech just before, in which you rejected my idea with fine scorn. It will help a bit if you will let me restate your arguments. They might be put as follows:

1.  As a small investor, you can't afford to sacrifice your coupon return, in order to get a profit on your principal ten years from now.
2.  Many contingencies might arise that would lead you to dispose of your bonds before 1933, in which case the expected profit would be lost.
3.  In any event you hope to obtain just as great a rise in the price of your 5s during the next few years—or very probably an even larger appreciation.

Is that a fair statement of your case?

*Byer: Perfect*

*Brokaw:* Well let us examine these three contentions in order. First about your not being able to afford to take a smaller coupon return. If you were a widow living on your income, or a lifetenant of an estate, that might sound plausible. But you do not spend every cent you get. If I am not mistaken, you pester me pretty regularly to recommend attractive investments.

*Byer: Oh, that is a different story. Like every ambitious man, I'm trying to build up a little estate. That's just why I need as large an income as possible.*

*Brokaw:* But don't you see that the few dollars a year you forego by switching into these B. & O. $4\frac{1}{2}$s are not lost. They are being invested precisely like a regular savings-bank deposit—but at a much higher interest rate. Observe what the proposition really amounts to. On each bond you are giving up only $5.00 per year. The first four years are taken care of by the two points in cash you get back when you make the exchange. So your whole sacrifice of income amounts to about $30 per bond and for that investment you are sure to recover $170 in increased value of your principal. Don't you think you can afford to invest $5.00 per year for six years in order to get back $170 at the end of the sixth year?

*Byer: Of course I can, but it means tying up the whole bond investment for ten years—*

*Brokaw:* One thing at a time.

We were considering only your first objection—and that was that you couldn't afford to take $45.00 per bond per year instead of $50.00. If it paid well enough in the end, wouldn't you be glad to do it?

*Byer: Well, if you consider point one just by itself, I admit it is not a very strong objection.*

*Brokaw:* That's too half-hearted an admission. Is Objection 1 answered or is it not?

*Byer: All right, you win. It's answered.*

*Brokaw:* Now for your second argument. You are afraid that you might want to sell the bond before the due date in which case the lovely 17 points profit would go to someone else. But do you really think you must hold the bonds until 1933 in order to realize any part of the advance in principal value?

*Byer: Why, sure. Suppose I sold them in 1926, how do I know whether they would be higher or lower than 81. I've got to strike a fair average and assume they will be worth the same price as now.*

*Brokaw:* Well on your basis of figuring an investor must calculate that his bonds will stay at 81 until 1933 and then suddenly be worth par on the day of maturity. Whoever buys them in 1933 will make a mighty fine profit in an awfully short time.

*Byer: Oh, I suppose that when maturity gets fairly near—a few years away maybe— the bond begins to advance in anticipation. But you don't mean to tell me that every year the bond must rise two points. I've seen bonds go down, instead of up, even though maturity was coming closer.*

*Brokaw:* You know that the changes in the price of any individual issue depend on two factors—the approach of maturity, and a rise or fall in the rate of interest. The effect of the nearer due date might be offset by an advance in interest rates generally or by a deterioration in the investment qualities of the bond.

*Byer: Yes, and if that's so, what assurance have I of getting any appreciation of principal if I sell out a few years from now?*

*Brokaw:* No absolute assurance, but the odds are greatly in your favor. What risk there is, is common to all investments. In fact there is a much greater likelihood of loss if you kept your refunding 5s and had to sell them out say in 1927.

*Byer: How can you demonstrate that?*

*Brokaw:* Consider the possibilities. Here it is March, 1927, and you must dispose of your B. & O. $4\frac{1}{2}$s. Suppose they were still quoted at only 81, you would think you had given up that one-half per cent coupon return for three years entirely for nothing, wouldn't you?

*Byer: Of course I would.*

*Brokaw:* But let's see how your refunding 5s would probably be faring. If these $4\frac{1}{2}$s were selling at 81 in 1927, with but $5\frac{1}{2}$ years to run, that would mean a 8.95% yield. Is it likely the 5s would still be selling at 83, to yield only 6.05 per cent?

*Byer: It's possible, isn't it?*

*Brokaw:* But how about those institutions you mentioned at the beginning? Some of them hold millions of the refunding 5s. Don't you think they would hasten to switch into the $4\frac{1}{2}$s in order to be sure of obtaining par for their holdings in only six years? Do you imagine they are going to let a discrepancy like that exist?

*Byer: I suppose not.*

*Brokaw:* If these $4\frac{1}{2}$s sold down from a 7.30 per cent to an 8.95% basis the same conditions should certainly cause the 5s to decline from a 6.05% basis to, say, a 7.50 per cent. Do you know what their price would be then? Let's look at the yield book . . . . Why, they would be selling at 67. So you see if you only broke even on the $4\frac{1}{2}$s you would be much better off than having to sell out the 5s at a 15-point loss.

*Byer: That's alright, but suppose the bonds go up?*

*Brokaw:* Not so fast. You're starting on objection three. First, I want to make it absolutely clear that you get the benefit of the gradual amortization of the discount even if you sell the bonds prior to maturity. Let me show you a few figures from the yield book. Suppose you dispose of the $4\frac{1}{2}$s in only two years. Assume they are still selling on a 7.30% basis, and the 5s are still yielding 6.05%. What would the prices be? Here they are:

| | |
|---|---|
| B. & 0. 5s | $83\frac{1}{4}$ |
| B. & 0. $4\frac{1}{2}$s | 84 |

The $4\frac{1}{2}$s will have advanced 3 points, while the 5s (their maturity still being a long way off) will scarcely have moved. That means the $4\frac{1}{2}$s will have brought in $1\frac{1}{2}$% per year in appreciation in addition to the coupon—a total of $60 per year against only $51 on the 5s. So you see that extra 1.15% I am trying to present you with would be money in your pocket even if you held on for only two years.

*Byer: Funny, I never worked it out that way before.*

*Brokaw:* Going further, look at it from another point of view. Suppose at the end of two years the B. & O. $4\frac{1}{2}$s and 5s are selling on the same basis—and that is where they logically belong. A 6.15% yield for the $4\frac{1}{2}$s would mean a price of 90, while the 5s are still at 83. That would be a 9-point profit obtained at a cost of only one point in coupon return.

*Byer: Do you really think the $4\frac{1}{2}$s are ever likely to sell on the same basis as the 5s?*

*Brokaw:* Why not? Take a look at the bond list. Here are two issues in an exactly similar position as the B. & O.'s, both being secured by the same mortgage.

|                                      | Price | Yield  |
|--------------------------------------|-------|--------|
| New York Central, 4s, due 1989       | 81    | 4.98%  |
| New York Central 4s, due 1942        | 86    | 5.18%  |

Here the shorter term issue yields only .20% more than the long term, instead of 1.15%. Now look at two Southern Pacific bonds:

|                                          | Price  | Yield  |
|------------------------------------------|--------|--------|
| Southern Pacific collateral 4s, due 1949 | 82$\frac{1}{2}$ | 5.25%  |
| Southern Pacific (convertible) 4s, due 1929 | 92$\frac{1}{4}$ | 5.58%  |

The 1929 issue is no longer convertible; and since it is unsecured, it really ranks below the collateral 4s. Still there is much less difference in yield here than in the case of the B. & O. bods.

*Byer: That's rather a convincing exhibit.*

*Brokaw:* By the way, those Southern Pacific issues present practical proof of my contention that it is not necessary to wait until maturity to benefit from appreciation in the case of a bond bought at a discount. I just recently dug out these comparative figures.

|                            | Price May 1917 | Price August 1923 |
|----------------------------|----------------|-------------------|
| Southern Pacific 4s, 1929  | 82             | 92$\frac{1}{4}$   |
| Southern Pacific 4s, 1949  | 82             | 82$\frac{1}{2}$   |

You will observe that in the past six years the Convertible 4s have made up more than half of their original 18-point discount, and that is not due to any fall in interest rates or improvement in Southern Pacific credit, since the longer-term bond has advanced very little.

*Byer: Well, I think I had better surrender unconditionally on Count 2. I admit the B. & O. 4$\frac{1}{2}$s yield really 7.30% and not merely the 5.40% straight return—and also that I ought to get the benefit of the higher yield even if I sell out before maturity. But I still think I would be better off with my refunding 5s even with their 1% lower yield—because I expect a rise in long-term bond prices.*

*Brokaw:* In other words you think that while the 4$\frac{1}{2}$s are going to par because of their maturity, the 5s will go to par because of a drop in money rates.

*Byer: Yes, and what's more they will probably sell above par, which you certainly cannot expect the 4$\frac{1}{2}$s to do.*

*Brokaw:* Are you positive that the 5s will reach par in the next few years?

*Byer: Well, pretty nearly. I am convinced that the long-pull trend of bond prices is upward.*

*Brokaw:* Then why don't you act upon your convictions?

*Byer: What do you mean by that?*

*Brokaw:* If long-term issues are so certain to have a big advance, you have a wonderful opportunity to make a killing. All you have to do is to put up five of your bonds and I'll buy you $20,000 of B. & O. 5s or some similar issue. Then, when they go to par, you will have a $3,400 profit, which means you will about double your investment.

*Byer: Say, are you trying to rope me into speculating on margin?*

*Brokaw:* Not at all. Where there is no chance of loss there is no speculation.

*Byer: But of course there is some chance of loss.*

*Brokaw:* That is just what I was driving at. You say you are positive your B. & O. 5s are going to advance, but when it comes to a showdown it seems you are not quite so sure. After all, don't you think that if long-term bonds have so much better prospects than the medium maturities, the bond market would reflect this fact generally in lower yields for the former?

*Byer: That would be logical.*

*Brokaw:* But it isn't the case at all. Dominion of Canada 5s of 1931 sell higher than the 5s of 1952. M-K-T prior Lien 6s of 1928 yield less than the identically secured 4s of 1950. As I pointed out before, the short-term issues of New York Central and Southern Pacific sell on nearly the same basis as the distant maturities. These B. & O. $4\frac{1}{2}$s are the only issue in the whole market I think that yields 1% more than another bond with the same security.

*Byer: Then how do you account for the discrepancy?*

*Brokaw:* Who can say? One of the numerous accidents or anomalies that appear from time to time in the bond market, but which few investors ever take advantage of, because they are either too lazy or too stupid. Which do you prefer to be?

*Byer: Neither, if you don't mind. You go right ahead and make that switch for me before your words of wisdom wear away. Of all the true things you've said in the last fifteen minutes, the truest is this: Ninety-nine per cent of all investors reason as I did, and they are all dead wrong.*

# 22

# THE UNSCRAMBLING OF READING

*A Problem for the Stockholders—
Earning Power before and after
Segregation—Mysterious Aspects
of the Coal Properties*

In September 1913, the Government instituted its famous suit to dissolve the so-called Reading Combination, for the purpose, first, of divorcing the Central Railroad of New Jersey from the Philadelphia & Reading Ry., and secondly, of terminating the control exercised by these carriers over their anthracite coal subsidiaries. As this article is written—almost exactly ten years later—the stockholders of Reading Company are about to approve a segregation plan, which apparently marks the complete triumph of the Government's long campaign.

As is well known, the present Reading Co. is a holding company, owning all the stock of three main subsidiaries, which for convenience we shall term the Railway, the Coal, and the Iron properties. Under the readjustment plan, Reading Co. loses its Coal and its Iron interests, but retains the Railway line, with which it will be merged. The stock of the new Coal Company (which will also own Reading Iron) will be offered for subscription to present Reading preferred and common stockholders, at $4 per share—one new share for two old. But to assure separate ownership, stockholders must dispose of either their Railway or their Coal shares before July 1, 1926. Reading General 4% bonds—now joint obligations of the holding company and its coal subsidiary—will be exchanged $^2/_3$ for new Railway General $4^1/_2$s and $^1/_3$ for new First 5s of the Coal Co. Various other inter-company settlements are to be effected, which will bring a net inflow of $27,100,000 of cash assets into the Reading Co. treasury.

The Jersey Central stock now owned by Reading is to be trusteed pending ultimate sale. (The Lehigh & Wilkesbarre Coal shares held by Jersey Central have already been sold.)

Such, briefly summarized, are the provisions of the scheme designed to create four separate entities in place of a single interest. The subscription rights constitute a welcome bonus for every Reading stockholder, but they also present a definite problem. He cannot retain his interest in both the railroad and the coal properties; he must cast his lot finally with one enterprise or the other. As procrastination is our favorite weakness, the natural tendency will be to defer all action at least until the time comes to subscribe to the Coal stock—probably soon after Jan. 1 next. For this very reason may not a special advantage be gained from an earlier survey of the situation; so that if any course of action is thereby revealed as clearly expedient, it may be availed of before competition grows too keen.

Apart from this special question of choice between the Coal and Railroad shares, a wider field of analysis is presented by all the important Reading issues, at their new prices and under their new conditions. How safe and how attractive will be the Reading Railway $4^1/_2$s obtainable at 86, the Coal 5s at 93, the First and Second Preferred at about 32 (ex-rights), the Railway Common at 56, and the Coal Shares at 50? (These prices for Reading Preferred and Common, ex-rights, are obtained by substracting from their present quotations of 55 and 79 respectively the value of the subscription rights, currently selling on the N.Y. Curb at 23.) To answer all these questions we must first examine some of the financial details of the segregation, and then refer to the available data bearing upon earning power and asset values.

Let us wrestle first with the problem of the present stockholder. Which should he retain—the Railway stock at its present price of 56 (ex-rights) or the new Coal shares at 50? Various answers to this question are available. In Wall Street, the "Insiders" are generally understood to favor the Coal shares— which are supposed to possess remarkable possibilities. Before the recent five point advance in Reading Common, expert tapereaders were wont to declare that this issue has been reflecting distribution, while the rights to the Coal stock were being accumulated. These statements the writer sets forth without prejudice and without responsibility—the reader must take them for what they are worth.

A second source of appraisal is provided by the evidence submitted to the U. S. Court on January 30 last, regarding the proper division of liability for the present Reading General 4% bonds, as between the Railway and the Coal companies. The question there considered was fundamentally the same as is before us now—namely, the relative value of the two properties. The Reading officials recommended that the Coal company assume one-third and the Railway company two-thirds of the total liability, supporting the proposal by sworn affidavits to the effect that the assets behind the new bonds would be worth not less than $100,000,000 and $200,000,000 respectively; and also that the earnings available for interest should average at least $6,000,000 and $12,000,000 respectively.

## FROM VIEWPOINT OF RELATIVE VALUES

While the artful phrase "not less than" in these affidavits allows the imagination to conjure up visions of enormously greater values, the testimony specifically asserts that in the opinion of the president of each company the Railroad properties to be subject to the new mortgage are worth about twice those of the Coal company. Hence the figures deserve serious consideration from the standpoint at least of *relative* values.

In Table I, is worked out the estimated value of the Railway and the Coal Common stocks, using the above estimates as a basis and allowing for the non-mortgaged assets, not considered in this testimony. These estimates are subject to the limitations inherent in all property appraisals. It is interesting to note, nevertheless, that there is indicated an asset value of $103 per share for the Railway Common and only $59 per share for the Coal stock—in the former case 47 points and in the latter case only 9 points above their present quotation.

As far as this evidence is concerned, therefore, the Railway shares appear by far the cheaper. The reader may very properly remark that he would be more impressed by a comparison of the *earning power* of the two issues, as indicated by these affidavits. But definite as appear these estimated profits of $6,000,000 and $12,000,000 respectively, on examination they are found to be fatally ambiguous, because one cannot tell whether or not they allow for numerous items, such as income from unpledged property, depletion, income taxes, and sundry other deductions. Nor indeed should it be necessary to rely for our conception of the earning power of the Railway properties on any such vague estimate, made even by the President of Reading Company, when we have such a wealth of past and current specific data to draw upon. More than

## TABLE I

ASSET VALUE OF READING (RAILWAY) COMMON AND READING COAL STOCK (AS OF NOVEMBER 30, 1922)

### Based on Estimates Submitted to the U. S. Court

|  |  | Railway Co. | Coal Co. |
|---|---|---|---|
| Value of assets to be applicable to new mortgages |  | $200,000,000 | $100,000,000 |
| Add value of other assets (as per appended exhibits) |  | 148,118,000 | 13,700,000 |
| Total assets |  | $348,118,000 | $113,700,000 |
| Deduct: |  |  |  |
| General mortgage bonds | $63,000,000 |  | $31,500,000 |
| Other obligations | 70,425,000 |  |  |
| Preferred stock | 70,000,000 |  |  |
|  |  | 203,425,000 | 31,500,000 |
| Balance for common |  | $144,693,000 | $82,500,000 |
| Per share |  | $108 | $59 |

a hint of mystery, it is true, attaches to the figures of the Coal company—but of this more will be said later.

How will the earnings of Reading Common be affected by the loss of the coal and iron subsidiaries? Is it likely that the $4 dividend can be maintained after the rights are received and the stock is marked down to 56? For a complete and rather startling answer to these questions the reader is referred to Table II, which seeks to summarize and interpret the rather complicated provisions of the Segregation Plan.

Boiled down to their very essence, these figures show that in the past $11\frac{1}{2}$ years the actual earnings available for Reading Common have averaged just over $10 per share, including all the profits of its three main subsidiaries. As a result of the segregation, Reading loses the earnings of the Coal and the Iron companies, averaging together $2.83 per share; but this loss is offset to the extent of $1.64 by the income value of the cash received and of the bonded debt transferred as part of the readjustment. Hence the net reduction of the average earnings would amount to only $1.19 per share, which would still leave a balance of $8.86, or well over twice the $4 dividend rate.

This is manifestly a reassuring exhibit, and indicates that the established dividend should be maintained without the slightest difficulty. Curiously enough, moreover, as far as the income of Reading company alone is concerned, the segregation plan actually INCREASES the average earning available for the Common stock. In other words, Reading company proper would have shown a

## TABLE II

EFFECT OF SEGREGATION ON EARNING POWER OF READING COMMON

a) Gain through segregation.

| | Cash Received | Bonded Debt Transferred | Total |
|---|---|---|---|
| To be received by Reading Co. | | | |
| For Coal Co. | $13,100,000 | $31,542,000 | $44,600,000 |
| For Iron Co. | 14,000,000 | | 14,000,000 |
| | $27,100,000 | $31,542,000 | $58,600,000 |

| | |
|---|---|
| Annual income value of new cash at 5% | $1,350,000 |
| Annual reduction in bond interest | 950,000 |
| Total increase in income through segregation | $2,300,000 |

b) Loss through segregation.

| | Value of Assets Surrendered (as earned Reading Co.) | Annual Average 1912–1922 | |
|---|---|---|---|
| | | Received by Reading Co. in Dividends and Interest | Earnings Applicable to Reading Com. |
| Coal Co. | $74,875,000 | $273,000 | $2,695,000 |
| Iron Co. | 1,000,000 | *875,000 | 1,270,000 |
| | $75,875,000 | $1,148,000 | $3,965,000 |

* Excluding $3,000,000 received Dec. 31, 1922, in anticipation of segregation.

c) Summary.

| | |
|---|---|
| Net gain in apparent average earnings through segregation | $1,152,000 |
| Net loss in actual average earnings through segregation | 1,665,000 |
| Net loss in book value of assets through segregation | 17,215,000 |

d) Income available for Reading Common before and after segregation.

Average 1912–1922

| | As Reported by Holding Company | Per Share | Consolidated Basis (Including Undisturbed Earnings of Subsidiaries) | Per Share |
|---|---|---|---|---|
| Before segregation | $7,050,000 | $5.04 | $14,067,000 | $10.05 |
| Net change through segregation | +1,152,000 | +.85 | −1,665,000 | −1.19 |
| | $8,202,000 | $5.89 | $1,240,000 | $8.86 |

larger dividend balance on the new basis—minus the coal and iron properties—than on the old basis, with the income of these companies included.

Substantial as is the past earning power as revealed by our analysis, it is far outshone by the phenomenal current profits reported this year. Table III presents the income account of the Railway company for the year ending

## TABLE III

INCOME ACCOUNT OF NEW READING (RAILWAY) CO.

**Year Ended August 31, 1923.**

| | |
|---|---:|
| Gross | $105,003,000 |
| Net after taxes | 31,243,000 |
| *Deductions, less other income | 4,096,000 |
| Preferred dividends | 2,800,000 |
| Balance for common | 24,347,000 |
| Per share | $17.89 |

* Combined 1922 figures of Reading Co. and Phila. & Reading Ry. Co., adjusted to reflect results of segregation.

August 31, 1923, adjusting the fixed charges to reflect the segregation details. The balance available for the common stock exceeds $17 per share, or more than 30% on its market price, ex-rights.

Almost equal significance should be attached to the very low fixed charges of the Railway company, on its new basis. The net deductions amount to only 4% of the gross business, indicating an unusually strong and conservative capitalization structure. It should be pointed out that a good part of the interest and rental payments previously reported by the Railway company has been received by the holding company as owner of equipment and various securities. Upon the consolidation of the Reading company with its railway subsidiary, these inter-company items will be eliminated.

## WHAT WILL THE COAL COMPANY EARN?

When we turn to an examination of the Coal company's position we find a sharp conflict between available facts and prevalent opinions, the figures being just as bearish as the tips are bullish. If reference is made to our second table, it will be seen that the combined annual earnings from 1912–1922, as reported by the coal and the iron companies, have averaged less than $4,000,000. After deducting $1,550,000 for interest charges on the new 5% bonds, the balance would have been equivalent to only $1.75 per share. Prior to the war boom the profits of the Coal company averaged only about $1,000,000 per annum, and those of the Iron company about $750,000. True to the history of the trade, the latter's profits rose to large proportions between 1916 and 1919, followed by two years of deficits and one of nominal earnings. The doubling of anthracite prices has been a boon to the Coal company, enabling it to quadruple its profits without increasing its production. From 1917 to 1921 income averaged about $4,400,000, but in 1922 the strike resulted in a small deficit.

As stated above, the president of the Coal company has estimated future earnings available for bond interests at not less than $6,000,000. While this figure is given as a minimum, the past record would scarcely warrant a higher estimate. Deducting therefrom $1,550,000 for interest and $750,000 for depletion, there remains a balance of $3,700,000 for the 1,400,000 shares of stock, or about $2.65 per share (possibly subject to income tax).

There is a widespread tendency to wave all the above considerations aside as misleading or immaterial. Great stress is laid on Reading Coal's enormous holdings of unmined anthracite and on its powerful position in a powerful industry. It is estimated that the reports heretofore published have deliberately understated the profits, and that in any event future earnings will greatly exceed those of the past.

Whether the anthracite producers can safely exploit their natural monopoly so as to obtain ever increasing profits must be left for the reader to judge. But as for any understatement by Reading Coal of its past earnings, the writer must confess—after careful scrutiny of the accounts—complete inability to find any basis for this belief. Nor is any such suspicion voiced in the recent report of the U. S. Coal Commission on costs and profits in the anthracite industry. The latter document significantly points out that margins of profit vary widely among the different companies, depending largely on their location, mining in the Schuylkill field, where Reading Coal has its properties, being much more expensive than in the Lehigh and Wyoming fields. This fact may account for the much larger profits per ton regularly reported by, say, the Lehigh & Wilkesbarre Coal Company.

Although the latter concern produces only about one-half the annual tonnage of Reading Coal, it has shown a larger average earning power, even in recent years of high anthracite prices. Nevertheless, Jersey Central holdings of Lehigh & Wilkesbarre Coal stock were sold at a price which gives a net valuation of about $28,000,000 for the mining properties, while the current quotation for Reading rights is equivalent to a price of $76,000,000 net for the corresponding assets of this company.

## THE BONDS AND FIRST PREFERRED

Our analysis has thus led us to the very definite conclusion that Reading (Railway) Common at 56 has apparently much more proven investment merit than the Coal shares at 50. Those stockholders who are guided by intrinsic values, as distinct from purely speculative considerations, should clearly hold on to their Reading Common and dispose of their rights. It follows also that the large average and current earning power shown by Reading, on its segregated basis, coupled with its exceptionally low fixed charges, together make this issue unusually attractive at current levels. If space permitted, this truth could be brought home more effectively by a detailed comparison with other issues—such as Chicago & North Western, Chesapeake & Ohio and even Norfolk & Western and Union Pacific.

Special reference should be made, however, to the position of the senior Reading securities—i.e., the new general $4\frac{1}{2}$s and the first preferred. The $4\frac{1}{2}$s are selling on the Curb at 86 "when issued." By buying \$3,000 of the present General 4s at $87\frac{1}{2}$, an investor would become entitled to receive \$1,000 of new Coal 5s, and \$2,000 of the new Railway $4\frac{1}{2}$s. If the 5% bonds were sold out at 93, the cost of the General $4\frac{1}{2}$s is marked down to only $84\frac{3}{4}$. That this price is abnormally low is evident from the fact that the new bonds should rank in quality with the gilt-edged issues, such as Norfolk & Western 4s and Atchison 4s, selling between 87 and 89. On this basis the Reading $4\frac{1}{2}$s would be entitled to sell above 90. The writer has reason to believe that they will be legal investments for savings banks and trust funds in New York State (a privilege denied the present 4s, as a collateral trust issue).

Reading First Preferred is selling at 32, ex-rights, or 64% of its \$50 par. As a preferred issue of the highest grade, it should rank with Union Pacific and Norfolk & Western preferred (also 4% non-cumulative), which sell at about 72. Hence the Reading shares appear about four points too low, especially as they still have some speculative prospects in connection with the eventual disposal of the Jersey Central stock.

While all the Reading issues have advanced materially during the writing of this article, they do not seem yet to have reached their proper comparative levels.

# 23

# HOW TO APPLY THE SCIENTIFIC THEORY OF SWITCHING TO CONCRETE CASES IN THE PRESENT MARKET

## *A Practical-Minded Scrutiny of the Comparative Merits of Many Securities Active in the Market Today*

The idea underlying security switches is a simple one. The investor or trader sells an issue he owns and buys another in order to obtain some definite advantage. The benefits sought may fall under one or more of the following heads:

1. *Increased Security,*
2. *Larger Yield,*
3. *Greater Chance for Profit,*
4. *Better Marketability.*

The ideal switch will secure the advantage desired without any offsetting loss. As a practical matter, however, it is often advisable to take a small sacrifice in one direction in order to effect a very substantial improvement in another.

Almost always it pays to accept a small decrease in yield if accompanied by greatly enhanced security. At times also, one is justified in transferring to an investment of slightly lower grade if the increase in income return and profit possibility is considerable.

In this article it is intended to point out the various types of switches which have been found to be desirable, to discuss some of the principles underlying each type, and to illustrate them by both past and current examples.

## SWITCHES THAT WOULD HAVE BEEN PROFITABLE

From time to time it is possible to establish the wisdom of a general form of switch applicable to a great many securities of a particular class. An excellent example is found in the bond market of 1921, when obligations of the highest grade were selling at an extremely high yield. It was evidently advantageous for investors to assure themselves of these high yields for as long a period as possible. Hence long-term issues were more attractive than short-term ones, and a general exchange from short maturities to long-dated obligations was bound to result profitably. To give the classic example, holders of VICTORY NOTES who switched from this issue at 98 into the long-term LIBERTY $4^1/_4$s at 87, thus obtained a 4.90% return on U. S. Government Bonds for seventeen years instead of two years. This benefit is now measured marketwise by an advance of 11 points in the price of the long-term issue.

Other comprehensive switches of a less obvious character sometimes suggest themselves. An unusually clear-headed analyst might have seen ten years ago the great advantages to be gained by a general exchange from railroad stocks into industrials. Last year a number of shrewd investors seized the opportunity to switch back into low-priced railroad shares when these were in an especially favorable position.

---

### PUTTING THE SEARCHLIGHT ON VALUES!

Switching from comparatively weak securities to others that are comparatively strong is, after all, the basic idea in sound investing.

This article not only explains how to identify "weakness" and "strength," but it gives specific instances illustrative of its theme.

The views expressed here should not be construed as speculative recommendations, but rather as investment conclusions reached after a careful comparison of individual security-values.

The exchanges mentioned above would have proved desirable for every investor; but in examining the security lists of an individual it is often found that some general type of exchange may be justified by his or her particular situation.

For example, a widow may be left an assortment of second-grade securities, all of which might have constituted rather attractive speculative commitments for her husband, but which are indubitably too risky to be held by herself. Hence, a general exchange into safer, if less remunerative, issues is obviously required. But, conversely, a business man who has for some time confined his purchases to gilt-edged issues yielding very low returns, might quite properly decide to assume the burden of careful selection and continuous supervision, as well as a slight unavoidable hazard, in order to obtain a substantially higher income return. In his case a wholesale exchange from 4% to 6% issues might well be justified by the special facts.

Under this heading, too, reference should be made to the important element of tax status. Undoubtedly there are many original subscribers to LIBERTY $3\frac{1}{2}$s to whom the surtax exemption is of slight importance, and who could increase their yield substantially by switching into the $4\frac{1}{4}$% issues at a negligible difference in price. On the other hand, a number of wealthy investors still include in their security list bonds of the type of ATCHISON GENERAL 4s, yielding only 4.65%, subject to normal and surtax. Deducting 8% normal tax, the yield is cut to 4.22%—less than that of LIBERTY $4\frac{1}{4}$s, which are free from normal tax and enjoy certain surtax exemptions. In other words, wealthy investors can increase their actual income by switching from gilt-edged rail-road issues into Liberty Bonds or completely taxfree municipals.

## SWITCHING INTO SENIOR CONVERTIBLES

The inherent advantages of convertible issues have frequently been stressed in these pages. As compared with the corresponding common shares, they provide the same opportunity of profit with much smaller risk of loss. Neverless, it is a curious fact that the public is still lacking in appreciation of the merits of convertible issues. The market price of such securities rarely reflects any considerable premium for the *potential* value of the conversion privilege (as distinct from the *immediate* conversion parity).

For example, DETROIT EDISON 6s, due 1932, will be convertible into common stock, par for par, after December 15, next. The common stock is currently selling at 105, and has reached 118 as recently as 1922; yet the 6% debentures can be bought at 104 to yield 5.40%—a price and return which reflects merely the strong investment rating of the issue, with scarcely any allowance for the undoubtedly attractive conversion feature.

Furthermore, the writer has found it extremely difficult to persuade the typical common stockholder to make even a slight and temporary sacrifice of income return in order to secure the added safety provided by a senior convertible issue. A few weeks ago, U. S. REALTY & IMPROVEMENT 7% PREFERRED (convertible into common at par) was selling at 103, with the common, paying 8%, at 102. Few common stockholders availed themselves of that opportunity of exchanging into the preferred shares, because they were unwilling to pay the one point difference or to accept a 7% dividend for a while instead of 8%. Yet the strategic advantage in holding the convertible preferred stock instead of the common is so great as to make the cost of the exchange an inconsequential factor. The preferred stockholder is virtually guaranteed against any cut in dividend or substantial market decline, while enjoying a continuous option of changing back into common stock if any favorable developments make this desirable. At this writing, Realty Preferred is selling at $102\frac{1}{2}$ and the Common at 96, so that an exchange made at one point difference would already have been amply justified.

In this matter of convertible issues we are dealing with such an ingrained prepossession on the part of investors that a special effort seems necessary to set the matter forth in a logical light. In the past five years, the writer has observed countless instances, where by switching—say from GENERAL ASPHALT common into the convertible preferred, or from SOUTHERN PACIFIC stock into the convertible bonds, or from PRODUCERS & REFINERS common into the participating preferred, all on about a parity—the stockholder could have saved himself a very substantial loss, or, otherwise stated, could have reversed his position later at a considerable profit. And in the nature of things, there is no example on record of such switches resulting in more than a nominal loss.

---

### THE UNDERLYING IDEA

"The idea underlying security switches is a simple one. The investor or trader sells an issue he owns and buys another in order to obtain some definite advantage."

---

Why then the reluctance of investors to embrace these opportunities? A psychologist might explain the situation as follows: A man buys or holds a common stock because he believes it is going to advance. If you suggest that he switch into a convertible bond or preferred stock, to guard against loss in a market decline, the idea will not appeal to him, *because he does not think the common is going down.* We may contend that, even admitting the *probability* of an advance in the common, it would still be wise to pay some slight insurance charge against the *possibility* of a drop—but this argument usually appears too refined or complicated to be effective.

---

### THIS ARTICLE CONTAINS PRACTICAL SUGGESTIONS TO HOLDERS OF THE FOLLOWING SECURITIES:

#### BONDS:

| | |
|---|---|
| Atchison 4s | Rock Island 4s, '54 |
| St. Paul 4s, '25 | Inter. Rap. T. 5s |

#### PREFERRED STOCKS:

| | |
|---|---|
| P. S. Corp. N. J. 7% | Ill. Central 7% |
| Cal. Petroleum 7% | Foundation Co. 7% |

#### COMMON STOCKS:

| | |
|---|---|
| Detroit Edison | Ontario & Western |
| Illinois Central | D. L. & W. |
| Foundation Co. | Pittsburgh & W. V. |
| Cal. Petroleum | Anaconda Copper |
| New Haven R. R. | Ray Copper |

Am. Ag. Chemical
General Electric Co.

---

I recall vividly an incident in April, 1920, when I pointed out to a large holder of CONSOLIDATED TEXTILE common, then selling at 45, that at a cost of only one point he could switch into an equivalent amount of the Convertible 7% Notes, due 1923, quoted about par—and thus combine all the price protection of a short-term note with the privilege of participating in any further rise in the stock. His reply was, "I am sure the Common is going to 60, so why should I waste the extra point?" The wisdom of "wasting" the extra point became evident before the year was out, for the common dropped thirty points to 16, while the notes declined the equivalent of only four points and were retired a few months later at $102\frac{1}{2}$. The switch suggested would have netted a handsome profit.

Let us apply the moral of this harrowing tale to a current situation. Would it not be prudent for a holder of ILLINOIS CENTRAL COMMON to switch into the CONVERTIBLE PREFERRED, even though he pay a fractional price difference and accept provisionally a one per cent lower income return? "Silly suggestion" retorts the typical common stockholder, "Illinois Central has been doing exceptionally well; the 7% dividend is absolutely safe; the stock is cheap rather than dear; so why should I throw away one per cent a year by switching into the preferred?"

He is indeed a bold man who can predict with absolute assurance future market action of any common stock. After all, only last December Illinois Central sold below par—five points under the preferred—and in 1921 reached as low as $85\frac{1}{2}$. The idea underlying this switch is not to turn a seven per cent investment into a six per cent one, but rather to provide a temporary position of safety from which the investor may observe market and railroad developments for a year or so. If a general decline should occur—something which, alas, is never impossible—he will undoubtedly be able to switch back into the common at a substantial difference in his favor. If all goes well, and the impregnable strength of Illinois Central's position is reflected in an advance to, say 120, he can exercise his conversion privilege and get back his common stock, at a small net cost for the valuable intervening illegible.

A more striking situation of the same kind is presented by the FOUNDATION COMPANY issues—though the public's interest in these is relatively small. The 7% Cumulative Preferred sells at 93, and is convertible into one and a quarter times as many shares of common, paying $6 and quoted at 74. The owner of ten shares of common could switch into eight shares of preferred for practically the same money. He would still have the right to get back his ten common through conversion (at any time up to December, 1925), but meanwhile would enjoy a much stronger investment position. If by any chance the common should again decline below 60, as it did last year, he could undoubtedly sell out his preferred and buy back the common at a very handsome saving.

An unusual switching opportunity is presented to owners of CALIFORNIA PETROLEUM common who can replace their holdings by the Participating Preferred stock at an actual cash profit—and thus obtain greater security without any cost at all. California Petroleum 7% Cumulative Preferred sells at 98 (par $100) and participates equally with the common (selling at its par, $25) in all dividends above 7%—one share of preferred being equivalent to four of common.

In other words, the preferred cannot receive a smaller dividend than the common; but for ten years the preferred paid an average of 7% while the common stockholders received nothing. The greater assurance of dividends on the preferred, together with the right to participate equally with the common in any increase, should entitle the preferred to sell appreciably higher than the junior shares. Nevertheless, the market has actually been paying more for the common. As the only possible excuse for this anomaly, we might mention that the preferred is callable at 120—twenty-two points above the present price. Considering that California Petroleum has a good-sized bond issue and has been spending money freely on plant account, the redemption of the preferred shares would appear a contingency of the remotest sort. It should be added that in former markets, when this issue (and the similar PRODUCERS & REFINERS PARTICIPATING PREFERRED) sold on a parity with the common, a switch into the senior issue would later have shown substantial profit.

Listed under this heading (in Table II) is one which partakes of the characteristics of the switches discussed above—namely, that from PUBLIC SERVICE CORPORATION 7% PREFERRED, to PUBLIC SERVICE ELECTRIC guaranteed 7% preferred. Since dividends on the latter are guaranteed by Public Service Corporation, this issue is virtually a bond, and ranks ahead of the parent company's preferred stock. Nevertheless, the guaranteed issue can actually be bought slightly below the price of the ordinary preferred, although it is clearly entitled to sell at a higher level. ARMOUR & COMPANY (DELAWARE) guaranteed preferred, for example, is quoted ten points above the price of ARMOUR & COMPANY (ILLINOIS) unguaranteed preferred.

But the field of desirable switches is not restricted to securities of the same company, such as heretofore considered, though these can be supported by more direct and simple arguments than any others. Most security exchanges involve two different companies and hence usually require a rather elaborate comparative analysis of both enterprises. But in discussing our various recommendations—which are intended to be representative rather than comprehensive—we shall have space to consider only the salient features of each case.

The switch to increase income is illustrated in our table by that from ATCHISON 4s at 87 to READING NEW $4\frac{1}{2}$s at 89. Here we have two issues of the highest grade. The Reading $4\frac{1}{2}$s still wear an air of novelty, because of their recent appearance as a result of the coal segregation. Hence they yield nearly one-half per cent more than other standard bonds of the same class. Eventually they should sell on the same basis as the Atchison 4s.

The exchange of ST. PAUL 4s of 1925 into ST. LOUIS SOUTHWESTERN 5s, due 1952, at about the same price, is recommended in the interests of caution.

## TABLE I

CONVERTIBLE-PARTICIPATING ISSUES

| *Switch From* | Price | Dividend | Yield % | *Switch Into* | Price | Dividend | Yield % |
|---|---|---|---|---|---|---|---|
| Cal. Pet. Com | 25 | $1.75 | 7.0 | Cal. Pet. 7% | 98 | $8.00 | 8.1 |
| Ill. Central Com | 105 | 7.00 | 6.6 | Ill. Central 7% | 105½ | 6.00 | 5.7 |
| Foundation Com | 74 | 6.00 | 8.1 | Foundation 7% | 93 | 7.00 | 7.5 |

## TABLE II

BOND AND PREFERRED STOCK EXCHANGES

| | Price | Yield | | Price | Yield |
|---|---|---|---|---|---|
| Atch., Top. & S'ta Fe, gen. 4s 1995 | 87 | 4.60 | Reading gen. & ref. 4½ s 1997 | 89 | 5.10 |
| Chicago, R. I. & Pacific ref. 4s 1934 | 77 | 7.46 | "Nickel Plate" System— | | |
| | | | Tol., St. L. & W. 4s 1950 | 79 | 6.40 |
| Interboro Rapid Transit ref. 5s 1966 | 65½ | 7.80 | B'klyn-Manhattan Transit 6s 1968 | 78 | 7.75 |
| | | | Third Avenue R. R. Ref. 4s 1960 | 55 | 7.70 |
| Chicago, Mil. & St. Paul 4s 1925 | 86 | 15.00 | St. Louis Southw't. Terminal 5s 1952. | 83 | 6.25 |
| Public Service Corp. of N. J. 7% Pfd. | 98 | 7.1 | Pub. Serv. Elec. Power Corp. gtd. 7% | 96½ | 7.2 |

## TABLE III

COMMON STOCK EXCHANGES

| | Price | Dividend | Yield | | Price | Dividend | Yield |
|---|---|---|---|---|---|---|---|
| New Haven | 18 | — | — | Kansas City Southern | 18½ | — | — |
| N. Y., Ontario & Western | 17 | — | — | Wabash | 17 | — | — |
| Del., Lackawanna & Western. | 116 | 6 | 5.1 | Reading | 55 | 4 | 7.2 |
| Pittsburgh & West Virginia | 44½ | — | — | Pere Marquette | 41½ | 4 | 9.6 |
| Anaconda Copper | 32 | — | — | Kennecott Copper | 35 | 3 | 8.5 |
| Ray Consolidated | 9¾ | — | — | Wright Aeronautical | 10½ | 1 | 9.5 |
| Am. Agric. Chemical | 10½ | — | — | Atlas Tack | 7 | — | — |
| General Electric | 220 | 8 | 3.7 | Westinghouse Elec. & Mfg | 61 | 4 | 6.5 |

There has been considerable buying of the St. Paul 4s by those hopeful of making a large profit in a year's time through their repayment at par. Yet a calm survey of the situation indicates that the redemption of this issue in cash next year is rather improbable; and that an involuntary extension is most likely, failing which a receivership might not be at all unthinkable.

The bondholder who bought this issue long ago for investment, now finds himself in a highly speculative position, with wide market possibilities in both directions. It would seem most prudent to take advantage of the twenty-point advance registered by this issue in the past year, by switching into a well protected 5% bond at the same price, such as St. Louis Southwestern Terminal 5s. This would mean accepting a one per cent higher coupon in place of the very speculative chance of a rapid price advance (not a bad offset), and at the same time effecting a great improvement safetywise.

Somewhat the same principle underlies the suggested switch from ROCK ISLAND 4s of 1934 into TOLEDO ST. LOUIS & WESTERN 4s, due 1950. The latter are assumed by N. Y. C. and ST. L. ("NICKEL PLATE"), a very prosperous system, paying 6% on its common. Rock Island has made an indifferent showing for some years, and the large junior bond issue must be considered as second grade.

This exchange can be made at about the same price, with the investor accepting a postponement of maturity in return for substantially increased security. Experience has shown that assurance of repayment is far more important than the date of repayment.

The switch from INTERBORO RAPID TRANSIT 5s has been selected to illustrate another important investment principle—namely, that the bondholder must of necessity pay more attention to unfavorable than to favorable factors. His return is limited and cannot be increased no matter how much the earnings may rise; but a severe reverse may endanger his interest payment. The I. R. T. set-up is fundamentally unsound from the standpoint of the bondholder, because the fixed charges are so heavy as to consume almost all the present available income—leaving a scant margin to meet any unexpected revenue losses.

No matter how optimistic we may be as to the future growth of earnings, the fact cannot be escaped that the bonds lack one prime requisite of safety— a large aggregate of junior securities to absorb fluctuations in earning power. For this reason an exchange into either BROOKLYN-MANHATTAN TRANSIT 6s, or THIRD AVENUE 4s, or both, appears logical, especially since it can be effected without loss of income. B. M. T. has earned its fixed charges about one and a half times; Third Avenue nearly twice; while Interboro's margin is only about fifteen per cent.

## COMMON STOCK EXCHANGES

Recommending common stock switches is a difficult, hazardous, and generally thankless job. No matter how complete and accurate an analysis may be,
there is always a possibility either of some new condition arising to belie your
conclusions, or else of the market refusing to act in accordance with your just
expectations. To illustrate the former point, an exhaustive comparison of
Norfolk & Western with Reading, made a few months ago, undoubtedly
indicated the latter to be far more attractive. But the Pennsylvania lease negotiations have of course entirely changed the situation, for if consummated it
will inject an entirely new element of value into Norfolk stock.

Again, with respect to the market action, the writer recalls pointing out
some time ago in this Magazine, that American Hide & Leather Preferred
was more attractive than Central Leather Preferred, then selling five points
higher. Nevertheless, the spread increased later to fifteen points in favor of
Central Leather preferred—though the switch recommended was fully justified in time by a twenty point decline in the latter and a twenty point advance
in Hide & Leather preferred.

Hence, the switches suggested in the accompanying table must be
accepted merely for what they represent—to wit, the result of a careful
analysis of all the available facts regarding the issues treated—and not as
infallible recipes for profit-making. These we must discuss with almost
indecent haste.

Kansas City Southern is preferred to New Haven because the latter has
serious financial problems from which the former is exempt; while the possibilities of increased earning power seem fuly as great in the smaller road. In
the Ontario & Western-Wabash exchange, the emphasis is the other way—
namely, that Ontario & Western's disproportionately large stock issue makes
it difficult to earn an appreciable percentage on its shares, while Wabash, with
its relatively small amount of common stock, easily translate favorable conditions into substantial per-share earnings. Nor is there any reason to prefer
Ontario & Western on the grounds of superior financial strength.

The contrast between Reading and D. L. & W. is very striking. Reading
earned over $10 per share last year, pays $4 and sells at 55, while Lackawanna
earned $7.50, pays $6, but sells over 120. Reading has been reporting larger
gross and much larger net earnings than D. L. & W., yet the latter's stock is
selling in the market for over $200,000,000 against $77,000,000 for Reading
common. Lackawanna's fixed charges are smaller, but Reading is so strongly
entrenched as to make this difference unimportant. A bullish argument
has been built on the possibility of a distribution of D. L. & W.'s coal bonds

(worth about $38 per share), but it is hard to see how the value of what is left can fail to be reduced by what is given away—especially as the loss of $2,400,000 per year income from the treasury bonds might well endanger the continuance of the $6 dividend.

A switch from PITTSBURGH & WEST VIRGINIA to PERE MARQUETTE seems justified, because Pere Marquette pays $4 while Pittsburgh & West Virginia has so far paid nothing; furthermore, Pere Marquette has been earning substantially more than the other road even though the latter has included in its income dividends from its coal subsidiary in excess of the latter's current profits.

A similiar switch in the industrial field from ANACONDA to KENNECOTT is based on the latter's ability to earn and pay $3 to shareholders under conditions necessitating the suspension of dividends by Anaconda. In the same way, the small likelihood of any payment being made by RAY COPPER, unless conditions change materially, would apparently justify a switch to WRIGHT AERO, whose $1 dividend has been maintained for some time. Wright is handicapped by a huge but very nebulous government suit, on the other hand, its cash asset position is extraordinary.

The AMERICAN AGRICULTURE-ATLAS TACK switch exemplifies a somewhat different idea. Both issues have declined because of poor earnings. But Atlas Tack has no prior securities; its market price is covered by net current assets; and it could resume dividends whenever profitable conditions return. (The president estimates earnings of $4.50 per share on a normal basis.)

American Agriculture Chemical has a heavy handicap of cumulative preferred dividends, and the presence of substantial amount of senior securities places it in a much weaker strategic position than Atlas Tack.

The GENERAL ELECTRIC–WESTINGHOUSE exchange is one of those propositions that ought to work out well but frequently don't. Westinghouse has been doing about one-half the business and earning about one-half as much per share as General Electric. Yet General Electric sells at nearly four times the price of Westinghouse. The latter yields a better dividend return. A through canvas of the situation—including such special features as General Electric's investments and depreciation charges, and the effect of the radio business on future profits, fails to disclose any convincing justification of the present spread. We are left to speculate upon a possible split-up of General Electric (which means nothing intrinsically) or else upon extraordinary results to be realized later from some new development, such as perhaps the mercury vapor engine. Looking at the matter through the eyes of the investor, the much larger present earning power of Westinghouse, in comparison with its price, would seem a sounder basis of purchase than any grandiose but shadowy hope of future miracles by General Electric.

Obviously a brief article such as this can do but scant justice to so comprehensive a subject as security switches. The aim has necessarily been, therefore, not so much to make out a complete and convincing case for each exchange suggested, as to illustrate a number of general ideas by specific examples.

# 24

# EIGHT STOCK BARGAINS OFF THE BEATEN TRACK

*Stocks that Are Covered Chiefly by Cash
or the Equivalent—No Bonds or Preferred
Stock Ahead of These Issues—An
Unusually Interesting Group of Securities*

*Note: This article discusses the position of a rare group of stocks character-
ized by two general features (1) the practical absence of liabilities ahead of
these issues and (2) the ownership of cash assets covering the major portion
of the prices at which they are selling in the market. We take this opportunity of pointing out that the stocks analyzed are not generally known to the
investing public, that their markets are consequently narrow, and that if
purchased it should be at a price and not "at the market."*

Suppose there were a company without liabilities of any sort, except
small current accounts and its capital stock. Suppose the stock sold at
$138 per share, while the company held cash and marketable securities
aggregating $175 per share. In other words, it had $30 per share more in cash

than the selling price of the stock. And suppose it held another $127 per share, represented by shares at par in a dividend-paying railroad. And another $120 per share in subsidiary investments. Finally, suppose it carried its own fixed assets at another $7 per share, although last year they returned net operating profits of $30 per share.

"What is the use of supposing," growls the Gentle Reader. "It is all too good to be true." *Au contraire,* the identical situation exists in the market today—except that the par of the stock happens to be $1 instead of $100, so that all the above figures, including the price, refer to 100 shares instead of to one share. The concern is the Tonopah Mining Company, listed in Philadelphia and on the New York Curb, and currently selling at $1^3/_8$, par $1.00.

A glance at the appended analysis of the latest balance-sheet will confirm our statement that the company actually has cash assets in excess of the selling price of its stock; and that its total assets are three times its market value, the smallest item being its mine and equipment. The company is paying dividends of 15% (15 cents per share) and has an uninterrupted dividend record of twenty years, during which it has paid out $15,550,000 on $1,000,000 of stock—an average of over 75% per annum. The earnings last year were 52 cents per share, or 37% on the market price; but about 30 cents per share was written off for exploration and development of new properties.

---

### EIGHT CASH ASSET STOCKS

#### No Bonds or Preferred Stocks Ahead of These Issues

| | Liquid Assets* Per Share | Market Price | Market |
|---|---|---|---|
| Tonopah Mining | $4.31 | $1.38 | {Phila. Stock Exch. N.Y. Curb |
| Transue & Williams | 24.62 | 28.00 | N.Y. Stock Ex. |
| Crex Carpet | 39.90 | 29.00 | N.Y. Stock Ex. |
| Cumberland Pipe Line | 88.20 | 128.00a | N.Y. Curb |
| Southern Pipe Line | 80.79 | 95.00 | N.Y. Curb |
| Pennok Oil | 8.36 | 15.50b | N.Y. Stock Ex. |
| Shattuck-Arizona Copper | 4.53 | 5.00 | N.Y. Stock Ex. |
| Wright Aeronautical | 19.79 | 10.50 | N.Y. Stock Ex. |

---

* Including current assets, after deducting current liabilities.
a Earned per share, 1923, $26.21.
b Earned per share, 1923, $5.28.

How is it possible that an issue with the splendid record of Tonopah Mining should sell at less than the company's cash assets alone? Three explanations of this strange situation may be given. The company's rich mines at Tonopah are known to be virtually exhausted. At the same time the strenuous efforts of the Exploration Department to develop new properties have met with but indifferent success. Finally, the drop in the price of silver last year has provided another bearish argument. It is this combination of unfavorable factors which has carried the price down from $7^1/_8$ in 1917 to its present low quotation.

Granting that the operating outlook is uncertain, one must still marvel at that triumph of pessimism which refuses to value the issue at even the amount of its cash and marketable investments; particularly since there is every reason to believe that the company's holdings in the Tonopah & Goldfield railroad and various other subsidiaries, are themselves intrinsically worth the present selling price. Perhaps there is a fear that this wealth of assets will be dissipated in the search for new properties.

The management's policy restricts exploration expenditures to a sum within the current income, and the cash assets will not be drawn upon without the approval of the stockholders. Some interests have been agitating for a liquidation of the enterprise and a distribution of the assets among the shareholders. Were this decided upon, the stockholders would certainly receive liquidating dividends well in excess of the current price. On the other hand, the writer believes with the majority of stockholders that "the thoroughly capable and experienced management" (to quote Weed in the Mines Handbook) is in the end more likely to multiply than to dissipate the company's assets through the development of new properties.

Tonopah Mining is representative of an unusual group of common stocks which are distinguished first by the virtual absence of any kind of liability ahead of them, and secondly by the ownership of cash assets covering the major portion of the selling price. Cash assets include call loans and readily marketable securities, besides money in the bank. (We do not list under this title accounts receivable or inventories).

Issues of this type are extremely rare. The cash and Liberty Bond holdings of U. S. Steel or General Electric, great as they are, still do not suffice to place them in this category. One might imagine, off-hand, that companies in such exemplary financial condition would be eagerly sought by conservative investors, and that their shares would be active and popular. Exactly the opposite is true.

Of the eight issues which are analysed in this article, as deserving the title of Cash Asset Stocks, not a single one may be called an investment

## Tonopah Mining

**Capitalization: 1,000,000 shares, selling at 1³/₈. Total market value $1,375,000.**
**No bonds or preferred stock.**

**Balance Sheet, Dec. 31, 1923.**

|  |  | Amount | Per Share |
|---|---|---|---|
| Cash Assets |  | $1,752,000 | $1.75 |
| Other Current Assets | $152,000 |  |  |
| Less All Liabilities | 66,000 |  |  |
|  |  | 86,000 | .09 |
| Tonopah & Goldfield R. R. Stock |  | 1,272,000 | 1.27 |
| Investments in Subsidiaries |  | 1,196,000 | 1.20 |
| Mine and Equipment |  | 69,000 | .07 |
|  |  | $4,375,000 | $4.38 |

**Income Account, 1923**

|  |  | Per Share |
|---|---|---|
| Gross (from own mine) | $1,262,000 | $1.26 |
| Net from Operations | 308,000 | .31 |
| Net from Investments | 211,000 | .21 |
| Total Income | 519,000 | .52 |
| Exploration Expenditures | 296,000 | .30 |
| Balance for Dividends | 223,000 | .22 |

## Transue & Williams Steel Forging

**Capitalization: 100,000 shares, selling at 28. Total market value, $2,800,000.**
**No bonds or preferred stock.**

**Balance Sheet, May 31, 1924.**

|  |  | Amount | Per Share |
|---|---|---|---|
| Cash Assets |  | $1,856,000 | $18.56 |
| Other Current Assets | $855,000 |  |  |
| Less All Liabilities | 249,000 |  |  |
|  |  | 606,000 | 6.06 |
| Fixed Assets, net |  | 1,259,000 | 12.59 |
|  |  | $3,721,000 | $37.21 |

**Income Account, 1923**

|  |  | Per Share |
|---|---|---|
| Operating Revenues | $6,247,000 | $62.47 |
| Operating Income | 506,000 | 5.06 |
| Depreciation | 116,000 | 1.16 |
| Net Operating Income | 390,000 | 3.90 |
| Investment Income | 69,000 | .69 |
| Total Income | 459,000 | 4.59 |

Net earnings for five months ended March 31, 1924, were at the annual rate of $2.64 per share.

favorite. In fact, most of them are practically unknown to the rank and file of security buyers. But on reflection this is found not to be surprising. After all, the standard, popular issues are rarely exceptionally attractive; and, conversely, the best bargains are usually found far off the beaten track. For how long can an issue sell substantially below its minimum intrinsic value after everybody knows all about it?

## TRANSUE & WILLIAMS

To support our thesis, let us introduce our readers to Transue & Williams Steel Forgings Corporation, selling on the New York Stock Exchange at 28, and paying dividends of $3 per share. Our analysis of the recent balance-sheet (dated May 31st last) shows that of this $28 per share, over $18.50 is covered by cash and security holdings alone—leaving only $9.50 as the market valuation of the remaining assets. But the company holds $6 per share more in other net current assets (after deducting all liabilites). Hence, the price of $28 is really equivalent to only $3$^1$/$_2$ per share or $350,000 in all, for the company's plant and going value.

When it is considered that the plant turned out last year products sold for $6,247,000, and that it showed a net operating profit of $506,000 before depreciation, this $350,000 market valuation appears ridiculously low. The company itself carries its fixed assets at the depreciated amount of $1,259,000, or $12.59 per share, which is only $63,000 more than the book value in November, 1916, and is apparently a very conservative figure.

The company has paid dividends regularly since organization, the lowest rate being $2 per share, paid in 1922. Incidentally, the present price of $28 is the lowest on record (except for 300 shares sold earlier this year) and compares with a high of 74$^7$/$_8$ in 1919, and of 40 last year. Surely the record, position, and dividend rate offered by Transue & Williams is more than satisfactory. Yet it is one of the inactive Stock Exchange issues—and necessarily so, since the purchase of a few thousand shares would probably put it back to 40, after which it would no longer be the outstanding bargain it is to-day.

## CREX CARPET

Another inconspicuous Stock Exchange issue, of the same general type, is Crex Carpet, makers of a well-known product. Compared with Transue & Williams, Crex has a more irregular dividend and earnings record, but its balance-sheet position is even stronger. As against the current selling price of 29, the last report shows $17 per share in cash and securities, together with $23 more in other current assets, after subtracting the mere $45,000 of current liabilities. Add to this the fixed properties, carried at $2,213,000, and the book value of 30,000 shares of capital stock works out at $113 per share.

 With this wealth of assets behind the issue, and the absence of prior liabilities, the bargain-hunter can afford to overlook the current lack of dividends and the peculiar fluctuations in the reported earnings. In the June 30, 1923 year, the profits equalled $3.25 per share. In the 1921 and 1922 period the company about broke even, but in 1920 the earnings reached $14.57 per share. The erratic dividend record includes $6 payments in 1911 to 1912 and 1913, and again in 1918, 1919 and 1920.

---

### CREX CARPET

**Capitalization: 30,000 shares selling at 29. Total market value $870,000.
No bonds or preferred stock.**

**Balance Sheet, June 30, 1923.**

|  |  | Amount | Per Share |
|---|---|---|---|
| Cash Assets |  | $509,000 | $16.97 |
| Other current Assets | $733,000 |  |  |
| Less All Liabilities | 45,000 |  |  |
|  |  | 688,000 | 22.93 |
| Fixed and Other Assets |  | 2,213,000 | 73.77 |
|  |  | $3,410,000 | $113,67 |
| Net Profits, 1923 |  | $98,038 |  |
| Per Share |  | 3.27 |  |

## CUMBERLAND PIPE LINE

**Capitalization: 30,000 shares, selling at 128. Total market value $3,840,000.**
**No bonds or preferred stock.**

**Balance Sheet, Dec. 31, 1923.**

|  |  | Amount | Per Share |
|---|---|---|---|
| Cash Assets |  | $2,517,000 | $83.90 |
| Other Current Assets | $153,000 |  |  |
| Less All Liabilities | 24,000 |  |  |
|  |  | 129,000 | 4.30 |
| Fixed Assets | 4,639,000 |  |  |
| Less Depreciation | 2,162,000 |  |  |
|  |  | 2,477,000 | 82.56 |
|  |  | $5,123,000 | $170.76 |

|  | Amount | Per Share |
|---|---|---|
| Earned 1923 | $1,022,000 | $34.07 |
| Less Depreciation | 236,000 | 7.86 |
| Balance for Dividends | $786,000 | $26.21 |

---

## SOUTHERN PIPE LINE

**Capitalization: 100,000 shares selling at 95. Total market value $9,500,000.**
**No bonds or preferred stock. Balance sheet Dec. 31, 1923.**

|  |  | Amount | Per Share |  | Amount | Per Share |
|---|---|---|---|---|---|---|
| Cash Assets |  | $7,873,000 | $78.73 | Earned 1923 | $718,000 | $7.18 |
| Other Current Assets | $207,000 |  |  | Less Depreciation | 170,000 | 1.70 |
| Less All Liabilities | 1,000 |  |  |  | $548,000 | $5.48 |
|  |  | 206,000 | 2.06 |  |  |  |
| Fixed Assets | $5,971,000 |  |  |  |  |  |
| Less Depreciation | 2,333,000 |  |  |  |  |  |
|  |  | 3,638,000 | 36.38 |  |  |  |
|  |  | $11,717,000 | $117.17 |  |  |  |

The company has large facilities and a popular reputation; one would imagine that with proper operating policies it should not be difficult to show a constant and substantial earning power on the small capitalization. Certain needed changes in management have apparently been initiated, and it does not seem possible that we shall indefinitely see the assets of this going concern priced in the market at far below their liquidating value.

## PIPE LINE STOCKS

There is one entire family of stocks and an aristocratic family at that, which is characterized throughout by an exceptional wealth of cash assets. These are the Pipe Line issues, erstwhile Standard Oil subsidiaries. In addition to their financial strength, they present numerous other attractive features. They combine the prestige of Standard Oil affiliation with a generous dividend return.

Engaged in a presumably stable transportation business, they have besides no labor problems, no fixed charges, and no need of capital expenditures. From the theoretical standpoint, therefore, the Pipe Lines would seem to combine all the requisites of an ideal stock investment. However, recent developments seem to be weakening the strategic position hitherto enjoyed by these oil carriers, for there is danger of diversion of business by their chief customers to other transportation agencies. This angle of the situation was the subject of an illuminating discussion in the May 24th issue of the Magazine of Wall Street.

One of this group, however, stands out as unaffected by the conditions which had recently been reducing the earnings of the others. This is the Cumberland Pipe Line, which as exclusive gatherer of crude from the long-lived Kentucky wells, has no need to fear loss of business to water-carriers or competing pipe lines. Its strongly entrenched position is demonstrated by the fact that its 1923 profits actually exceeded the excellent showing of 1922, the figures being $26.21 and $24.12 per share, respectively. At the present price of 128, the $12 dividend supplies a yield of over 9%.

That this company amply deserves a place in our collection of Cash Asset Stocks is clear from the appended balance-sheet analysis, which shows holdings of no less than $83.90 per share in cash and its equivalent. Adding in the fixed properties, which are conservatively valued and liberally depreciated, the total assets work out at $171 per share. It is significant that liabilities of all sorts total only $24,000 (8 cents per share). There is indeed an "oil purchase and sale contingent reserve" of $868,000, but investigation shows this to be really part of the surplus account. Cumberland Pipe Line combines all the attractive features of this Standard Oil Group, and is apparently immune from the threatening adverse influences. With its splendid exhibit of assets, earnings and dividends, it can hardly fail to prove a profitable investment.

## SOUTHERN PIPE LINE

From the standpoint of cash assets alone, the showing of Southern Pipe Line is even more striking. Our analysis indicates that of the present price of 95, no less than $78 per share (or over 80%) is covered by cash and marketable investments. The commitment in the fixed assets is thus marked down to only $15 per share, which seems low enough to discount almost any possible future loss of earnings. The fact is, however, that although the 1923 profits were but $5.48 per share, traffic has increased so far this year and the $8 dividend is probably being earned.

## CRESCENT PIPE LINE

In this connection, mention must certainly be made of Crescent Pipe Line, which reports net cash assets of $15.85 per share, as against current sales at 13. Here we have a 100% plus Cash Asset Stock. But while most attractive from this single standpoint, Crescent is weakest of all the Pipe Line companies in other respects. As a small connecting line, it seems in danger of losing its business entirely due to changing conditions. Its earnings last year were only 73 cents per share, and it recently broke the long tradition of Standard Oil stocks by passing its dividend.

Crescent Pipe Line furnishes a good illustration of certain qualifying considerations which should be borne in mind in connection with cash asset issues. It is a very fine thing to be able to buy a certificate representing $1 cash in the bank for 90 cents—but your profit on the deal is strictly limited to 10 cents. And if a long interval must elapse before the $1 is paid over, you may find your profit a very small one, considering the time involved.

For a real "killing," you must pick out just the opposite kind of a proposition—an enterprise with little surplus cash, because its funds are all in its business, and with large liabilities, i.e., using other people's money to increase the earning power of yours. It is this sort of pyramiding (well exemplified by many Public Utility common stocks), which, *when successful*, will increase the value of the junior shares, not by 10%, but by 1,000% and more. But if not successful—a Receiver quickly appears, and the common stock disappears.

Cash assets then are a great source of strength, but a moderate source of profits. They will appeal strongly to the investor, but their speculative possiblities are limited. For this reason, if a stock represents $16 in cash and little else, the writer would not call it an outstanding bargain at 13. In the case of the stocks especially recommended above, the strong cash asset position is reinforced by other attractive features. With Tonopah Mining and Crex Carpet, the emphasis is laid on the large excess of total assets over market value. On the other hand, Cumberland Pipe Line and Transue & Williams combine substantial earning power, and dividend returns with their wealth of cash holdings.

## PENNOK OIL

This point is well exemplified also by Pennok Oil, which has recently been coming into deserved prominence on the New York Curb. The jaded analyst, accustomed to the recurring financial problems of the minor oil companies, is agreeably surprised to note in Pennok's March 31st balance-sheet the outstanding item: "Cash, collateral loss, tax-exempt securities: $3,030,644.93"— against which liabilities of every sort are covered by the single entry, "Accounts payable: $157,003.66."

---

PENNOK OIL

**Capitalization: 375,000 shares, selling at 15½.\* Total market value $5,813,000. No bonds or preferred stock. Balance sheet March 31, 1924.**

|  |  | Amount | Per Share | Income Account | 1923 | 1st Qu'ter 1924 |
|---|---|---|---|---|---|---|
| Cash Assets |  | $3,031,000 | $8.08 | Gross | $3,874,000 | $558,000 |
| Other Current Assets | $264,000 |  |  | Net | 3,396,000 | 464,000 |
| Less All Liabilities | 157,000 |  |  | Reserves and |  |  |
|  |  | 107,000 | .28 | Write Offs | 1,398,000 | 152,000 |
| Fixed Assets | 5,425,000 |  |  | Balance for |  |  |
| Less Depreciation, etc. | 2,670,000 |  |  | Dividends | 1,998,000 | 312,000 |
|  |  | 2,755,000 | 7.35 | Per Share | 5.28 | .83 |
|  |  |  |  | Annual Rate | 5.28 | 3.32 |
|  |  | $5,893,000 | $15.68 |  |  |  |

\* Before allowing for 20% stock dividend payable July 25. Regular cash dividend is $1 per annum.

Here we have, as our table shows, cash holdings aggregating $8.08 per share and covering more than half of the current market price of $15^1/_2$. This is an imposing nest-egg, with good possibilities, but at present it supplies only a small part of the company's income. Its operating properties are responsible for practically all the excellent earnings of the last year and a half.

In 1923, the profits per share were $5.28. This despite the collapse in the oil price, and after depletion and other charges aggregating over 25% of the entire property account. These phenomenal results were due to a special cause—the development of large flush production in the Tonkawa field. Yet in the first quarter of 1924, with its output stable, earnings were at the rate of nearly $5 per share before reserves, and $3.32 after such deductions. More important still, the company has recently brought in a deep sand-well, which has more than doubled its total production and probably tripled the current profits.

This flush output will not last, of course, but other wells will be drilled to the same sand and the outlook from the producing end is now immeasurably improved. General over-production with possibilities of price-cuts, pro-ratings or shut-downs may cloud the immediate horizon; but the fact remains that Pennok Oil has to-day not only the most cash on hand, but also the largest current earnings in comparison with its selling price, of all the petroleum stocks known to the inquiring statistician.

## SHATTUCK-ARIZONA

Coming back to the New York Stock Exchange, brief attention may be paid to Shattuck-Arizona Copper, a modest issue selling at only $5 per share, but not without its peculiar merits. Here again the analysis shows cash and Liberty Bonds covering more than one-half of the market price, while the other current assets, net, supply practically all the remainder. Hence, the market refuses to give any value to the mining properties, which are carried by the company at $17 per share after substantial deductions for depletion and depreciation.

The market price of zero for the Shattuck mines and equipment appears unduly conservative when it is considered that these properties have not only shown very large profits under favorable conditions, but are actually bringing in a net cash income in the present depressed metal market. In fact, the net operating cost of its copper production was only 7.95 cents per pound in the first quarter of 1924. It should be mentioned that the company now produces more lead than copper, and that while the life of its copper reserves is uncertain, it undoubtedly possesses a large tonnage of lead-ores. In every past rise

## SHATTUCK-ARIZONA COPPER

**Capitalization: 249,390 shares selling at 10¹/₂. Total market value $2,618,595.**
**No bonds preferred stock. Balance Sheet Dec. 31, 1923.**

|  |  | Amount | Per Share | Income Account, 1923 |  |
|---|---|---|---|---|---|
| Cash Assets |  | $1,008,000 | $2.88 | Operating Revenues | $847,000 |
| Other Current Assets | $648,000 |  |  | Operating Profit | 222,000 |
| Less All Liabilities | 69,000 |  |  | Income from Investments | 38,000 |
|  |  | 579,000 | 1.65 | Total Income | 260,000 |
| Fixed Assets | 9,056,000 |  |  | Depreciation, Depletion |  |
|  |  |  |  | and Development | 262,000 |
| Less Reserves | 3,097,000 |  |  |  |  |
|  |  | 5,959,000 | 17.02 | Loss After Reserves | 2,000 |
|  |  | $7,546,000 | $21.55 |  |  |

Earned 1923 before reserves, 70c per share
Earned 1st quarter 1924 before reserves at annual rate of 85c per share

in the metal shares this issue has crossed 10—and the prospects are good for
a similar advance in the next favorable market.

## WRIGHT AERONAUTICAL

No enumeration of Cash Asset Stocks would be complete without including
Wright Aeronautical. This enterprise is selling in the market at $2,700,000,
while its treasury holds more than $4,000,000 in cash and investments.
In other words, there are $16.25 of cash assets applicable to each share now
selling at 10¹/₂.

The fly in the ointment is the threatened Government suit for the recovery of some $4,700,000, alleged to have been overpaid the predecessor com-
pany. The Government's chief contention seems to be that certain provisions
of the war contracts, although undeniably agreed to by the War Department,
were contrary to public policy, and therefore ineffective.

Of this pending litigation it may be said that the company itself, its special
counsel, and, more significantly its Certified Public Accountants, are positive
that the case of the United States is without merit. And it is also noteworthy

---

WRIGHT AERONAUTICAL

**Capitalization: 249,390 shares selling at 10¹/₂. Total market value $2,618,595.
No bonds or preferred stock. Balance sheet Dec. 31, 1923.**

|  | | Amount | Share Per | Income Account, 1923 | |
|---|---|---|---|---|---|
|  | | | | Operating Revenue | $2,227,000 |
| Cash Assets | | $4,049,000 | $16.25 | Operating Income | 238,000 |
| Other Current Assets | $1,024,000 | | | Investment Income | 186,000 |
| Less All Liabilities | 143,000 | | | Total for Dividends | 424,000 |
|  | | 881,000 | 3.54 | Per Share | 1.70 |
| Due from U. S. G'v't | | 1,181,000 | 4.75 | | |
| Plant, etc. | | 669,000 | 2.68 | | |
|  | | $6,780,000 | $27.22 | | |

Earnings 1st quarter, 1924, were at the annual rate of $1 per share.

---

that, although two and a half years have elapsed since the Attorney-General advertised his intention of bringing these proceedings, no legal action has as yet been taken. The Government is furthermore admittedly liable to the company for $1,181,000 for certified claims, which money is being withheld pending the outcome of the suit, and will be applicable against any judgment which might be rendered against Wright Aeronautical.

In the meantime, the company's balance-sheet position is certainly extraordinary. The current assets (including the amount due from the U.S. Army) are nearly $25 per share, and fixed assets are carried at only $2.68 per share. These moderately valued operating properties have each year yielded net profits of over $1 per share after liberal depreciation. Investment income brought the total profits last year to $1.70 per share, amply covering the $1 dividend which has regularly been paid since August, 1921.

Even a brief summary of Wright Aeronautical's position must not omit reference to the company's prominent place in an industry with a limitless future, nor should tribute be withheld from its shrewd and conservative policy, which has closely guarded the large cash reserves and refrained from expensive pioneering. Hence it stands prepared either to expand its business substantially whenever commercial aviation is placed on a profitable basis, or to liquidate without sacrifice if its present source of earnings—U. S. Government orders—should be lost.

It is the writer's considered view that, should the government suit prove unsuccessful, Wright Aero will be worth at least $30 per share. In this litigation it would appear that the odds strongly favor the company; and it is difficult to imagine any outcome, however unfavorable, which should reduce the value of this stock below its present market price.

# 25

# EIGHT LONG-RANGE OPPORTUNITIES IN LOW-PRICED ISSUES

*Two Varieties of "Cheap Stocks"—Eight Interesting Issues Discussed—Intelligent Speculation versus Wild Gambles*

Low-priced stocks hold a perennial fascination for the small investor. He regards them as best suited to his modest means, and as involving smaller risk of loss than more pretentious issues. While in the cold light of logic, both of these grounds for preference will be found somewhat fallacious, nevertheless the cause of low-priced issues might be successfully pleaded on rather different grounds.

It is undoubtedly true that in bull markets the cheap stocks enjoy the largest *proportion* of advance. Glancing at my newspaper as I write this, I observe that the first stock quoted is Ajax Rubber, which has risen from $4\frac{1}{2}$ to $9\frac{3}{4}$; while the next issue, Allied Chemical, has ranged from 65 to 79. Hence Ajax has more than doubled in price while Allied Chemical has been advancing about 20%.

The reader may think of numerous issues of the low-priced group—such as General Motors, Loew's and Nevada Copper—which have been persistently sluggish, even in this active market. A study of the situation reveals that there are really two kinds of low-priced stocks, which may be termed—semi-seriously—the artificial and the genuine type. The "artificially" low-priced issue has been made to sell at a small figure by the simple device of issuing a great many shares.

This is well illustrated by General Motors. Here the number of common shares was increased fifty-fold to over 20,000,000, presumably to obtain the market advantages commonly attached to the cheaper issues. But the stimulus of low prices was more than offset by the burden of innumerable shares, so that the way is now being retraced in part by a new exchange of one old share for four new.

The "genuinely" low-priced issue is one with a small valuation in comparison with the company's assets and turn-over. To return to Ajax Rubber, the price of $4\frac{1}{2}$ was genuinely low, because it represented an aggregate value of only $1,915,000 for the common stock of a company with total assets of $11,000,000 and annual sales of $16,000,000. The reason for the low price in such cases is usually found in poor earnings, due to a small margin of profit; or to the presence of heavy prior obligations; or both. Ajax Rubber exemplifies the former reason; Interboro Rapid Transit the latter; Wickwire Spencer Steel the two combined.

## WHAT EARNINGS IMPROVEMENT MEANS

It should be evident from the above that genuinely low-priced issues will yield a most pronounced response to favorable developments. Any small improvement in sales or profit margin may make a substantial difference in the status of the common stock. If Ajax Rubber could again realize the standard 10% margin on sales, it would show $3\frac{1}{2}$ earned per share of stock. If I. R. T. increased its revenues but 10%, with the same operating ratio, the additional income would be nominally equivalent to $10 per share. This is the secret of some of the phenomenal advances that have dazzled Wall Street in recent years, as illustrated by American Water Works, McCrory and many others.

---

This article was prepared in response to a widespread demand that we publish a list of attractive low-priced issues. Special care has been given the treatment of this subject in view of the fact that it is not generally well understood by investors. Attention should be given the educational features in connection with this article as well as the purely specific recommendations which are given. In order to cover a wider field than usual in this department, these issues have not been confined to merely the industrial group but contain selections as well from railroads and the oils.

The prudent will object immediately that these opportunities for large profit are offset by corresponding risks; and just as a small improvement in the company's affairs may mean a large increase in the price of the stock, so any adverse development may result in its complete elimination through receivership. One answer might be that it may be good business to risk (where such risk can be afforded) a few dollars now and then if there is a fair chance of a profit of several hundred per cent. But even this reasonable risk may be largely eliminated through careful choice. Let us discuss this point concretely, by reference to the possibilities of a number of low-priced issues representing different fields of industrial activity.

## INTERNATIONAL AGRICULTURAL

This common stock issue, now selling around $5 per share, came into being last year as the result of a voluntary adjustment, which provided:

1. *For the extension of maturity of the First Mortgage 5% Bonds from 1932 to 1942. (Over 85% have been so extended.)*
2. *For the conversion of $9,000,000 of bank loans into $10,000,000 of new 7% cumulative preferred stock.*
3. *For the replacement of $20,300,000 of old preferred and common by 433,000 shares of new common, without par.*

Of these three provisions, the most important was the second, which supplanted a fixed and overdue obligation by a non-maturing preferred stock, dividend payments on which are of course discretionary. Thus the company was placed in a healthy financial condition, and its total interest charges reduced to a small fraction of its average net operating profit.

It is this arrangement which makes the new common stock so interesting. At $5 per share, the entire common is selling at only $2,165,000, representing equity ownership of a corporation which has had a $30,000,000 annual turnover.

If the long-awaited agricultural revival is at last at hand, and if the fertilizer companies are finally to emerge from their protracted depression, it is evident that a substantial earning power may soon be developed for the common. In the meantime, the fact that the banks have been willing to surrender their fixed claims in exchange for preferred stock at $90 per share, must indicate great confidence on their part in the future solvency of the enterprise. In the writer's view, therefore, International Agricultural new common at 5 represents an interesting speculation because (a) it can easily advance four or five-fold under favorable trade conditions, while (b) even if the recovery is delayed, this company should find little difficulty in keeping out of financial trouble.

## WABASH

Somewhat similar considerations apply to Wabash common, selling at 16, and make it unusually attractive from the standpoint of "conservative speculation." Here again we have the entire common issue selling in the market for about $11,000,000, and controlling a property with annual gross receipts of $66,000,000. All that is needed is a little imagination to grasp the future possibilities of a set-up like this. Given only the inevitable growth of traffic—with operating expenses kept under control—and earnings far greater than the $2.70 shown last year are bound to follow. In the meantime, the fixed charges are not excessive, so that financial difficulties are most improbable; and the withholding of dividends from the non-cumulative preferred has been storing up equity and treasury strength for the benefit of the common.

St. Paul and Wabash, both currently selling at 16—offer perfect examples respectively of a wild gamble and an intelligent speculation. Consider on the one hand Chicago, Milwaukee & St. Paul, with its continuous deficits, its desperate financing, its approaching $45,000,000 maturity—surely here receivership must be accounted perhaps less than a certainty, but more than a mere possibility.

Compare Wabash, with small fixed charges, lower operating costs, larger working capital, an immeasurably better earnings record in recent years, its reorganization behind it instead of before it—and yet it sells no higher. This contrast throws a sidelight on a peculiar weakness of the stock market—its propensity for paying attention to only a single factor governing an issue, and losing sight of other and frequently more important elements. Wabash has been sluggish in the recent buoyant stock market, because its friends have been hoping for a preferred dividend this year, and the falling off in earnings has made such action seem doubtful. The St. Paul enthusiasts, having no dividend to look forward to, need fear no disappointment on this score; and are blithely pinning their faith on improved Northwestern conditions, plus general railroad prosperity, to tide over the crucial maturity of the 4s, due 1925.

A little reflection should make it clear that failure to pay a dividend on the non-cumulative Wabash preferred could not be very harmful to the common. At worst it means that a little more patience is needed before the possibilities of the junior shares are realized. But there are many in Wall Street who would rather bet gayly on St. Paul's escaping the sheriff, than make a safe and sound commitment in the future of Wabash.

## SIMMS PETROLEUM

A different type of low-priced issue is illustrated by Simms Petroleum, selling at 14. This has the appearance of a straight bargain, judging from current earnings and financial condition. The common stock has virtually no obligations ahead of it, and the net current assets exceed $6 per share, of which half is in cash and Liberty Bonds. The earnings in the first six months of 1924 were at the annual rate of about $5 per share of common, after deducting amortization charges of $2.50 per share.

This company has had a hectic history, including a price range in a single year of from 73 to 6. It has settled down, however, under new management, to

### TABLE I.

STATISTICAL POSITION OF THREE OIL COMPANIES: SIMMS PETROLEUM

| Capitalization: | | | |
|---|---|---|---|
| Guaranteed Bonds | | | $564,000 |
| Stock, 669,065 shares, no par, selling at 14 | | | 9,367,000 |
| Total | | | $9,931,000 |

#### BALANCE SHEET, JUNE 30, 1924

| | | | Per share |
|---|---|---|---|
| Cash Assets | | $2,053,000 | 3.06 |
| Other Current Assets | $2,520,000 | | |
| Less Current Liabilities | 373,000 | 2,147,000 | 3.19 |
| Fixed Assets, Net | | 11,510,000 | 17.20 |
| Total Assets | | $15,710,000 | 23.45 |
| Less Bonds | | 564,000 | .84 |
| Balance for Stock | | $15,146,000 | $22.61 |

| Income Account | Year 1923 | 1st 6 mos. 1924 |
|---|---|---|
| Gross | $4,050,000 | $3,887,000 |
| Net after Taxes | 1,278,000 | 2,479,000 |
| Depreciation, Depletion, etc. | 1,244,000 | 824,000 |
| Balance for Stock | 34,000 | 1,654,000 |
| Earned per share before charge-offs | 1.91 | 3.71 |
| Earned after charge-offs | .05 | 2.47 |

## Facts in Brief About Eight Low-Priced Stocks

INT. AGRICULTURAL

1. As result of 1923 readjustment, company is placed in stronger financial position.
2. Interest charges reduced to small fraction of average net operating profit.
3. Agricultural improvement warrants belief in increase for fertilizer demand.
4. Common stock at $5 will be favorably influenced by improved conditions.

WABASH R. R.

1. Control of operating expenses combined with growth of traffic should increase earnings over period of years.
2. Financial difficulties improbable. Non-payment of preferred dividends has added strength.
3. Common stock at 16 earned $2.70 per share last year and is attractive.

SIMMS PETROLEUM

1. Earnings this year at annual rate of $5 per share. Stock now selling at 14.
2. Production quadrupled since 1921.
3. Dividend probable this year in view of good earnings and strong financial position.

WALDORF SYSTEM

1. Prosperous and growing chain-restaurant system.
2. Should earn in 1924 double the $1.25 dividend.
3. Stock selling at 15 and yields over 8%. Attractive at the current price.

SALT CREEK PRODUCERS—MOUNTAIN PRODUCERS

1. Strong cash position.
2. Steadily increasing production and properties in Salt Creek field only 20% developed and seem sure of long life.
3. Favorable arrangement with Midwest Refining Co. (see text.)
4. Salt Creek Producers stock slightly more attractive than Mountain Producers, though latter yields a little more. Salt Creek pays $2 and yields 8.51%. Mountain Producers pays $1.60 and yields 8.89%.

METRO-GOLDWYN

1. Preferred stock to receive $1.89 in dividends and sells at 15. Yield is $12\frac{1}{2}$%.
2. Total assets nearly three times amount of preferred stock.
3. Combined earnings four and one-half times preferred dividend requirements.
4. Stock to be listed.

LANDOVER HOLDING CORP.
1. Outgrowth of liquidation of Willys Corporation.
2. Has in treasury 1 share Willys-Overland common for each share of own stock.
3. Possibilities for cash distribution (see text).
4. An attractive longpull speculation.

a very successful development of its holdings in Texas and Arkansas. Its production has grown from 1,000,000 barrels in 1921 to nearly 4,000,000 last year.

Perhaps nothing is more indicative of the quality of a company's management than its accounting methods—especially in the matter of charge-offs, and those followed by Simms Petroleum are conservative in the extreme. In view of the excellent earnings and large cash holdings, a dividend should be paid this year (as intimated in the last report), unless the general oil situation grows considerably weaker. But in connection with a strongly entrenched company, such as Simms is today, it should be remembered that the temporary demoralizations, to which this industry is especially prone, can mean only a passing diminution of profits, to be followed almost inevitably by the return of prosperity. As stated above, Simms at 14 is rather unusually cheap for long-pull speculation.

## WALDORF SYSTEM

Interesting possibilities are presented by this chain-restaurant issue, which sells at about 15, and pays a dividend of $1.25 per year. The company operates about 115 "stores," mainly in New England, with gross sales last year of close to $14,000,000. The capitalization consists of only $1,546,000 of 8% preferred, and 441,600 shares of common, no par, with a total market value of $6,625,000. Last year the profits equaled $2.38 per share of common; in the first six months of 1924 they ran at the annual rate of $2.58.

The company thus is earning 16% and paying 8% on the market price of the common. These would be satisfactory figures for any industrial, especially in view of generally poor results this year. But when it is considered that Waldorf System is a chain-store proposition, and deserves comparison with other companies in that favored class, then its exhibit takes on a more favorable significance.

Well established chain-store stocks are selling as a group to yield an abnormally low return, considering either dividends or earnings. Woolworth pays less than 3% on its market price and last year earned about 7%. United Cigar Stores has been called very attractive at 53, *because* current earnings are estimated at about $3 per share—less than 6%. And so with many other examples. Practically all chain-store stocks sell much higher than current results would justify—because the public is confident that future growth will make even present prices cheap. The peculiar strength of these merchandising companies is their ability to increase sales and maintain profit margins in good times and bad. Their tangible assets are usually scanty, but most of them have a resource of the highest value in their experience and efficient management.

There would seem every reason to place Waldorf System in the charmed circle of chain-store issues. The business has been in existence for many years; it has shown steady expansion in stores, sales and profits. Its cash position, while not brilliant, is adequate. **The stock sold last year at the equivalent of over 22, and might very properly reach an even higher figure in due course.**

## SALT CREEK PRODUCERS-MOUNTAIN PRODUCERS

These companies originally constituted a single enterprise and are still closely related from many standpoints. They control together more than 50% of the production of the prolific Salt Creek oil field in Wyoming and are both beneficiaries of an unusual contract with Midwest Refining (Standard Oil of Indiana subsidiary), running until 1934. Under this agreement, Midwest Refining assumes all the cost of development and production on the properties of the two companies, and purchases all the output at prices based on Chicago quotations for gasoline, etc. Hence the income reported by Salt Creek Producers and Mountain Producers is all net profit, except for minor expenses, taxes and amortization charges. This arrangement was entered into in order to foster orderly drilling of the Wyoming field; and in addition to other advantages, assures these two companies of a long life and efficient exploitation of their valuable holdings.

The capitalization and earnings of the two companies are quite similar, as indicated in the appended table. Owing to the rather uncommunicative character of their reports, it is not an easy matter to get at all the basic facts. A careful investigation brings to light a number of favorable features, which may be enumerated as follows:

1. *Large earnings in 1923 despite the low price for oil. In addition to nearly $7,000,000 reported as received from the sale of oil (free of all operating expenses) it would seem that each company's assets were increased by over $3,500,000, representing value of oil stored but not sold. An indicated income account for 1923 is given here-with, based on the data available, but its accuracy is not guaranteed.*

2.  *Remarkably strong cash position, especially in the case of Salt Creek Producers.*

3.  *Steadily increasing production, despite curtailment policies. Their proven properties in the Salt Creek field are but 20% developed, and are apparently assured of a long life.*

4.  *The unusually favorable operating contract with the Standard Oil interests, referred to above, which insures most efficient and profitable operation.*

5.  *An excellent dividend return of over 8%.*

While in most respects there seems but little ground for preference between the two companies, the stronger cash position of Salt Creek Producers makes it appear somewhat more attractive.

## LOW-PRICED PREFERRED STOCK

In Metro-Goldwyn preferred (née Goldwyn Pictures), we have a very different issue of a very different industry. A consolidation has recently been arranged between Goldwyn Pictures and Metro Films, the producing subsidiary of Loew's Inc. Under its terms, Goldwyn is being exchanged, on a share for share basis, for Metro-Goldwyn new 7% cumulative preferred, par $27. The initial dividend of $1\frac{3}{4}\%$ is to be paid on the new stock on September 15. As a preferred issue, Goldwyn will now receive $1.89 per share. Its present price of 15 is equivalent to only 56% of its new par value, and the dividend yield will be just $12\frac{1}{2}\%$.

Goldwyn represents an original cash investment far in excess of the current price. The company did a large business, but on a losing basis—presumably due to unwise policies. It is understood that at the time the merger was arranged the company had been placed on a paying basis. At this writing, the listing application of the new stock, containing complete figures, is not yet available.

It has been stated that the two companies combined have current earnings of $1,600,000 per annum, or four and a half times preferred dividend requirements. Of this sum, Goldwyn is said to contribute $450,000, and Metro $1,250,000. The total assets behind the preferred stock are valued at $8,000,000, while the issue is selling in the market for $2,800,000.

The desire to give the Goldwyn stockholders share for share in new preferred has resulted in the peculiar par value of $27 for this issue. Considering the reported large margin of earnings for dividend requirements, and the generous yield, 15 would appear an unduly low price for the new preferred. While Metro is not contributing a very substantial volume of tangible assets to the new corporation, its earning power will be an important factor. It is

## TABLE II.

STATISTICAL POSITION OF THREE OIL PRODUCERS (CONT.): SALT CREEK PRODUCERS AND MOUNTAIN PRODUCERS

### Salt Creek Producers     Mountain Producers

*Capitalization:*

| | Salt Creek | | Mountain | |
|---|---:|---:|---:|---:|
| Bonds and Preferred Stock | | None | | None |
| Common Stock, par $10 | | $14,968,600 | | $16,821,820 |
| Price | | 23½ | | 18 |
| Total Market Value | | $35,176,000 | | $30,279,000 |
| Cash Assets | | $7,135,000 | | $3,157,000 |
| Other Current Assets | $7,452,000 | | $4,274,000 | |
| Less Liabilities | 943,000 | 6,509,000 | 579,000 | 3,695,000 |
| Fixed Assets | $30,154,000 | | $35,210,000 | |
| Less Reserves | 15,044,000 | 15,110,000 | 11,141,000 | 24,069,000 |
| Total Assets | | $28,754,000 | | $30,921,000 |

| | Production | Net Earnings from Oil Sales | Production | Net Earnings from Oil Sales |
|---|---|---|---|---|
| 1st Quarter, 1924 | | | bbls. 2,209,000 | $2,280,000 |
| Year 1923 | bbls. est. 7,540,000 | est. $6,888,000 | 7,582,000 | 6,923,000 |
| Year 1922 | 4,250,000 | 4,617,000 | est. 4,293,000 | est. 4,650,000 |

| Indicated Income Account 1923 | | Per Share | | Per Share |
|---|---:|---:|---:|---:|
| Net from Oil Sold | $6,888,000 | | $6,923,000 | |
| Value of Oil Stored | 3,846,000 | | 3,684,000 | |
| Interest on Liberty Bonds | est. 800,000 | | 200,000 | |
| | $11,534,000 | | $10,807,000 | |
| Deduct indicated figures for Taxes and Expenses | 1,301,000 | | est. 1,300,000 | |
| | $10,233,000 | $6.84 | $9,507,000 | $5.65 |
| Depreciation and Depletion | 4,610,000 | | | |
| Balance for Dividends | $5,623,000 | 3.76 | | |
| Dividends—Cash | $2,245,000 | 1.50 | $1,850,000 | 1.10 |
| New Bradford Stock | 2,993,000 | | 2,403,000 | |
| Surplus increased | $387,000 | | | |
| Current Dividends | 2.00 | | $1.60 | |
| Yield | 8.51% | | 8.89% | |

understood to account for over one-half of the profits of Loew's Inc.—so that to an important extent, Metro-Goldwyn preferred may be considered senior to the one million odd shares of Loew's, selling in the market for over $16,000,000, and is undoubtedly an attractive speculation.

## LANDOVER HOLDING CORP.

The last in our nondescript gathering of low-priced portraits is perhaps the most unique of all. Landover Holding Corporation, class "A," is selling on the New York Curb at $8\frac{1}{2}$. It is an outgrowth of the liquidation of Willys Corporation, that ill-starred investment enterprise of the dynamic auto builder. The story is a long one, but suffice it to say that all the established claims have been paid in full, and a separate arrangement made with the Willys 1st preferred stockholders, whereby their shares were exchanged equally for the present Landover stock.

Landover Holding has in its treasury one share of Willys Overland common (also selling at $8\frac{1}{2}$), for each share of its own stock. These Overland holdings are distributable after July, 1928. But it is also heir to any cash remaining out of the liquidation of Willys Corporation. The receiver of the latter enterprise has on hand about $1,800,000, or $12 per share of Landover stock, this amount being subject only to a certain claim by the U. S. Government. There were originally two such claims, one for a large amount of unpaid taxes—but this has been dropped by the Revenue Bureau, and is definitely disposed of. There remains a suit involving $1,548,000, alleged to have been overpaid by the War Department to Duesenberg Motors, a former subsidiary of Willys Corp. The receiver shows an additional contingent liability of $560,000 for five years' interest on this claim.

The litigation is pursuing its leisurely way through the courts of New Jersey. It is understood that the defense is confident of a favorable outcome, on the grounds (1) that the alleged over-payments were not actually made. (2) The amount sued for is an arbitrary maximum, the sum really involved being much smaller. (3) Any judgment awarded the Government will be collected only from the assets of Duesenberg Motors itself, as far as they can be traced into the possession of Willys Corporation. These are asserted to amount to only a few hundred thousand dollars at most.

The reader must form his own opinion from the above as to the eventual outcome of this litigation. As in the Wright Aero case, the company at least has the cash, and the burden is on the U. S. to collect. It may be pointed out that so far these war-contract suits have proved generally unsuccessful.

In any event, the purchaser of Landover Holding stock at $8^1/_2$ has an interesting speculation. His commitment is fully covered by deposit of an equivalent amount of Willys Overland common. In addition, he has a good chance to receive a cash distribution ranging up to a possible maximum of $12 per share. It may be a year or so before the matter is finally settled; but it looks as if a handsome reward may be reaped for a little patience.

# 26

# SIX BARGAINS IN LOW-PRICED DIVIDEND PAYING STOCKS

## *Profitable Purchases among Business Men's Investments*

Herewith is presented brief analyses of a sextet of attractive dividend-paying common stocks, selling within a price range of 14 to 41. There is a special type of security buyer to whom such a selection will appeal. He is not the conservative investor of the old school—rightly careful, but a little hidebound—who holds anything but a mortgage bond to be a wicked gamble.

Nor is he the typical Wall Street speculator, buying and selling quotations only, to whom the property behind the price means little or nothing. Well within either extreme, there is a shrewd, intelligent class who recognize that wisely chosen, strongly entrenched dividend-paying common stocks prove on the whole the most profitable purchases, considering both income and principal value. For in the last analysis they are the real investments in the prosperity of the United States.

## 1. AMER. STEEL FOUNDRIES

Starting first with the Steel industry, the writer's choice falls upon American Steel Foundries, paying $3 and selling at 37. The dividend yield is therefore over 8%. This issue has everything to recommend it. The company is the leader in its particular section of the railroad-equipment field, comprising steel casings and car wheels—the latter providing a stable replacement demand.

There are no bonds, and the preferred issue is only one-third the size of the common. The 1923 earnings were $9.55 per share, over three times the dividend. In the first half of 1924, despite the severe shrinking in the steel business, it earned $2.81—or nearly twice the dividend. Cash and Liberty Bond holdings aggregate $12,000,000. On December 1 last current assets totalled 23.9 millions and current liabilities only 3.8 millions.

The attractive features of a security can often be best emphasized by comparing it with some other—particularly a standard, well-known issue. If American Steel Foundries at 37 be compared with Bethlehem Steel at 45, the desirability of the former becomes apparent. We have space here for only a superficial comparison, but it should serve our purpose. Bethlehem Steel sells 8 points higher but pays no dividend. It has 213 millions of bonds and 59 millions of preferred stock, ahead of 81 millions market value of common. So here the common stock represents only 23% of the total capitalization, against 75% for Steel Foundries.

During 1922, 1923 and the first half of 1924, American Steel Foundries in each period earned from 40% to 140% more per share than Bethlehem. Nearly 60% of its capitalization is represented by net current assets alone, while the figure for Bethlehem is 34%. And last, but not least, American Steel Foundries paid dividends of $3 per share since 1920. It is a decidedly attractive common stock.

---

*Though many stocks have advanced to very high levels, good opportunities still exist for the careful investor, particularly among the medium and low-priced issues. Each of the stocks herein selected and offered for the consideration of investors has been subjected to a strict test as to value of principal and security of dividend. It will be noted that only one stock has been selected from each of the six industries covered, thus offering the required element of diversity. An investment in each of these six issues would give a combined yield of 8.4% in addition to a good opportunity for enhancement of value.*

## 2. CUBAN AMERICAN SUGAR

The next issue carries the same dividend and sells at nearly the same price. Cuban American Sugar at 32, paying $3, yields 9.40%. This company is the second largest in the industry, and ranks first from the standpoint of financial stability. Its low production cost has enabled it to make a creditable showing of sustained earning power, despite the kaleidoscopic variations that have marked the last decade of sugar production. In 1921, of course, it took a severe licking; but even this deficit leaves average earnings for ten years at about $4.50 per share on the present stock.

There are one million shares of common, par $10, selling for $32,000,000. The 9 millions of bonds are likely to be called at any time and paid out of treasury assets. This would leave only 7.9 millions of preferred stock ahead of the common. On September 30, 1923, net current assets were 18.4 millions, covering both the bonds and preferred stock. In that fiscal year, earnings were $7.45 per share of common, well over double the current dividends. No figures are available regarding profits for the current year. As usual, sugar prices have varied considerably, and have recently had a substantial advance. In June last, profits for this year were estimated at about $5 per share.

The price of this stock has fluctuated widely since 1920, in line with changing sugar conditions. The high was 60⅜ in 1920, the low 14½ two years later. For the past year the price has been stable at around the 30–35 level. At this price it seems attractive, not only for its high dividend and satisfactory recent earnings, but also in view of the company's favored position in a basic industry, as evidenced by its ten-year record.

## 3. WHITE EAGLE OIL

From sugar we turn to petroleum. Here attention might well be called to the merits of White Eagle Oil, paying $2, and selling at 24. The company's record is really remarkable when placed against the background of its industry. Since 1919, when White Eagle Oil was organized, oil has been a feverish business. Few companies, outside of the Standard Oil group, bear a recognizable likeness to their semblance of five years ago. Many have grown several times as large; many have gone bankrupt; not a few have done both.

Yet, through all this era of ups and downs, of sweeping changes and instability, White Eagle has pursued a singularly tranquil course. It has paid its $2 dividend continuously since its first year, 1919—with one cash extra of

25¢. and one stock extra of 25%. It has made but one public sale of stock, and its only bond issue has been the recent offer of $3,000,000 of $5\frac{1}{2}\%$ notes. Finally, in each year, including the 1922 boom and the 1923 depression, it has carried something to surplus after paying its dividend.

This record of stability is especially noteworthy, considering that White Eagle is but a small company. Its sales of 14.7 millions and total capitalization of 14 millions are far from negligible, but they cannot be compared with even the large independents, to say nothing of Standard Oil. Yet White Eagle has built up a complete organization from crude production to retail sales, including three refineries, pipe lines and tank cars. But the key to its strength is its distributing system. At the end of last year it owned 472 service and bulk stations throughout the Middle West. It has steadily been building up this end of its business with a view to providing dependable outlets for as much as possible of its refining capacity. Hence, while in 1922 it sold 17% of its gallonage direct to the consumer, this figure reached 40% in 1923. This fact would explain its ability to make profits even under demoralized conditions, where the scanty margin between crude oil and *wholesale* gasoline prices bears heavily on the average small refiner.

In the first half of 1924, White Eagle earned $3.52 per share before amortization and taxes. This would mean about $2 per share after all deductions. In other words, the year's dividend was earned in the first six months. The recent cut in crude oil prices has undoubtedly benefited the company on the whole, for its own production supplies only $\frac{1}{3}$ of its refinery requirements, and it should save considerably on outside purchases.

It has recently been reported that the company is sold out of gasoline, having no excess inventory, and in fact holds $1,700,000 in cash against $681,000 last May. If this statement is true it indicates how valuable the service stations have been to White Eagle Oil in meeting the current problems of over-production.

The attractiveness of White Eagle may be illustrated by a comparison with Cosden, which sells higher and pays no dividend. Cosden reported a deficit last year while White Eagle earned $2.93 per share. Cosden's earnings in the first half of 1924 were less than $1.50 a share after estimating depletion, etc., on the same basis as 1923. This company has also over 9 millions of bills payable and its current liabilities almost equal its quick assets. On the other hand, White Eagle had 5.4 millions of current assets against only $740,000 of current liabilities. Obviously, White Eagle Oil is a sound oil stock and is recommended at current levels of 24.

| SIX UNUSUALLY ATTRACTIVE LOW-PRICED STOCKS | | |
|---|---|---|
| **Am. Steel Foundries** | **White Eagle Oil** | **Weber & Heilbroner** |
| Price.......$37 div.............$3 / Yield, 8.1% | Price.......$24 div.............$2 / Yield, 8.3% | Price.......$16 div.............$1 / Yield, 6.2% |
| **Cuban-American Sugar** | **Paige Detroit Motor** | **Columbian Carbon** |
| Price.......$32 div.............$3 / Yield, 9.3% | Price.......$14 div.............$1.20 / Yield, 8.3% | Price.......$41 div.............$4 / Yield, 9.8% |

## 4. PAIGE-DETROIT MOTOR

A natural transition brings us from Oil to Motors. The issue selected here is Paige-Detroit common, selling at 14 (par $10), paying $1.20, and yielding over $8\frac{1}{2}\%$. The company's products—the Paige and Jewett cars—are well known to motorists, but the New York public is not well acquainted with its stocks, although they are listed on the Curb. On the Detroit Stock Exchange, however, the common is fairly active. It has just been reported that the issue is to be listed on the New York Stock Exchange.

The investigator is immediately struck by the surprisingly strong showing for the first half of 1924. Sales were 25.5 millions, against 46.3 millions for all of 1923. Net profits after preferred dividends were $1,854,000, or $3.09 per share of common—at the annual rate of over $6 per share. These profits were about equal to those of Chandler, which sells at nearly three times the price of Paige. They were four times larger than the per share earnings of Hupp, which also sells at about 14. Particularly note-worthy is the fact that the second quarter's earnings were substantially larger than those of the first three months— in direct contravention of the general experience of motor companies this year. The 1923 earnings were given as $4.99 per share, but apparently certain deductions should be made, bringing the figure to about $3.90 per share.

Paige has recently experienced a remarkable growth. In only two years—1921 to 1923—sales rose from 8,700 to 42,900 cars. The introduction of the lower-priced Jewett model has proved a very successful step. This second line is being turned out in a new factory, which is claimed to be one of the finest in the country. Of course, expansion at this rapid rate has required a considerably heavier investment. Nevertheless, the large earnings above cash dividends, aided by the sale last Spring of $3,000,000 of bonds, have sufficed to keep the company in excellent liquid condition. On June 30, 1924, current assets were 9.1 millions against 2.8 millions of current liabilities. The working capital thus covers fully both the bonds and preferred stock.

Both on its separate showing and on a comparative basis, Paige-Detroit appears to be one of the most attractive of the motor issues.

## 5. WEBER & HEILBRONER

This issue is representative of the merchandising or retail group, which has made so excellent a record in recent years. Weber & Heilbroner operates a chain of 13 stores (12 in New York City) selling men's clothing and furnishings. The stock is quoted at 16, pays $1, and yields 6%. The earnings in the year ended February last were $2.60 per share, against $2.40 a year before. At the beginning of the current fiscal year Weber & Heilbroner purchased the business of Brokaw Bros., paying $300,000 in preferred stock, and $1,134,000 in cash, part of which was raised by the sale of 52,000 shares of additional common at $15 per share. The company now has outstanding $960,000 preferred stock and 225,000 shares of common, making an aggregate capitalization of $4,570,000.

Total sales of the present company are about 8 millions annually. The indicated net profits of Brokaw Bros. alone last year were only about $70,000; but the average for eight years was about $150,000. Certain changes in policy are expected to add substantially to future profits under new control. Combined net earnings have accordingly been forecast at approximately $800,000, or $3.25 per share. If these figures are realized, the dividend of $1, paid since November 1919, may easily be increased.

The financial condition is sound, current liabilities of one million being covered by quick assets of 2.7 millions. The tangible value of the stock is only $7.50 per share, but this is a fair showing for a retail store issue. Compared with others of this class, Weber & Heilbroner is selling at an attractive level and appears to have excellent possibilities of price enhancement through the steady growth of its business.

## 6. COLUMBIAN CARBON

The program will be concluded by an analysis of an issue representing no group in particular, unless it be that conveniently labeled "Miscellaneous." Columbian Carbon sells at 41, pays $4, and so yields close to 10%. The business has been in existence since 1907, but the shares are relatively new to the New York Stock Exchange, having been listed only last year. Due to the possible unfamiliarity of our readers with the business of the company, a brief description of its properties and products may be in order.

Its chief product is carbon black, which is the main constituent of printers' ink. In the past few years, carbon black has also become a major ingredient in tire manufacture, producing the standard "black tread." It is used in many other rubber products, in paints, varnishes and polishes, and a myriad other items. The company also produces lamp black, which has many industrial uses, and other black pigments.

Carbon black is obtained from natural gas, which the company produces on its large holdings in various fields, chief of which is the Monroe Gas Field of Louisiana. The company controls about 48,000 acres of proven lands and

HOW SIX ATTRACTIVE LOW-PRICED DIVIDEND PAYERS COMPARE

| Capitalization | Am. Steel Foundries | Cuban-Amer. Sugar | White Eagle Oil | Paige Detroit Motor | Weber and Heilbroner | Columbian Carbon |
|---|---|---|---|---|---|---|
| Bonds | — | $9,035,000 | $3,000,000 | $3,000,000 | — | — |
| Preferred | $8,951,000 | 7,874,000 | — | 2,338,000 | $960,000 | — |
| Com. No. Shares | 722,200 | 1,000,000 | 460,000 | 600,000 | 225,520 | 402,131 |
| Market Value | $26,721,000 | $32,000,000 | $11,040,000 | $8,400,000 | $3,608,000 | $16,480,000 |
| Total Capitalization | 35,672,000 | 48,909,000 | 14,040,000 | 13,738,000 | 4,568,000 | 16,480,000 |
| 1923 Report | | | | | | |
| Sales | $63,592,000 | $36,063,000 | $14,693,000 | $46,296,000 | $6,500,000† | $8,597,000 |
| Bal. for Common. | 6,987,000 | 7,450,000 | 1,348,000 | 2,352,000* | 442,000 | 3,376,000 |
| Earned per Share. | 9.55 | 7.45 | 2.93 | 3.92 | 2.60† | 8.40 |
| First Half of 1924 | | | | | | |
| Sales | — | — | $6,632,000 | $26,559,000 | — | — |
| Bal. for Common. | $2,046,000 | | 1,017,000* | 1,854,000 | | $1,228,000 |
| Earned per Share. | | | | | | |
| (annual rate) | 5.62 | — | 4.42 | 6.18 | — | 6.10 |
| Balance Sheet Figures | | | | | | |
| Date | Dec. 31,1923 | Dec. 31, 1923 | May 31, '24 | June 30, 1924 | Feb. 29, 1924 | Dec. 31,1924 |
| Cash Assets | $10,097,000 | $1,793,000 | $681,000 | $1,724,000 | $662,000 | $1,245,000 |
| Total Curr. Assets | 23,901,000 | 25,051,000 | 5,438,000 | 9,113,000 | 2,771,000 | 3,189,000 |
| Current Liabilities. | 3,767,000 | 6,633,000 | 739,000 | 2,763,000 | 1,063,000 | 875,000 |

* After estimating deductions. †Year ended Feb. 29, 1924, before Brokaw acquisition. Sales partly estimated.

53,000 acres unproven. It owns 26 factories, as well as pipe lines and tank cars. As a by-product, the company produces large quantities of gasoline, and it also sells about 10% of its natural gas production to outsiders.

The capitalization structure is simplicity itself—402,000 shares of stock, no par, selling for $16,480,000. There are no bonds or preferred stock. Reports for the past five years show a remarkable expansion in production, sales and profits. Natural gas output was more than quadrupled. Sales increased from 3 millions in 1918 to 8.4 millions in 1923. Profit before taxes rose from $1,386,000 to $3,866,000. After all deductions, including 1.4 millions for amortization, earnings per share last year exceeded $8, or twice the dividend. The recent industrial depression has of course somewhat reduced 1924 profits, which for the first half ran at the annual rate of $6.10 per share. On this account the price of the stock has declined from a high of 55 to its present level of 41 which is about the low.

The working capital position on December 31 last was excellent. Current assets totalled $3,189,000, while current liabilities consisted only of $394,000 accounts payable, and $480,000 estimated taxes. In view of the strong cash position, and the fact that earnings are still 50% above dividend requirements, there would seem no reason to expect a change in the current rate.

The company has been steadily adding to its productive capacity and the uses for its output have been constantly expanding. Hence it is in a position to take full advantage of renewed business activity, and should have no difficulty in exceeding the excellent earnings for 1923.

# 27

# READING—THE MARKET'S "SLEEPING BEAUTY"

*Reading's Powerful Exhibit Obscured by
Misleading Comparisons—Investment
Facts and Speculative Possibilities*

An interesting comparison can be made between Reading common and two groups of railroad stocks. Those in one group—comprising Delaware, Lackawanna & Western, Norfolk & Western and Southern Pacific—are earning about the same amount per share as Reading, but are selling at much higher prices. On the other hand, Lehigh Valley and Chicago & Northwestern are selling at about the same price as Reading, but are earning considerably less. Reading yields higher dividend return than any of the other five, excepting Norfolk.

Why should Reading sell so much lower than these other rails, in comparison with its current earnings? Are this year's results abnormally favorable due to special causes? Is it burdened by much heavier fixed charges than the others? Is its past record less satisfactory? None of these reasons will apply. The strong exhibit is by no means a phenomenon of 1924 alone; in fact the 1923 figures were far more impressive. With one exception its fixed charges are the lowest of the group; and everyone knows that because of its record and financial position, Reading ranks with the strongest roads of the country.

As far as the writer can see, the actual explanation of Reading's backwardness marketwise is to be found in one of its points of strength—namely, its phenomenal earnings in the first eight months of 1923. To clear up this paradox, a little of Reading's recent history must be retold. From January 1 to August 31, 1923, Reading was reporting gross and net earnings of unprecedented magnitude, which indicated a balance for the common of fully $20 per share. At that time this powerful exhibit was obscured by two factors: the severe decline in the general market, and, more important still, the litigation and consequent uncertainty regarding the segregation plan. For since the coal properties had long been the basis of speculative interest in Reading, the question as to how these would ultimately be handled overshadowed the more commonplace factor of current earnings.

It was not until October, 1923, that the segregation difficulties were finally disposed of. Almost coincidentally, however, the company began to spend enormous sums on maintenance of equipment—which fact, coupled with a brief coal strike and the general falling off in business, resulted in negligible profits in the last four months of the year. Instead of $20 per share, as previously indicated, the final result worked out at the still satisfactory figure of $13$\frac{1}{2}$, on the segregated basis.

Beginning with January, 1924, the earnings reported this year had to bear comparison not with the poor figures of the last part of 1923, but with the phenomenal earnings of the earlier months. Reading began to show an apparent falling off of 20% in gross and fully 50% in net. Hence, investors quite generally received the impression that Reading was having a very poor year—when in fact the earnings will be considerably better than its past average.

If it is true that Reading has been handicapped marketwise by a series of misleading monthly comparisons, it may well be that the tide is now about to turn. For the September, 1924, figures will be considerably better, not only than those of any month this year, but also of September, 1923. The same favorable comparison is likely to continue for the rest of the year, and should serve to correct the popular misapprehension on the score of Reading's exhibit.

The moment may therefore be propitious for an analysis of the real earning power of Reading, as shown by a comparison of its current results with those of the five representative roads mentioned at the outset. Table I gives actual earnings per share for 1923 and the estimated figures for 1924, expressed also as a percentage of the recent selling price. The most important fact is that both last year and this Reading's earnings are proportionately

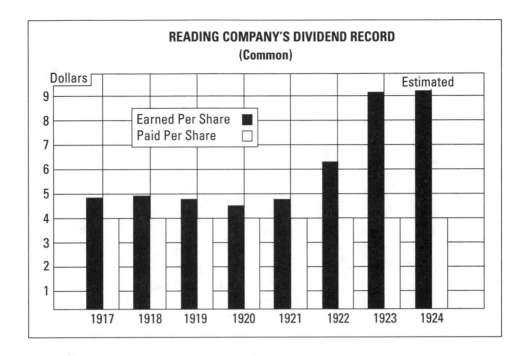

larger than those of any of the other five roads, by margins ranging from about 50% in the case of Southern Pacific, to 700% for Lehigh Valley in 1923.

Especially interesting is the comparison with Norfolk & Western and Lackawanna. As shown by Table II, here are three roads presenting nearly the same figures for the number of shares outstanding, gross revenues and net profits—with unimportant differences in fixed charges. On this showing one would expect them all to be quoted at about the same level. Yet the very stock which is actually doing somewhat better than the other two sells at less than half their price.

When earnings are suspiciously high or low, look at the maintenance account. Here the results are the opposite of what might be expected. Up to September 30 Reading has devoted this year 36.4% of its gross to maintenance—an abnormally high figure for this road, and larger than that of all the others except Norfolk. Incidentally, Reading makes the best showing of the group in respect to the control of transportation expenses. The advantage of Reading over D., L. & W. in this respect has been fully 9% of gross—an extraordinary indication of superiority when it is considered that both roads presumably operate under the same conditions. From the standpoint of financial position Reading rates with the strongest roads of the country. It has not sold a bond issue in years. The various segregation payments have poured cash into the treasury in addition to reducing its bonded debt by over $30,000,000.

Brief as this analysis has been, the facts disclosed would seem to justify the conclusion that, on the basis of earning power and financial strength, Reading is selling far out of line with the other roads. We have sought to account in some measure for this discrepancy by referring to the peculiarly misleading development of Reading's monthly earnings in 1923 and 1924. But other factors enter into the situation which deserve discussion, not only for their bearing on the question of Reading's comparative value, but also for the light they shed on the vexing question of how the mind of the market works.

Chief of these factors is the dividend return. Reading's yield of 6% is the same as that offered by Norfolk, Southern Pacific and Northwestern. Buyers of investment stocks habitually pay more attention to the rate of dividend than to the rate of earnings. This is particularly true of high-grade railway issues, dividends of which change very rarely in comparison with the fluctuations in earnings. The income statements exert a prominent influence marketwise only when the belief becomes prevalent that the figures foreshadow either an increase or a cut in the dividends. Hence, even though investors recognized that Reading was earning considerably more on its price than Southern Pacific, they would not be willing to accept a substantially lower dividend return on Reading unless they believed, either that its rate would soon be advanced, or Southern Pacific's reduced. The latter is out of the question; and while Reading's earnings would seem to justify fully an increase in dividend to $6, no one can predict whether or when this will happen.

In the case of the two other issues which yield less than Reading—namely, Lehigh Valley and Delaware, Lackawanna & Western—other considerations appear to enter. About these stocks are hovering the twin angels of Wall Street—Merger and Distribution. Though the one denotes addition and the other subtraction, the beautiful inconsistency of the market finds a bullish argument in both. Attention has been called to Lehigh Valley's ownership of Coxe Bros. (Coal) stock, which must be disposed of after February 1, 1926. The average earnings for this subsidiary for the ten years ending in 1922 were about 70 cents per share of Lehigh Valley, practically all of which has been paid over to the parent company in dividends. To the calm observer this is hardly a matter for wild excitement, especially since if this asset is presented to the stockholders it is lost to the company. Furthermore, nothing can be done in this direction until February, 1926, when the maturity of a bond issue will release the stock now pledged as collateral.

Lackawanna has a very formidable treasury asset in the shape of $60,000,000 of Glen Alden Coal 4% bonds, distribution of which among the shareholders has frequently been predicted. Valuing the bonds at 80, such a melon would amount to about $30 per share—a sizeable figure. But it must not be forgotten that any such action would mean the loss to the company of $2,400,000 income per year, or $1.50 per share. Without this investment income D., L. & W. would not have earned even its $6 dividend in 1923, and would cover it this year with a dangerously small margin. The market tends to regard an asset of this kind both as a source of income to the company and as a subject of possible distribution to the stockholders. This means valuing the same thing twice—a logical fallacy which in the end must be exploded.

Merger talk seems also to have played a leading part in establishing the high price of the two issues. The Van Sweringens are said to be after Lackawanna; New York Central (and even Wabash) after Lehigh Valley. As far as the future is concerned, anything is possible. No one can say with absolute certainty that the Van Sweringens or J. P. Morgan or the New Haven are not going to offer $200 per share for D., L. & W. Hence, in a speculative market, what counts is imagination and not analysis. But for those interested, it may be said that most large roads will be found to have been taken over at something approaching their reasonable comparative value— and that fancy prices are likely to prove the exception rather than the rule.

Curiously enough, even from the speculative standpoint of segregation and mergers, Reading is by no means an outsider. It still has its holdings of Jersey Central, valued in the market at $36,000,000, and by enthusiasts at fantastic figures. These shares, like Lehigh Valley's interest in Coxe Bros., must eventually be disposed of. In the pending consolidation plans, Reading is to go to the B. & O.—although there has been some opposition thereto on the grounds that Reading is too valuable to be given to any one system.

It appears therefore that the reasons advanced above may explain but will not justify Reading's comparatively low price. Furthermore, Reading is amply supplied with speculative attractions which can easily be exploited when public interest is turned in their direction. These include the current change in earnings from much smaller to much larger figures than last year; the possibility of a distribution of Jersey Central stock; and merger developments which may conceivably involve a battle for possession of this exceptionally prosperous road.

*In the stock market facts are important, but emphasis is all important. In the parlance of the fairy tales (well suited to Wall Street) Reading is a Sleeping Beauty awaiting its Prince Charming (in the prosaic form of a bull pool) to stir it into life and reveal its charm to an appreciative public.*

## TABLE I

EARNINGS AND DIVIDEND YIELDS OF SIX RAILROAD COMMON STOCKS

| | Price | Div. | Yield % | Earned per share | | Earned on recent market price | |
| | | | | 1923 | Est. 1924 | 1923 % | Est. 1924 % |
|---|---|---|---|---|---|---|---|
| Chic. & N. W. | 68 | $4 | 5.88 | $4.94 | $5.50 | 7.3 | 8.1 |
| Lehigh Valley | 70 | $3^1/_2$ | 5.00 | *1.90 | 7.00 | 2.7 | 10.0 |
| Reading | 65 | 4 | 6.15 | *13.50 | 9.25 | 20.8 | 14.2 |
| Norfolk & West | 122 | 8 | 6.54 | 11.80 | 9.00 | 9.7 | 7.4 |
| Lackawanna | 138 | 6 | 4.35 | 7.10 | 9.00 | 5.2 | 6.5 |
| Southern Pacific | 104 | 6 | 5.77 | 12.90 | 10.25 | 11.4 | 9.9 |

*Segregated basis.

## TABLE II

RESULTS FOR 9 MONTHS OF 1924

(000 Omitted)

| | Gross | Net op. income | Charges and pfd. divs. (est.) | Balance for common | Indicated balance for year | Number of shares common outstanding | Indicated earnings per share |
|---|---|---|---|---|---|---|---|
| Chic. & N. W | $111,426 | $11,699 | $6,505 | $5,194 | $8,000 | $1,432 | $5.50 |
| Lehigh Valley | 56,709 | 8,684 | 3,013 | 5,681 | 8,500 | 1,210 | 7.00 |
| Reading | 68,319 | 13,828 | 5,000 | 8,828 | 13,000 | 1,400 | 9.25 |
| Norfolk & West | 68,399 | 12,320 | 4,299 | 8,021 | 12,000 | 1,328 | 9.00 |
| Lackawanna | 64,213 | 11,463 | 704 | 10,759 | 15,400 | 1,691 | 9.00 |
| Southern Pacific | 202,693 | 33,449 | 7,500 | 25,949 | 38,000 | 3,724 | 10.25 |

# 28

## SIMPLE TESTS FOR DETERMINING THE VALUE OF RAILROAD PREFERRED STOCKS

*What Investors Should Know—*
*Recommendations and Cautions*

If you had approached the average careful bond buyer with the suggestion that he purchase 'Frisco Income 6s at 76, yielding over 8%, he would probably have rejected the idea with the remark that he does not like Income bonds because interest payments thereon are not obligatory. He might have added that, besides, the company earned its interest charges last year only $1\frac{1}{4}$ times over and that this margin is too small for safety.

At the same time 'Frisco 6% noncumulative preferred was being bought continuously, also at 76, by "investors" who were impressed by the fact that in 1923 the company earned the current dividend 8 times over, and this year will probably cover it 10 times over. A stock that earns 8 or 10 times its dividend appears well secured—much safer in fact than the mere Income bonds of a company which covers its interest only $1\frac{1}{4}$ times.

Nothing could sound more plausible—and nothing could be more ridiculous. Of course we all know that St. Louis & San Francisco Preferred could not possibly be better secured than the Income 6s, for the simple reason that the Incomes must first receive their interest before the Preferred can get any dividend. And, in fact, the Income bonds have received interest regularly for eight years while nothing whatever was being paid on the noncumulative preferred.

That this 6% preferred should sell fractionally higher than the 6% bonds is a strong indication that there is something wrong with the average investor's method of valuing preferred issues. A good share of the blame should rest on the shoulders of us financial analysts, who have been emphasizing earnings per share in articles and manuals thus giving investors the impression that this is a real test of safety.

In the writer's view this practice is a relic of the Dark Ages when security analysis was a branch of stocktipping and figures could be and were made to prove any given conclusion. It was only recently that the good old fashion prevailed of stating impressively in bond circulars the number of times that the interest on that particular issue was being earned. The investor was importuned to buy a third mortgage bond because it was earning its interest no less than five times, although he was not told that at the same time the first mortgage charges were hardly covered twice. This sort of honest misrepresentation has been quietly frowned out by the Investment Bankers Association. It seems about time to try to apply a similar corrective to prevalent notions regarding the safety of preferred dividends.

---

*The virtue of this article consists of its freedom from the conventional method of analyzing railroad preferred stocks. It points out the common-sense methods of appraising the value of issues of this type and presents several simple and important tests by which the investor may be guided in his dealings in this field. We urge thoughtful investors not only to read this article but to study it. They will find in it many points which they should be able to apply with great advantage not only in their purchases of railroad preferred shares but in all their security purchases.*

---

## WHAT THE FIGURES SHOW

Let us explain briefly how the current fallacy arises by reference to the St. Louis & San Francisco situation. Here are the figures in a nutshell:

| | |
|---|---|
| Balance for Bond Interest, 1923 | $18,611,000 |
| Bond Interest | 14,577,000 |
| Balance for Preferred | 4,034,000 |
| Preferred Dividend Requirements | 471,000 |
| Interest Earned | 1.27 times |
| Preferred Dividend Earned | 8.57 times |
| Interest and Preferred Dividend Earned | 1.25 times |

'Frisco has a large funded debt, but a small preferred stock issue. The margin of 4 millions above fixed charges is rather narrow compared to the interest requirements, but appears more than ample as against $471,000 needed for preferred dividends. In a case like this, it is evident that figuring earnings on the preferred shares alone will give entirely deceptive results. It must either be meaningless or misleading to state that a preferred dividend is being earned 8 times over, when the bond interest of the same road is covered only $1^{1}/_{4}$ times.

*Evidently there is only one scientific way to measure the margin of safety behind a preferred dividend—and that is to figure the number of times that earnings will cover the fixed charges and preferred dividend combined.* This is precisely the same procedure as is now universally used in measuring the safety of any junior bond—i. e., the number of times that earnings cover interest requirements of that issue and all senior securities combined. In the case of 'Frisco, it is much more informing to say that earnings in 1923 amounted to 1.25 times the bond interest *and* preferred dividend, than that they equaled $50 per share on the preferred alone.

The size and consequent per-share earnings of a preferred issue, considered separately, do assume importance at such times as the directors must exercise their discretion as to initiating or suspending payments. If only a small sum is needed for preferred requirements, these are likely to be maintained, despite a slender margin above fixed charges—if only for the credit advantage that the road would enjoy as a dividend payer. Hence at times the earnings on the preferred shares alone exert a considerable market influence.

Yet, if we study the record of these issues over a period of years, it is striking to observe how irregular have been the dividend payments on the preferred shares of the less prosperous roads. Whenever earnings fall off, the temptation to save cash at the expense of the senior stockholders is almost irresistible, especially if their claim is non-cumulative. *In fact, of all the roads not paying on their common, Kansas City Southern is the only one that has a ten-year record of regular preferred dividends.*

## TABLE I

ANALYSIS OF LISTED RAILROAD PREFERRED ISSUES

| PREFERRED. ISSUE GROUP I | Dividend Rate Entitled to | Receiving | Appox. Price | Yield (%) | Arrears to 12–31–24 | Earned Per Share of Preferred Year Ended Dec. 31, 1923 | Sept. 30, 1924 | Net Charges and Pfd. Divs. Covered Year Ended Dec. 31, 1923 Times | Sept. 30, 1924 Times |
|---|---|---|---|---|---|---|---|---|---|
| Atchison | $5 N | $5 | 93 | 5.38 | | $33.9 | $30.5 | 5.2 | 4.7 |
| B. & O. | 4 N | 4 | 63 | 6.35 | | 38.1 | 26.1 | 1.7 | 1.4 |
| Ches. & Ohio | 6½ C Co | 6½ | 107 | 6.08 | | 71.5 | 85.7 | 1.8 | 1.9 |
| 'Frisco | 6 N | 6 | 76 | 7.90 | | 50.2 | 58.7 | 1.22 | 1.29 |
| Ill. Central | 6 N Co | 6 | 114 | 5.27 | | 72.5 | 80.8 | 3.0 | 3.0 |
| Nickel Plate | 6 C | 6 | 90 | 6.67 | | 24.2 | 14.5 | 1.7 | 1.4 |
| Norfolk | 4 N | 4 | 76 | 3.27 | | 70.4 | 57.2 | 11.5 | 4.1 |
| Chi. & N. West | 7 N P | 7 | 110 | 6.35 | | 39.0 | 44.6 | 1.6 | 1.7 |
| Pere Marquette Prior | 5 C | 5 | 81 | 6.15 | | 46.5 | 43.6 | 2.0 | 1.9 |
| Pere Marquette Prior (Second) | 5 C | 5 | 71 | 7.05 | | 37.4 | 34.8 | 1.8 | 1.7 |
| Reading First | 2 N | 2 | 36 | 5.33 | | 94.3 | 50.3 | 11.3 | 4.8 |
| Reading (Second) | 2 N | 2 | 35 | 5.72 | | 49.0 | 24.9 | 6.3 | 3.0 |
| GROUP II. | | | | | | | | | |
| Col. & So. First | 4 N | 4 | 63 | 6.35 | | 14.8 | 31.1 | 1.73 | 2.35 |
| Col. & So. First (Second) | 4 N | 4 | 57 | 7.02 | | 10.8 | 27.1 | 1.50 | 2.03 |
| Culf, Mobile & N | 6 C | 5 | 82 | 6.10 | $24½ | 8.2 | 9.4 | 1.23 | 1.38 |
| Omaha | 7 N P | 5 | 90 | 5.57 | | 5.5 | 7.9 | .95 | 1.03 |
| Rock Island | {7 C* | 7 | 97 | 7.22 | | 8.2 | 10.0 | 1.05 | 1.10 |
| | 6 C* | 6 | 86 | 6.95} | | | | | |
| St. L. Southwest | 5 N | 5 | 74 | 6.77 | | 15.4 | 10.4 | 1.75 | 1.34 |
| Kansas City So | 4 N | 4 | 58 | 6.90 | | 13.2 | 12.2 | 1.37 | 1.31 |
| Western Pac. | 6 N Co | †6 | 86 | 7.00 | | 6.7 | 6.0 | 1.08 | 1.00 |
| GROUP III. | | | | | | | | | |
| Chi. & East. Ill. | 6 C | None | 55 | | 6 | 5.04 | Def. | .98 | .57 |
| Chi. Gt. West. | 4 C | None | 29 | | 35 | 1.22 | 1.87 | .73 | .79 |
| Erie First | 4 N | None | 41 | | | 15.1 | 12.3 | 1.45 | 1.31 |
| Erie Second | 4 N | None | 40 | | | 33.1 | 24.8 | 1.39 | 1.25 |

| M. K. & T. | 7‡ | None | 68 | | | 11.4 | 14.2 | 1.12 | 1.16 |
|---|---|---|---|---|---|---|---|---|---|
| Miss. Pacific | 5 C | None | 71 | 32$\frac{1}{2}$ | | .17 | 6.90 | .78 | 1.08 |
| Seaboard | 4 N | None | 39 | | | 3.22 | 7.84 | .98 | 1.08 |
| Soo | 7 N P | None | 62 | | | 9.85 | Def. | 1.18 | 1.10 |
| St. Paul | 7 N P | None | 29 | | | .18 | Def. | .77 | .70 |
| Wabash | 5 N Co | None | 54 | | | 7.67 | 6.55 | 1.10 | .79 |
| West. Md. (Second) | 4 N Co | None | 22 | ** | | 4.29 | Def. | 1.01 | .83 |
| Wheeling & L. E. (Second) | 6 N | None | 30 | *** | | 8.55 | 7.18 | 1.11 | 1.06 |

C=Cumulative
N=Non-Cumulative
Co=Convertible
P=Participating
*=Cumulative up to 5%. 7% issue is preferred over 6% issue as to 1%

**= 45$\frac{1}{2}$ % accrued on Prior Pfd. (not listed)
***= 57% accured on Prior Pfd. (not listed)
†= Will receive a stock dividend after completion of Denver reorganization
‡=Cumulative from January 1, 1928

---

### MAIN POINTS SUMMARIZED

1. *From an investment viewpoint, this analysis indicates the following to be the three most attractive railroad preferred stocks in each of the three groups:*
   *Group 1:  Pere Marquette (2nd) Preferred.*
   *Group 2:  Colorado & Southern (2nd) Preferred.*
   *Group 3:  Erie 1st Pfd., or M. K. T. Pfd.*
2. *From the standpoint of the immediate progress of the railroad share market, investment analysis is of little value when applied to the more speculative issues.*
3. *From a long-pull viewpoint, speculative railroad preferred shares do not appear logical purchases at these levels.*

## A COMPLETE PICTURE

In order to illustrate this idea further, and at the same time give a comprehensive picture of the entire group of railroad preferred stocks, we append a table which analyzes every listed issue of this class, excepting a few in receivership, or very inactive. To show the different results arrived at by the two standards of measurement, we present both the earnings per share (as currently used) and the margin of safety above fixed charges and preferred dividends together. The figures are given for the calendar year 1923 and for the 12 months ended September 30, 1924. Where the actual interest and other deductions for 1924 have not been published, they have been taken as the same as in 1923.

It should be mentioned that the bond interest paid by a railroad is not always an accurate indication of its real fixed charges. The company may have also to disburse large amounts for rentals (including guaranteed dividends) which are virtually equivalent to additional interest charges; conversely, it may receive substantial sums as "other income" (interest on investments, rental credits, etc.) which are properly an offset against its deductions. The writer has found from experience that instead of considering bond interest alone, the better measure of fixed charges is found by simply taking the difference between Net After Taxes and Surplus for Dividends. Our table shows how many times this figure (termed "Net Deductions" or "Net Fixed Charges") and preferred dividends combined are covered by earnings.

The roads illustrated in our table fall naturally into three groups: those paying dividends on both preferred and common; on preferred only; and on neither. At the alphabetical head of the first group come Atchison and B. & O. preferred. Those who are guided only by the earnings per share may be surprised to note that, whereas B. & O. preferred yields 1% more than the Atchison issue, its profits per share in 1923 were the larger. The real facts are revealed in our additional columns which show that Atchison's margin of safety above fixed charges and preferred dividends combined was three times as great as that of B. & O.

In fact, it will be found that in this group the differences in yield are pretty well accounted for by corresponding differences in the safety margin, on our suggested basis. An interesting exception is provided by Pere Marquette (2nd) preferred. At 71, the 5% dividend returns a yield of just over 7%, the highest in the group. Yet the earnings in the past two years afford somewhat better protection than those of B. & O., Southern Railway, or Chicago & Northwestern, all of which yield appreciably less. The Pere Marquette dividend is cumulative, while that of the other roads is non-cumulative. Incidentally, Pere Marquette preferred is offered 90% in new Nickel-Plate preferred stock, which is selling "When issued" at 85. The latter price is equivalent to $76\frac{1}{2}$ for Pere Marquette preferred, and indicates that if the Van Sweringen merger is consummated, this issue should be worth several points more than 71.

The safety of the dividend, while perhaps the most important factor, is by no means the only one which enters into the valuation of a preferred issue. Other questions which arise from time to time are:

1. Is the dividend cumulative?
2. How much back dividends have accumulated?
3. Is it participating?
4. Is it convertible?

The value of a conversion or participating privilege is rarely susceptible of accurate measurement. It all depends on the position and prospects of the common. While the conversion privilege constitutes the chief attractiveness of Illinois Central preferred, it seems of negligible importance in the case of Western Pacific preferred. Other things being equal, a cumulative preferred is always more desirable than a non-cumulative issue. But the value of this provision varies greatly with the character of the road.

It matters very little that Atchison preferred is non-cumulative, since it is well-nigh impossible to imagine its dividend ever being suspended. On the other hand, the cumulative feature of Missouri Pacific preferred has recently been a vital factor in the advance of the issue, for the current upturn in earnings has raised strong hopes of ultimate payment of the $32 per share cumulated since 1918.

But this leads us to another important truth about preferred stocks which investors and speculators are often disposed to ignore. It is evident, as stated before, that a preferred stock cannot be any safer than a bond ranking ahead of it. It is equally true, but not so evident, that a preferred stock cannot be worth more than a common stock in the same position. Suppose Missouri Pacific common stockholders gave up their rights and turned over the property to the holders of the preferred. The preferred stock would then be in effect a common issue (as Great Northern "Preferred" is today). But as a new common it would be worth intrinsically more than now as a preferred—for, in addition to having all the equities and rights to back dividends that the preferred stock now has, it would be entitled to whatever real value may eventually attach to the present common shares.

If the reader will consider the matter carefully he must recognize the soundness of this argument. The word *preferred* does not add anything to the value of an issue. If a common stock has just as large earnings applicable to it and no greater deductions ahead of it, it must be more valuable than a similarly situated preferred—because the common stock is entitled to *all* future earnings and the preferred only to a restricted portion thereof. Concretely, if Missouri Pacific preferred were the only stock issue, it should be worth as much as the present preferred and common combined—which would mean $100 per share, if the current quotations are justified.

## APPLYING A NEW TEST

When we apply this critical reasoning to present preferred stock prices, some of them begin to appear in a rather new light. Consider further Missouri Pacific Preferred. Its rise this year from 24 to 72 has been based in good part

## TABLE II

RAILROAD PREFERRED AGAINST COMMON ISSUES

| ISSUE | Price | Dividend Paid | Yield (%) | Earned per Share Year Ended | | Prior Ch'ges Cov'd Year Ended | |
|---|---|---|---|---|---|---|---|
| | | | | Dec. 30, 1923 | Sept. 30, 1924 | Dec. 31, 1923 Times | Sept. 30, 1924 Times |
| {Missouri Pacific Pfd. | 71 | | | $0.17 | $6.90 | 1.01 | 1.38 |
| {St. Louis Southwestern Common | 52 | | | 14.75 | 8.71 | 1.75 | 1.34 |
| {Chi. & E. III. Pfd. | 55 | | | 5.04 | Def. | 2.00 | .86 |
| {Reading Common | 68 | $4 | 5.88 | 14.50 | 7.25 | 6.30 | 3.00 |
| {Omaha Pfd. | 90 | 5 | 5.57 | 5.50 | 7.90 | 1.24 | 1.34 |
| {Southern Railway Common | 76 | 5 | 6.58 | 10.10 | 10.60 | 1.60 | 1.70 |
| {Soo Pfd. | 62 | | | 9.85 | Def. | 1.24 | .89 |
| {Pere Marquette Common | 65 | 4 | 6.15 | 8.93 | 8.21 | 1.80 | 1.70 |

on the great improvement in earnings which has encouraged hope of dividends—not only at 5%, but also to clear up arrears. a potential common stock, the facts appear modest enough. In 1923 Missouri Pacific earned 13c per share of Pacific earned 13c per share of preferred; in the 12 months ended September 30 last, the figure has risen to $6.90. Correspondingly, the deductions ahead of the preferred have been earned 1.01 times in 1923 and 1.38 in the current period.

This showing is not nearly as good as that of St. Louis & Southwestern common which sells 20 points lower. The "Cotton Belt" earned $14.75 per share in 1923, and, despite the traffic shrinkage this year, the September 30, 1924, figure is still $8.71 per share. Furthermore, all the charges ahead of the common (including preferred dividends) were earned 1.75 times and 1.34 times in the two periods.

If Reading common were compared with Missouri Pacific preferred, it would make a still more impressive showing, especially from the standpoint of margin of safety over prior charges. We may allow for the expectation of larger earnings for the Missouri Pacific preferred in the last three months of 1924 (current estimates being $9 per share for the full year), and yet these conclusions would be little affected.

Now in a comparison of this kind, back dividends do not enter at all. If Missouri Pacific preferred were a common stock it would have better than a claim to 32% in back dividends—it would have the right to all the dividends that can ever be paid in the future. *It should be apparent, therefore, that from a comparative standpoint, the current earnings of Missouri Pacific do not justify the price of 71 for the preferred—especially if the very poor record of past years is taken into account.* It is well to recognize, therefore, that the rise in this issue reflects very largely the discounting of a hoped-for continuance of the recent improvement, together with other benefits expected from the road's expansion plans. The price of Missouri Pacific preferred, therefore, looks more to the future than to the present, and certainly not to the past. Hence its basis is primarily speculative rather than analytical.

In Table II we set forth other comparisons of railroad preferred with common stocks, which indicate that perhaps the market is paying too much attention to the nominal priorities of many preferred issues without considering their real limitations. As the writer sees it, the situation may be summed up as follows:

1. Our analysis indicates that from the standpoint of investment merit, the most attractive issues in each of the three groups appear to be:
   *Group* 1.   Pere Marquette 2nd Preferred.
   *Group* 2.   Colorado & Southern 2nd Preferred.
   *Group* 3.   Erie 1st Preferred or M. K. T. Preferred.
2. From the standpoint of the immediate progress of this railroad share market, investment analysis is of little value when applied to the more speculative issues.
3. From a "long-pull" viewpoint, the speculative railroad preferred shares do not appear logical purchases at these levels.

For the prospective buyer must espouse one of two views. Either he is confident that a new era of great prosperity is opening for all the railroads, or else his native caution makes him doubt that all the difficulties under which the carriers are laboring can be dispelled over night. If he takes the latter attitude, then most of the preferred issues of weaker roads would seem too risky to be bargains at these levels. But if he is a thoroughgoing optimist on the future of the railroads, then well-selected common issues would seem to offer better opportunities for realizing on his convictions.

# PART IV

# JANUARY 1925–
# JANUARY 1927

# INRODUCTION

BY DAVID DARST

B y 1925, Benjamin Graham had amicably departed Newberger, Henderson, and Loeb (in 1923, at 29 years of age) and had established, with the backing of the Harris family, a private investment account, the Graham Corporation, which was dissolved two years later in favor of a new structure, the Benjamin Graham Joint Account, in which Graham's only compensation was a percentage of the profits. From 1925 to 1927, Graham contributed eight articles to *The Magazine of Wall Street*.

The middle of the new century's second decade were heady times and the twenties were beginning to roar. Buoyed by burgeoning consumer demand for motor vehicles and a +42% revenue increase, General Motors common stock rose +130% and similarly dramatic advances were registered by other automakers (including Nash and Hudson Motor) as well as tire and rubber shares and oil stocks. Other groups reflecting the nation's prosperity included retailers, chain stores, cement and gypsum companies, and railroad stocks. Even though the market stumbled somewhat in November after the Federal Reserve raised the discount rate to 4%, the Dow Jones Industrial Average closed at 156.66, up +30.0% for the year.

The next year's stock market performance was much more muted, a +0.3% pause of sorts for the Dow Jones Industrials in 1926, before they gained +28.8% in 1927 (and another +48.2% in 1928, to close at 300.00). The six-week −17% correction in February-March 1926 turned out to be the most severe market selloff from 1921 up to the market's secular peak in late 1929.

Even though the famous Florida real estate bubble began to burst in the third quarter of 1926, several stocks rose significantly for the year, including Warner Brothers, which almost sextupled, and Butterick (the pattern maker), which almost quadrupled.

American Telephone & Telegraph's launch of commercial telephone service between New York and London (and its successful demonstration of television between New York and Washington, D.C.) and Charles Lindbergh's historic nonstop solo airplane crossing of the Atlantic (on May 20–21, from Roosevelt Field in New York to Le Bourget Field in Paris) in 1927 seemed to epitomize a growing national confidence which also found expression in the investment realm. Even as the Dow Jones Industrials rose +28.8% and the Dow Jones Rail Index surpassed its all-time high (set in January 1906), several heretofore non-standout companies rose to investment prominence. Among them were International Harvester, +90%; Celanese, +166%; Macy & Co., +97%; Johns-Manville, +123%; and Wright Aeronautical (whose Whirlwind engine powered *The Spirit of St. Louis*), +276%.

At this point, it may be worthwhile to set forth some biographical information about Benjamin Graham. He was born on May 9, 1894, in London, the youngest of three boys, and moved at age one to New York City with his family. In 1914, he graduated second in his class from Columbia College, Phi Beta Kappa. Declining three different offers from Columbia to teach Philosophy, Mathematics, or English, Graham began his Wall Street career in 1915 at Newberger, Henderson, and Loeb.

In his 45 years in the investment business, Graham applied his acumen, work ethic, and creativity to stocks; bonds; put and call options; international securities; liquidation, arbitrage and hedging strategies; and on occasion, proxy contests (among the most notable being his successful campaign against Northern Pipeline). Graham taught a course in Advanced Security Analysis at Columbia for 27 years (from 1927 to 1954) and later served for 15 years (1956–1971) as Regents Professor at the UCLA Business School. Graham was a man of prodigious energy and voracious intellectual curiosity. Married three times, father of five children (the eldest, Isaac Newton Graham, died in 1927 at age 9, of meningitis), he authored at least three plays (*Baby Pompadour* made a brief appearance on Broadway, in 1934), the translation of a Uruguayan novel (Mario Benedetti's *The Truce*), six books (including his memoirs and his two widely read masterpieces: *Security Analysis,* first published in 1934 with subsequent editions in 1940, 1951, 1962, 1988, and 2008; and *The Intelligent Investor,* first published in 1949, with subsequent editions in 1954, 1959, and 1973), and numerous articles for *Barron's, Economic Forum, The Financial Analysts Journal,* and other publications in addition to the ones collected here from *The Magazine of Wall Street.* He bought a controlling interest in GEICO Insurance Company (in 1948), helped found the New York Society of Security Analysts (in 1935), and was a devout supporter of the CFA Institute. Graham compiled a stellar multi-decade investment record in spite of portfolio declines of –20% in 1929, –50% in 1930, –16% in 1931, and –3% in 1932 (a total four-year decline of –77%), compared to declines in the Dow Jones Industrial Average of –17.3%, –33.8%, –52.71%, and –23.1%, respectively, over the 1929 through 1932 period. He taught and mentored Warren Buffett and hired him from 1954–1956 to work for Graham-Newman Corporation.

Some of his home addresses included: 115th and 125th Streets in Manhattan; Brooklyn; the Bronx; Mt. Vernon, New York; Deal, New Jersey; the Beresford and the El Dorado apartments in New York City; 611 North Maple in Beverly Hills, California; London, England; 7811 Eads Avenue in La Jolla, California; Funchal, Madeira; and Aix-en-Provence, France, where he died on September 21, 1976.

On his tombstone at the Stephen Wise Free Synagogue Westchester Hills Cemetery in Hastings-on-Hudson, New York, are written the last four words of one of Graham's favorite poems, Alfred, Lord Tennyson's magisterial *Ulysses:* "And not to yield."

■    ■    ■

"A Diversified List of Low-Priced Stocks" sets forth in brief form the rationale for recommending seven "low-priced dividend-paying stocks which are intrinsically worth their present prices and which should yield very satisfactory results in the long run." Graham hastens to point out that *investing*, rather than *speculating*, in low-priced stocks is much less simple than selecting seasoned bonds, which requires a greater degree of discernment and analysis. When stock prices are trading at elevated levels, "the lowest price issues are likely to prove the dearest; for many a dead issue, awaiting a decent burial, has suddenly been galvanized into deceptive vitality."

Graham's first low-priced stock (he attaches no significance to the order in which these analyses appear) is American La-France Fire Engine common, priced at $10.00 per share and yielding 10%. The company manufactures various kinds of fire apparatus and trucks, sold primarily to municipalities. American La-France has enjoyed steady revenue and earnings growth, its three-year note and preferred stock obligations are completely covered by working capital, and net tangible assets are fully equal to the stock price.

Douglas-Pectin Corporation sells at $16.00 per share and yields 6.67%. The company manufactures pectin, used in the making of jams and jellies, and is also the largest manufacturer of vinegar in the Untied States. The book value of the stock is $10.00 per share, and its working capital position is good. Although the stock has advanced from a low of $9.38 per share based on anticipation of the introduction of a new product, Douglas-Pectin "is not without intrinsic merit, and its stock may benefit substantially from favorable developments in its special field."

Metro-Goldwyn Pictures 7% cumulative preferred stock is quoted at $18.50 per share and yields 10.22%. Loews Inc. owns the entire common stock of the company, a consolidation of Goldwyn Metro Films—the producing and distributing subsidiary of Loew's. The preferred dividend was earned three times over and its face value is fully covered by net

current assets. Beginning in 1926, 2% of the total issue in each year is to be
retired in a sinking fund by lot at $27.00 per share, equivalent to an
additional 1% yield on the investment.

Wright Aeronautical, trading at $16.00 per share, yields 6.25% and is
attractive to Graham for three reasons: (i) the company has the "prestige,
experience, physical facilities, cash resources, and everything else needed"
to secure a leading position in the commercial aviation industry; (ii) Wright
Aeronautical possesses extraordinary liquidity, having net current assets of
$24.00 per share, of which $17.00 (more than the entire market price) is in
cash and marketable securities; and (iii) "there seems good reason to believe
that only a small part, if any" of the $4.7 million claimed in an overcharging
lawsuit by the U.S. government will ever be awarded.

Waldorf System, a chain of 116 restaurants located chiefly in the East,
sells for $19.00 per share and yields 6.58%. Its sales and earnings have
shown steady growth, and a recent investment in the company by a
prominent financial firm should promote continued expansion.

U.S. Hoffman Machinery, the largest U.S. producer of garment-pressing
equipment, sells for $24.00 per share and yields 8.33%. The book value of
the common stock slightly exceeds the common stock price, although a
good part of the book value is represented by the capitalization of basic but
valuable patents. "The company's excellent management and strong
financial condition seem to afford assurance that the satisfactory results of
the past will continue in the future."

Fifth Avenue Bus is priced at $11.50 per share and yields 5.56%, "with
the prospect of an early advance in the dividend rate." Like a public utility,
Fifth Avenue Bus "has a permanent business, steadily expanding, subject to
few and minor recessions," and unlike a public utility, most of its plant and
equipment can be sold or moved. The company has no long-term debt or
preferred stock outstanding, and nearly 50% of its total capitalization is
represented by working capital. Fifth Avenue Bus has applied for a
comprehensive additional franchise, and "if the company is permitted thus

to enlarge its operations, the stockholders should undoubtedly obtain a corresponding benefit from increased profit and dividends."

■　　■　　■

In "Are C. & O. Holders Unfairly Treated?" Graham seeks to determine the fairness of the merger offer made by the Van Sweringen interests of Cleveland to the Chesapeake & Ohio (C. & O.) stockholders as part of the Van Sweringens' plans to combine several railroads: the Nickel Plate, the Erie, the Pere Marquette, the (small) Hocking Valley, and the C. & O.

Graham finds that the merger offer values the C. & O. Railroad at only 8 times earnings, lower than the valuation placed on the Pere Marquette and the Nickel Plate roads. Upon closer inspection, he also finds a further significant discrepancy in that C. & O.'s 1923 stated earnings were lowered by its paying maintenance charges amounting to 40.7% of revenues (due to a one-time charge for retirement of freight cars) compared to less than 35% of revenues for both Nickel Plate and Pere Marquette. Upon adjusting the maintenance charges to 35% for all the to-be-merged railroads, "then the superiority of Chesapeake's earning power becomes pronounced indeed."

On this basis, the price being paid for Chesapeake & Ohio is *only five times earnings,* as opposed to ten times earnings for the other railroads. Based on 1924 earnings:

> We find in sum that the Chesapeake shareholders are being asked to accept for their holdings less than one quarter as favorable—based on the adjusted current results—as that offered for the Nickel Plate properties; while Pere Marquette stockholders are treated three times as liberally. Even Erie, with its immeasurably poorer history, is getting 50% better treatment, from this point of view, than is Chesapeake & Ohio.

Graham forcefully reprises his unfavorable assessment of the inequitable treatment meted out to C. & O. shareholders:

And the common stockholders have some cause to wonder why their shares, on which $17 was earned last year, are offered new securities worth $94 per share—while Nickel Plate common, which earned about $13, is valued at $128. Pere Marquette earned just half of the Chesapeake figure, yet it is offered the equivalent of $72 per share.

Relying on the average revenue and earnings figures for the previous ten years, Graham finds that "the pre-eminence of Chesapeake would be fully maintained, and probably heightened." Graham's detailed analysis also reveals that Chesapeake's superiority in net earnings available for dividends follows directly from corresponding advantages in the underlying elements which produce net profits, including: gross earnings; fixed charges; the physical valuation of properties; and operational efficiency. With admirable restraint given the vastly inferior valuations offered to C. & O. shareholders, Graham concludes that his work irrefutably shows "substantial justification for the dissatisfaction that exists with respect to the treatment accorded Chesapeake stock."

■    ■    ■

In "Effect of Rail Consolidations Upon Security Values," Graham reviews the main influences affecting railroad consolidations in the wake of the Transportation Act of 1920, passed five years earlier. Thus far, however, due to vague guidelines and a general lack of regulatory direction, the Interstate Commerce Commission's grand plans for powerful, prosperous super-systems "have been more honored in the breach than in the observance." Only seven carriers have followed the I.C.C.'s General Consolidation Plan, and "perhaps the only thing certain is that the consolidation question teems with uncertainties."

After reviewing the I.C.C.'s probable attitude toward departures from its tentative consolidation plan, as well as the legislative environment at the state level, Graham considers the stockmarket consequences for various railroad companies. While recognizing the possibilities of exceptions, Graham lays out the case for purchasing selected shares:

> There is ground for believing that proportionately the largest profits are to be gained in the shares of small lines strategically desirable to powerful systems, to whom the amount involved in paying a liberal price would be of little moment.

Graham does not foresee equivalent profit opportunities in mergers involving large railroads, especially the largest (the Pennsylvania Railroad) because of its "inherently unsound" policy of guaranteeing dividends on (or exchanging bonds for) the common stocks of acquired lines. Citing the "grossly inadequate" terms offered to C. & O. shareholders in the proposed Nickel Plate merger, Graham also warns of the possibility of unfavorable treatment of minority stockholders. In conclusion about the I.C.C.'s initiative, Graham notes that the "effect on permanent investment value is not likely to be nearly as great as the temporary speculative stimulus."

■     ■     ■

"Bargain Hunting Not Thrilling—But Immensely Profitable" illustrates a variety of bargain investment opportunities and describes some of the factors which render a security a bargain. Graham concedes that "buying bargains is undoubtedly a safe and satisfactory way to make money in the market; but it is by not means the only way—and it may not be the best way." For Graham, "*the essence of a bargain is the price*" [his emphasis], and "most bargains exist *because* and *in spite* [his emphases] of some unfavorable feature" which analysis reveals to be either imaginary, overemphasized, or important, but "far outweighed by elements of strength."

One special arena in which Graham looks for bargains is among sound bonds or preferred stocks which have an adequate yield and which also have conversion or participation privileges. Another category of securities bargain can be found in issues, which due to neglect or erroneous analysis, return too high a yield relative to the degree of safety offered. Moreover, some bonds may represent true bargains even in the face of poor earnings, if the asset values are so large that the junior security holders (usually, the stockholders) would not conceivably allow default. In an example cited by Graham, the $714,000 of Superior Oil 7% bonds are covered more than six times by the company's assets.

Graham next turns to the simplest form of bargain opportunity, in which improving values are not reflected in the stock price. Examples include the wide fluctuations in the stock prices of Cudahy Packing and Consolidated Gas & Electric of Baltimore, whose prices appear "amply justified by any reasonable method of appraisal."

A very different type of bargain is represented by Industrial Finance common stock, whose common shares trade for an extraordinarily depressed two times earnings due in part to the fact that they have never paid a dividend and the company's preferred shares have been in arrears on their dividend for six years. In a situation such as this, a moderate increase in revenues or the profit margin tends to have a startling effect on the earnings of the common stock.

As examples of asset-driven rather than earnings-driven bargains, Graham presents Northern Pipe Line, yielding 7.5%, with no debt or preferred outstanding, and cash plus marketable securities equal to the market price of the stock. In essence, the company's bargain status can be traced to investors' concerns about competition from then recently completed Panama Canal. In Graham's opinion, a bargain has been created by investors attaching too much importance to an unfavorable development. An overly emphasized unfavorable development (rising raw material prices and the expiration of some leases) has driven down to bargain levels the share price of Waldorf System, a restaurant chain. Finally, bargains are created by a company's not making the most of its opportunities, leading to investor neglect, as in the case of copper mines Calumet & Arizona and Salt Creek Producers, an energy play.

■    ■    ■

In "A Victory for the Small Stockholder," Graham discusses the implications of the Interstate Commerce Commission's denial of the gigantic Nickel Plate railroad merger scheme put forth by the Van Sweringen brothers, Oris and Mantis. The I.C.C.'s rejection was based on: (i) unjust ratios of exchange; (ii) the newly issued preferred stock was not granted voting rights; (iii) the Nickel Plate remained a holding company, thus permitting pyramiding of control; and (iv) The Erie coal properties should have been left out, while the Erie short line railroads should have been included.

In the Commission's words, "the applicants have not sustained the burden of showing that the ratios are just and reasonable as between stockholders of the responsible lesser companies." The Van Sweringens had been hoping to turn their minority ownership of the separate constituent companies into majority control of the consolidated system, which directly violated the Commission's opposition to control without majority ownership, and its insistence that preferred stockholders be entitled to voting rights. The Commission also pointed out the poor treatment meted to two of the four roads, commenting that "there was an utter lack of independent and impartial representation of all the stockholders of the Chesapeake and Hocking."

Graham goes to some length to point out the "propriety—more, the necessity—of the Commission's adverse decision:

> But it does signify that age-old rules of equity are still in force—that though minorities may have no power, they still have rights; and that though directors may represent single interests, they still have obligations towards every stockholder.

In studying the reactions of the investing community to the details of the Commission's opinion, Graham notes that the *concept* of rail mergers had not been subsumed, none of the Commission's objections would likely prove insuperable, and some other important mergers may actually be "consummated while the fate of the greater Nickel Plate is still in doubt."

■   ■   ■

"The Riddle of U.S. Steel's Book Value" contrasts the book value of U.S. Steel ($281.00 per share as of December 31, 1925) with its recent record high stock price ($140.00 per share). Graham reiterates the time-honored principle that "prosperous enterprises sell for more than their assets, and unsuccessful ones sell for less," with the two major sectoral exceptions being the railroads and the steel companies.

In a series of insightful tables, Graham traces U.S. Steel's: (i) aggregate income-statement results over a ten-year period; (ii) their effects on the balance sheet; and (iii) their effects on the company's earning power. This line of analysis produces the startling finding that "the half billion dollars reinvested in the business have purchased only fifteen million of added profits." Graham issues an important reminder:

> All experienced investors know that earning power exerts a far more
> potent influence over stock prices than does property value. The worth
> of a business is measured not by what has been put into it, but what can
> be taken out of it.

The failure to grow operating income despite the significant increase in plant investment boils down to a higher expense ratio, which stems primarily from a disproportionate growth in labor costs. In turn, U.S. Steel's expanded wage expenses had their origin in: (i) the abolition of the twelve-hour work day in 1923, resulting in a great relative expansion in the number of employees; (ii) the large proportion of labor costs in the company's total cost of goods sold makes an expansion in payroll "a more serious factor here than in other lines;" and (iii) U.S. Steel only increased its ingot production 15.5% over the ten-year interval, as against a 42% rise nationally over the same time frame.

It appears to Graham that a substantial part of U.S. Steel's plant expenditure has been devoted not to *increasing capacity*, but to retiring obsolete and uneconomic units and/or to attempting to improve its manufacturing processes to increase its competitiveness with other steel manufactures. At the same time,

> To the extent that the undistributed profits are required to offset plant investment grown obsolete (and not amortized by depreciation and contingent reserves), the true earnings would have to be regarded somewhere lower than the reported figures.

Graham concludes that "competitive pressure has been gradually undermining the margin of profit on sales and the rate of return on capital," which is most likely be the "fundamental reason for the relatively moderate improvement in the position of Steel stockholders over the past years." The inescapable facts of the matter are that the steel industry necessitates a steady expansion of assets without assurance of a similar increase in earnings. Because of this, "it is inevitable, and by no means unjust, that the stock market should appraise these assets at less than their face value."

The bottom line for Graham is that "the essential character of Steel common remains the same today as in the past—a surer investment than most, but slower than many to grow in value."

■    ■    ■

In "Mr. Shareholder—Do You Know *When* Periodic Stock Dividends Help and *When* They Hurt You?" Graham examines the purpose, effect, usefulness, and possible abuse of paying dividends at regular intervals in stock rather than cash. While the primary theoretical reason for paying dividends in stock is "to reconcile the two conflicting aims of a company's management: to reward the stockholders and to build up the business," the intrinsic worth of a share depends on factors besides dividends. Such factors include earnings, future prospects, the quality of management, and the issue's marketability.

Graham points out that regular income is the fundamental aim of investment, an argument in favor of paying dividends in cash. Increasing investor focus on future earning power instead of current dividends leads to an emphasis on retaining earnings in the business and capital appreciation rather than paying out income in the form of dividends.

Because a company's overall dividend policy is ultimately determined by its Board of Directors, Graham acknowledges:

> That this situation has all too frequently operated against the small stockholders and in favor of the large investors; against the outsider in favor of the insider; even against the shareholders as a body and in favor of the management in their capacity as officials.

Regular dividends payable only in stock produce a yield independent of its market price. For example, "North American, paying 10% per annum, will ostensibly yield 10% whatever be its price." At the same time, one of the fundamental contradictions of periodic stock dividends is that "corporations usually think they are paying out less than shareholders think they are receiving." Graham favors the general concept of periodic stock dividends but he argues that the *appearance* of a stock dividend-paying company, thus, distributing to shareholders more than it is currently earning per share produces misleading, illusional, and basically unsound perceptions on the part of the investor. As a result, Graham calls for standards of sound practice in paying dividends and a more discriminating, less formulaic application of regular-payment stock dividend policy, the chief principle of which is that the current value

of the stock dividend paid should be conservatively less than the
reinvested earnings.

■    ■    ■

"The New Era of Discrimination in the Selection of Securities" reviews the
wide dispersion of price movements during many months of 1926 among
the major sectors of the equity market, and even among leading companies
within a given sector. Graham asks "whether any new controlling
influences, any new principle of action, can be discerned in the price
movements of the past year, which may have some valuable bearing on
future markets."

Graham seeks answers from the perspective of the various forces
influencing equity price movements:

(a)  Corrective—readjustments necessitated by previous market excesses;
(b)  Reflective—corresponding to current developments affecting the issue;
(c)  Anticipative—discounting expected future occurrences; and
(d)  Manipulative—representing large scale market operations independent
     of influences affecting intrinsic value.

The significant market correction of March 1926 applied to virtually all
issues, with the causes traceable to the high speculative advances of 1925
being unwound by margin and collateral calls. Extravagant overvaluations
and speculative excesses led to sharp *Corrective* price retreats in, among
other groups, the chain stores issues, the large scale public utility holding
companies, the larger baking companies, and most of the dairy products
and ice cream stocks.

As for *Reflective* price movements driven by reference to coincident
operating results, Graham cites advances in copper, sugar, tobacco, and
New York traction issues sparked by improving fundamentals and results,
with declines noted in the building equipment, coal, leather, and rubber

groups "because of unsatisfactory developments in these industries." In fact, the stock exchange list contained many pairs of companies in the same industry which moved in opposite price directions reflecting positive or negative current developments: in industrials, General Electric rose while Westinghouse declined; in meat packing, Armour fell and Cudahy rose; National Distillers retreated while U.S. Industrial Alcohol moved ahead; in motion pictures, Pathé advanced while Warner Brothers slipped; and in the railroad sector, Atchison, Norfolk, and Rock Island were up, while Seaboard and Atlantic Coast Line declined.

Noting that in the 1926 market prices "moved quite generally not before but along with industrial developments," with a few exceptions Graham identified only U.S. Steel's upward price behavior as derived from *Anticipative* forces expecting an increased cash dividend in 1926 and a probable stock dividend in 1927.

The unusual price movement of Interborough Rapid Transit shares relative to that of a similar enterprise, Manhattan Elevated Modified guaranteed shares indicates to Graham that *Manipulative* influences were at work preventing normal price relationships from asserting themselves.

Perhaps partly recognizing that the 1920s bull market had further to go in price and in duration, Graham concludes by classifying the year 1926 as "at bottom more logical and intelligent than most of its predecessors."

> Nevertheless, the writer imagines that experienced observers would demand more proof than a single twelve months can afford that the days of wild speculation and ensuing general liquidations are definitely behind us.

# 29

# A DIVERSIFIED LIST OF LOW-PRICED STOCKS

*Seven Dividend Payers Selling Under
$25 per Share Which Are Attractive
for Immediate Income and
Long Pull Prospects*

Kipling's "nine and sixty ways of constructing tribal lays" are easily exceeded by the available methods of investing money. Unfortunately, we cannot say of the latter that "Every bloomin' one of them is right." Yet the field of sound investment is by no means restricted to the single group of "gilt-edged securities" but offers a wide variety of approach to those of enterprise and judgment. To speak of *investing* in low-priced common stocks may seem to many like an absurd contradiction. Nevertheless, the idea is practicable and the results may be most satisfactory; but it is much less simple than selecting seasoned bonds, requiring as it does a greater degree of discrimination and study.

At this point in the market, when price levels appear generally high, if not prohibitive, the selection of really attractive common stocks is becoming especially difficult. In particular, the lowest price issues are likely to prove the dearest; for many a dead issue, awaiting decent burial, has suddenly been galvanized into deceptive vitality. Are there any stocks left that can be bought without undue risk?

The answer depends essentially upon the reader's point of view. No issue, however skilfully chosen, can well escape the influence of a general set-back. Yet, disregarding the question of immediate fluctuations (which of course may be upward as well as downward), the small investor may still be able to acquire an assortment of low-priced dividend-paying stocks which are intrinsically worth their present prices and should yield very satisfactory results in the long run. Seven issues of this type are discussed in the following paragraphs:

---

**1. *AMERICAN LA-FRANCE FIRE ENGINE common (par $10).***
   ***Price*** $10, *dividend* $1, *yield* 10%.

---

This company manufactures various kinds of fire apparatus and also commercial motor trucks. Most of its product is sold to municipalities. The present company began operations in 1912. Its sales have increased steadily from $1,500,000 the first year to above $8,000,000 in 1924. During this period it has never failed to report a surplus after dividends. The common has received regular disbursements for ten years, the present $1 (10%) rate having been in effect since February, 1920.

---

*The seven low-priced stocks included in this article represent practically the only attractive opportunities remaining among this class of stock so far as New York Stock Exchange securities are concerned. Several of these issues have been recommended at somewhat lower prices in past issues of this Magazine but are considered still to hold possibilities. No significance should be attached to the order in which these analyses appear.*

---

Earnings for the first nine months of 1924 were at the annual rate of $1.70 per share. In 1923 about the same figure was earned on a somewhat smaller capitalization. Net tangible assets are fully equal to the present price, and the company enjoys excellent management and financial backing.

The 345,000 shares of common stock are preceded by two millions of three-year notes, and about four millions of preferred. These senior obligations, however, are fully covered by working capital. *The exceptionally stable nature of the company's business, and its excellent record of continued expansion, would seem not only to justify the present capitalization structure, but also to offer good possibilities of an enhanced value for the common stock.*

---

**2. *DOUGLAS-PECTIN CORP.***
   ***Price*** 16, *dividend* $1, *yield* 6.67%.

---

This company manufactures "Pectin," an essential element in the making of jams and jellies. This product is sold also in bottles under the name of "Certo," and has shown a rapid sales growth in recent years. In addition, the company is the largest manufacturer of vinegar in the United States.

The capitalization consists of $475,000 of 7% bonds, due 1932, and 300,000 shares of no-par stock. The book value of the stock is about $10 per share. Its working capital position is good. In 1922 and 1923, the net earnings were about $1.70 per share. In the first nine months of 1924 they amounted to $1.35 per share, indicating about the same results for the full year as in 1923. The $1 dividend has been paid since organization of the present company in April, 1923.

The stock has advanced from a low of $9^3/_8$, partly in sympathy with the general market, and partly on a recent announcement that the company is placing a new product on the market a palatable form of castor oil, which is expected to have a large sale. *While hardly in the bargain class, Douglas-Pectin is not without intrinsic merit, and its stock may benefit substantially from favorable developments in its special field.*

---

**3. *METRO-GOLDWYN PICTURES* 7% *Cumulative Preferred (par $27).***
   ***Price*** 18$^1/_2$, *dividend* $1.89, *yield* 10.22%.

---

The rather outlandish $27 par value arose from a share for share exchange of Goldwyn Pictures for this issue, at the former's appraised value.

The company is a consolidation of Goldwyn Metro Films—the producing and distributing subsidiary of Loew's Inc.

There is $4,971,000 of preferred, which at $18^{1}/_{2}$ is selling at 70% of its face value. Loew's owns the entire common issue of $3,100,000, and has an additional investment of $3,700,000 in the form of permanent advances. Last year Metro-Goldwyn reported about $20,000,000 of gross business, and net earnings of about $1,000,000. In other words, the preferred dividend was earned about 3 times over. The face value of the preferred stock is fully covered by net current and working assets.

Although the predecessor companies have enjoyed a large gross business for many years, their profits have been quite irregular—particularly in the case of Goldwyn. There seems good reason to believe, however, that the new conditions growing out of the merger should do much to stabilize the earning power of the present company, so that there should be little difficulty in covering the preferred dividend. The close relationship with Loew's Inc., owning so many theaters, should prove of the greatest value.

*Metro-Goldwyn preferred has recently advanced from about 15 to $18^{1}/_{2}$, partly in sympathy with the great strength and activity in Loew's. Although naturally not as attractive as at its lower price, the yield of 10% still to be obtained on this issue remains a strong recommendation. Beginning in 1926, 2% of the total issue in each year is to be retired by a lot at $27 per share. The value of this sinking-fund provision is equivalent to an additional 1% yield on the investment.*

---

**4.  *WRIGHT AERONAUTICAL.***
    ***Price*** 16, *dividend* $1, *yield* 6.25%.

---

Despite the recent advance of this stock from a low of about 10, it still holds possibilities which deserve consideration. There are three main elements in the Wright Aeronautical situation:

1.  The stock offers a most attractive medium for those who have confidence in the future of commercial aviation. The company is amply supplied with the prestige, experience, physical facilities, cash resources, financial backing, and everything else needed to place it in the forefront of the industry. Furthermore, this is not a new, untried venture, but a company with a five-year record of stable profits and uninterrupted dividends dating from May, 1921. Its capitalization consists simply of 249,000 shares of no-par stock.

2. The company is in an extraordinary liquid position, having net current assets alone of over $6,000,000, or $24 per share, of which $17 (the entire market price) is in cash and marketable securities. But—

3. Three years ago the United States Government announced its intention of suing the company for over $4,700,000, alleged to have been overpaid the predecessor enterprise on war contracts. Despite the long interval since elapsed, no proceedings have actually been started. There seems good reason to believe that only a small part, if any, of this sum will ever be awarded the government.

*Aside from the possible continuance of the recent market activity of this stock, it seems to have exceptional long-pull prospects. If and when the government claim is disposed of without serious cost to the company, as the management confidently expects, then the enormous cash assets and strategic trade position of Wright Aeronautical should raise the price of the stock considerably above its present level.*

---

### 5. *WALDORF SYSTEM.*
*Price* $19, *dividend* $1.25, *yield* 6.58%.

---

This company operates a chain of 116 restaurants, located chiefly in the East. Its capitalization consists of about $1,550,000 preferred and 442,000 shares of no-par common, valued at $8,400,000. Its gross business amounts to about $14,000,000 annually. The net profits in each of the last three years have been $1,150,000, or over $2.30 per share.

These earnings amount to about 12% on the present market price. This is a relatively large ratio for a chainstore proposition, practically all of which tend to sell in the market on the basis of profits expected in the future rather than current results. A banking firm, prominent in the chain-store field, has recently acquired a substantial interest in Waldorf System. *This should mean ampler resources and experience to take advantage of the wide possibilities of expansion for an enterprise of this character.*

---

### 6. *U. S. HOFFMAN MACHINERY.*
*Price* $24, *dividend* $2, *yield* 8.33%.

---

This enterprise is by far the largest producer of garment-pressing machinery in the United States. It sells its output to tailoring establishments,

SEVEN ATTRACTIVE LOW-PRICED DIVIDEND-PAYING STOCKS

| Issue | Price About | Div. Rate | Yield (%) | Earn'gs Per Sh. 1924* | Ear'd on Market Price |
|---|---|---|---|---|---|
| Am. La France Fire Eng. | 10½ | $1.00 | 8.70 | $1.60 | 13.8 |
| Douglas Pectin | 16 | 1.00 | 6.33 | 1.70 | 10.7 |
| Fifth Ave. Bus | 11½ | .64 | 5.56 | 1.77 | 15.4 |
| U. S. Hoffman Mach | 24 | 2.00 | 8.33 | 4.00 | 16.7 |
| Waldorf System | 19 | 1.25 | 6.58 | 2.32 | 12.2 |
| Wright Aero | 16 | 1.00 | 6.25 | 1.65 | 10.0 |
| Metro-Goldwyn Pfd. (Par 27) | 18½ | 1.89 | 10.22 | 5.44 | 29.4 |

* Estimated.

laundries, hotels, clothing factories, and many others. Since 1908 annual sales have grown without interruption from $94,000 to over 5 millions. Its capital consists of $1,300,000 of 7% cumulative preferred (convertible into common at $30), and 180,000 shares of common. On the present setup, the net profits in each of the past three years have exceeded $4 per share, after deducting $1 per share for amortization of patents.

The book value of the common stock somewhat exceeds the market price, though a good part is represented by capitalizing patents. None the less, these patents, which are basic, have a very real value, as shown by the steadily increasing and constantly profitable business based thereon. *The company's excellent management and strong financial condition seems to afford assurance that the satisfactory results of the past will continue in the future.*

---

**7. FIFTH AVENUE BUS.**
*Price* 11½, *dividend* $.64, *yield* 5.56%.

---

The low yield of this issue is offset by many favorable factors, not the least being the prospect of an early advance in the dividend rate. Fifth Avenue Bus is one of an intricate series of holding companies controlling the well known green buses of New York City. Under a plan of merger of the New York and Chicago enterprises, most of the Fifth Avenue Bus shares were acquired by the new Omnibus Corp. But the Fifth Avenue Bus Company retains, its separate interest in the New York properties; and since a considerable number of shares were not turned in, they continue to be traded in on the New York Stock Exchange.

Fifth Avenue Bus is a most unusual enterprise in that it appears to combine all the advantages of public utility companies with none of their drawbacks. Like every public utility, it has a permanent business, steadily expanding, subject to few and minor recessions. But instead of being committed to a fixed plant investment equivalent to several times its annual business, Fifth Avenue Bus takes no more than $2 of revenue for each dollar of plant and equipment, and nearly all of it is in a form which can be readily sold or moved. For this reason the company has been able to avoid issuing those large amounts of bonds and preferred stocks which nearly always characterize and often burden the typical public utility.

Eliminating the meaningless holding company structure, the Fifth Avenue Bus enterprise is seen to be capitalized at 728,500 shares of no-par, which at $11\frac{1}{2}$ have a total value of $8,378,000. There are no bonds or preferred stock. Furthermore, of this total capitalization, nearly 50% is represented by working capital, and 40% by cash and marketable securities (chiefly Liberty bonds). The peculiarly favorable nature of the company's business is seen from the fact that it has been able to increase its annual receipts from about $600,000 in 1912 to nearly $6,000,000 in 1924, without raising any new capital—and at the same time to accumulate a surplus cash fund of 3 million dollars available for further expansion.

In the calendar year 1923 net profits were $1.77 per share for Fifth Avenue Bus stock, or $15\frac{1}{2}$% of the market price. For 1924 the figure will be about the same. But it should be borne in mind that the Security Fund of 3 million dollars, which represents over 40% of the capital, provided only about 13% of the income. This means that on that part of the present capitalization actually invested in the business, the net earnings were fully 20%. This figure, which would be very satisfactory for an industrial enterprise, is little short of remarkable in the case of a public utility, very few of which earn as much as 10% on their total capitalization.

Investors may hesitate to buy into this company on account of the tangled transit situation in New York City. Uncertain as are many of its aspects, there seems little reason to fear for the future of Fifth Avenue Bus. Its franchises are for the most part permanent, and possibly exclusive. It seems very unlikely that other companies will be permitted to operate over its present routes. On the other hand, the local administration contemplates a wide extension of bus facilities throughout the city, and the Fifth Avenue Bus company has made a bid for comprehensive additional franchise. While there are many rivals in the field, this company appears to have reason for bearing off the main prize. For its offer is backed by plenty of capital, long experience, and— best of all—the decided good-will of the public. *If the company is permitted thus to enlarge its operations, the stockholders should undoubtedly obtain a corresponding benefit from increased profits and dividends.*

# 30

# ARE C. & O. HOLDERS UNFAIRLY TREATED?

*Analysis of the Van Sweringen Merger—How the Earnings of the Constituent Companies Compare with Their Purchase Price*

That the completion of the Greater Nickel Plate Merger, announced early in August last, has been delayed by a variety of difficulties should occasion neither surprise nor concern to those familiar with the vast amount of detail and the numerous technical obstacles inherent in a corporate transaction of this magnitude. A keen observer of the proceedings, however, cannot have failed to note a rather striking peculiarity about the negotiations of the past few months.

It will be recalled that when the merger terms were originally announced, they were regarded as quite favorable to each of the constituent companies with the exception of Chesapeake & Ohio. These views were registered in the stock market by advances in the shares of Nickel Plate, Erie and Pere Marquette, while Chesapeake common and preferred declined substantially. At the same time there was considerable tentative discussion of possible organized opposition to the Plan by minority stockholders, particularly since it apparently made no provision whatever for compensation to dissenting interests.

It appears that the problem of caring for non-participating stockholders has since constituted the chief obstacle to the progress of the Plan. It has necessitated numerous conferences, culminating in new agreements. But strangely enough, these discussions have all taken place between the Van Sweringens and the Erie or Pere Marquette directors, on behalf of possible Erie and Pere Marquette dissenting stockholders.

The directors of Chesapeake apparently had not considered it necessary to take any similar steps on behalf of their stockholders—although it was generally anticipated that owners of Chesapeake would be more likely than any others to dissent. This fact was perfectly obvious in the case of Chesapeake preferred. Under the Plan, each share of this issue was offered 1.15 shares of new Nickel Plate preferred. At the opening price of 83 for the new preferred, this meant an offer of $95\frac{1}{2}$ for Chesapeake preferred—which was not only 13 points below its then market quotation, but 5 points below its lowest recorded price. Under these conditions it would seem that Chesapeake preferred stockholders could not be blamed if they elected not to turn in their shares; and it would also appear that they were at least as well entitled to have their interests safeguarded as were the possible Erie or Pere Marquette minorities. It was not, however, until the recent announcement of the new lease terms that Chesapeake stockholders learned that they, too, were to be included in the concessions made to the Pere Marquette and Erie objectors.

As it happens, the original rather scattered opposition of Chesapeake stockholders, after a period of silent vigilance, has recently again been given voice in circulars distributed by a somewhat mysterious Protective Committee in New York, and by a southern investment house. The time seems propitious therefore for a careful analysis of the situation, with a view to determining whether the offer made the Chesapeake & Ohio stockholders under the merger plan is adequate and fair.

The question appears forbiddingly complicated, involving as it does a comparative valuation of four important railways. (Hocking Valley is not considered here because of its smaller size and the limited public ownership of its stock.) The Plan contains no hint of how the Van Sweringens themselves arrived at their bases of exchange. It is understood, however, that a simplified procedure was followed, whereby the amount offered for each road was determined primarily by its net earnings in 1923, this on the theory that the results of previous years were either too abnormal or too remote to be of value. The logical approach for us therefore would be first to accept provisionally this

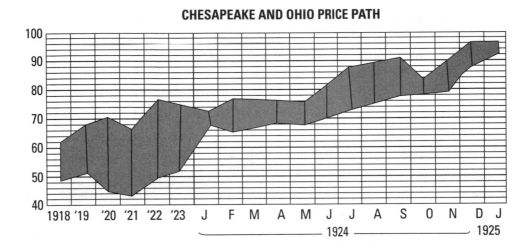

**CHESAPEAKE AND OHIO PRICE PATH**

1923 criterion of value, in order to see what conclusions it would justify, and then to consider how these results are confirmed or modified by the exhibits of other years.

First, what is being paid for each road? To simplify matters we shall consider that the new company is really buying the stocks of the various constituent systems, paying for them in its new shares, which we shall value at the recent price of 86 for the preferred and 85 for the common. Here the old Nickel Plate presents a slight complication. For this company is receiving two lots of new stock—one for its physical properties and one for its investment holdings of Pere Marquette and Chesapeake. For the latter holdings costing $17,900,000 (which cost is assumed by the new company) it is given new shares worth $23,200,000. This profit of $5,300,000 is not open to question here and should be credited against the total purchase price. As shown by Table I, therefore, the amount paid for the stock equity in the Nickel Plate properties should be taken as 66 millions. This is exactly the same as the offer made for the Erie stocks. On the other hand, Pere Marquette issues are together valued at 52 millions, while C. & O. preferred and common are valued at 74 millions.

Table II summarizes the 1923 Income Accounts of the four roads and shows that the net earnings available for dividends represent the following percentages of the total price offered for the stocks:

| | |
|---|---|
| Erie | 16.05% |
| Chesapeake & Ohio | 12.47% |
| Pere Marquette | 10.10% |
| Nickel Plate | 9.59% |

These figures might indicate, superficially at least, that the Erie stocks have received less favorable treatment than their earnings would warrant. But in reality they bring home the fact that a single year's results do not determine a railroad's value, either comparative or actual. It would be absurd to maintain that if two railroad stocks happen to earn the same amount in any year they immediately become worth the same price, regardless of their past records.

## THE INFLUENCE OF MAINTENANCE CHARGES

Assuming therefore that Erie's 1923 showing is too exceptional to have any conclusive force, we find that Chesapeake shows somewhat larger earnings on its offered price than the two remaining roads. The price to be paid for Nickel Plate stock is over ten times the 1923 earnings; in the case of C. & O. it is only eight times these earnings. But if the 1923 reports are analyzed more carefully an element appears which makes the actual discrepancy in treatment far greater than that indicated by our first comparison. This element is the portion of gross revenue devoted to maintenance expenditures. As is well known, the maintenance ratio during any moderate period of time is largely within the control of the management, so that the net earnings for any given year can easily be expanded or contracted by the simple expedient of restricting or increasing expenditure on upkeep. Hence the analysis of the results of any single year—especially if to be used as a measurement of *permanent* earning power—must not fail to take into account the maintenance policy followed during that period.

Table II shows also the percentage of 1923 gross expended for maintenance by the four roads considered. Chesapeake's ratio was the highest of the group; its figure of 40.7% being especially striking in comparison with the less than 35% shown by Nickel Plate and Pere Marquette. As it happens, the greater part of this difference admits of a very simple explanation. In 1923, C. & O. charged to maintenance of equipment a lump sum of $3,533,000 for retirement of freight cars. This is obviously an unusual and non-recurrent charge (in fact, Nickel Plate's Freight Car Retirement account in that year amounted to only $36,000, and that of Chesapeake itself in 1922 to but $174,000). This large item was essentially a bookkeeping entry which fell accidentally in 1923 instead of some other year.

A fair comparison of the earnings of these four roads can only be made if the maintenance expenditures are adjusted to approximately the same basis for all. If we select 35% as a representative ratio (that being about the figure for the roads of the country) and if the net results are revised accordingly, then the superiority of Chesapeake's earning power becomes very pronounced indeed. On this basis Chesapeake would have earned over 20% on the price offered for its shares—a figure more than *twice* as great as that shown by either Pere Marquette or Nickel Plate.

## TABLE I

THE VAN SWERINGEN MERGER TERMS

(000 omitted)

| Issue | Offered per Share | Total Pfd. | New Stk. Of'ed Com. | Value of Pfd. at 86 | New Stock Com. at 85 | Total Offered Price for Old Stocks |
|---|---|---|---|---|---|---|
| N. Y. Ch. & St. L. pfd. | 1 sh. pfd. | $34,391 | $49,130 | $29,577 | $41,760 | $71,337 |
| N.Y. Ch. & St. L. com. | 1 sh. com. | Less Profit on Investments | | | | 5,348 |
| Invest. Holdings of C. & O. and Pere Marq | (See text) | Net Pd. for old Nick. Plate | | | | $65,989 |
| Ches. & Ohio pfd. 1.15sh.pfd. | | | | | | |
| Ch. & Ohio com. | .55 sh. pfd. | 50,430 | 35,985 | 43,370 | 30,587 | 73,957 |
| | .55 sh. com. | | | | | |
| Erie 1st pfd | .50 sh. pfd. | | | | | |
| Erie 2nd pfd | .50 sh. pfd. | 31,952 | 44,993 | 27,479 | 38,244 | 65,723 |
| Erie com | .40 sh. com. | | | | | |
| Pr. Marq. pr. pfd. | 1 sh. pfd. | | | | | |
| Pere Marq. pfd | .9 sh. pfd. | 22,386 | 33,289 | 19,252 | 32,546 | 51,798 |
| Pere Marq. com. | 85 sh. com. | | | | | |

## TABLE II

ANALYSIS OF 1923 RESULTS

(000 omitted)

| | Nickel Plate | C. & O. | Pere Marquette | Erie |
|---|---|---|---|---|
| Gross | $57,477 | $101,978 | $45,966 | $132,978 |
| Net after Taxes | 10,677 | 18,369 | 9,232 | 20,539 |
| Deductions (net) | 4,346 | 9,487 | 4,029 | *10,000 |
| Balance for Dividends | 6,331 | 8,979 | 5,203 | 10,542 |
| Ratio to Gross: | | | | |
| Maintenance | 34.9% | 40.7% | 34.4% | |
| 37.9% | | | | |
| Other Expenses and Taxes | 46.5 | 41.3 | 45.5 | 46.7 |
| Earned on Purchase Price of Stocks, (a) Reported Basis. | 9.59 | 12.47 | 10.10 | 16.05 |
| Ditto (b) Maintenance Restated at 35% of Gross | 9.50 | 20.33 | 9.66 | 20.30 |

*Excluding $3,324,000 charged in 1923 income for Sinking Fund and U.S. Guaranty settlement.

**TABLE III**

ANALYSIS OF 1924 RESULTS

(000 omitted)

|                                          | Nickel Plate | C. & O.   | Pere Marquette | Erie      |
|------------------------------------------|-------------:|----------:|---------------:|----------:|
| Gross                                    | $53,992     | $108,033  | $41,798        | $119,097  |
| Net after Taxes                          | 10,960      | 20,463    | 8,799          | 18,699    |
| Deductions (net)                         | 5,091       | *7,963    | 3,864          | *9,399    |
| Balance for Dividends                    | 5,869       | 12,500    | 4,935          | 9,300     |
| Ratio to Gross: Maintenance              | 33.3%       | 42.3%     | 33.0%          | 36.6%     |
| † Other Expenses and Taxes               | 47.4        | 38.9      | 46.1           | 47.4      |
| Net Deductions                           | 9.6         | 7.1       | 9.2            | 7.9       |
| Earned on Purchase Price (a)             |             |           |                |           |
| Reported Basis                           | 8.90%       | 16.89%    | 9.52%          | 14.16%    |
| Ditto (b) Maintenance Restated at        |             |           |                |           |
| 35% of Gross                             | 7.02        | 27.45     | 7.90           | 17.08     |

*Partly estimated. 12 mos. ended Nov. 30, 1924.

## THE 1924 FIGURES

If the 1923 results were used in formulating the Merger Plan, those of 1924 deserve equal attention in deciding the fairness of the terms proposed. These figures are presented in Table III, the interest charges of Chesapeake being based on the sum reported for the first six months. The reports show an increase in gross and surplus earnings for Chesapeake & Ohio and a falling off in both these items for each of the other lines. The dividend balance shows 16.89% on the price offered for Chesapeake stock, being nearly twice the figure shown by Nickel Plate and 75% more than that earned by Pere Marquette.

But this is not all. During this twelve-month period Chesapeake continued its policy of ultra-liberal maintenance expenditures while the other three roads curtailed theirs further. In the year ended November 30 last (December figures not being available) Chesapeake's maintenance ratio reached the exceptionally high figure of 42.03% of gross against only 33.3% in the case of Nickel Plate and 33.0% for Pere Marquette. If Chesapeake had restricted its maintenance outlay to the same relative figure as the other roads, its net income would have been about $9,500,000 higher—which would have meant an increase of fully $14 per share in the earnings available for the common, bringing the year's figure above $30 per share.

To realize the full significance of the 1924 results, as compared with those of 1923, they must be restated on the basis of an equalized maintenance ratio. Taking 35% of gross again as the standard, it is found that the revised net earnings of Chesapeake are not less than 27% of the offered price, as against only 6.4% for the old Nickel Plate. We find in sum that the Chesapeake stockholders are being asked to accept for their holdings less than one quarter as favorable—based on the adjusted current results—as that offered for the Nickel Plate properties; while Pere Marquette stockholders are treated three times as liberally. Even Erie, with its immeasurably poorer history, is getting 50% better treatment, from this point of view, than is Chesapeake & Ohio.

If these figures have any value at all, they mean that the results of 1923 and 1924 lend strong support to the claim for better treatment voiced by the Chesapeake stockholders. Owners of the preferred shares, with their potentially valuable conversion privilege, can hardly be convinced by this exhibit that they should accept new preferred stock worth in the market so much less than their present holdings. And the common stockholders have some cause to wonder why their shares, on which $17 was earned last year, are offered new securities worth $94 per share—while Nickel Plate common, which earned about $13, is valued at $128. Pere Marquette earned just half of the Chesapeake figure, yet it is offered the equivalent of $72 per share. If Chesapeake received the same proportionate treatment as Pere Marquette it would be worth $144 per share; and comparing it with the present price of old Nickel Plate its value would appear to be over $170. Nor does this calculation take into account the greatly increased superiority of Chesapeake's earning power that would result in equalizing its abnormally higher maintenance expenditure.

## OTHER CONSIDERATIONS

We have confined the above analysis to the results of 1923 and 1924 because it is understood that the terms of the Plan were based mainly upon the earnings of recent years. If the comparison were carried back to the average figures of, say, the past ten years, the pre-eminence of Chesapeake would be fully maintained, and probably heightened. For C. & O. has by far the best record of established and sustained earning power. In particular, the relatively favorable showing of Erie in the past two years loses greatly in importance when averaged with its extremely erratic exhibit prior to 1923. Pere Marquette began the decade in receivership, and attained common dividends only two years ago. The present Nickel Plate is a merger of three smaller systems which, before the Van Sweringens waved their magic wand, were considered distinctly second grade. The "Clover Leaf" in fact had just emerged from receivership; Lake Erie & Western had paid no dividend since 1907; the original New York, Chicago & St. Louis common had received nothing since 1912. Chesapeake, on the other hand, has earned more than $6\frac{1}{2}$ per share in each year since 1915, and in the past ten years has averaged over $10 per share.

A really exhaustive comparison of the merging system would of course include many considerations in addition to the net earnings available for the year. The purchase price would be studied in relation to the gross earnings, the fixed charges, the physical valuation of the properties, the technical operating results, and numerous other details which cannot be treated at length within the limits of this article. A few concise facts will show, however, that Chesapeake's superiority in net earnings available for dividends follows directly from corresponding advantages in the underlying elements which produce net profits.

While the purchase price of Chesapeake is fixed at 10% above that of Nickel Plate, its gross business last year was fully twice as large. Furthermore, its actual operating costs were so much lower than Nickel Plate as practically to offset its self-imposed handicap of tremendously larger maintenance outlays. Similarly, while the Chesapeake stockholders are offered in the aggregate 40% more than those of Pere Marquette, C. & O.'s gross was $2\frac{1}{2}$ times as great—and its advantage in lower actual operating costs was about as striking as in the case of Nickel Plate. Although Erie's gross revenue is somewhat larger than Chesapeake's, the latter consistently shows a greater net operating income because of its lower transportation costs. As compared with total receipts, Chesapeake's, net fixed charges are proportionately lower than those of Nickel Plate and Pere Marquette, and as compared with net earnings, they are the lowest of all four roads.

While the extremely large earnings reported per share of common stock would be reduced somewhat by the conversion of the Chesapeake & Ohio 5% bonds, due 1946, this difference would be largely offset by the correspondingly stronger financial structure which always follows the replacement of funded debt by share capital.

The above analysis, somewhat brief as was necessitated by limitations of space, must still be regarded as affording substantial justification for the dissatisfaction that exists with respect to the treatment accorded Chesapeake stock. Whether the special terms provided for dissenting stockholders in the modified lease will amply meet their objections cannot be determined at this moment, in the absence of the complete text of the lease agreement.

# 31

# EFFECT OF RAIL CONSOLIDATIONS UPON SECURITY VALUES

*How Merger Problems
Are Being Solved*

As the mind looks back to the passage of the Transportation Act in 1920, under the leadership of Senator Cummins, one is irresistibly reminded of Moses laying down the Law to the Children of Israel on Mount Sinai. For had not the carriers been wandering for twenty-six months in the wilderness of Federal Control, and were they not nearing the promised land of private operation, flowing with milk and honey—(profit content $5\frac{3}{4}$%)? And certainly the Act of 1920 is a veritable Deuteronomy of prescription, injunction and regulation.

## THE PROVISIONS

Of all its 294 paragraphs, none lay nearer to the heart of the venerable Senator than the five which provide "for the consolidation of the railroad properties of the continental United States into a limited number of systems." The grouping was to be arranged in such a way as to preserve competition, but also to equalize the operating costs of the various systems in order to secure a uniform rate of earnings on capital. The procedure included the publication of a tentative plan by the I. C. C., the holding of hearings thereon, and the final adoption of a definitive plan. The Act then states that "it shall be lawful" for two or more carriers to consolidate, provided their union is in accordance with the final plan and the securities of the new system at par do not exceed the value of the properties merged.

The passage of this legislation was hailed by the country as ushering in a new era for the railroads. Powerful, prosperous super-systems were to replace the present medley of lines—some weak, some strong; some big, some little. Numerous advantages were to be gained through higher operating efficiency, improved service, and greater financial strength. Undeniably a new speculative factor had been injected into the railroad situation, of the kind which Wall Street loves most dearly.

The spirit in which the Transportation Act was passed certainly afforded a legitimate basis for these great expectations. Nevertheless, a study of the text of the relevant sections would have disclosed serious limitations and ambiguities. In the first place, the Bill did not create or even require any consolidations at all. It merely asked the Commission to adopt a plan, in accordance with which the roads "may" effect mergers. In strict truth, the Act was much more specific in prohibiting consolidations not consonant with the plan than in facilitating mergers of the character approved. Indeed, because of its peculiar phraseology, the contention was soon advanced that no combinations of any kind could be permitted until the I. C. C. had finally adopted its definitive plan. Hence, a paradoxical situation threatened in which the only concrete effect of the Act would be to prevent all mergers for an indefinite period.

> *This article is an authoritative review of the main factors affecting railroad consolidations. Inasmuch as the unfolding of this situation is exerting a pronounced effect on the value of railroad securities, it is essential that investors obtain a clear view of what is going on.*

This was one of the problems which faced students of the consolidation question five years ago. Other difficult points related to:

a.  The procedure of the Commission in formulating its tentative plan and deciding on the final grouping.

b.   Whether the plan would actually stimulate railroads to consolidate.

c.   The general treatment to be accorded security holders in roads to be taken over.

d.   The rights of dissenting stockholders and of objecting States.

It seems pertinent to ask what light the developments of the past five years have shed upon these and kindred questions involved in the consolidation idea. Some of them affect the railroad investor in direct and obvious fashion. Others seem highly technical, yet they may conceivably contain corollaries of great practical significance. In this brief review of the situation, we shall endeavor to touch upon all these considerations, but from the standpoint primarily of their moment to the holder of railroad securities.

## PREPARING THE GENERAL PLAN

In the first place, what has been done toward the adoption of a comprehensive consolidation plan? The Interstate Commerce Commission lost no time in tackling the problem, and in August, 1921, published its tentative proposal, as prescribed in the Act. The scheme provides for 19 systems to replace some 150 existing lines. It is based largely upon recommendations made by Professor Ripley, the railroad expert, which are incorporated in an elaborate report and discussion. In due course, hearings began before the Commission and proceeded for many months, eliciting a great variety of views from numberless witnesses. The plan was criticized in general and in detail many amendments were offered, including a comprehensive substitute scheme by the banker, John E. Oldham.

The railroad officials, as representatives of the lines to be merged, were naturally leading figures in the inquiry. The executives of the strong lines exhibited a generous disposition to waive all claim to the weak sisters allocated to their systems, but argued persuasively in favor of enlarging their quota of desirable roads. Some of the leading railroad men of the country expressed themselves as unequivocally opposed to the whole idea of consolidations, claiming that the benefits were illusory and the practical objections unsurmountable.

A recent feature of these discussions has been the controversy precipitated between the Pennsylvania Railroad and certain other Eastern systems over a proposed substitute plan covering the consolidations in this district. This matter will require our attention elsewhere.

Since the hearings were formally closed a long time ago, rumors have arisen from time to time that the Commission was about to announce its final plan. It may be that the differences among the Eastern lines are partially responsible for the delay but in any event it is impossible at this moment to make a prediction as to when the final scheme will appear and how it will resemble or differ from the tentative proposals published four years ago.

Such is the present rather indefinite status of the General Consolidation Plan. In the meantime, however, a number of individual combinations have taken place or are pending, and to these we must look for whatever concrete information is available respecting the real progress of the merger idea. In the appended table we present a fairly inclusive list of specific consolidation developments during the past four years. (Changes in the form or extent of control previously existing are not included.) The list divides into three sections, comprising respectively the consolidations actually completed, those pending, and those projected. Pending plans are those which have been announced in detail and await approval. The projected schemes have reached the stage only of enumerating the proposed constituent lines.

In separate columns we compare the systems by which the various roads have been or are to be acquired with those to which they are assigned in the I. C. C. tentative plan. A survey of this list inspires the reflection that the Commission's ideas have been more honored in the breach than in the observance. Of twenty-nine carriers listed only seven are allocated exactly as the tentative plan prescribes. Under these circumstances it is particularly interesting to review the attitude of the Commission in those combinations which have been before it for approval.

## THE COMMISSION'S ATTITUDE

The over-shadowing question of course has been that of the Commission's right to authorize any mergers before adopting the final plan. The I. C. C. has been prone to follow the good old Supreme Court tradition of never deciding a major issue if the particular case can be disposed of on minor grounds. Only one of the acquisitions passed upon has involved a consolidation in the legal sense; the others have been effected by purchase of stock, lease, or operating agreement. In all the latter cases the Commission has seized upon this technical distinction (which is undoubtedly employed in the Act itself), to avoid the question of whether preliminary consolidations are permissible.

In the original Nickel Plate-Clover Leaf-Lake Erie & Western merger, the problem was presented in unescapable form. This was a consolidation in every sense. In an opinion in which a slight truculence evidently disguises an underlying uneasiness, the Commission decided definitely that it was

## SPECIFIC CONSOLIDATION DEVELOPMENTS TO DATE

### A. COMPLETED

| Line Acquired | Acquired by | Parent Company of System in I.C.C. Plan |
|---|---|---|
| Int. & Gt. Northern | N. O. Tex. Mexico (Miss. Pac.) | Missouri Pacific |
| New Orleans Tex. & Mexico | Missouri Pacific | Missouri Pacific |
| Denver & Rio Grande | ($^1/_2$) Miss. Pacific} ($^1/_2$) West. Pacific | Atchison-West. Pac. |
| Carolina Clinchfield & O. | Atlantic Coast Line-L. & N. | Atlantic Coast Line-L & N. |
| Clover Leaf | Nickel Plate | Nickel Plate |
| Lake Erie & Western | Nickel Plate | Nickel Plate |

### B. PENDING

| | | |
|---|---|---|
| Chesapeake & Ohio | New Nickel Plate | C. & O.-Virginian |
| Hocking Valley | New Nickel Plate | C. & O.-Virginian |
| Erie | New Nickel Plate | Erie-Lackawana |
| Pere Marquette | New Nickel Plate | Pere Marquette-Ann Arbor |
| Nickel Plate | New Nickel Plate | Nickel Plate-L. Valley |
| Virginian | Norfolk & Western | C. & O.-Virginian (Prof. Ripley assigned it to Norfolk). |
| Alabama & Vicksburg | Illinois Central | Southern Railway |
| Vicksburg Shreveport & Pac. | Illinois Central | So. Pacific-Rock Island |
| Gulf & Ship Island | Illinois Central | III. Central |

### C. PROJECTED

*1. Eastern System Plan*

| | | |
|---|---|---|
| Lehigh Valley | N. Y. Central | Nickel Plate-L. Valley |
| N. Y. Ontario & Western | N. Y. Central | New Haven |
| Norfolk & Western | Pennsylvania | Norfolk & Western |
| Alton (East Lines) | Pennsylvania | Frisco |
| Lackawanna | Nickel Plate | Erie-Lackawanna |
| Reading-Jersey Central | B. & O. | B. & O. |
| Western Maryland | B. & O. | N. Y. Central |
| Ann Arbor | B. & O. | Pere Marquette |
| Buff. & Susq. | B. & O. | Erie-Lackawanna |
| Wabash (East. Lines) | B. & O. | Erie-Lackawanna |
| Chic. & East III. | N. Y. Central & Nickel Plate | Missouri Pacific |
| Wheeling-Lake Erie | Three systems | Nickel Plate-L. Valley |
| Pittsburg & West Virginia | Three & Four Systems | Nickel Plate-L. Valley |
| Delaware & Hudson | Four Systems | Erie-Lackawanna |

*2. Changes in above suggested by Pennsylvania*

| | | |
|---|---|---|
| Lehigh Valley or Lackawanna | Pennsylvania | Nickel Plate-L. Valley Erie-Lackawanna |
| Virginian | Pennsylvania | C. & O.-Virginian |
| Chic. & E. III. | Pennsylvania | Missouri Pac. |
| Buff.-Susq. | Pennsylvania | Erie-Lackawanna |
| Lackawanna | N. Y. Central & Nickel Plate | Erie-Lackawanna |

not empowered or directed to prevent desirable consolidations which had been effected under valid State laws. Commissioner Eastman has consistently espoused the opposite view, even in cases involving acquisition by stock purchase, and in this case adduced cogent arguments against the majority's stand.

The next important question is the Commission's attitude towards departures from its tentative plan. Curiously enough, although so many of these divergencies appear in our list, the Commission has had occasion to pass upon but two such instances involving roads of any importance. The first covered the 'Frisco's application to acquire the stock of International & Great Northern, which had been assigned to Missouri Pacific. The Commission refused to approve this deal. The second was the purchase by Missouri Pacific of one half the stock the Denver & Rio Grande Western, a line which had been allocated to the greater Atchison system. This acquisition was approved, although four of the eleven commissioners dissented. The opinions show that the opposing decisions in the two cases were based primarily on the fact that the first plan would have prejudiced, while the second would maintain, an existing "route and channel of trade and commerce." All the other combinations approved to date do not conflict with the tentative plan.

The reader may draw his own conclusions as to the probable attitude of the I. C. C. towards pending mergers which do not follow its original proposal. Perhaps the best that can be said is that the Commission is likely to require convincing evidence that such combinations are in the public interest. It may also be said that the more important are the lines involved, and the nearer its approach to perfecting its final plan, the more likely is the Commission to withhold approval until the definite scheme is published.

At various times, the I. C. C. has been called upon to consider the attitude and legislation of certain States, bearing upon proposed acquisitions. In general it has taken the stand that the views of any State are merely one of the elements to consider in determining whether a combination is in the public interest, and that the Transportation Act empowers it to nullify adverse State legislation in carrying out its merger plans. It may be charged that the Commission in the same decisions has treated an acquisition as a legal consolidation for the purpose of denying authority to adverse State laws, and as not a consolidation (but only a lease or stock purchase) in order to avoid the question of the legality of preliminary consolidations. Furthermore, it has finally decided this last question in the affirmative by upholding the validity of State laws, while at other times apparently disqualifying them when they conflict with its decisions. This is one of the bewildering aspects of the consolidation problem.

## INFLUENCE ON SECURITY VALUES

We turn now from legal to financial considerations. How are consolidation developments affecting the pocketbooks of security holders? The possibility of mergers has certainly been a stock-market influence of prime importance, more potent indeed than the actuality. We may list Norfolk & Western, Lehigh Valley, D. L. & W., Chicago & East Illinois, Rock Island and Pittsburgh & West Virginia as issues which have consistently sold above comparative levels because of merger influences. In the case of the first four mentioned the Pennsylvania appears as the "angel." It has admittedly negotiated for the Norfolk; Chicago & East Illinois it wants instead of the Alton assigned it in the Eastern substitute merger plan; and it demands either Lackawanna or Lehigh Valley—both already claimed by other systems. No doubt the expectation of competitive buying for control of these disputed lines (if not such buying itself) has caused their market buoyancy.

It seems more logical to ask what has been the real influence on market values of the mergers actually announced. In most cases the purchase price or exchange value of the shares acquired has been higher than that previously obtaining. Of these however it might be observed that nearly all the lines have been either of minor extent or without wide public interest. The acquisition of control of Cotton Belt by Rock Island and of Katy by Kansas City Southern is of prime importance, but these have been effected without any general offer to stockholders. In the case of Cotton Belt at least, this development has been as yet entirely without market results.

Foremost in point of size and general interest is the Nickel Plate merger, now the subject of hearings before the Commission. From the market standpoint it may be said that Erie and Pere Marquette are selling at about where they would probably stand if no merger were in process; that Chesapeake & Ohio is apparently below and Nickel Plate undoubtedly above its market value ex-merger. It is obviously most difficult to generalize from the above instances. There is ground for believing that proportionately the largest profits are to be gained in the shares of small lines strategically desirable to powerful systems, to whom the amount involved in paying a liberal price would be of little moment. In the case of larger combinations, the writer does not believe it safe to count on a figure being paid for the shares much in excess of that justified by their comparative earning power. It is possible, but by no means certain, that in some cases a large property valuation may offset poor operating results.

Because of the present market importance of the announced desire of Pennsylvania to acquire various lines, a word of caution seems permissible.

The expansion plans of Pennsylvania—is are subject to opposition on two grounds—first because the system is already larger than any competitor, secondly because its method heretofore employed of guaranteeing dividends on (or exchanging bonds for) common stocks is inherently unsound. It has already resulted in a disproportionate increase in Pennsylvania's fixed charges and is understood to have excited adverse comment from substantial stockholders. Moreover, the I. C. C. has itself intimated (notably in the Panhandle Lease decision) that it is not in full sympathy with this policy. I The recent leasing of the Virginian by Norfolk—on a guaranteed dividend basis, and as a possible preliminary to a similar lease of Norfolk by Pennsylvania,—is likely to elicit a definite opinion from the Commission on both Pennsylvania's strategic plans and its financial methods.

## WHERE MINORITIES STAND

Against the prospect of enhanced market values due to merger developments must be set the possibility of declining in some issues because of unfavorable treatment. Such an example is of course provided by Chesapeake & Ohio, which has been included in the Nickel Plate deal on terms denounced by the minority as grossly inadequate. (In a recent analysis in The magazine of Wall Street the writer expressed his view that these objections appear well supported by the facts.) The question of the rights of dissenting minorities is one of the most important in the whole consolidation situation, and the progress of the Chesapeake & Ohio struggle will merit careful attention.

There has been a widespread impression that protesting stockholders will have to rely exclusively upon the courts, since the I. C. C. is likely to scrutinize the terms from the stand-point only of the public's interest and not as between security owners. This view rests largely on the action of the Commission in approving the Panhandle Lines despite objections by certain shareholders. Careful study of the records fail to substantiate such a conclusion. In the Panhandle case the Commission stated:

*"We do not consider it necessary to discuss our responsibility in protecting the interests of minority stockholders … inasmuch as it is our view that the granting of the authority herein requested will not be inimical to the interests of any of the interested stockholders."*

The above is a typically Delphic utterance of the kind previously referred to, in which the Commission avoids passing on the scope of its authority by deciding that its conclusion would be the same whether it had the authority questioned or not. In the decision permitting the purchase of

Big Four stock by New York Central, another oracular pronouncment of the same subject reads:

*"In a case involving dealings between two corporations under common control, we may even, perhaps, scrutinize the proposed transaction to determine whether the bargain is fair from the standpoint of protesting minorities."*

It may properly be said, therefore, that up to now the Commission has avoided committing itself on the question of minority interests. The last opinion cited seems to imply a leaning towards the view that its jurisdiction does apply to these matters. The wide liberty accorded counsel for the Chesapeake minority to cross-examine witnesses before the Commission would seem to strengthen this interpretation. In the interest of fairness it appears desirable that protesting minorities could obtain relief from the Commission, instead of being relegated to the more tortuous justice of the courts.

A review of this article suggests that every point considered is left unanswered, and the conclusions arrived at are too indefinite to be of much value. Perhaps the only thing certain is that the consolidation question teems with uncertainties. By way of summary we append a brief resume of the situation, in the form of question and answer:

1. Q  Will consolidations be beneficial to the country and the railroads?
   A. The weight of authority is strongly in the affirmative, but the evidence is not nearly so conclusive.
2. Q  Will the Transportation Act stimulate consolidations?
   A. Undoubtedly, despite its limitations in this field.
3. Q  Will I. C. C. tentative plan be closely followed?
   A. Apparently not.
4. Q  Will the consolidations enhance the value of railway securities?
   A. In general, the effect on permanent investment value is not likely to be nearly as great as the temporary speculative stimulus.
5. Q  Will the consolidations be worked out along sane lines and on a basis generally fair to all stockholders concerned?
   A. Decidedly, this remains to be seen.

# 32

# BARGAIN-HUNTING NOT THRILLING BUT—IMMENSELY PROFITABLE

*Some Current Examples of Bargains*

A bargain is something which can be bought well below its ascertained value. The conception of bargain involves essentially a comparison of the current price with a *definite* value—i.e. one not chiefly speculative or anticipatory. To recite a homely example: The housewife who buys Uneeda Biscuits at 4 cents per box considers justly that she has found a bargain, because the price is lower than the accepted value of the article. On the other hand, those who are amassing fortunes in Florida real estate transactions may be alert and keen, but they clearly are not dealing in bargains.

This distinction is especially important in Wall Street. Buying bargains is undoubtedly a safe and satisfactory way to make money in the market; but it is by no means the only way—and it may not be the best way. Quicker and larger profits are often made either by adroitly swimming with the tide of popular favor, or by shrewdly anticipating future industrial developments. The former type of opportunity has recently been illustrated by the Public Utility stocks, the latter by the Electrical Refrigeration issues. Although these shares have yielded such handsome profits, at no time could they have been characterized as bargains, for *the essence of a bargain is the price.* But in the purchase of these issues the price has played a very minor role. They are to be bought at one *time* and sold at another *time;* not cheap at one *price* and dear at another *price.*

The bargain-hunter keeps his nose to the grindstone of established facts. He analyzes recent balance-sheets and past income accounts. His idea of the future is obtained chiefly by averaging the past. He holds aloof from the hue and cry of the market; popularity means little to him for he generally buys the unpopular. He is a plodder—unimaginative and perhaps shortsighted; *but he averages an excellent return on his capital and sleeps well at night.*

Bargain opportunities are rarely, if ever, undisputable and obvious. We cannot expect to find issues which are exceptionally attractive from every point of view, including their price. Most bargains exist both *because* and *in spite* of some unfavorable feature, which upon analysis is found to be (a) imaginary; or (b) over emphasized; or (c) important, but far outweighed by elements of strength. Let us hasten, however, to concrete illustrations.

> *The primary object of this article is to illustrate the different types of bargain opportunities and how to determine that which makes a bargain in securities. The examples given are not intended to supply a complete list of current opportunities but rather to illustrate the main varieties of the genus Bargain. Although bargain-hunting may not offer the hectic excitement which attaches to the more speculative Wall Street operations, it is not without its pecular form of mental thrill—and financial reward for those who take the trouble.*

## BARGAINS IN SENIOR SECURITIES

In general there are two types of bargain opportunities in bonds or preferred stocks. The first is afforded by sound issues yielding an adequate return, and which also possess special features in the form of conversion or participation privileges. In such instances the buyer is getting a valuable right without paying for it. As a recent example we may mention the International Telephone & Telegraph $5\frac{1}{2}$s, convertible into stock at 125 after next April, which were offered at 99. The large margin shown above interest requirements made this issue reasonably attractive merely for the income yield of 5.58%. Hence, the price included no charge for the ten-year privilege of conversion into stock of this rapidly growing enterprise, at a figure below its recent quotation. This issue was therefore one of the rather rare instances of a bond offered to the public at a price clearly below its comparative value.

Bargains of the other type are presented by issues returning too high a yield in comparison with the security afforded. Sometimes such discrepancies arise through pure neglect, but they are usually due to the public's failure to appraise the facts correctly. In other words, it is the familiar story of undue weight being attached to unfavorable factors, which in reality are unimportant. Take the case of Congoleum preferred, which sells at 102, yielding 6.85%. The reader will probably recall that Congoleum has not done as well this year as last, and that the common dividend has been cut and its quotation fallen more than one-half from its previous high. How then can its 7% preferred be a bargain above par? The answer is simple. There is only $1,780,000 of preferred stock outstanding which ranks ahead of 1,641,000 shares of common, now worth about $40,000,000. Here are the earning figures:

| Year | Balance for Preferred Dividend | Preferred Requirements |
|------|-------------------------------|------------------------|
| 1922 | $4,893,000 | $243,000 |
| 1923 | 6,863,000 | 129,000 |
| 1924 | 6,388,000 | 136,000 |
| 1925 (1st half) | 2,777,000 | 68,000 |

Hence the shrinkage in earnings which caused all the weakness in the common stock has still left the preferred dividend covered over *forty times*. This margin is so enormous as to give the issue a much greater assurance of safety than that enjoyed by many standard preferred stocks selling ten points higher. It will undoubtedly be redeemed in due course at its call price of 107.

## THE BOND FIELD

A bond issue may be a bargain even in face of poor earnings if the asset values are so large that the junior security holders could not conceivably permit default. When Pierce Oil was recapitalized last year by raising some $6\frac{1}{2}$ million dollars of new cash through the sale of common stock, its 8% bonds were selling at 92. The issue then amounted to $1,700,000, subject to an annual sinking fund of $200,000, assuring eventual redemption at 110. The refinancing resulted in 2,500,000 shares of new common, selling in the market for $17,500,000, or ten times the amount of the bond issue.

Come what may, the bonds were bound to be taken care of eventually, because the stockholders, having just made so large an investment, would certainly not permit the holders of so small a claim to take possession of the property. The realization of this state of affairs has since raised the price of the bonds to 106—even though Pierce stock has declined.

At the present time a somewhat similar situation appears in Superior Oil 7s, due 1929, selling at 92, and so yielding $9\frac{1}{2}$%. Of the original one million dollar issue, there is now only $714,000 outstanding, of which $200,000 must also be redeemed each year. The bonds are followed by 1,091,000 shares of stock, with a market value of some $3,200,000. The bonds are more than covered by net current assets, while the producing properties are carried at six times the issue. The steady losses reported by this company are due to very heavy depreciation and depletion charges. In 1924, for example, the company showed a profit of $826,000 before these charges—an amount exceeding the total bond issue. There is a distinct chance of a substantial payment being received from Atlantic Refining in consequence of a $3,500,000 verdict won by Superior Oil in a damage suit. The logical use of any such funds would be the redemption of the small bond issue at 105. But apart from this possibility—by no means remote—the assets are undoubtedly worth so much more than the $714,000 of bonds, that the latter appear certain to be taken care of in any contingency.

## CUDAHY PACKING

The simplest form of bargain opportunity is created by improvement in value not yet reflected in price. Such instances, while always difficult to find at the height of a bull market, are especially rare at this moment. For the protracted upswing, having a relatively restricted industrial improvement as its basis, has left few genuinely favorable situations unexploited. One of these would seem to be Cudahy Packing, selling at par on the New York Stock Exchange, and paying $7 per share. The steady recovery of this company from its postwar deflation losses is seen from the following table of earnings per share of the common stock:

| 1921 | Deficit $12.49 |
|------|------|
| 1922 | + 3.78 |
| 1923 | + 8.32 |
| 1924 | + 16.13 |

No official figures for 1925 are available, but seemingly authoritative reports indicate an improvement over the excellent showing of last year, with prospects equally encouraging. The ratio of recent earnings to price places Cudahy in the bargain class because this percentage (16.1% for 1924) is unusually high when compared with:-

1. The average of all industrial stocks in the present market.
2. The present exhibit of other packing stocks.
3. The normal earning power required for an issue of this class.

The only weakness in Cudahy's armor lies in the relatively low average profits for, say, the past seven years. Were these figures an indication that the business is one inherently subject to wide fluctuations, then it would be hazardous to buy the stock on the basis of 1924–25 results. It is generally accepted, however, that the difficulties of the 1920–21 period were abnormal and non-recurrent, and that the packing industry is returning to the stability and steady growth which characterized it before the war. If we view Cudahy in the same light as the mail-order stocks (which experienced even severer deflation losses) it seems substantially out of line at this price.

## Various Types of Bargains

| | Recent Price | Dividend Per Share | Chief Bargain Characteristic |
|---|---|---|---|
| **Bonds** | | | |
| Int. Tel. & Tel. Convertible 5½ s | *99½ | | Valuable conversion privilege not reflected in price. |
| Superior Oil 1st Mortgage 7s | 92 | | Small size of mortgage issue compared with total investment insures safety despite unfavorable developments. |
| **Preferred Stocks** | | | |
| Congoleum Nairn | 103 | $7.00 | Earned dividend 40 times in the first half of 1925 and 50 times in 1924. |
| **Common Stocks** | | | |
| Cudahy Packing | 100 | 7.00 | Earned 16.1 per cent on market price: a large rate for this class of business. |
| Con. Gas & Elec. of Baltimore | 45 | 2.00 | Earnings large in themselves, and especially so as compared with other public utilities. |
| Industrial Finance | 13 | | Earnings of over 50 per cent on market price and good prospects offset poor record. |
| Northern Pipe Line. | 80 | 6.00 | Cash assets equal market price, with nominal liabilities. |
| Waldorf System | 15½ | 1.25 | Despite recent slump, earnings are proportionately much larger than those of other chain enterprises. |
| Calumet & Arizona | 50 | 1.00 | Price entirely covered by value of New Cornelia holdings and liquid assets, leaving its great mine as a bonus. |
| Salt Creek Producers 26 | 2.00 | | Unusual physical and financial situation, assuring large earnings for many years. |

* Recent offering price

## CON. GAS & ELECTRIC OF BALTIMORE

Just what percentage of earnings on market price is required to put an issue in the bargain category must vary, of course, with the types and the times. While 16% is an attractive figure for a packing stock, it would not be conclusive if shown by an automobile issue in the first six months of 1925. For in this group the seasonal variation in earnings and the repeated ups and downs of individual companies would make a single half-year's figure a doubtful indication of established earning power. Conversely, the sweeping change in the investment position of Public Utility enterprises must receive some recognition in (analyzing companies of this class, by requiring a) smaller earnings ratio than in former days.

Consider Consolidated Gas & Electric of Baltimore, which in the past four quarters earned some $5.75 per share, or nearly 13% on the market price of 45. This is a much larger percentage than that shown by other utilities. American Water Works, for example, for the same period earned only $3 per share, or less than 5% on the price of 62. Not only are the Baltimore company's current earnings so satisfactory, but its average profits for the past three years—$5.50 per share—are an earnest of stability. Furthermore, it is conservatively capitalized with respect to senior obligations. The current dividend of $2 yields only 4.40%, but this should not prove a decisive factor, especially as the earnings would permit a substantial increase. Consolidated Gas of Baltimore has evidently not shared the spectacular advances of other public utility stocks. Judged from present valuation standards of such issues, it seems ridiculously low; but what is of chief importance from the standpoint of this article, its price is amply justified by any reasonable method of appraisal.

## INDUSTRIAL FINANCE

The same underlying principle is illustrated by a bargain of a very different type, namely, Industrial Finance common, selling at 13 (par $10). Here we are confronted with one very unfavorable and one very favorable feature. On the debit side we note immediately that not only has this stock never paid a dividend, but the company is even in arrears of six years on the 6% preferred stock. Against this, set the fact that earnings last year were $7.45 per share of common—over 55% on the market price. This is a situation calling for further study.

Industrial Finance is the parent organization of the Morris Plan companies operating throughout the United States in the field of small loans to individuals and business. The distinguished board of directors shows that the enterprise has the best of sponsorship, as fulfilling a useful public function. At the same time, the system followed has enabled the company to transact an increasing business with a remarkably small ratio of loss. Industrial Acceptance Corporation, a subsidiary, has an exclusive contract with Studebaker Corporation to finance purchases by its dealers and customers. The financial results in earlier days were meagre—probably due to development expenses—and necessitated the withholding of preferred dividends from 1917 to 1923. In the latter year excellent profits were returned, equivalent to $4.50 per share of common. As told above, the 1924 results were even better ($7.45 per share). The last annual report anticipates another prosperous year in 1925, and intimates that the back dividends on the preferred will shortly be taken care of.

These developments make the stock appear exceedingly attractive, not only because the earnings for the last two years are in themselves so large, but equally because the company gives every evidence of being now strongly entrenched in a profitable field. The whole story can be summed up in the observation that the Morris Plan companies last year transacted a volume of business of $120,000,000, while the entire common stock issue of the parent company is selling for only $1,500,000. In a situation like this a moderate increase either in the turnover or the margin of profit has a startling effect upon the earnings of the junior shares.

The inherent difference between a bargain in the proper sense and an ordinary opportunity for profit is well illustrated by comparing Industrial Finance with the similarly named Industrial Fibre common, which has also recently sold around 13. The latter company manufactures Rayon and has begun to participate in the growth of the new industry. The earnings per share are given as follows: 1922, 25 cents; 1923, 38 cents; 1924, 36 cents; and the first half of 1925, $1.55 (annual rate). These results show encouraging recent progress, and when joined to the optimistic predictions for the future, invest the issue with no little appeal. But considered by themselves the earnings are relatively small. Hence, the purchase of Industrial Fibre must be motivated chiefly by the buyer's view of the *future;* in the case of Industrial Finance the actual results of the *recent past* afford the primary recommendation. It is enough that future prospects are not unfavorable to stamp this issue as obviously undervalued.

## BUYING CASH ASSETS

Although earnings are rightly considered as in general more important than assets, the latter frequently play a major part in the creation of bargain opportunities. This principle is at present illustrated by an entire group of issues, namely the Standard Oil Pipe Line stocks. Perhaps the best individual example is furnished by Northern Pipe Line. This stock sells at 80, pays $6, and thus yields 7.50%. It has paid at least $6 in every year since the Standard Oil segregation in 1912, averaging over $10 annually. It has no capital liabilities ahead of its common shares. Its cash and marketable securities alone amount to $80 per share—the full market price. The total liabilities are only $12 per share, of which undoubtedly half is in the form of miscellaneous reserves.

What is wrong with this picture? The trouble lies in the recent earnings. In common with all companies of the group, Northern Pipe's business has been adversely affected by Panama Canal shipments of surplus California oil. Reported net income per share fell from $12.05 in 1922 to $7.70 in 1923 and $5.35 in 1924. On examination, however, there appears no warrant for the belief that figures for the last three years reveal a definite trend towards disappearing earnings. In fact, the statistics for oil traffic for the first half of this year already show substantial improvement, the increase in Northern Pipe's deliveries amounting to 14%. The effect of California competition is likely to wane as its flush production settles down; and there is no indication that the pipe lines are to be superseded in their established function of transporting crude from the great Mid-Continent field to the Eastern refineries.

### How Nine "Cash Asset Stocks" Acted
Since Recommendation in The Magazine of Wall Street, Issue of July 19, 1924

|  | Cash Assets per share | Price when Recommended July, 1924 | Recent Price | % change |
|---|---|---|---|---|
| Crescent | $15.85 | 13 | 17 | +31% |
| Crex Carpet | 16.97 | 29 | 52 | +79 |
| Cumberland Pipe | 83.90 | 128 | 153 | +20 |
| Pennok Oil | 8.08 | $15\frac{1}{2}$ | *$20\frac{1}{2}$ | +32 |
| Shattuck-Arizona | 2.88 | 5 | 6 | +20 |
| Southern Pipe | 78.73 | 95 | 78 | −18 |
| Tonopah Mining | 1.75 | $1\frac{3}{8}$ | 5 | +264 |
| Transue & Williams | 18.56 | 28 | $26\frac{1}{2}$ | −5 |
| Wright Aero | 16.25 | $10\frac{1}{2}$ | $30\frac{1}{2}$ | +190 |
| Average Advance |  |  |  | +68% |
| Standard Statistics |  |  |  |  |
| Aver. 231 Stocks | 104.7 | 130.1 |  | +24% |

* Allowing for recapitalization.

We have here an example of the creation of a bargain situation by attaching excessive importance to an unfavorable development. With the price of Northern Pipe Line down to its cash assets, and with current earnings probably covering the liberal dividend, the stock is evidently selling well below any conservative appraisal.

Northern Pipe exemplifies a type of stock which should always exert a powerful appeal to the bargain-hunters—namely, those with no liabilities and cash assets representing the bulk of the selling price. A number of stocks of this kind were recommended in The Magazine of Wall Street about a year ago. To illustrate the possibilities of this type of commitment there is appended a comparison of the present quotations of this group with their prices of 1924. It is interesting to note that while these issues represented anything but speculative favorites, they have advanced on the average considerably more than the general stock market, while at the same time they could properly be regarded as carrying very slight risk of loss.

## WALDORF SYSTEM

This stock of a chain restaurant enterprise affords another illustration of a bargain being created by an unfavorable development. The earnings of the company have fallen off recently because of an advance in food prices and the expiration of some leases. Accordingly, the price has declined from 20 to $15^{1}/_{2}$. At the current quotation the $1.25 dividend yields 8%. The earnings of the first half of 1925, which have been regarded as so unsatisfactory, are nevertheless at the rate of 11% on the price. This is considerably higher than that shown by other chain store enterprises. In this period, Child's earned at the rate of less than 6%, and Shattuck at less than 5% on their market quotation. By comparison, therefore, Waldorf appears very cheap even at its present showing and especially so on its past record. Considering that the company has the advantage of strong and experienced financial sponsorship, there would seem to be no reason for pessimism with respect to its future.

## CALUMET & ARIZONA

Sometimes an issue possesses bargain qualities for a reason not readily apparent in a quick scrutiny of either the income account or the balance-sheet. Take Calumet & Arizona for example, a copper stock selling at 51. Here the chief factor is the company's control of New Cornelia, a porphyry mine with possibilities of large production at low cost.

New Cornelia sells at 20, and since Calumet & Arizona holds 1.9 shares of this subsidiary for each share of its own, it is evident that $38 of the price of Calumet is represented by the market value of its holdings in New Cornelia. Furthermore, the other investments and net current assets of Calumet & Arizona are worth over $12 per share. Hence, only $1 per share, or $650,000, is left as the market valuation of Calumet & Arizona's mine and equipment, which can produce 70 million pounds per annum and which even in 1924 earned nearly $1,000,000 net, before depreciation. The Calumet & Arizona mines have not only a wonderful record, but a promising future besides; and the present price of the stock means that the purchaser is getting this great property virtually thrown in as a bonus with an investment in New Cornelia at $20 per share. Incidentally, the stock pays $4 dividends with a yield of nearly 8%.

## SALT CREEK PRODUCERS

This stock sells on the Curb at 26, pays $2.50, and yields over 9%. Here is an oil issue which is a bargain because it is not making the most of its possibilities. Most companies owning acreage in a valuable field exploit their holdings as rapidly as possible, partly for the sake of quick profits, but chiefly for protection against drainage by competitors. This company and its companion, Mountain Producers, completely control the heart of the remarkable Salt Creek field in Wyoming. Its acreage is being developed by a Standard Oil of Indiana subsidiary, from the primary standpoint of securing a supply of oil for years to come. Hence, the property is being drilled up very gradually, and actual production has been held well below the potential figure. Although a prolific deep sand was discovered some time ago, no real attempt has been made to exploit what are certain to be tremendously valuable additional resources.

Despite its carefully restricted production, Salt Creek Producers earned well over $4 per share in each of the last two years. It has over 17 million dollars (or $11 per share) of net current assets, more than half in cash and Liberty bonds. The stock appears exceptionally attractive, first because it has demonstrated its ability to show good returns, under favorable conditions, and secondly, because its future is assured from both the financial and the operating standpoint.

# 33

# A VICTORY FOR THE SMALL STOCKHOLDER

*Vital Defects of the Van Sweringen Scheme—Effect on the Merger Situation—Value of Ches. & Ohio, Erie and Pere Marquette*

The denial of the Nickel Plate Merger came as an unpleasant surprise to Wall Street and served to intensify the severe unsettlement in stock prices which had commenced just previously. Yet whatever may have been its temporary effect on the speculative structure, it was undoubtedly a great victory for the real Wall Street—the intelligent, conservative security owners of the country.

For them, the decision means that fair dealing must rule in railroad finance, and that large interests, merely because they are large, cannot enforce their unrestrained will upon their smaller partners. Nor is the decision a set-back to the fundamental trend towards railroad consolidation. On the contrary, in approving the Nickel Plate grouping from a transportation standpoint (while condemning it as financially unsatisfactory), the commission has displayed a distinctly liberal and elastic spirit towards merger schemes, whether or not in accord with its preliminary general consolidation plan. The technical obstacles in the way of railway combinations have been considerably lessened by the decision; hence, the failure of Van Sweringens does not mean that pending merger plans must be abandoned, but only that they must be equitable.

Readers of The Magazine of Wall Street are no doubt familiar with the broad outlines of the Nickel Plate case. It is fully a year and a half since the Van Sweringens surprised the country with their New York, Chicago & St. Louis lines with the Pere Marquette, the Erie, the Chesapeake & Ohio and the Hocking Valley. The scheme contained many elements to appeal to the romantic imagination. The rapid rise of the Cleveland brothers, their rather mysterious personalities, their spectacular entrance into a financial field presumably reserved to prosaic bankers—all provided human interest "copy" of the first order.

More sober judgment, as usually happens, found occasion for regret as well as rejoicing. The Van Sweringens' plan was not without its faults. Objections, at first scattered and tentative, finally crystallized into determined opposition to the treatment accorded stockholders of Chesapeake & Ohio and Hocking Valley. The adequacy or inadequacy of these terms appeared to the general public to be the overshadowing question at issue in the long hearings before the Interstate Commerce Commission. Without minimizing either the importance of the specific question, or the strength of the dissenting minorities' case—which, in fact, the writer had supported in The Magazine of Wall Street as far back as February, 1925—it should be recognized that there were several other elements in the Nickel Plate proceedings which were equally open to criticism. These refer to both the provisions of the plan and the methods employed in carrying it out.

---

*"WHATEVER may be said in favor of the Van Sweringens as men of enterprise and constructive talent, it cannot be denied that they have displayed a callous disregard of the legitimate rights of their smaller partners… it is impossible to understand how in these enlightened days a deal of such magnitude and public interest could be engineered with a ruthlessness and lack of finesse reminiscent of the old-time captains of industry."*

## THE COMMISSION'S OBJECTIONS

The opinion of the Interstate Commerce Commission enumerates various defects which led to its vetoing the proposal. The chief of these were:

a.  *The ratios of exchange were not just.*

b.  *The new preferred stock should have been given voting rights.*

c.  *The old Nickel Plate remained a holding company, thus permitting pyramiding of control.*

d.  *The Erie coal properties should have been left out; and*

e.  *The Erie short lines should have been taken in.*

The commission's finding on the exchange ratios is vigorously expressed: "But it is evident from the record that inadequate consideration was given to the terms from the point of view of the stockholders of the Chesapeake and Hocking." There is severe criticism of the methods employed in determining and ratifying the various offers. Reference is made to the growth of Chesapeake's and Hocking Valley's traffic, and to their large earnings as compared with dividends paid. Against this the opinion cites an increase of 68 points in the price of Nickel Plate common from August, 1924, to December, 1925, while Chesapeake was advancing but 32 points. Finally, the general conclusion is reached that "the applicants have not sustained the burden of showing that the ratios are just and reasonable as between stockholders of the responsible lesser companies."

The next two provisions specifically disapproved are both related to a single objectionable purpose of the Van Sweringens—namely, to turn their minority ownership of the constituent companies into majority control of the consolidated system. This was to be accomplished in part by exchanging the voting preferred stocks of Erie, Pere Marquette and Chesapeake into non-voting new preferred. The other device is more subtle. The old Nickel Plate was to receive share for share in new common and preferred stock, as well as additional blocks for its holdings of Pere Marquette and Chesapeake. But instead of distributing this new stock to its shareholders in lieu of their old holdings—as was to be done by the other roads—it was planned to retain the new stock in the treasury of the old Nickel Plate, thus keeping it alive as a holding company. In this way the Van Sweringens, through ownership of about 54% of the old company's stock, would retain control of all the new Nickel Plate shares given for its properties. By these two artifices, a 32%

interest in the old companies would have been transferred into a 51% control of the consolidated system.

Delving further into the control situation, the commission notes that the Van Sweringen holdings are themselves vested in a separate corporation—the Van Ess Company, of which the brothers own 80%—the stock of which in turn is tied up in a voting trust in such a way that they would continue to exercise control thereof without owning a single share. The commission sets itself on record as emphatically opposed to control without majority ownership, and insists that preferred stockholders are entitled to voting rights.

In voicing strong objection to the inclusion of the Erie properties, the opinion raises an issue to which little attention had previously been paid. The Interstate Commerce Commission takes the stand that railroads should confine themselves to railroading, and sees no reason why it should authorize securities of the new Nickel Plate for the purpose of acquiring coal subsidiaries. On the other hand, the decision contains a rather unpleasant reminder to merger promoters that one of the primary purposes of the whole consolidation theory was to solve the problem of the weaker roads by including them in the larger systems. As students of the question have frequently pointed out, consolidation plans to date have uniformly passed over the lesser lines in polite silence—so that the American Short Line Association was moved to tearful remonstrance in the present case. The commission does not indicate to what extent it is prepared to insist on the inclusion of smaller lines, but it particularly condemns the failure of the new company to assume operation of the unprofitable subsidiaries now controlled by the Erie.

## THE VAN SWERINGENS' METHODS

In addition to discussing the various provisions which failed to win its approval, the opinion has a good deal to say about the methods employed in formulating and ratifying the plan. It is here that the decision is of chief interest to the rank and file of railroad stockholders. Whatever may be said in favor of the Van Sweringens as men of enterprise and constructive talent, it cannot be denied that they have displayed a callous disregard of the legitimate rights of their smaller partners. To the writer, the proceedings have remained from their inception a source of genuine amazement—it is impossible to understand how in these enlightened days a deal of such magnitude and public interest could be engineered with a ruthlessness and lack of finesse reminiscent of the old-time captains of industry.

The first announcement of the plan contained no reference to the position of non-assenting shareholders. It was even stated informally that those failing to join in the plan would receive nothing whatever for their hold-ings—a threat so obviously absurd as to require a later denial. The ratios of exchange were devised with a cavalier indifference to appearances. The terms for Chesapeake & Ohio common were undoubtedly inadequate, yet at least there was material for argument on this point. But the treatment accorded the Chesapeake & Ohio preferred stock was intolerable on its very face. While the exchange for Erie and Pere Marquette preferred issues meant a substantial increase in market values, Chesapeake & Ohio preferred was alloted new shares worth 13 points *under* its then current quotation. For a mere 4/10% increase in dividend it was asked to surrender its exceptional security, its voting power, and chief of all, an extremely valuable conversion privilege;—while Pere Marquette prior preferred, having no conversion priv-ilege, was given a 1% larger dividend.

There was also good reason for Erie 1st preferred stockholders to feel dissatisfied at receiving no more than was given to the 2nd preferred. This complete ignoring of their prior claim appeared especially illogical since Pere Marquette 1st preferred received 10% more than the junior issue. The fact that the Van Ess Company owned 52,600 shares of Erie 2nd and only 24,700 shares of Erie 1st, constituted an excellent explanation of this arrangement, but a very poor justification.

One of the most exasperating details of the plan was the arrangement whereby the old Nickel Plate received separate blocks of new stocks in exchange for its holdings of Chesapeake and Pere Marquette, while Chesapeake & Ohio was given nothing additional for its majority holdings of Hocking Valley. To accentuate the inequality, the records showed that the Nickel Plate had just acquired and not even paid for these shares of Pere Marquette, and that the cost of both lots was to be borne by the new company. This discrimination of the Van Sweringens in favor of their concern was so patent as to occasion wonderment that they did not at least take the trouble to disguise it by some of the many means available.

## C. & O. STOCKHOLDERS IGNORED

Whether or not these provisions were really as unfair as they seem might con-ceivably have been a matter of opinion. The Van Sweringens did not lack experts before the commission to defend their reasonableness in every respect. But the procedure they followed in effecting confirmation of their plan by the Chesapeake's board can inspire but one sentiment. While the Pere Marquette and Erie directors were deliberating, negotiating and demanding modifica-tions here and there, the Chesapeake & Ohio board—controlled by the Van

Sweringens—accepted the plan in toto without delay or question. In his original article on the Nickel Plate Plan, the writer, referring to this "striking peculiarity," employed the following language, which might have been less moderate had its aim not been a strictly dispassionate analysis of the case:

> *"But strangely enough these discussions have all taken place between the Van Sweringens and the Erie or Pere Marquette directors on behalf of possible Erie and Pere Marquette dissenting stockholders. The directors of Chesapeake apparently had not considered it necessary to take any similar step on behalf of their stockholders—although it was generally anticipated that owners of Chesapeake would be more likely than others to dissent."*

The language of the commission is identical in purport, but more forceful in tone: "The contrast between the manner in which the interests of all the stockholders of the Chesapeake and of the Hocking Valley were represented, and the manner in which the interests of Pere Marquette and Erie was protected, is striking." And again "there was an utter lack of independent and impartial representation of all of the stockholders of the Chesapeake and Hocking."

The opinion directs especial censure towards the president of the Chesapeake & Ohio, who was not a Van Sweringen nominee, and whom the stockholders might have excusably expected to make some effort to secure adequate consideration for those who for so many years had employed and trusted in him. But whereas the directors of Pere Marquette had obtained a substantial increase in the exchange ratios for each of their issues, the president of the Chesapeake confined his activities to issuing a statement approving in every respect the terms offered his stockholders. This part of the record makes painful reading.

We have dilated upon this aspect of the merger proceedings, not for the pleasure of criticism, but to indicate clearly the propriety—more, the necessity—of the commission's adverse decision. This was not a victory for mere obstructionism. It does not mean that any disgruntled stockholder can block important desirable developments by claiming some minor hurt. *But it does signify that age-old rules of equity are still in force—that though minorities may have no power, they still have rights; and that though directors may represent single interests, they still have obligations towards every stockholder.*

## EFFECT ON OTHER MERGERS

The effect of the decision upon the merger situation must be viewed from two angles: that of the Nickel Plate Plan alone and that of railroad consolidation plans in general. After its first disappointment Wall Street was quick to realize

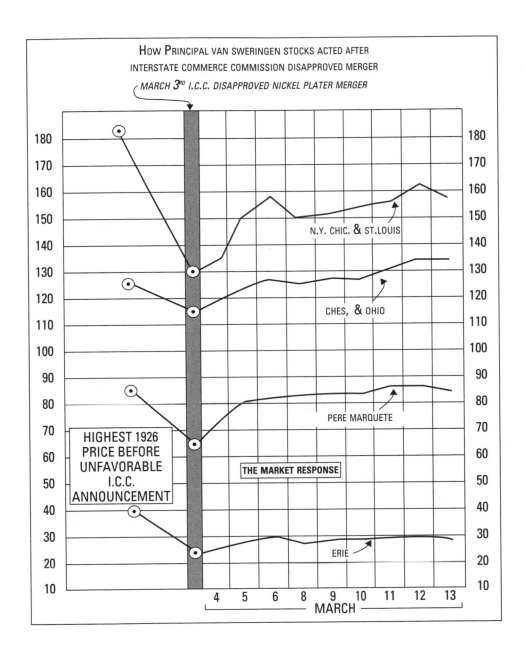

HOW PRINCIPAL VAN SWERINGEN STOCKS ACTED AFTER
INTERSTATE COMMERCE COMMISSION DISAPPROVED MERGER
MARCH 3RD I.C.C. DISAPPROVED NICKEL PLATER MERGER

N.Y. CHIC. & ST.LOUIS

CHES, & OHIO

PERE MARQUETE

HIGHEST 1926
PRICE BEFORE
UNFAVORABLE
I.C.C.
ANNOUNCEMENT

THE MARKET RESPONSE

ERIE

MARCH

that the opinion by no means constituted a setback to the merger idea as a whole. The question whether important single groupings can be effected in advance of the adoption of a comprehensive plan for the whole country, and whether the commission would admit departures from its own tentative proposals, have both been answered in the affirmative.

Most comments, however, have overlooked the exceedingly narrow margin of approval of the transportation feature of the plan—if margin it can be called. For of eleven commissioners, three did not participate and four refused to approve even the transportation setup. This means that somehow or other the remaining four members were able to announce the "majority opinion." From this point of view the situation is a bit confusing; suffice it to say then that the decision marks, if not a sweeping victory, at least a step in advance for the consolidation idea.

"What will the Van Sweringens do now?" has been the universal question in the financial district. Their chief counsel, in evident pique at their rebuff, intimated at first that his principals would abandon the whole project. Later statements were less extreme and in a few days Wall Street heard that a modified plan was already in the making. It seems fair to assume that any new proposal will endeavor to meet all the commission's objections. This means that Chesapeake and Hocking Valley must have better terms; that the preferred stock must have voting power and the holding company idea be abandoned; and probably also that the Erie subsidiary lines be included and the coal properties segregated. Some of these changes will present serious difficulties, but none should be insuperable. For example, the problem entailed by the pledge of the Erie coal stocks under its bond issues might be met by distributing to its stockholders certificates of interest in these properties. Naturally they should then accept some compensating reduction in their allotment of new Nickel Plate stock.

The Chesapeake & Ohio stockholders now hold the upper hand. After their recent galling defeat, it is not likely that the Van Sweringens will submit a new plan to the commission without first having reached an agreement with the Chesapeake and the Hocking minorities. (Because of the relatively small public interest in the Hocking Valley situation, we cannot discuss it here, beyond paying tribute to the able presentation of the dissenting stockholders' case by their counsel.) When new terms are discussed for Chesapeake & Ohio, attention will have to be given, not only to the original justification for more liberal treatment, but also to the greater earning power developed since the plan's inception.

## VALUE OF C. & O. COMMON

In the writer's view, the committee which has so energetically and successfully championed the cause of Chesapeake & Ohio, would remain well within the bounds of moderation if it now demanded 150% in new common. (The original offer of 55% each in new preferred and common was not only inadequate in the aggregate, but unsatisfactory also in asking the stockholders to surrender half of their equity in future earnings for a security with limited return.) *A new arrangement such as this—which represents, of course, only an individual view—would make Chesapeake common worth upwards of $150 per share.* The writer believes that apart from all merger developments, the exhibit of Chesapeake during recent years would fully justify this figure.

The increase in the Pere Marquette dividend has more than offset the severely adverse initial influence of the merger denial. With earnings last year of $11\frac{1}{2}$ and a $6 dividend rate, the common stockholders may face future developments with equanimity.

The position of the Erie issues is, of course, not nearly as strong, especially that of the common stock, which reported only $3.70 earned last year on account of the smaller dividends received from the coal properties. But the market decline from 40 to 25 amply reflected its less favorable status, nor can the stock be called unduly high at the current level of 30. Erie 1st preferred is properly establishing a level above the second, and since the way is now clear for a dividend on this issue, holders of these shares will in the end have suffered comparatively little.

Now that Chesapeake & Ohio has just increased its dividend and has thus followed Pere Marquette's dividend example, the result will, of course, be favorable, to their stockholders, but is likely to complicate the merger situation still further. Whether the commission will permit an increase in the Chesapeake & Ohio ratios without some compensating reduction elsewhere, and whether on the other hand the Pere Marquette directors, having raised the common dividend, may now claim more liberal terms for their stockholders, it is difficult to forecast. With the steam roller out of commission, the Van Sweringens are likely to find a second Nickel Plate Plan a more arduous undertaking than the first. Indications are not wanting of a possible withdrawal of the banking support so indispensable to the execution of their project. Hence the public should not be surprised to find some other important mergers actually consummated while the fate of the greater Nickel Plate is still in doubt.

# 34

# THE RIDDLE OF U.S. STEEL'S BOOK VALUE

*Is the Common Stock Worth
$280 Per Share?—Assets Contrasted
with Earnings—Essential
Characteristics of the Steel Industry*

The wide discrepancy between the book value and the market price of U.S. Steel has been of perennial interest to Wall Street. On December 31st last the net assets applicable to the common stock were equivalent to $281 per share—nearly twice its current record high level. Having existed for many years, this situation has from time to time been variously interpreted. Whenever Steel assumes its intermittent market leadership—as recently—the huge book value is cited as proof that the shares have all along been grievously undervalued. On other occasions, the persistent failure of these accruing equities to find adequate market recognition has given rise to criticism of the management's policy of turning back into the property so large a portion of the annual earnings.

The probabilities are, of course, that neither of these arguments is sound. It is unlikely that the market has for years remained completely blind to the merits of its most prominent industrial; it is equally unlikely that the directors of the Steel Corporation have pursued a reinvestment policy opposed to the best interests of their stockholders. We have here, it appears, something of a riddle—and an interesting one. For it involves not only the true worth of Steel common—itself a subject of no little importance—but also the general question of asset values and their relation to investment values.

While the Stock Exchange list exhibits the widest diversity, in both directions, between market prices and book values, the underlying explanation is simple enough. In general, prosperous enterprises sell for more than their assets, and unsuccessful ones sell for less. Two chief exceptions are the railroads and the steel companies. In these groups the shares of even the strongest concerns sell below their book value. The railroad issues of course belong to a separate class, their destinies affected primarily by regulation. It is a fact worth pondering that save for a few other steel companies, U. S. Steel is practically the only prosperous industrial now selling for much less than the tangible assets behind the shares.

This unique market position of Steel common is undoubtedly the result of exceptional conditions affecting the corporation's business. The situation can best be understood by tracing its development over a period of years—on the one hand from the balance-sheet viewpoint (the physical and financial factors) and on the other hand from the income-account angle (the operating and profit factors). We have selected a ten-year period, both as a customary interval and as one well adapted to comparative study. In the appended tables are succinctly set forth: (A) The aggregate results for the past decade; (B) Their effect upon the balance-sheet; and (C) Their effect upon the earning power, to the extent indicated by a comparison of the 1925 operations with those of 1915.

Considering the period as a whole, the results are most satisfactory. The average annual earnings of $18.40 per share of common are excellent; the average dividend of $8 is undoubtedly adequate; and the aggregate increase in surplus of $104 per share is most impressive. The latter large figure is reinforced by 124 millions, or $24 per share, added to miscellaneous reserves, part of which are undoubtedly equivalent to surplus. As part B of Table I shows, a total of 650 millions, or $128 per share, has been poured back into the business for plant investment, added working capital, and bond retirement. On the other hand, the market price of U. S. Steel common on December 31st last was only $47 per share (or 240 millions) greater than ten years before. This figure is less than the increase in working capital alone; it is considerably below the

## TABLE I

### A. Summary of U. S. Steel Corp. Financial Results 1915–1925:

|                          |               | Per Share |
|--------------------------|---------------|-----------|
| Earned for Common Stock  | $936,019,000  | $184.10   |
| Common Dividends Paid    | 409,181,000   | 80.50     |
| Surplus Increased        | $526,838,000  | $103.60   |

### B. Balance Sheet Changes; December 31, 1925 versus December 31, 1915:

| Plant and Misc. Assets Increased. | $264,317,000 | Surplus Increased        | $526,838,000 |
|-----------------------------------|--------------|--------------------------|--------------|
| Cash and Investments Increased    | 197,502,000  | Misc. Reserves Increased | 124,268,000  |
| Other Current Assets Increased    | 83,198,000   |                          |              |
| Funded Debt Decreased             | 106,089,000  |                          |              |
|                                   | $651,106,000 |                          | $651,006,500 |

### C. Income Account 1925 Compared with 1915:

|                                 | 1915          | 1925            | % Increase |
|---------------------------------|---------------|-----------------|------------|
| Sales, etc. (Excl. Inter Company) | $552,700,000 | $1,064,400,000  | 93%        |
| Wages                           | $176,800,000  | $456,700,000    | 158        |
| Taxes                           | 13,600,000    | 50,900,000      | 274        |
| Depreciation                    | 32,400,000    | 56,100,000      | 73         |
| Other Expenses                  | 225,400,000   | 396,500,000     | 76         |
| Total Expenses                  | $448,200,000  | $960,200,000    | 114        |
| Balance Before Interest         | $104,500,000  | $104,200,000    | Dec. 00.3  |
| Interest Paid, net              | 28,700,000    | 13,600,000      | Dec. 52.   |
| Preferred Dividends             | 25,200,000    | 25,200,000      |            |
| Balance for Common              | $50,600,000   | $65,400,000     | +29%       |
| Earned per Share                | $9.96         | $12,86          |            |

sum that has gone into cash assets and bond retirement; it is scarcely 50% of the amount added to surplus, and less than 40% of the increase in surplus and miscellaneous reserves combined.

These figures all support the repeated claim that Steel common has been sadly undervalued. In part C of Table I, however we view the matter from another angle and we obtain a different result. Here it appears that the half billion dollars reinvested in the business have produced only fifteen millions of added profits. Despite the tremendously increased asset value of Steel common, its earnings in 1925 were hardly $3 per share greater than in 1915.

Though the market price of Steel common has risen so much more slowly than the property values behind it, it has actually advanced faster than the earning power. In 1915, Steel earned $9.95 per share, or 11% on the closing price of 89; in 1925, it earned $12.86, or $9^{1}/_{2}$% on the last sale at 136.

These figures, however contradictory, undoubtedly contain the clue to the discrepancy between Steel's asset value and market value. *All experienced investors know that earning power exerts a far more potent influence over stock prices than does property value.* The worth of a business is measured not by what has been put into it, but by what can be taken out of it. So much is this true that many an unprofitable company sells in the market for less than the working capital alone—less than the liquid assets, which presumably could be readily turned into cash if the business were discontinued. Such companies, and they are by no means rare, are worth more dead than alive. Even cash assets, therefore, are not a dominant factor in market value, unless there are distinct possibilities of a special distribution therefrom. Hence Wall Street's refusal to recognize in full even the increased specie holdings of the Steel Corporation—which to the reader of the balance-sheet must appear like so much added cash in the pockets of its stockholders.

Granting that we can explain the lagging market price by the lagging profits, we are only introduced to a new problem—how to account for the very moderate growth in the Steel Corporation's earnings as compared with the enormously increased investment. But before we address ourselves to this difficult question it may be desirable to consider whether our premises are sound. Have we the right to attach any significance to the comparative prices of U. S. Steel on December 31, 1915, and December 31, 1925? Quotations fluctuate constantly, reacting often illogically to all sorts of temporary and even trivial influences. Objection may well be lodged against any attempt to base serious conclusions on a comparison of sales prices taken arbitrarily ten years apart. It may also be questioned whether the growth of Steel's earning power in the past decade can properly be measured by comparing earnings of the single years 1915 and 1925, in view of the widely varying results of the steel industry as between good and bad times.

Fortunately for our purpose, it can readily be shown that both the prices and the earnings selected are well suited to our comparative study. The price of $89 at the close of 1915 was itself a kind of average figure representing the mid-point in the upswing then under way. Ten years later, however, the price of $136 registered a high peak after a long bull market. The difference of 47 points between these two levels reflects very generously, therefore, the improvement in the market position of Steel common during the past decade. Similarly, 1925 should properly be regarded as a better business year than

1915. The latter, opening in gloom and ending in boom, showed for the whole twelve months a moderately favorable result. But 1925, with its new high record of production in steel and many other lines, was undoubtedly a year of more than average prosperity. Hence, the figures used for comparing both earning power and market value are, if anything, relatively more favorable to average present-day conditions than to those of ten years ago.

The conclusion appears inescapable that holders of U. S. Steel common have not derived concrete benefits proportionate to the vast equities that have been poured back into the property since pre-war days. Neither the earning power, dividend rate nor market value has increased to an extent commensurate with the growth of surplus and balance-sheet strength. This three-fold discrepancy is speedily reduced to a single problem—that of earnings, upon which both the dividend rate and the market price essentially depend. Is it possible to determine the causes underlying the failure of earnings to keep pace with the growth of assets? The task is not a simple one, and an exhaustive inquiry is precluded by the character of this article. Yet, even a brief study of the records may serve to shed some light on this important and perplexing question.

In the first place, in tracing the relation between reinvested profits and increased earnings, the former may usefully be divided into two parts: (A) The portion which has been used to improve the corporation's financial position; and (B) The portion devoted to expansion of operations. Division A includes funds utilized for debt retirement and increased cash assets. In Division B belongs the surplus invested in additions to plant, inventories and receivables. This segregation immediately discloses an interesting situation—

|  | Increase in Assets 1915 to 1925 | Increase in Earnings 1925 over 1915 |
|---|---|---|
| Class A "Financial". | $303,600,000 | $15,088,000 |
| Class B "Operating". | 347,416,000 | Dec. 319,000 |
|  | $651,016,000 | $14,769,000 |

It appears that the entire increase in earnings for 1925 over 1915 was supplied by the surplus devoted to "financial" purposes, and none at all by the still greater sum reinvested in "operating" assets. The full 15 millions of larger profits are accounted for by added interest received and smaller interest paid. As may expected, this income is equal to some 5% on the new capital involved. To this point we will recur later.

## TABLE II

### COMPARISON OF SELECTED ITEMS IN 1925 AND 1915 REPORTS

|                            | % Increase 1925 over 1915 |
|----------------------------|---------------------------|
| Property Account           | 17.7%                     |
| Capacity: Ingots           | 10.6                      |
| Capacity: Finished Steel   | 5.9                       |
| Production Finished Steel  | 12.8                      |
| Receipts per Ton           | 73.9                      |
| Total Sales                | 93.0                      |
| No. of Employes            | 30.7                      |
| Average Annual Wage        | 97.6                      |
| Total Pay Roll             | 158.3                     |

The failure to increase operating income despite the huge sum added to plant investment is necessarily due to a higher expense ratio. Some comparative figures on this score are arresting, as seen in Table I (C) and Table II.

These comparisons show clearly that the lower profit margin follows primarily from a disproportionate growth in labor costs. (The heavy increase in the tax item is an additional important factor, though this burden no doubt bears just as grievously on other lines of industry.) The labor difficulty goes deeper than the increase of 98% in the average annual wages, against the rise of 74% in indicated selling prices.

These relative figures are not far different from those of other businesses which have, nevertheless, succeeded in reporting large increases in net profits.

The special handicap of U. S. Steel in the matter of wages arises from three conditions. First, the abolition of the twelve-hour day in 1923, the effect of which is seen in the great relative expansion in the number of employees. This means a corresponding reduction in the output per man; or otherwise stated, that the hourly wage has increased much more than the annual wage. Secondly, the large proportion that wages bear to the total costs in the steel industry makes the expansion of the pay-roll a more serious factor here than in other lines. Finally, it must be pointed out that U. S. Steel has not enjoyed the advantage of greatly augmented output which has helped other companies to absorb the higher wage scale. In fact, the increase of $15\frac{1}{2}$ % in ingot production for 1925 as against 1915 is undeniably a disappointing figure, especially when compared with the 42% rise in the output of the whole country.

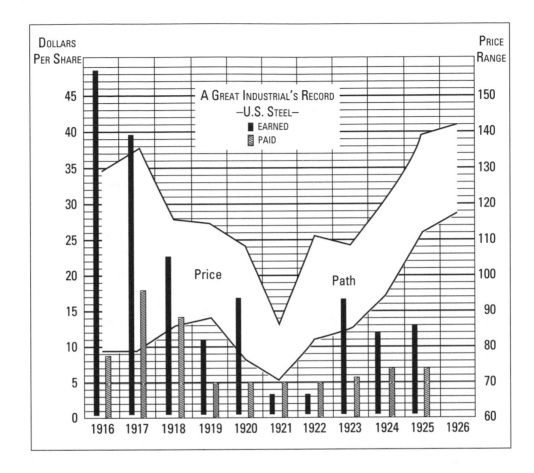

DOLLARS PER SHARE

PRICE RANGE

A GREAT INDUSTRIAL'S RECORD
—U.S. STEEL—
■ EARNED
▨ PAID

Price        Path

This production ratio leads us to a consideration of the results achieved by the corporation's large expenditures on new plant facilities. Judge Gary has effectively disposed of the charge of over-expansion by pointing out that in twelve years Steel's ingot capacity has increased but 20%, against 60% by its competitors. This fact raises in turn the question of the cost of each ton of added output. We have seen that the additional capital invested in operating assets since 1915 amounts to 347 millions. Against this the increase of ingot capacity is reported at 2,200,000 tons, and that of finished steel at only 900,000 tons. While exact comparisons are not feasible, it is significant to note that Republic Iron & Steel, with a total capitalization selling in the market for 60 millions, reported last year an output of 932,000 tons of finished and semi-finished products.

Evidently, a substantial part of the corporation's plant expenditure has been devoted not to increasing capacity but to improving the manufacturing processes. It is also true that a good part of the additions to capacity are offset by reductions due to the retirement of obsolete and uneconomical units. The effect of the outlays for improvements is visible in the fact that since 1915 operating expenses other than wages have increased at a somewhat smaller rate than the gross receipts, although the exhibit here can hardly be called impressive.

But, however, the capital expenditures are divided as between additions and betterments, the fact remains that no commensurate benefit can be traced either in capacity or costs—either in output or profit margin. The fundamental reason for this unsatisfactory state of affairs is to be found in the competitive character of the industry, or more exactly in the combination of keen competition with elaborate manufacturing processes. Where so many different operations are involved, technical improvements are constantly being devised, which, as soon as adopted by one company, must straightway be followed by the rest. This necessitates incessant outlays for new equipment and the rapid obsolescence of old facilities. An outstanding example is the development of the by-product coke process replacing the beehive ovens. In the end, however, the competitive pressure prevents any increase in the margin of profits as the result of this greater efficiency, so that the chief benefit therefrom is reaped by the consumer.

Hence, it may be questioned whether the Steel Corporation's yearly charges for maintenance and depreciation, enormous as they appear, have fully provided for this obsolescence factor, which is not capable of annual calculation. To the extent that the undistributed profits are required to offset plant investment grown obsolete (and not amortized by depreciation and contingent reserves), the true earnings would have to be regarded as somewhat lower than the reported figures.

Again, the integrated character of the steel industry, together with the great variety of its products, supplies a constant incentive to expansion. Nearly every company can always find a good reason for branching out in some department which it had previously neglected, or "strengthening its position" at some point in the chain from raw material to finished goods. In the aggregate this means a continuous increase in the country's steel capacity, beyond that required by the growth of demand.

These basic factors probably explain the attitude of combined helplessness and disapproval which now and then qualifies the constitutional optimism of the leaders of industry. Judge Gary expresses a desire to spend less on property account, but insists that the activities of his competitors force the Steel Corporation to fall in line, or else lag behind. President Campbell of the Youngstown Steel & Tube—a concern enjoying an earning power above the average—states that under present conditions of high costs, plant expenditure must be financed out of earnings and not by sale of securities. The skeptic would inquire, "Why make these improvements if they cannot be expected to return a fair profit on their cost?" The answer is, no doubt, that competitive conditions demand them.

Mr. Schwab, of Bethlehem Steel, has recently called attention to the relatively small return per dollar of capital invested in the steel industry, and has not hesitated to blame it on the practice of making plant expenditures without the prior assurance of a suitable return. Very possibly, however, the situation arises not from errors in policy, but from the steady working of economic laws. Adam Smith pointed out long ago that in a developed community the long-term tendency is for the rate of profit on capital to decline. It may well be that beneath the welter of war dislocation and post war fluctuations, the steel industry in the past decade has been illustrating this principle.

This question is of vital interest to those alert investors who buy for appreciation as well as for income. A trend towards diminishing returns is by no means noticeable in every field. In the past decade countless companies have been able to increase their earnings, and, therefore, the price of their shares, in far greater ratio than the growth of their assets. These include enterprises as diverse as American Tobacco, Corn Products Refining, Railway Steel Spring—to say nothing of obvious examples like Woolworth and General Motors. American Tobacco, for example, in the past ten years has added 53 millions to the assets behind its common stock, which meanwhile increased in market price over 140 millions—a difference explained by the growth in net earnings from 8 to 19 millions.

Where a company is unusually prosperous the reason will generally be found in a special growth of demand—a growth more rapid than the normal, secular, or populational rate. This may be due to new or intensified public tastes—as in cigarettes, autos and various trade-marked goods; or to advantages enabling certain types of organization to secure an increasing proportion of the total business in their field—as illustrated by chain systems, department stores and many small efficient enterprises. In such cases expanding volume keeps competition within "healthy" bounds, and permits maintenance of a satisfactory profit margin on the growing turnover.

Neither the steel industry, as a whole, nor U. S. Steel in particular, belongs to this class. Their growth has been sure and by no means slow; yet in the absence of any special stimulus to demand, the tendency has been for augmented capacity to keep well abreast of rising volume. Hence, competitive pressure has been gradually undermining the margin of profit on sales and the rate of return on capital. This would seem to be the fundamental reason for the relatively moderate improvement in the position of Steel common stockhold-ers over the past ten years, as compared with that of many other companies operating, it would seem, under no more favorable auspices.

It might be well, finally, to point out the practical bearing of this situa-tion on the value of Steel's cash assets. We have seen that in the past decade the corporation's financial position (as distinct from its operating assets) has been improved to the extent of over 300 millions, or $60 per share, from which it has derived added annual income of 15 millions, or about 5%. Yet, investors would generally expect Steel common to earn on the average some 10% on its market price—this being regarded as a fair ratio in the case of stocks with nor-mal prospects and subject to fluctuations in earning power. Nor is it custom-ary to reduce the required percentage because of the existence of large cash assets, unless there is a definite likelihood of a large *distribution*. This being the case, a peculiar and wide discrepancy results between the face value of the corporation's holdings in cash, or cash equivalents, and their practical value to the stockholders. There is no room here for a thorough discussion of this point, but it is worth considering that there may be such a thing as excess financial strength in the same way as excess plant capacity.

In the absence of strong indications to the contrary, it must be assumed that the Steel Corporation's management is thoroughly aware of the consider-ations outlined above, and has held them clearly in mind when apportioning the annual profit between dividends and reinvestment. With respect to the sums applied to plant account, a good part of these seem to have been dictated more by necessity than by choice, and their failure to produce a commensurate growth in profits must be attributed to conditions inherent in the industry rather than to faulty judgment. Frankly speaking, it is not so obvious that all the sums applied to cash assets and bond retirement have been indubitably needed therefore. The accepted argument in favor of ultra conservatism—that the stockholders must ultimately reap the benefit—fails to take the time element into account. According to this view, it is immaterial to a shareholder whether his equities take realizable form in one year or ten. Nothing could be more fallacious; for in this respect stocks are identical with bonds, the return from which is invariably calculated on an annual basis. Hence, in a real sense delay means loss; and to the extent that a stockholder's reward is postponed, its value to him is diminished.

Needless to say our conclusions in no wise question the impregnable strength of U. S. Steel Corporation or its ability to earn a fair return on a capital-ization undoubtedly far below the actual investment. We have been concerned rather with the cause and significance of the persistent disparity between the book value of Steel common and its market quotation. Our investigation indicates that the steel industry is one which necessitates a steady up building of assets without assurance of a comparable increase in earnings. This being the case, it is inevitable, and by no means unjust that the stock market should appraise these added assets at less than their face value.

This may explain why Steel common does not and should not sell at $280 per share. Whether the present record price, around $140, is intrinsically low or high, constitutes an entirely different question, on which this article sheds at best an indirect and partial light. Looking beyond the immediate market furore, and the accompanying stock dividend prospects, the writer hazards the view that the essential character of Steel common remains the same today as in the past—a surer investment than most, but slower than many to grow in value.

# 35

# MR. SHAREHOLDER—DO YOU KNOW *WHEN* PERIODIC STOCK DIVIDENDS HELP AND *WHEN* THEY HURT YOU?

The practice of paying dividends in stock at regular intervals has become increasingly prevalent. The leading example is General Electric, which for several years has been making an annual distribution in special stock in addition to the quarterly cash payment. This policy has gained most adherents in the public utility field, including such notable enterprises as North American Co., Cities Service, etc. So far this year several companies have initiated quarterly or semi-annually stock dividends in addition to the customary cash payment, while in recent weeks Lorillard and Hartman have announced their intention of substituting stock for cash. In view of their growing importance these periodic stock dividends deserve study. What is their purpose and effect; to what extent are they useful and wherein lies their possible abuse?

The fundamental purpose of paying dividends in stock is to reconcile the two conflicting aims of a company's management: to reward the stockholders and to build up the business. But that these objects, while both praiseworthy, are mutually hostile is evident from the fact that stockholders are ordinarily rewarded by paying out the profits, while building up the business usually requires that the profits be retained. The stockholder wants both income and appreciation, but in general the more he gets of one the less he realizes of the other. The periodic stock dividend ingeniously gives him the equivalent of a regular income while retaining the cash itself for purposes of corporate expansion. The stockholder "eats the cake" and the company still has it.

To many this artifice will appear merely a snare and a delusion. In their view, what the stockholder thinks is really income is only a piece of paper, which the Supreme Court has held to make him no richer than before. While aiming below the surface, this criticism does not go deep enough. In pure theory even cash dividends represent no real increase in the shareholders' wealth, for they are paid at the expense of the company's assets, and the value beyond his stock is diminished accordingly. But this notion fails to recognize that the worth of an issue depends on other things besides the net assets on the company's books. Current earnings, future prospects, management, marketability are all factors more or less independent of assets which contribute their share to the intrinsic value.

The dividend rate is another such separate element of value. It seems superfluous to argue that dividends are important; nevertheless the extreme diversity of dividend policies indicates that the financial community's ideas on this subject are confused and unstandardized. To understand stock dividends one must first understand cash dividends, and a short discussion of this question may also shed some light on a needlessly obscure phase of corporate practice.

> *The newer tendency toward periodic stock dividends is sufficiently important to require the detailed analysis which appears in this article. Investors have the right to know under which conditions these periodic dividends attain a greater market value than justified and under which conditions their payment is in direct harmony with real earnings.*

That the investing public attaches great significance to the dividend rate, as distinguished from earnings and all other considerations, cannot be denied. Of two companies with similar earnings and prospects the one paying the greater dividend will nearly always sell higher in the market— i. e., it will be preferred by security buyers. Now if this view represented a mere baseless prejudice—a sort of financial superstition—it would still deserve recognition by the company's directors; for their prime duty is to try to satisfy their shareholders, not to chasten or reform them. This certainly is the hope of the investor.

But the desire for distribution of profits is based on sounder grounds. For regular income, after all, is the primary and fundamental aim of investment. In the field of bonds and preferred stocks, this is almost the exclusive consideration and it is only among admittedly speculative common shares that fluctuations in principal value claim the leading importance. It is the ingrained and justifiable expectation of investors that good common stocks should pay dividends fairly proportionate to their earnings and intrinsic value.

But against this basic principle a powerful counter-current has long been operative in American corporate finance, which has laid the emphasis upon future earning power instead of current dividends and has viewed the stockholders' reward in terms of appreciation rather than income. Hence, directors have felt perfectly free to retain and utilize all or any part of the profits, whenever future advantage seems likely to result. While we accept this attitude as natural and largely praiseworthy, it is worth noting that it is peculiar to American finance and is not generally followed abroad. The English or Dutch shareholder expects that after adequate reserves (including those for contingencies but not for new capital) the year's earnings will be distributed to him virtually in toto. If funds are needed to expand the business, they are raised by the sale of additional securities—usually new shares at an attractive subscription price.

The development of the opposite American practice can be traced to a number of causes. It originated in the early days at the large "trusts," whose common stock was predominantly water and which were burdened with excessive issues of bonds and preferred shares. Under these conditions the upbuilding of assets out of earnings was urgently necessary to correct an initially unsound capitalization. Many of the stronger corporations, moreover, were controlled by one of several wealthy stockholders, who had no need of dividends and permitted the profits to accumulate as in a private business. (For the proverbial apathy of the small American shareholder rendered unnecessary any consideration of his rights.) The war period, with its high surtaxes, added another compelling influence in the same direction, since the dominating interests could save enormously in personal taxation by foregoing dividends.

Through the operation of these diverse causes, the practice of accumulating earnings has in various degrees superseded and obscured the original obligation to distribute them. It may be said that there is now no accepted standard in this vital matter, which conscientious directors will endeavor and others can be compelled to observe. However necessary the retention of earnings may have been in individual cases, and however advantageous in many others, it cannot be denied that the prevalence of this policy has in general given rise to grave abuses and injustice. For although the dividend rate has become a matter of practically arbitrary determination by the directors, yet, through its inherent importance, it has remained of prime interest to the investor —especially the small investor. Hence, the attractiveness of a stock issue—which means not only the market price, but in some sense the intrinsic value as well—has been in no small measure dependent upon the discretion, whim, or personal interest of the directors.

It cannot be denied that this situation has all too frequently operated against the small stockholder and in favor of the larger interests; against the outsider and in favor of the insider; even against the shareholders as a body and in favor of the management in their capacity as officials.

From the standpoint of the investing public as a whole it is highly desirable that our corporate practice should be more nearly standardized in the direction of a normal relationship between earnings and dividends. Strong arguments can be adduced in favor of the general foreign practice of devoting the profits as a whole to dividends and of expanding the business by new security issues. There are, however, a number of obstacles—some real and others imaginary—to the adoption of this policy by typical American corporations, and for practical purposes the same object can be accomplished by the artifice of the periodic stock dividend.

Here our digression brings us safely back to the original subject. All the preceding arguments have been directed towards creating a correct comprehension of the basic function of the regular stock dividends—not as a sop or idle gesture, but as an effective recognition of the legitimate interests and desires of the shareholders. In this connection a sharp distinction must be made between stock dividends paid at regular intervals (once, twice or four times a year) and those of a sporadic or "melon" type. The latter must be considered not in the light of income but as a readjustment of capital. They may serve a useful purpose in reducing the market price of a stock to a more convenient figure, and their object is sometimes to raise the actual cash dividend while maintaining the same nominal rate per share—though this would scarcely appear of any real importance. In general, however, large, infrequent stock dividends are part of the unstandardized distribution policy against which criticism has been directed above. They are authorized at arbitrary times and in arbitrary amounts, and generally exert an undue, frequently sudden effect upon the market price out of proportion to their real significance.

## Issues Paying Regular Stock Dividends

| Name | Dividend Rate | | | Current Market Price | Total Value of Dividend | Latest Annual Earnings | | Ratio to Market Price | |
| --- | --- | --- | --- | --- | --- | --- | --- | --- | --- |
| | Cash | Stock | Stock Div. Payable | | | Year Ended | Earned per Share | Dividend | Earnings |
| American Gas & Elec. | $1.00 | 4% | S. A. | 104 | $5.16 | June, '26 | $6.84 | 4.96% | 6.58% |
| American Power & Light | 1.00 | 4 | S. A. | 71 | 3.84 | June, '26 | 4.69 | 5.41 | 6.61 |
| American Rolling Mill | 2.00 | 5 | A. | 48 | 4.40 | Dec., '25 | 2.35 | 9.17 | 4.90 |
| American Waterworks & Elec. | 1.20 | 5 | S. A. | 59 | 4.05 | June, '26 | 4.51 | 6.86 | 7.64 |
| Assoc. Gas & Elec. "A" common | 2.50 or | 10 | Q. | 37 | 3.70 | June, '26 | †3.73 | 10.00 | 10.08 |
| Canada Dry Ginger Ale | 2.00 | 5 | Q. | 46 | 4.30 | Mar., '26 | 3.22 | 9.35 | 7.00 |
| Childs | 2.40 | 4 | Q. | 52 | 4.48 | June, '26 | 4.00 | 8.61 | 7.69 |
| Cities Service | 1.20 | 6 | M. | 44 | 3.84 | July, '26 | ‡3.38 | 8.73 | 7.68 |
| Electric Investors | | 10 | A. | 44 | 4.40 | May, '26 | 3.18 | 10.00 | 7.23 |
| Electric Refrigeration | 2.00 | 5 | Q. | 67 | 5.35 | June, '26 | 5.25 | 8.00 | 7.84 |
| Famous Players | 8.00 | 2 | A. | 115 | 10.30 | Dec., '25 | §13.67 | 8.95 | §11.88 |
| Federal Light & Traction | 0.80 | 4 | Q. | 34 | 2.16 | June, '26 | 3.48 | 6.35 | 10.24 |
| Federal Motors | 0.80 | *10 | *Q. | 33 | 4.10 | June, '26 | 3.90 | 12.42 | 11.82 |
| General Gas & Electric "A" | 1.50 or | 6 | Q. | 50 | 3.00 | July, '26 | †2.35 | 6.00 | 4.70 |
| General Electric | 3.00 | $1 (a) | A. | 91 | 4.10 | Dec., '25 | 5.12 | 4.51 | 5.63 |
| Hartman "B" | | 10% (b) | Q. | 29 | 2.60 | June, '26 | 3.19 | 8.97 | 11.00 |
| Kraft Cheese | 1.50 | 6 | Q. | 69 | 5.64 | Dec., '25 | 4.28 | 8.18 | 6.20 |
| Lorillard | | 8 | Q. | 32 | 2.56 | Dec., '25 | 3.90 | 8.00 | 12.19 |
| McCrory Stores "A" & "B" | 1.00 | 3 | (c) | 80 | 3.40 | June, '26 | 5.82 | 4.25 | 7.27 |
| North American | | 10 | Q. | 56 | 5.60 | June, '26 | 3.40 | 10.00 | 6.07 |
| Schulte Retail Stores | | 8 | Q. | 47 | 3.76 | June, '26 | 4.37 | 8.00 | 9.30 |
| Seagrave | 1.20 or | 10 | Q. | 13$^1/_2$ | 1.35 | June, '26 | 2.75 | 10.00 | 20.37 |
| Standard Gas & Elec. | 3.00 | 2 | Q. | 56 | 4.12 | Dec., '25 | 6.38 | 7.36 | 11.40 |
| United Cigar Stores | 2.00 | 5 | Q. | 100 | 7.00 | June, '26 | 5.03 | 7.00 | 5.03 |
| Utilities Power & Light "A" | 2.00 or | 10 | Q. | 31 | 3.10 | Feb., '26 | †2.52 | 10.00 | 8.13 |
| Utilities Power & Light "B" | 1.00 or | 10 | Q. | 14 | 1.40 | Feb., '26 | 1.81 | 10.00 | 12.93 |

§ On stock outstanding December 31.   †Available under participating rights.   ‡Before reserves.   *Indicated rate.   (a) In special stock, par $10, selling at 11.   (b) In A stock, selling at 26.   (c) In three quarterly payments of 1%.

But the *periodic* stock dividend appeals to the investor in terms of regular income. It is the practical equivalent of cash—readily salable by those who want money rather than stock. To this point the Supreme Court could pay no attention; for legal expediency compelled the general dictum that dividends if in cash were income and if in stock were merely paper. But good law may be poor psychology; in the investor's mind the notion of income depends not on cash payments as against stock, but upon receipt at regular, dependable intervals.

There is submitted herewith a fairly complete list of the companies now paying periodic stock dividends. Certain variations in procedure may be noted, although they are hardly of real consequence. The stock dividends are paid in some cases annually, in others semi-annually and in others quarterly; in the two former cases they usually supplement a quarterly cash disbursement. Some companies give their stockholders the option of taking either cash or stock at fixed rates; others declare a cash dividend with the accompanying right to subscribe to an equivalent amount of new stock. Since in all such cases the stock offered is worth in the market considerably more than the cash alternative, and since all but the most careless stockholders invariably take the stock, such arrangements are practically identical with a straight stock dividend declaration.

The data contained in the appended list will serve to illustrate both the advantages of a stock dividend policy and its possible defects. Taken as a whole, these issues sell higher than other common stocks in comparison with their earnings. This point substantiates the obvious fact that regular stock dividends are appreciated by the public and constitute a separate source of attractiveness which benefits the market price of the shares. But a critical scrutiny of our list raises the question whether these stock dividends may not be too efficacious in upholding market quotations.

The price of many of these issues appears higher than would be conservatively justified by the current earnings. In each case, no doubt, champions will arise to assert that the future prospects are such as to warrant the present level; nevertheless prudence suggests that the dividend policy may sometimes lend an undue stimulus toward discounting the future, thus adding dangerous fuel to the speculative flames.

One of the peculiar features of regular dividends payable in stock is that the yield is independent of the market price. An issue like North American, paying 10% per annum, will ostensibly yield 10% whatever be its price. For if the price advances the value of the dividend increases proportionately. Hence no matter how high such issues may be selling they will always appear attractive from the dividend standpoint. This consideration suggests that the stock dividends are not as simple as they look, nor as innocent as they sound. From an accounting angle the subject teems with complications; and while most of these can fortunately be ignored by the investor, he should not be blind to their wider consequences. One of the basic contradictions is that corporations usually think they are paying out less than stockholders think they are receiving. Recurring to North American, which pays 10% in stock, since the par value is $10, the company's accounts carry the payment at $1 per share, but since the market price is $50 the stockholder regards his dividend as worth $5. The same is true of certain issues without par value such as American Power & Light. Here the common is arbitrarily carried in the balance sheet at $10 per share. Hence the annual stock dividend of 4% is charged by the company at the rate of 40 cents per share although it is worth in the market (and valued by the stockholders) at $2.40 per share.

This accounting detail has made it possible for so many of these companies to follow a dividend policy that apparently pays out to the stockholders more than is currently earned on the shares. Our table shows this condition to obtain in the case of half of the common issues listed, while a good proportion of the remainder show a dividend rate very close to the reported earnings. Although the writer is strongly in favor of the general idea of periodic stock dividends, he feels that the situation just disclosed is certainly misleading if not basically unsound, and indicates the crying need of a more discriminating and less mechanical application of this valuable device.

> "… although the dividend rate has become a matter of practically arbitrary determination by the directors, yet, through its inherent importance, it has remained of prime interest to the investor—especially the small investor. Hence, the attractiveness of a stock issue—which means not only the market price, but in some sense the intrinsic value as well—has been in no small measure dependent upon the discretion, whim, or personal interest of the directors."

If North American Company is currently earning some $3.50 per share, then a dividend rate equivalent to $5 must be open to question. (Whether or not the actual earnings are larger because of excessive reserves is beside the point, which is fundamentally that of real dividends as opposed to bookkeeping dividends.) The directors may claim that they are paying only $1 per share (10% of $10 per share); yet if this is so, then the greater part of the value of the dividend arises at the expense of the stock previously outstanding. But brushing aside theoretical attacks and technical defenses, the vital defect of such a policy is its over-subtlety. On its surface it is opposed to the commonsense judgment of the investor, and it offers too great opportunities for delusion and illusion to be entirely safe.

In this connection the record of American Light & Traction carries a salutary warning. This company was perhaps the pioneer in the field of regular stock dividends. From 1909 to May, 1920, it paid uninterrupted quarterly dividends of 2½% in cash and 2½% in stock. At the end of 1916 the shares were selling at 380. Hence the annual dividends, while $20 at par, were worth in the market about $48 per share. In that year—the best to date—the earnings were equivalent to about $26 per share, against a previous average of some $22. One effect of this liberal stock dividend policy was to increase the common shares outstanding from about nine million dollars in 1910 to twenty-seven million dollars in 1920. Toward the end of this period the post-war rise in public utility expenses cut severely into the system's net earnings, which in 1920 declined to only $8 per share. This finally necessitated a reduction in the annual dividend rate to 4% in cash and 4% in stock, and was accompanied by a drastic decline in the market price to a low of 78 in 1921.

Beginning in 1924 the earnings recovered sharply, and are now larger than ever before. Nevertheless, early in 1925 the management abandoned stock dividends entirely and is now paying only $8 in cash. So while others were flocking to the cult, its virtual founder recanted.

The spectacular decline in the price of this issue from 1917 to 1921 has been pointed to by some as indicating that a policy of continuous stock\dividends must be fundamentally unsound, in that it involves a cumulative increase in the size of the stock issue until an unwieldy total is reached. Evidently a great part of American Light & Traction's troubles were in no sense related to the dividend policy, but followed from the widespread difficulties of the public utilities under inflationary conditions. But it is clear also that the aggregate dividend was too liberal in comparison with the earnings; and that the practice of repeatedly presenting, the shareholders with stock worth $38 in the market, but representing only $12 to $16 reinvested in the property, was clearly bound sooner or later to result unpleasantly.

But such disastrous consequences are by no means inherent in stock dividend policies generally; nor can the practice of capitalizing reinvested earnings be validly attacked, provided due conservatism is exercised. When profits are voluntarily retained in the business, there is no reason why the stock should not be issued against them, for they should be able to earn a profit and pay cash dividends in the same way as the original capital. If this procedure must ultimately stop, it is because the limit of profitable reinvestment is reached; and at this point the earnings should go to the stockholders in cash instead of back into the business. Whenever earnings must be retained and yet cannot be safely capitalized, i. e., cannot be counted upon to increase future profits—then these are not real earnings at all, but represent necessary reserves to make good obsolescence or some other hidden impairment.

It may be noted that the accumulation of earnings in the form merely of undisturbed surplus tends to obscure the stockholders' view of what constitutes a satisfactory earning power and to over-simplify the problem of the

management. In many cases the stockholders, by foregoing possible dividends over a period of years, have really invested twice as much as the par
value of their shares; yet since the amount of stock has remained unchanged,
they habitually compare the current earnings and dividends with the original
capitalization instead of with the total cash actually invested to date. Two
years ago Judge Gary, discussing the dividend on Steel common, spoke of a
7% rate as "very good for any stock." That may be quite true if the stock represents an investment of $100 per share, but when there is actually $200 per
share contributed to the business, a $7 rate is much less adequate than it
appears on the surface.

What we clearly need, and what we have yet to attain, is some definite
standard of sound practice in paying regular stock dividends. The chief of
these is the principle that the current value of the stock dividend paid should
be conservatively less than the earnings reinvested. Hence in fixing the rate
the market price of the stock to be distributed should be considered, rather
than the par or book value,—especially when the former is a much higher figure. It is interesting to know that Famous Players has recognized this point in
its recently adopted dividend policy of paying an extra $2 per share in stock at
a price to be fixed by the directors. A simple means to avoid this troublesome
divergence between book and market figures is to pay the stock dividend in
preferred shares with relatively stable value. General Electric is the leading
exponent of this plan, having for years paid an extra dividend in its 6% special
stock. This policy was recently adopted by Hartman and was followed for a
while by Schulte before the split-up of the common shares.

It is strongly to be hoped that the future will bring a better understanding of the whole subject of dividends. This is certain to involve a clearer
delimitation of the rights of stockholders and the duties of directors,
together with an approach to a standardized dividend policy, flexible in
detail but more or less uniform in the underlying recognition of the stockholder's claim to a return commensurate with the value of his investment.
For this purpose the periodic stock dividend will be utilized to an increasing
extent to give the shareholders concrete evidence of that part of their profits
voluntarily reinvested in the business.

The trend towards such a dividend policy is inevitable. As the financial
community becomes more familiar with its various features, the possibilities
of misconception or misuse will steadily diminish. Eventually the regular
stock dividend should gain thorough understanding by the investment community and wide adoption by business heads as an integral part of corporate
procedure.

# 36

# THE NEW ERA OF DISCRIMINATION IN THE SELECTION OF SECURITIES

*Lessons of the 1926 Market That Should
Prove Valuable in 1927*

It has already become a commonplace that for the greater part of 1926 there was no such thing as a "Market Trend." The old conception of the stock market as a single entity, responding as a whole to bullish or bearish influences, was practically valueless throughout the year, except during the cataclysmic break of last February and March. In the other months each group of stocks has fluctuated with little regard to any other group, and even among companies in the same industry the diversity of their price range has been extraordinary. In summing up the 1926 market one is tempted to revise the familiar line to read: "Every little issue had a movement of its own."

Because of these conditions the much discussed "Stock Market Averages" have taken on a far different and much less vital significance than of yore. In the olden days the averages gave us a pretty good picture of the price changes in most representative stocks, taken individually. If the industrial average had advanced five points in a month, it meant nearly always that Steel, Baldwin, American Can, American Sugar, etc., had each experienced a fair-sized upswing.

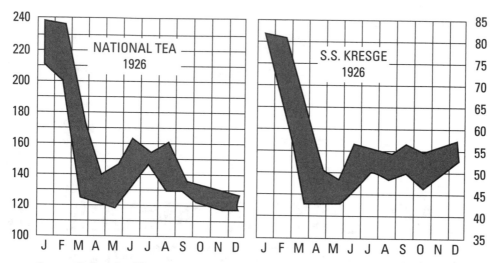

**1.**    ***Corrective Movement*** *— representing the application of a less visionary standard of value to over-exploited issues and definitely establishing them on a lower market plane.*

## "AVERAGES" LOSE VALUE

But during the most of 1926 the "Industrial Average" was not a picture but an arithmetical abstraction. It no more reflected the market action of any one particular stock than the figures for the average weight, height and income of all New Yorkers would be applicable to the first man in the street.

As one result of this situation we find that various averages behaved quite differently depending upon how they were constructed. The Standard Statistics Index, based on 230 issues, showed a slightly higher level towards the end of November than at the beginning of the year. On the other hand, THE MAGAZINE OF WALL STREET STOCK Indexes, based on 238 stocks, showed a decline of some 9%.

As a separate check the writer compared the November 30 and January 1 quotations of 515 issues, and found there had been 245 declines against 170 advances—a ratio of about three losses for each two gains. Furthermore, analyzing the price changes by groups of industries, there were found eighteen groups with a predominating downward range, nine groups enjoying a general advance, and ten having gains and losses in fairly equal proportions. These observations would tend to bear out the general impression among traders that stock prices are for the most part lower now (January, 1927,) than at the beginning of 1926, despite the general strength near the close.

## 1926 A MANY-SIDED MARKET

Starting with the fair premise that the many-sidedness of the 1926 market distinguishes it from all its predecessors, the question presents itself whether any new controlling influences, any new principle of action, can be discerned in the price movements of the past year, which may have some valuable bearing on future markets. Do the scores of fluctuating price variations signify that the market is more complicated, more inscrutable than ever—or do they reflect perhaps a general rearrangement of quotations to conform with new but recognizable standards of value? These are interesting questions and worth pondering, even though the answers be but fragmentary and tentative.

The 1926 market has already been analyzed to good effect from the standpoint of the action of various industrial groups. It will serve the writer's purpose better if we approach the subject from the angle of the diverse forces governing price movements. These influences may conveniently be considered as of four kinds:

(a)  *Corrective—readjustments necessitated by previous market excesses;*

(b)  *Reflective—corresponding to current developments affecting the issue;*

(c)  *Anticipative—discounting expected future occurrences;*

(d)  *Manipulative—representing large scale market operations independent of influences affecting intrinsic value.*

Of course not all market developments can be classified under one of these four headings; in many instances more than a single influence is at work, nor can it be definitely asserted which is controlling. Yet the majority of price movements may be related fairly definitely to some one of these forces, and not a few of the vagaries of the 1926 market become more comprehensible when considered in this light.

## CORRECTIVE MOVEMENTS IN LAST YEAR'S MARKET

The break of last March was a corrective process applied to all issues, and during this period alone the market acted as a unit. The drastic collapse was induced by the too violent and indiscriminate speculation of the previous months, reflected in rapidly mounting collateral loans and many over-extended pool positions. The real diversity of the 1926 market became evident after the decline was over, in the widely varying degree in which the losses were later recovered. In analyzing the issues which failed to regain the greater part of their shrinkage, we can see that some were subject to corrective influences of an individual kind, distinct from and more enduring than those behind the general market shake-out of last Spring.

An obvious example is presented by the chain store issues, nearly all of which are selling below their January 1, 1926, prices, the average decline being some 25%. Yet sales have exhibited sustained expansion and profits were undoubtedly ahead of 1925. In this group, therefore, the market action ran counter to current developments, because the extravagances of the previous year (1925) demanded correction. The tremendous advances of 1925 had sent their quotations to a level entirely unwarranted not only by the current earnings, but even by any increases which one could legitimately expect for years to come. Kresge, for instance, opened the year at 885 ($88\frac{1}{2}$ for the split-up shares) against earnings of $31.70 per share; an earnings ratio of only 3.6%. At these dizzy levels the chain store group was especially vulnerable to deflationary forces. Hence the March decline in these issues proved more than a technical setback; it represented the application of a new and less visionary standard of value to their statistical exhibits, which definitely established their quotations on a lower plane.

The market action of Kresge, National Tea, etc., throws an interesting sidelight on the hazards necessarily involved in buying issues on their expected future earning power. The theory that a low current rate of profit can be disregarded, provided there is strong assurance of steady future increase, has the peculiar weakness that it proves too much. For it could be

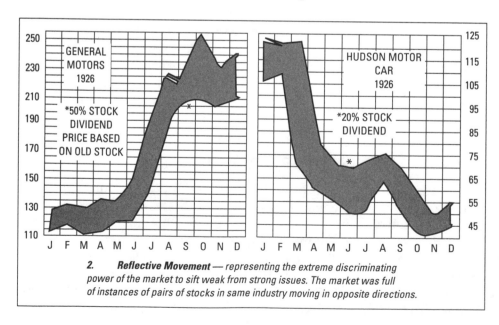

2.　**Reflective Movement** — representing the extreme discriminating power of the market to sift weak from strong issues. The market was full of instances of pairs of stocks in same industry moving in opposite directions.

used to justify any price, no matter how fantastic, merely by looking far enough ahead and making these remote profits the basis of current investment. The danger is of course that at any time the market may turn a little less far-sighted and look to the present or the near future for its measure of value. This is precisely what happened to the chain store issues,—the change in the market's viewpoint being stimulated by the general shattering of speculative idols last Spring.

At first glance the action of the public utility group appears hopelessly contradictory, in that substantial advances are found side by side with severe declines. Closer inspection shows that this group is itself divided into two distinct sub-classes—the large scale holding companies and the local enterprises. Nearly all the latter type are selling higher and nearly all the former type are selling lower than at the beginning of 1926.

The cause of this divergence lies also in the market of 1925. In those hectic days the large holding companies (e. g., North American, American Water Works) became such speculative favorites that unsound price levels were reached which clamored for correction. The situation here was precisely similar to that obtaining in the chain store issues, and although the profits of 1926 exceeded the 1925 figures, the year's price trend was downward, because it started from an excessive level.

But the local utilities (e. g., Brooklyn Edison, Laclede Gas) had not held the same speculative attraction the year before as the large holding companies, and hence their advance had been more orderly and conservative. They were thus in a position to reflect the continuance of favorable operating conditions in 1926 (including the winning of the New York rate litigation), so that their price trend was predominantly upward.

The larger banking issues have suffered a severe decline from their January 1, 1926, prices which was also the result of undue enthusiasm in 1925. Here the deflation has been accentuated by the 1926 earnings. For, while not less favorable than those of the year before, they nevertheless failed to register the gains confidently expected during the precipitate rise of the shares. Somewhat the same description applies to most of the dairy products and ice cream stocks.

The speculative excesses of 1925 were of two types: first, those affecting whole groups of issues which caught the public's imagination and enjoyed a wide, if misguided, following; and secondly, over-valuations of isolated issues, which in most cases perhaps were the affair of private manipulation. To the latter class belongs a miscellaneous list of speculative skyrockets, headed by such extreme instances as Devoe & Raynolds and New York Canners, and including American Linseed, International Combustion, Savage Arms, Simmons Bed,

White Rock, Worthington Pump, etc., etc. In all these examples, the market shrinkage during the past year has been due primarily not to current unfavorable results, but rather to unwarranted advances in 1925. There are some issues, such as Jordan Motors, in which previous over-valuation and disappointing earnings both played a part in the price collapse, it being impossible to say which deserves greater emphasis.

Because of the buoyant character of the 1925 market there were not many instances of the December 31 prices being palpably too low and needing correction through an upward adjustment. Oppenheim Collins may be cited as one of the few examples, for at 49 it was clearly out of line with other department store issues, and accordingly it has advanced 12 points despite the general downward trend in its group.

## REFLECTIVE MARKET MOVEMENTS

There is little doubt that the majority of last year's price changes can be adequately explained by reference to current operating results. The copper and sugar issues advanced as a group because of improvement in the price of the commodity; the tobaccos rose as usual because their remarkable growth has continued; the New York tractions spurted sharply on the expectation of relief through fare increase or otherwise.

Conversely, the building equipment, coal, leather and rubber groups suffered general declines because of unsatisfactory developments in these industries. In these examples the trend is practically universal, with only scattered exceptions. But there is a larger number of groups in which the results vary greatly between individual companies. A comprehensive study of these situations yields striking evidence of the individual character of American enterprise, and of the ability of single companies better favored by natural advantages or executive skill to outstrip their competitors, and even to prosper while their industry as a whole is depressed.

Undoubtedly the outstanding example of our thesis was General Motors, which registered its most brilliant exhibit while most of its competitors were showing a substantially lower earning power. In this case a minor recession in the trade as a whole meant a major setback for most units, because General Motors' increased sales came entirely at their expense. A few companies like Packard held their gain fairly well; only Nash and Hupp in the passenger field and Federal Motors among the truck companies were able to follow the giant along the path of continued growth in both sales and profits.

The list is full of pairs of issues in the same industry which moved last year in opposite directions. In most cases the discrepancy can be explained by reference to current earnings or other specific developments. The net advance of General Electric against the decline in Westinghouse is readily ascribable to the split-up and increased dividend of the former, together with its better exhibit of new business booked.

More striking is the contrast between Armour and Cudahy. The latter not only has given two shares for one and declared a larger cash dividend, but also has reported a substantial increase in profits; while Armour was compelled to suspend dividends on its A stock and has undoubtedly earned less in 1926 than in 1925.

Similarly the severe shrinkage in National Distillers preferred and common was accompanied by a sharp decrease in the quarterly earnings, while U. S. Industrial Alcohol's advance is explained by the resumption of dividends, bearing out the reports of a prosperous year. In comparing the diverse movements of Pathe and Warner Brothers Pictures, it is clear that the former's weakness was occasioned by the poorer earnings of 1926, while the buying of Warner Brothers has ignored its current deficits in the enthusiasm over the possibilities of the Vitaphone.

In the railroad list most of the substantial advances, as in Atchison, Norfolk, Rock Island, etc., can be correlated with an equally decisive expansion in net income. On the other hand, the chief declines took place in the Southern group, including Seaboard and Atlantic Coast Line, and are readily explained by developments in Florida.

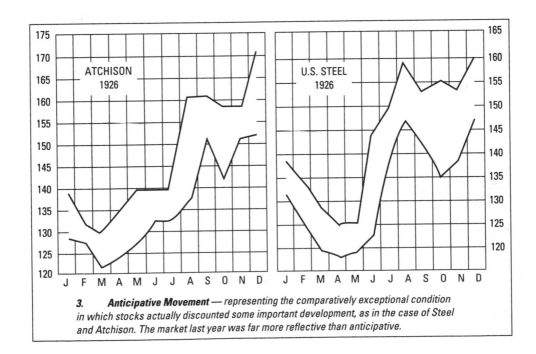

3.   *Anticipative Movement* — representing the comparatively exceptional condition in which stocks actually discounted some important development, as in the case of Steel and Atchison. The market last year was far more reflective than anticipative.

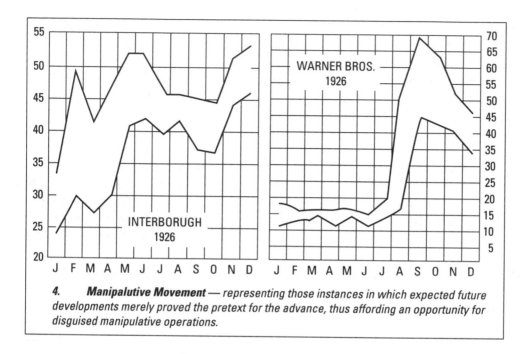

**4.** ***Manipalutive Movement*** *— representing those instances in which expected future developments merely proved the pretext for the advance, thus affording an opportunity for disguised manipulative operations.*

One of the interesting results of our analysis has to do with the market's action in discounting future developments in individual companies or groups. Until recently the stock market was supposed to function as a general business barometer, anticipating by several months at least the changes that were due in the industrial situation. But since the last major depression of 1920–21 this traditional characteristic of the market has not been so much in evidence— largely, perhaps, because there have been no really wide business swings to anticipate. Where stocks as a whole have fluctuated in recent years, these variations seem for the most part to synchronize rather closely with, instead of forestalling, industrial changes.

## ANTICIPATIVE INFLUENCES IN 1926

In 1926, with no single stock market trend to refer to, and with similarly confused and contradictory business developments, the question whether stock prices anticipate industrial changes must be transferred from the general to the specific field. We have already stated that the majority of price movements can apparently be accounted for by current developments affecting the issues; i. e., the market influences have for the most part been reflective rather than anticipative.

Of course, there have been numerous instances where a stock has had a substantial move up or down without explanation and the reason has been found in some subsequent earnings report or dividend action. But such anticipation merely reflects the exploiting of advance knowledge by insiders. This is not the intelligent discounting of the future for which the market has often claimed credit, but in essence a species of financial "wire-tapping."

Of anticipation in the barometric sense there seems to have been remarkably little in the 1926 market. The sugar stocks advanced, not because the price was expected to go up, but because it was going up. The motors rose sharply as a group from May to July, because of good Spring business. They did not reflect the poorer third quarter and the sharply contracted year-end business until the results were coming to hand. So in most individual issues. Advance-Rumely preferred had a wide upswing while business was good, and then lost 50% of its price coincident with a slump in the second half-year. *Prices moved quite generally not before but along with industrial developments.*

The sensational rise in U. S. Steel for months preceding the stock dividend announcement constitutes one of the few well defined instances of anticipatory market action in 1926. The same is probably true of the advance in Atchison, which reflected the increase in the cash dividend and probable stock dividend later this year. It would also seem that the rise of the Erie issues was bound up with the expectation of a favorable merger outcome. Yet, the strength in the other Van Sweringen issues, while ostensibly discounting the success of their unification plan, might with equal plausibility be attributed to the excellent operating results for 1926.

## ANTICIPATION OR MANIPULATION?

In quite a few instances, the expected future developments which seem to have occasioned the rise in an issue may have been more truly a pretext or talking-point, disguising manipulative operations. Let us take the New York City tractions as an example. Third Avenue has advanced 200% and Interboro nearly 100%, although the actual financial results show little change. The inference is that the pronounced strength of these issues represents intelligent anticipation of the much discussed transit relief. But if the market were here merely reflecting expected future values it would be hard to understand why Interboro stock should have been selling at times within a point of Manhattan Elevated Modified Guaranteed shares. For the latter must receive $5 per share (cumulative) before I. R. T. can get any dividend, nor may the latter pay more than $7 before 1950. And if the $7 maximum were paid, Manhattan stock would be entitled to 7% also. A discrepancy of this kind usually means that some artificial or manipulative influences are at work which prevent the normal relation of values from asserting itself in the market.

For different reasons one suspects such a rise as was registered by Butterick from 22 to a high of 72, ostensibly in anticipation of increased earnings from some new and ill-defined executive policy. Such gyrations remind one too much of the rise of New York Canners in 1925 from 32 to 81 and its disastrous aftermath.

In the preceding discussion we have shown by examples how our various types of price influences were operative in the 1926 market; and have endeavored to appraise their relative importance. Does our study lead to any conclusions of value with respect to the future? Naturally, an understanding of the vagaries of 1926 will be of value in 1927 only if we have the same kind of market as in the preceding year.

If we are going to see an orgy of indiscriminate speculation on the one hand, or a protracted and equally uniform bear market on the other, the fine distinctions called for by last year's complexities will be of no avail. The ruling opinion seems to be, however, that the character of the market is not likely to change radically in the current year. If this assumption is correct certain useful ideas are suggested by our study of the 1926 record.

To begin with, if price changes for the most part will reflect current developments rather than the future—as seems to have been the case last year—then good judgment as to what is in store should prove unusually profitable. In other words, there should be excellent opportunities to act ahead of the market. The man who is sure improvement is coming can buy on the basis of current less favorable conditions, and thus derive the full benefit of the betterment—if it materializes. For example, from the low price of the rubber stocks one would ordinarily imagine that the market expects poor results in 1927; but it may be that these low prices reflect simply the small earnings and inventory losses of 1926. Hence, it is more than possible that conditions are going to be stabler and profits larger this year, in which case there is an opportunity to make a substantial profit in these issues by buying them at current depressed levels.

The same would be true if one expected higher prices for oil or copper, or a real turn in the textile or fertilizer industries. On the other hand, if a trader rightly anticipated a slump in the steel industry, he has a similar chance for real profit on the short side.

The second point is that just as the 1926 market corrected in many cases excessive price advances of 1925, so exaggerated moves in either direction last year may be corrected in 1927. To an analyst of values it seems that in reflecting current unfavorable results the market has in many instances swung too far on the destructive side, and has marked down the price of solvent issues to a figure below their minimum intrinsic value. Such opportunities are being constantly discovered and discussed by THE MAGAZINE OF WALL STREET. The writer will merely mention as examples such issues as Atlas Tack, Hartman Corporation, Kinney Shoe, Lee Rubber, National Cloak & Suit, Transue & Williams. Given fairly favorable general market conditions, discrepancies of this type should adjust themselves in due course and the purchaser of such issues at bargain prices should reap a handsome reward.

There are undoubtedly far fewer examples of fantastic and purely speculative over-valuations in the stock list today than a year ago. Of those that currently exist, time and reason will doubtless rectify a goodly percentage. Hence, it is important to make sure that one is not lured by rash enthusiasm into commitments at levels greatly above those soundly warranted by the financial set-up and the earnings record.

A study of stock prices in relation to earnings and past history would tend to support the widely held opinion that the rails appear more attractive at current levels than the industrials. While the shares of those carriers showing increased income have had substantial advances, on the whole, their prices are lower compared with earnings than in the case of strong industrials. As far as we can judge, future fluctuations in the transportation field should not be as wide as with the industrials, so that from an investment viewpoint the former issues present more conservative opportunities.

With all its contradictions and vagaries, the market of 1926 was at bottom more logical and intelligent than most of its predecessors. It would be interesting indeed if last year has really ushered in a New Era of Discrimination in Wall Street. Nevertheless, the writer imagines that experienced observers would demand more proof than a single twelve months can afford that the days of wild speculation and ensuing general liquidations are definitely behind us.

# INDEX

## A

Ajax Rubber, 259, 260
All America Cables, 210
Allied Chemical, 259
Allied Packers, 157
American Agricultural Chemical
  asset value of, 71
  capitalization of, 70, 71
  dividend policy, 67
  dividend records of common stock, 67
  dividend returns, 72
  effect of war on earnings of, 68
  investment rating of, 65
  market yields of securities, 66
American Can, tax reserve of, 45–46
American Ice Co., 210
American International, 111–112, 169
  comparative balance sheet, 172
  comparative income account 1916–19, 170
  investment holdings and gross earnings,
    172
American La-France Fire Engine, 314–315
American Light & Traction, 377
American Smelting & Refining, 45
American Steel Foundries, 165
  current assets of, 272
  stock of, 117
    low-priced dividend paying, 271
American Sugar Refining, 162
American Telephone & Telegraph, 298
American Water Works, 260, 344
Associated Dry Goods, 210

## B

Bargain
  and bond issue, 341–342
  and buying of cash assets, 345–347
  concept of, 339
  different types of, 340
  features of, 340
  opportunities, 340
  in securities, 340
  various types of
    Calumet & Arizona, 347
    Consolidated Gas & Electric of
      Baltimore, 344
    Cudahy Packing, 342
    Industrial Finance, 344–345
    Salt Creek Producers, 348
    Waldorf System, 347
Benjamin Graham Joint Account, 297
Bethlehem Steel, 272
Bond(s)
  attractive yields, 76
  cheap industrial, 96–97
  of Chesapeake and Ohio, 95
  East Tennessee, Virginia & Georgia 1st 5s,
    94–95
  interest payments, 117
  investing, principle of, 117
  market, 75
  prices, 13
    discrepancies in, 16
  quotations, 75
  selection, 62

Bond(s) (*Cont.*)
    selling on high income basis, 76
    yields, 217
    (*See also* Mortgage bonds)
Brokaw Bros., 276
Brooklyn Union Gas, 87

# C
California Petroleum, 238
Calumet & Arizona, 347–348
Capital gains, effects on bonds purchased at
        discount, 8
Capitalization, indirect method for,
        212–213
Capital stock, 245
Capital structure, comparison of, 211
Cash assets, 254
Cash asset stocks, 121, 247, 256
    balance-sheet analysis, 252
    Crescent Pipe Line, 253–254
    Crex Carpet, 250–252
    Pennok Oil, 254–255
    Shattuck-Arizona Copper, 255–256
    Southern Pipe Line, 253
    Tonopah Mining, 246
    Transue & Williams Steel Forgings
        Corporation, 249–250
    Wright Aeronautical, 256–258
Certified public accountants, 256
Chesapeake & Ohio, 322
    formulation of merger plan, 326
    stockholders of, 353
*Chiaroscuro* effect, 11
Chile Copper, 77, 97–98
Coal stocks, estimated value of, 227
Columbian Carbon, 127
    capitalization, 278
    low-priced dividend paying stocks,
        276–278
Common stock exchanges, 242–244
Company, factors determining essential
        merits of, 5
Congoleum, 341
Consolidated Copper mines, treatment of
        ores in, 36
Consolidated Gas & Electric, 306, 344

Consolidated Gas System
    asset value of, 88
    balance-sheet, 85
    companies comprising, 84
    contingency and renewal reserves of, 86
    elements adding to asset value, 85
    elements adding to earning power, 85
    hidden assets of, 63
    important bond issues of, 90
    income account of, 86
    incorporeal rights, 88
    intrinsic value of, 84
    operating costs of, 87
    and subsidiaries combined balance sheet,
        89
Consolidated Textile, 237
Convertible debenture, 89
Convertible issues, advantages of, 235
Convertible preferred stocks, and
        opportunities for hedging, 158
Corporate Property Tax, 87
Corporation bonds, 99
Corporation earnings, 208
Cosden, 274
Crescent Pipe Line, 122
    cash assets of, 253
Crex Carpet, 133, 254
    capitalization, 250
    dividend rate offered by, 250
Cuba Cane, 118, 162
    earnings per share, 163
    percent earned on total capitalization, 164
    prices and dividends on common and
        preferred shares, 166
    relation of capital structure to earnings, 164
Cuban American Sugar, 138, 162
    earnings per share, 163
    as low-priced dividend paying stock, 273
    percent earned on total capitalization, 164
    prices and dividends on common and
        preferred shares of, 166
    relation of capital structure to earnings, 164
Cudahy Packing
    bargain issues in, 342
    stock price of, 306
Cumberland Pipe Line, 252, 254
    capitalization, 251

## D

Daily Quotation Sheet, 93
Debentures, 114
Detroit Stock Exchange, 275
Devoe & Raynolds, 385
Douglas-Pectin Corporation, 300, 315
Dow Jones Industrial Average, 3, 59, 103, 297
Dow Jones Rail Index, 298
Duesenberg Motors, 269

## E

East Tennessee, Virginia & Georgia bonds, 94–95
Equity capitalization, 106
Equity investors, 104
E. T. Va. Ga. Bonds (*See* East Tennessee, Virginia & Georgia bonds)
Excess profits tax, 29, 43

## F

Fifth Avenue Bus, 301, 318–320
Ford Motor Company, 113

## G

GEICO Insurance Company, 299
General Asphalt, 236
General Chemical Pfd., 135
General Electric, 82, 104, 243
  book capital and surplus, 46
General Motors, 260, 297
Gilliland Oil, 117, 158
Goldwyn Pictures, 267
Goodyear Tire and Rubber, 113
  balance sheet, 180
    after reorganization, 184
  financial history of, 182
  issuance of bonus stock, 186
  present position of, 183–185
  readjustment plan, 114, 179
  working capital and fixed charges after reorganization of, 185
Graham, Benjamin
  analysis of
    degree of attractiveness of bonds, 64
    issues concerning Nevada Consolidated, 10–11
    stock values, 116
  bargain opportunity for stock price, 305
  business model analysis for Inspiration Copper, 9–10
  capital structure analysis, 60
  concept of periodic stock dividends, 310
  contribution in determining corporate's profits, 3
  determination of factors influencing merits of company, 5
  factors effecting vagaries of business cycle, 59
  investment analysis by, 59
  investment approach, 60
  investment principle, 304
  opinion on long-term investment, 6
  standard of assessing value of preferred stock, 106
  valuation of Great Northern Ore certificates, 9
  views on
    Consolidated Gas's earnings, 63
    downside risk of any investment operation, 6
    patterns of investor behavior, 60
Graham Corporation, 297
Granby Copper, bonds of, 96
Great Northern, 139
  earnings under federal control, 141
  gross and net revenues of, 143
  land holdings, 144
  miscellaneous charges and income, 144
  transportation costs, 141
Great Northern Iron Ore Trust
  certificates
    annual dividend, 25
    appraisal of, 24
    steps for valuating, 21
  comparison with porphyries, 25
  earnings in 1914, 21
  formation of, 20
  Graham's opinion on annual reports of, 9
  income for 1916, 23
  leasing of property, 20
  royalties, 20
  shares, 20
  state of unsettlement, 21–22
  steps for valuating certificates for
    actual earnings, 21–22
    determination of life of mines, 22–23

"The *Great Steel Tax Mystery: Secrets of Invested Capital—Part 2*", 11
Great Western Mining Company
  earnings from properties, 22
  fluctuations of stock, 25
  operating management of, 23
  ore reserves, 24
Griffin Wheel Co., 165

## H

Hedging, 155
  between bonds and stocks, 156–158
  convertible preferred stocks and opportunities for, 158
  types of, 159
"High Yield and Safe Investments," 62

## I

Income statement factors, and effect on company's going concern value, 5
Income tax, corresponding to tax reserve, 43
Industrial Acceptance Corporation, 345
Industrial Alcohol, 312
Industrial common stocks
  approximate tangible asset values of, 44
  assessment of, 108
  general features of, 245
  investments in, 81
  low-priced, 259
  low-priced dividend paying
    American Steel Foundries, 272
    book value of, 318
    Columbian Carbon, 277–278
    comparison of, 277
    Cuban American Sugar, 273
    Paige-Detroit Motor, 275–276
    Weber & Heilbroner, 276
    White Eagle Oil, 273–274
  low-priced stocks
    American La-France Fire Engine, 314–315
    Douglas-Pectin Corp., 315
    Fifth Avenue Bus, 318–320
    Metro-Goldwyn Pictures, 315–316
    U. S. Hoffman Machinery, 317–318
    Waldorf System, 317
    Wright Aeronautical, 316–317
  margin of safety for, 105
  net earnings for, 108
  preferred, 77
  price rise in, 109
  purpose of paying dividends in, 371
  security analysis for, 105–106
  for sugar industry, 110–111
  which are conservative investments, 81
  yielding 7% or more, 79
Industrial Fibre, 345
Industrial Finance, 306
Industrial preferred stocks
  attractive, 133
    list of, 135
  cumulative *vs.* non-cumulative, 136–137
  disadvantages of non-cumulative, 106
  dividends on, 80, 134
  equity capitalization-to-total par value of, 106
  factors influencing value of investment in, 132
  investment quality of, 132
  price per share of, 134
  standard of assessing value of preferred stock, 106
Inflation-indexed securities, 4
Inspiration Copper
  conditions during war and peace, 32
  dividend policy, 31
  features of annual report of, 28–29
  investment value of stock, 31–34
  mining, 27
  ore reserves, 31
  ore valuation and war taxes, 29–30
  price range, 27
  probable costs and profits, 30–31
  production and prices, 28
  profits per share for stock, 30
  taxes levied against 1917 income, 29
*The Intelligent Investor,* 104, 299
Interborough Rapid Transit, 260, 312
Intrinisic value *vs.* book value, 105
Invested capital
  asset value of, 41
  book figures for, 54

mathematical process involved in
    determining, 43
method employed for calculation of, 43–45
under War Revenue Act, 47
Investment
    definition of, 105
    misconception about, 14
    prices and compensation, 42
    real capital, 42
    *vs.* speculation, 104–105
Iron Mountain, 80

## J

J. P. Morgan, 283

## K

Kresge
    assets and earning power of, 150
    capitalization and dividends of, 152
    percentage of 1918 earnings to market
        price of, 149
    tangible asset values of, 151
    working capital of, 152
Kress
    assets and earning power of, 150
    capitalization and dividends of, 152
    percentage of 1918 earnings to market
        price of, 149
    tangible asset values of, 151

## L

Lackawanna Steel, 156
Landover Holding Corporation, 125,
    269–270
Liberty Loan Drive, 4
Liggett, Louis K., 189, 191
Loews Inc., 300
Low-priced preferred stock
    Landover Holding Corporation,
        269–270
    Metro-Goldwyn, 267–269
Low-priced stocks, 264
    long-range opportunities in, 259
        International Agricultural, 261
        Mountain Producers, 266–267
        Salt Creek Producers, 266–267

Simms Petroleum, 263–265
Wabash, 262
Waldorf System, 265–266

## M

Mack Truck, 214
Manati Sugar, 162
    percent earned on total capitalization, 164
    prices and dividends on common and
        preferred shares, 166
    relation of capital structure to earnings, 164
Market prices, role of, 105
May Department Stores, 210
McCrory, 147
    capitalization and dividends of, 152
    comparative earning power of, 149–150
    market prices, 148
    percentage of 1918 earnings to market
        price of, 149
    reasons for backwardness of, 151
    tangible asset values of, 151
    working capital of, 152
Merger and acquisitions, 302
    effect on purchase of stock, 332
    market values due to, 336
Metro-Goldwyn Pictures, 315–316
Midwest Refining, 266
Missouri Pacific, 80, 291
Mortgage bonds, 64, 66, 71, 114
Mortgage lien, 95
Mutual funds, 4

## N

National Distillers, 312, 387
National Sugar Refining, 146
Nevada Consolidated
    book value of assets per share, 39
    charges for depreciation, 39
    dividend, 35
    earnings of, 37
    income account for 1917, 37
    liquidating proposition, 39
    mining expense due to war causes, 37
    net operating costs, 37
    open pit ore, 36
    recoverable ore, 36

New Haven, 283
New York Canners, 390
New York Stock Exchange, 93, 114
Nickel Plate, 322
  Interstate Commerce Commission,
    objections of, 351–352
  railroad merger scheme, 307
Non-cumulative preferred stocks,
    disadvantage of, 136
Northern Pacific, 140
  earnings under federal control, 141
  financial advantage under federal
    control, 142
  gross and net revenues of, 143
  land holdings, 144
  land sales, 142
  miscellaneous charges and income, 144
  transportation costs, 143
Northern Pipe Line, 306
N. Y. Edison Company, 86
  mortgage security of, 89

**O**

Oil stocks, 159, 274
Omnibus Corp., 319
Oppenheim Collins, 386

**P**

Paige-Detroit Motor, 126
  low-priced dividend paying stocks, 275
Pan American Petroleum, 158
Peerless Truck and Motor Corp., 100
Pennok Oil, 122
  capitalization, 254
  cash holdings, 255
Pere Marquette, 322
Periodic stock dividends, 309
Pipe line stocks
  characterization of, 252
  Crescent Pipe Line, 253–254
  dividend return on, 252
  Pennok Oil, 254–255
  Southern Pipe Line, 253
Preferred stock, 114
Premium bonds, 14
  market value of, 15
Prior preference stock, 114, 185

Producers & Refiners, 236
Public utility stocks, 63, 339
Punta Alegre Sugar, 111, 162
  earnings per share, 163
  percent earned on total capitalization,
    164
  prices and dividends on common and
    preferred shares, 166
  relation of capital structure to earnings,
    164

**Q**

Qualitative factors, and effect on company's
    ability to survive and prosper, 5
Quotation Sheet, 94
  (*See also* Daily Quotation Sheet)

**R**

Railroad
  common stocks, 199
    earnings and dividend yields of, 284
    estimated values of, 227
    relative values of, 227
  earnings in year 1921, 203
  mergers and acquisitions, 332
    influence on security values on,
      335–336
    market values due to, 336
  operating costs, 200–206
  preferred stocks
    analysis of listed, 288–289
    bond ranking of, 291
    against common issues, 292
    per-share earnings of, 287
    test for determining value of, 128, 285
  securities, value of, 330
    influence of merger and acquisition on,
      335–336
  six selected low-priced issues of, 201
    Chicago & Eastern Illinois, 205–206
    Missouri, Kansas & Texas, 203–204
    Pere Marquette, 205
    Rock Island, 205
    St. Louis Southwestern, 202–203
    Toledo, St. Louis & Western, 204–205
  specific consolidation developments, 333
Railway Steel Springs, 55–56

Reading Company, 128
  dividend record of, 281
  earning power and financial strength of, 282
  earning power of stockholders of, 225
Republic Iron & Steel, 365

## S

Salt Creek, 266, 348
"Secrets of Invested Capital," 11
*Security Analysis*, 108, 299
Security switching
  benefits of, 233
  profitable, 234
  into senior convertibles, 235–241
  types of, 234
Shares, preferred
  asset value and earning power of, 81
  criteria of selecting, 81
Shattuck-Arizona Copper, 123
  capitalization, 256
  issues of, 255
Simms Petroleum, 124, 169, 263, 265
Sinclair Oil, 158
Southern Cotton Oil Company, 68, 70
Southern Pacific Co., 94, 109
  bonds, 222
Southern Pipe Line, 251, 253
Standard Oil, 253, 348
Standard Statistics Index, 382
Steel Foundries, tangible value of, 55
Steel War Tax, 50
Stock dividends
  advantages and disadvantages of, 376
  issues paying regular, 375
Stock Exchange Quotation Sheet, 98
Stockholders
  earning power before and after segregation, 225
  effect of inter-company settlements on earning power of, 226
Stock market averages, 381
  anticipative influences during year 1926, 388
  corrective movements for improving, 383–385

Stock prices, in relation to earnings, 391
Stock quotations, 181
Stocks (*See* Industrial common stocks)
Studebaker Corporation, 345
Sugar stocks, 161
  earnings per dollar of market price, 163
  reports for year 1918–19, 162–164

## T

Tax
  law for differentiating real and imaginary assets, 42
  rates of, 43
  reserves
    and determination of invested tangible capital, 49
    of leading industries, 42
  return, 54, 131
Tax-exempt securities, 254
Tonopah Mining, 121, 247, 254
Transportation Act of 1920, 304, 329
Transue & Williams Steel Forgings Corporation, 121, 248
  balance sheet, 249
  dividend rate offered by, 250
  market valuation of, 249

## U

Union Bag and Paper Company, 97
Union Pacific, 199
United Cigar Stores, 135, 266
United Drug
  asset value of, 193
  balance sheet, 191, 193
  business prospects of, 189
  current liabilities of, 193
  depreciation of inventories, 192
  growth of retail business, 195
  history of, 191–193
  listing in New York Stock Exchange, 190
  plant and inventories, 115
  stock dividend, 115
  stock prices, 114, 190
United Fruit Co., 162
U.S. Hoffman Machinery, 301, 317–318
U. S. Industrial Alcohol, tangible asset value of, 45

U.S. Steel Corporation
  balance sheet changes, 361
  book value and market price of, 359
  capital expenditures, 366
  deviation of treasury figures for
    1917 earnings, 53
    1916 invested capital, 55
  financial results, 361
  income account, 361
  net income, 50
  production ratio, 365
  reinvestment policy, 360
  tax reserve, 50
  transcription of tax return of, 50
  wages, 364

**V**

Van Ess Company, 352
Van Sweringens, 283, 302
Virginia-Carolina Chemical
  asset value of, 71
  business diversification, 70
  capitalization of, 70, 71
  debentures, 80
  decline in percentage of net profits, 67
  dividend records of common stock, 67
  effect of war on earnings of, 68
  growth of working capital, 69
  investment rating of, 65, 72–73
  market yields of securities, 66
  working capital of, 72

**W**

Wabash, 262
Waldorf System, 124, 301, 317
  bargain opportunities, 347
  capitalization, 265
  profits per share, 265

Warner Brothers, 312
War Revenue Act, 29, 41
  invested capital provisions of, 47
War taxes, of coppers, 29
War Tax Reserve, 41
  approximate tangible asset values of
    common stocks as determined
    from, 44
  for determining approximate valuation of
    intangible assets, 45
Wartime Excess Profits Tax Revenue, 11
Weber & Heilbroner, 126
  business growth, 276
  low-priced dividend paying
    stocks, 276
Westchester Lighting Company, 88
  mortgage security of, 89
Westinghouse, 82
White Eagle Oil, 126
  capitalization, 274
  low-priced dividend paying stock, 273
White Motor, 214
Wickwire Spencer Steel, 260
Willys Corporation, 125, 269
Willys-Overland Pfd., 135
Wilson & Co., 76
Woolworth, 147
  capitalization and dividends, 152
  comparative earning power of, 149–150
  market prices, 148
  percentage of 1918 earnings to market
    price of, 149
  tangible asset values of, 151
Wright Aeronautical
  capitalization, 257
  cash asset stocks, 256
  dividend yields, 301
  market activity, 317
  profits and dividends, 316